The cross on the sword

Catholic Chaplains in the Forces

TOM JOHNSTONE AND JAMES HAGERTY

Hope you enjoy this.

Love Oenee . 1997

**GEOFFREY
CHAPMAN**

Geoffrey Chapman
A Cassell imprint
Wellington House, 125 Strand, London WC2R 0BB
215 Park Avenue South, New York, NY 10003

First published 1996

British Library Cataloguing-in-Publication Data
A catalogue record for this book is available from the British Library.

ISBN 0-225-66824-6 (hardback)
    0-225-66825-4 (paperback)

Cover picture: Fortunino Matania, *The Last Absolution of the Munsters at Rue Du Bois 1915*
Father Francis Gleeson is shown giving the Last Absolution to the Munsters on their way to Aubers Ridge on 8 May 1915. After, the Regiment sang the *Te Deum*. In the subsequent attack, the Munsters lost nineteen officers and 374 men.
Originally painted as a Christmas supplement to the *Sphere*, this dignified picture became one of the most famous of all war illustrations.
© Principal RC Chaplain (Army), to whom grateful acknowledgement is made.

Typeset by BookEns Ltd, Royston, Herts.
Printed and bound in Great Britain by Redwood Books, Trowbridge, Wiltshire.

Contents

To the 69 Catholic priests of Great Britain, Ireland and the British Commonwealth, killed in action, died of wounds and died on service in the Crimea, India, and during two World Wars, while ministering faithfully to their flock, this book is respectfully dedicated.

The good shepherd giveth his life for the sheep.
(John 10:11)

Foreword

The Right Reverend Francis J. Walmsley CBE, RN Retd
Bishop-in-Ordinary to Her Majesty's Forces

The Acts of the Apostles describes how St Paul persuaded the seamen and soldiers in the storm-battered ship off Malta to have something to eat, assuring them 'Not a hair of your head will be lost'. He then 'took some bread, gave thanks to God in front of them all, broke it and began to eat'. Whether or not St Paul was the first minister of Christ to serve those who go down to the sea in ships, and the soldiers who accompany them, the care of men at arms has a history as long as the Church itself.

The word 'chaplains' derives from the 'Cappellani', or those who guarded the *cappa* or cloak, a relic of the soldier-saint Martin who became Bishop of Tours. We are told how Martin shared his military cloak with a poor beggar by cutting it in half. He is the patron saint of chaplains.

During the Second Crusade, among the orders for the venture can be found the following: 'Every ship should have its own priest, and there should be orders to observe the same practices as in a parish ... That everyone should confess weekly and go to Communion on the Lord's Day.' At the Battle of Crécy in 1346 the army of King Edward III was accompanied by three grades of chaplains, whilst 32 chaplains were at the Battle of Agincourt in 1415.

During the English Civil Wars in the seventeenth century, Catholics generally fought on the side of the King. Serving them was Fr John Huddleston OSB. Fr Francis Pavier was killed ministering to the wounded at the Battle of Marston Moor (2 July 1644), whilst Fr Henry Starky lost a leg, shot off by a cannon ball. At the time Catholics were subjected to the rigours of the Penal Laws. Fr Edward Cary served King James II as Chaplain General and on the King's deposition fled with him to exile in Paris. Still later in penal times, the Scot Fr Alexander MacDonnell helped his clan Chief of the same name to raise a regiment of fencibles to defend the country against Napoleon. Such are the beginnings of the great tradition of which the Catholic Chaplains serving today are the proud legatees.

Having served for many years both as a Naval Chaplain and as Bishop to the Forces, I am proud of the service Roman Catholic priests have given to the Royal Navy, the Army and the Royal Air Force during the last 150 years of this nation's turbulent history. From the war in the Crimea, through the South African and Boer wars, the two World Wars and subsequent conflicts including Korea and the Gulf, to the present deployment of British forces in Bosnia, hundreds of Catholic priests from dioceses, religious orders and religious congregations and societies in the United Kingdom, the Empire and Commonwealth and the Republic of Ireland have responded to the immortal words of Lord Kitchener: 'Your Country Needs You.' Having answered in their youth the command of Christ to 'leave all things and follow me', they have gone still further and left the comparative security of parish or religious house to minister to fighting men and women, serving far from home and in peril of their lives. Some, like their spiritual brothers and sisters, made the supreme sacrifice. This book, *The Cross on the Sword*, is the story of these Catholic Chaplains, told for the first time.

Military chaplaincy in support of sailors, soldiers and airmen and their dependants, wives and children is an integral part of our Church's service to the nation. The fact that Catholic Chaplains and their people have the exclusive care of a Bishop of their own and of a 'diocese' crafted to meet their own very special needs is testimony enough of the Church's love, support and pastoral care. Pope John Paul II has said: 'The presence of Chaplains in the military world is very important. Through their ministry the Church lavishes her saving means upon the faithful who serve in that particular type of life and, at the same time, helps them to form an upright conscience in regard to vitally important ethical questions, especially in the matter of education for peace. Pastoral work with military personnel should therefore be highly esteemed.'

Catholic Chaplains and their flock rejoice with their Anglican, Church of Scotland and Free Churches colleagues at the bicentenary of the Royal Army Chaplains' Department's service of God, King and Country. It is in the spirit of this anniversary that our authors offer their work.

Preface: Christianity, war and military service

The morality of Christians serving as soldiers has long been questioned. Christ preached the theology of peace and rejected war in the advance of His Kingdom (Matt 26:52). But the New Testament writers also insisted that Christians had a duty to God and Caesar (Matt 22:21; Rom 13:1-7; 1 Peter 2:13-17). John baptized Roman soldiers, telling them, in passing, not to abuse their power (Luke 3:14). Peter instructed and baptized the centurion Cornelius in Christ's teaching without demanding the surrender of his sword (Acts 10:1). St Paul's attitude towards temporal authority is given in Romans 13:1-4 which tells us: 'you must obey the governing authorities since all government comes from God', assuming, of course, that Paul delivered his strictures believing that the 'governing authorities' ruled justly and fairly to all and however authoritarian Caesar might be he was fundamentally benevolent and protective towards those who obeyed the laws.

> If Paul says nothing here about the legitimacy of government, the rights of rulers or Christian involvement in the exercise of temporal power, he at least views such power as a source of justice, and he reminds the Christians that they are subject no less than other men to those agencies which preserve a form of order.[1]

Jesus marvelled at the order and discipline of the legion as expounded by the centurion at Capernaum, and for his beliefs the centurion's servant was healed (Matt 8:9-13). St Paul would have suffered a lashing had it not been for a centurion, and might have been murdered but for another (Acts 22:25; 23:17). In the light of his experience with Roman soldiers as related in Acts 22 and 23, it is hardly surprising that Paul used many military metaphors in his epistles.

Indeed, the use of the legions as a role model for Church order and discipline can be seen very early in its history:

> It is interesting to note that Pope St Clement I, writing in 76 AD to the Church in Corinth and calling for discipline in the church and obedience to the bishop, uses as his ideal the image of the soldier and the army,

pointing out that it is through obedience that the few command the many. If he had a low moral opinion of military service he is unlikely to have chosen the illustration he did.[2]

Notwithstanding the gospels of Matthew and Luke and the writings of Paul, together with the evidence of the Acts, early theologians such as Tertullian were against all military service, probably because the soldier's oath linking duty to idolatry was incompatible with Christian belief. However, Tertullian (c. 160-220) did acknowledge that only Rome's legions stood guardian to civilization against the teeming hordes of restless barbarians on the frontiers.

> We know that Rome's continuance holds back the great force which menaces the world, that is, the very end of time which threatens frightful calamities. We have no desire to experience these things, and while we pray for their deferral, we are prompting the continued existence of Rome.[3]

Nevertheless, although foreseeing the coming of the barbarians and the dark age which was to blight western Europe within two centuries, Tertullian dogmatically held fast to the principle of non-violence, even unto death and the possible extinction of Christianity.

> What kind of war would we, who willingly submit to the sword, not be ready or eager for despite our inferior numbers, if it were not for the fact that according to our doctrine it is more permissible to be killed than to kill?[4]

However, the conversion of Constantine and the imperial edict of toleration for Christians changed almost overnight the Christian attitude towards war and their participation in it. Recognition by Christians of the need to support the maintenance of law in peacetime and the security of frontiers during war followed swiftly. The Council of Arles (314) decreed excommunication for deserters, even in peacetime. It was a watershed in Christian attitudes towards war. Shortly after the Council of Arles, in 315, St Martin of Tours was born. The word 'chapel' and 'chaplain' are derived from the Roman military cloak or *cappa* of St Martin. A soldier and the son of a soldier, Martin cut his cloak in two, giving half to a shivering beggar. The other half became a relic, venerated in what became known as a chapel.

Divisions within the Roman world, and the removal to Constantinople of Rome's most vigorous administrators, resulted in the eventual invasion of the western Roman Empire. There followed the personal confrontation between Pope Leo I and Attila's Huns at the gates of Rome during AD 452. It was the first evidence of a Christian spiritual leader exercising leadership in war.

The Venerable Bede mentions priestly participation in war extending back to the Dark Ages. On Good Friday 1014, priests inspired the Irish to victory under Brian Boru in their final confrontation with the Norsemen at Clontarf. During the Norman invasion of England, Bishop Odo of Bayeux accompanied his half-brother William of Normandy. Odo, we are told, was careful to use only a mace in obedience with the Old Testament interdiction against priests 'smiting with the edge of the sword'. During 1138 Archbishop Thurstan rallied Yorkshire under the ecclesiastical banners of York, Beverley and Ripon to confront the Scots invaders at the Battle of the Standard. One hundred and sixty years later, during an invasion of Scotland, Anthony de Beck, Prince-Bishop of Durham, in defiance of the Synod of Westminster's ruling in 1175 against clergy bearing arms or wearing armour, said Mass in full armour just before the Battle of Selkirk. Froissart relates that King Edward III, the Prince of Wales and most of the army confessed and received Communion before the Battle of Crécy.[5] At Poitiers, Sir John Chandos, one of the foremost knights in Christendom, wore the badge of Our Lady on his surcoat. It was he who told the Black Prince: 'Sir, sir, ride on ahead, the day is yours, thanks to God it will be in your hands.'[6]

While Edward and the Black Prince were harrying the French, the Scots invaded England and Queen Philippa raised an army for the defence of the realm. As most of the nobility were in France, the host was led into battle by the Archbishops of Canterbury and York, and the Bishops of Lincoln, Carlisle and Durham. During a later war against France, Henry V had no fewer than thirty priests with the army, all of whom gave absolution and said Mass before Agincourt.[7]

At the height of the Cold War, following Vatican II, an historic pronouncement was made concerning Catholics and military service:

> Those who devote themselves to the military service of their country should regard themselves as agents of security and freedom of peoples. As long as they fulfil their role properly, they are making a genuine contribution to the establishment of peace. (Constitution on the Church in the Modern World, 79)

At that time there were tens of thousands of Catholic servicemen in Her Majesty's Forces. They, and indeed most Christian soldiers of the NATO armies facing the might of the Communist Soviet Union, or serving with United Nations troops on thankless peace-keeping missions in several parts of the world, must have been greatly encouraged that their services in the cause of peace and justice were recognized at the highest levels of Christian society.

References

1.   Louis J. Swift, *The Early Fathers on War and Military Service* (Wilmington, DE,

    1983), p. 23.
2.   Fr Michael Masterson, 'The Just War v Pacifism' (unpublished paper), p. 7.
3.   Tertullian, *Apology* 30.4.
4.   Ibid., 37.4.
5.   J. Jolliffe (ed.), *Froissart's Chronicles* (London, 1967), p. 140.
6.   Ibid., pp. 165–8.
7.   RAChD Museum, Bagshot Park.

Abbreviations

(in the References and Bibliography)

AAA	Archdiocese of Armagh Archives
ABA	Archdiocese of Birmingham Archives
ADA	Archdiocese of Dublin Archives
ASA	Archdiocese of Southwark Archives
AWA	Archdiocese of Westminster Archives
COA	The Catholic Ordinariate of Great Britain Archives
DAA	Downside Abbey Archives
DAB	*Dictionary of Australian Biography*
DCB	*Dictionary of Canadian Biography*
DNB	*Dictionary of National Biography*
ECD	*Catholic Directory of England and Wales*
ICD	*Irish Catholic Directory*
IWM	Imperial War Museum
JAD	Jesuit Archives, Dublin
RCCA	Roman Catholic Chaplains' Department Archives, Bagshot
SCD	*Scottish Catholic Directory*
Statistics	*Statistics of the War Effort of the British Empire*
WWH	*Who Was Who*
WW	*Who's Who*

Acknowledgements

The authors wish to thank the many people who made this book possible. In the course of three years' detailed research the response to our appeals has been magnificent. Without exception, everyone approached has responded generously with their valuable time, freely given to enquiring strangers. Without such unstinting and helpful co-operation the task might have been possible, but less enjoyable, and most certainly the results would have been sadly impoverished. Mere words of thanks seemed, to us, inadequate for the help so readily given.

It would be invidious to single out any one person, diocese, or Order; however, the authors owe a heavy debt to Sister Eileen M. Grant RCE, of the RAChD (RC); the Archivists of the Archdioceses of Armagh, Dublin, Southwark and Westminster; and the Benedictines and the Jesuits. More particularly, grateful thanks is due to the Abbot of Downside for permission to quote from the Rawlinson Papers; and the Father Provincial of the English Province, and the Father Provincial of the Irish Province of the Society of Jesus, for permission to quote from their house journals, *Letters and Notices* and *Interfuse*; the Trustees of Ampleforth for permission to quote from the papers of Dom George Forbes OSB; the Trustees of Fort Augustus for permission to quote from the diary of Dom E. Denys Rutledge OSB; and the Abbot of Prinknash for permission to quote from *Pax*; the Commanding Officer and officers of the 14th/20th King's Hussars for permission to quote from the *Regimental Journal*; the Rt Rev Mgr A. J. Harris SCA, VG, Principal Chaplain (RC) RAF; Rt Rev Mgr G. Lavender VG, Principal Chaplain (RC) RN; Rt Rev Mgr S. H. Louden VG, RAChD, Principal Chaplain (RC) Army. The Rt Rev Francis J. Walmsley, Roman Catholic Ordinariate to HM Forces, who from the inception of the project has given his support throughout, deserves a special thanks. Undoubtedly, without the help of those mentioned above and below, this book would not have been possible.

Rev Francis Barber CF; Dr Anthony Barling; Mr Michael Conroy; Mr Milan Davidovic; Rev Ian Evans CF; Mr V. J. L. Fontana; Mr Michael Graves; Gen Sir John W Hackett; Rev Alfred Hayes SCF; Dr M. E. M. Herford; Mrs Catherine P. Johnstone; Mr Eamonn McIntyre; Rev Michael K. Masterson SCF; Mrs Susan Milner; Mrs Patricia Moorhead; Mr Sean

Murphy; Mr Hugh Norwood; Mr Dermot I. O'Sullivan; Maria Raissiguier; Lt Col J. P. Riley; Rev Phelim Rowland SCF; Maj G. E. M. Stephens; Mr David Stevens; Mr Tony Storan; Leila Thorpe; Mr Vincent de Paul Vokes; Mr Peter Wiseman.

England and Wales: Archdioceses: Birmingham, Rev Petroc Howell and Rev Anthony Jones; Cardiff, Rev Bernard Whitehouse; Liverpool, Mr Brian Plumb; Southwark, Rev Michael Clifton; Westminster, Rev Ian Dickie. Dioceses: Arundel and Brighton, Mgr John Hull; Brentwood, Miss Jane Neely; Clifton, Rev A. M. Daley and Rev Dr J. A. Harding; Hallam, Rev Desmond Sexton; Hexham and Newcastle, Mr Robin Gard and Rev Michael Wymes; Lancaster, Rev Stephen Cross; Leeds, Mgr George Bradley, Mr Robert E. Finnigan, Rev Bernard Funnell, Mgr Patrick J. Hennessey, Mgr Edward Wilcock and Rev Dr Michael Williams; Menevia, Rev Patrick Daly; Middlesbrough, Rev George Foster; Northampton, Mrs Margaret Osborne; Nottingham, Rev A. P. Dolan; Plymouth, Rev Christopher Smith; Portsmouth, Rev F. P. Isherwood; Salford, Rev David Lannon; Shrewsbury, Mr Brian Plumb; Wrexham, The Very Rev Canon James Mulroy. Ushaw College, Rev Michael Sharratt. Religious Orders: Rev Fabian Binyon OSB, Prinknash; Rev Anselm Cramer OSB, Ampleforth; Rev Nigel Cave IC; Rev R. C. Cheals OP; Rt Rev Charles Fitzgerald-Lombard OSB, Abbot of Downside; Rev Charles Fitzsimons OSB, Quarr; Rev W. W. Gandy CSSp; Rev Philip Graystone SM; Rev Jerome Hodkinson OSB, Belmont; Rev Geoffrey Holt SJ; Rev Placid Hooper OSB, Buckfast; Rev Philip Jebb OSB, Downside; Rev Ignatius M. McCafferty OSM; Rev Thomas M. McCoog SJ; Rev Bernard P. Nann IC; Rev Henry Parker CSSR; Rev Didacus Pierce OFM; Rev E. Denys Rutledge OSB, Fort Augustus; Rev Geoffrey Scott OSB, Douai; Rev Hugh Simon-Thwaites SJ; Rt Rev Laurence Soper OSB, Abbot of Ealing; Rev Frederick Turner SJ; Rev Michael Walsh SMA; Rev A. Whitehead CRL.

Scotland: Archdioceses: St Andrews and Edinburgh, Dr Christine Johnson; Glasgow, Dr Mary McHugh. Dioceses: Aberdeen, The Rt Rev Mgr J. F. Copland VG; Argyll and the Isles, The Rt Rev Canon Roderick Macdonald; Dunkeld, Rev Michael J. Milton; Galloway, The Rt Rev Bishop Maurice Taylor; Paisley, The Very Rev Canon Bernard J. Canning. Religious Orders: Rev B. Bailey OP; Rev Michael Walsh SMA.

Ireland: Archdioceses: Armagh, Rev Eugene Sweeney, Rev E. McCamley; Cashel, Rev Christopher O'Dwyer, St Patrick's College, Thurles; Dublin, Mr David C. Sheehy; Tuam, Mgr Dominick Grealy. Dioceses: Achonry, Most Rev Bishop Thomas Flynn; Ardagh, Rev Owen Devaney; Clogher, Rev Denis Dolan and Rev Liam S. MacDaid; Clonfert, Very Rev P. K. Egan AP; Cloyne, Sr M. Cabrini Delahunty; Cork and Ross, Sr M. Angela Bolster, Rev Ted O'Sullivan; Derry, Rev Peter McLoughlin; Down and Connor, Very Rev George O'Hanlon; Dromore, Rev Anthony Davies; Elphin, Rt Rev Mgr Gerard Dolan; Ferns, Very Rev John V. Gahan; Galway, Rev Noel Mullin;

Kerry, Rev Kieran O'Shea; Kildare and Leighlin, Rev Thomas McDonnell; Killaloe, Most Rev Bishop Michael A. Harty; Kilmore, Very Rev Daniel Gallogly; Meath, Rev Paul Connell and Mgr John Shortall; Ossory, Miss Ann Lalor; Raphoe, Rev John McGlynn and Rev John J. Silke; Waterford and Lismore, Rev Gerard Chestnutt. All Hallows College, Dublin, Rev Kevin Rafferty; Clonliffe College, Rev Peter Briscoe; St Kieran's College, Kilkenny, Rev Joseph Gallavan; St Patrick's College, Maynooth, Rt Rev Mgr Patrick Corish and Mrs Penelope Woods, Russell Library. Religious Orders: Rev Thomas Cooney OSA; Rev Vincent Denny OMI; Rev Séan Farragher CSSp; Rev Hugh Fenning OP; Rev Peter Haughey OSA; Rev Michael Healy SSC; Rev E. M. Hogan SMA; Rev Fabian McCormack OCD; Rev Felix X. Martin OSA; Rev Benignus Millett OFM; Rev Patrick O'Donnell CSSR; Rev Peter O'Dwyer OCarm; Rev Kieran O'Mahony OSA; Rev Henry O'Shea OSB; Rev Stephen Redmond SJ.

Australia: Rev T. Daly SJ; Mgr Francis Lyons; The Most Rev Geoffrey F. Mayne, Catholic Ordinariate to the Australian Defence Forces; The Most Rev Bishop John A. Morgan; Bridget and John Patrick; Mgr Patrick Walsh.

Canada: Mgr Roger Bazin CD OSJ Chaplain General (RC).

Malta: Mgr Joseph Lupi.

New Zealand: Rev M. A. Cahill.

Rome: Rev Thomas Davitt CM; Rt Rev Mgr James Sullivan, English College, Rome.

South Africa: Rev J. Brady OMI; The Rt Rev Bishop Reginald Cawcutt; Mgr J. G. Maginnis VG.

USA: Rt Rev H. Alban Boultwood OSB, Abbot of St Anselm's Abbey; Professor Kevin J. Keaney, Georgetown University.

The staff of the Reading Room, British Library, Boston Spa, Yorkshire; the staff of the Reading Room, Imperial War Museum; the staff of the Linen Hall Library, Belfast; the staff of the Reading Room, National Library of Ireland, Dublin; the staff of the Public Record Office of Northern Ireland; the staff of the Reference Section, State Library of Victoria, Australia.

Our grateful thanks are extended to Fiona McKenzie of Cassell and to Stephen Ryan, the proof-reader, who saved the authors from many errors.

Finally, to our wives, whose forbearance, especially during the last year, has been saintly.

1

The first Catholic chaplains and the Royal Army Chaplains' Department

The first Catholic chaplains

In 1794 the first Catholic chaplain to serve in the British Army since the reign of King James II was commissioned, Fr Alexander MacDonnell of Glengarry. His commission was signed by King George III, and his appointment to the Glengarry Fencibles was confirmed. He had worked in Lochaber and Badenoch since 1791, and moved with his clansmen to Glasgow, the first resident priest there since the Reformation. After the Peace of Amiens in 1803 the Glengarrys were disbanded, and most went to Canada.[1]

Alexander MacDonnell followed his clansmen and settled in Upper Canada in 1804. There he played a pivotal role in forming an alliance between French Canadian and British settlers, and Indians[2] for the protection of Upper Canada during the American War of 1812. MacDonnell persuaded his clansmen to take employment under the government and formed the Glengarry Light Infantry,[3] becoming regimental chaplain and taking part in four engagements against the American invader.[4]

'Big Sandy' was not, however, the first British Catholic chaplain in Canada; even before the Catholic Relief Acts Fr John McKenna had accompanied the Loyalists from the State of New York who fled to Canada during the American Revolution, and 'contrary to the regulations of the times, was paid for his services'.[5] In 1798, Fr Edmund Burke was named as chaplain to the soldiers in Niagara, in addition to being Vicar-Apostolic of Nova Scotia.[6]

Formation of the Chaplain-General's department

The history of the Royal Army Chaplains' Department really begins in 1796 when an Anglican Chaplain-General was appointed to control Army chaplains. Regimental chaplains were then abolished in favour of brigade chaplains, almost all being Church of England and naturally unacceptable to 'dissenters'. Catholic priests somehow managed in various ways to minister spiritually to their flocks without causing anxiety to either the ruling or military establishments. Following the second Catholic Relief Act, and although his father King George III was totally against Catholic Emancipation, during 1806 the Duke of York, Commander-in-Chief of the British Army, granted permission for Catholic troops to attend Mass in Catholic chapels close to their barracks, provided the commanding officer approved.[7]

Notwithstanding these measures, there were still officers who punished Catholics for attending Mass. In Dublin in January 1795 Trooper John Hyland of the 14th Light Dragoons, who had complained about not being allowed to attend Mass, was court-martialled and sentenced to receive 200 lashes.[8] On the other hand, an officer of the Royal South Down Militia was court-martialled and reprimanded for not allowing his soldiers to attend Mass.[9]

The Wellingtonian period

After the departure of Fr MacDonnell, officially Catholics in the army had no chaplains until 1836, although they were ministered to unofficially by local priests in the United Kingdom. Overseas, as has been mentioned, there existed paid chaplains, both in Canada and in Australia.

The first widespread ministration to Catholic troops in the field took place during the Peninsular War. The British Government, responding to the national appeal from both Spain and Portugal, in 1808 despatched two British armies to the Peninsula, one under Sir John Moore, the other under Sir Arthur Wellesley (the future Duke of Wellington). Moore led his army directly into Spain. Wellesley, hereafter called Wellington, arrived at Mondego Bay. Lord Burghersh, one of Wellington's staff, was ordered ashore on a special mission. On his arrival at Coimbra four young Irishmen offered their assistance immediately: Frs Austin M'Dermott, James Warren Doyle (later Bishop of Kildare and Leighlin), Nicholas Clayton, and a Mr Hanlon, all Austin Friars at Coimbra University.[10]

> Sir A. Wellesley deputed me, … to proceed through Coimbra and the central Portuguese provinces, all of which were in insurrection against the French, and report to him the troops which were collected and the general state of armament of the country. I proceeded immediately to Coimbra … and the students of the University had formed themselves into a corps, which was joined to the regular troops … amongst the leaders of these students was Mr M'Dermott, and Mr, afterwards Bishop, Doyle. These young men, with several Portuguese, offered to accompany me as an escort to the provinces, and I gratefully accepted their patriotic proposal.[11]

M'Dermott and Doyle accompanied Lord Burghersh on his fact-finding mission on the Portuguese resistance. General Barcellor, commanding a force of Portuguese and Spanish, was contacted, and through his Irish aides Burghersh arranged for Barcellor to co-operate with Wellington for an advance on Lisbon.

Rejoining the army, Burghersh introduced M'Dermott and Doyle to Wellington, who attached them to his staff as interpreters and gallopers. Fr M'Dermott was present at the Battles of Caldas, Rolica, and Vimeiro. At Rolica,

> I was entrenched behind a strong windmill, ballproof, employed in giving spiritual assistance to a number of soldiers, who knowing that I was in priest's orders, sought my aid. But at Vimeiro ... I was greatly exposed to the fire of the enemy, as I was obliged to keep going to and fro with orders and despatches to the Portuguese General.[12]

At a critical phase of the Battle of Vimeiro, Fr M'Dermott guided Anstruther's division from the beaches where they had just landed to hold an exposed flank. Without its presence, the British might well have been defeated.[13] At the Convention of Cintra, Doyle and Clayton acted as interpreters.[14] General Junot capitulated on good terms, and, to the fury of the British Government, the French were transported home in British ships.

After Vimeiro, Fr M'Dermott became ill and took no further part in the campaign. However the three other priests continued to serve Wellington's army for a considerable time until joined by others from Spain.

As the political and military situation in Spain intensified, the Scots and English Colleges at Valladolid closed, students and professors went home and the buildings were occupied by the French. At Salamanca the faculty of the University authorized the formation of a university military unit and the students of the Irish College and the Diocesan Seminary enlisted, Alexander Hore of the Irish College becoming its commander. General Sir John Moore, aiming for Madrid, reached Salamanca on 13 November 1808. Napoleon, exasperated at the failure of his marshals, personally reoccupied Madrid, and advanced to intercept Moore. Moore retired northwards with his troops on 10 December; but before his departure 'all the Irish Students joined his force as interpreters'.[15] The Rector, Dr Curtis, remained alone at the college. When the French occupied Salamanca, the Irish College was requisitioned; Curtis was expelled but returned and was later twice exiled by the French to Ciudad Rodrigo.

Moore had no recourse but to retire towards the sea, marching 250 miles in the depth of winter through the frozen mountains of Galicia, his army suffering dreadfully. Moore stood before Corunna in January 1809 and defeated Soult, but was killed in the hour of victory. His army embarked for England unmolested. The Irish religious, professors and students, having little to look forward to in England, went south to find Wellington. Their adventures and privations on this long journey have not been recorded, but they managed to escape Soult's troops, survive the hardship, and join Wellington's army. Young, spirited, educated and speaking Spanish, their value would have been grasped immediately. They became part of the Intelligence Service under Colonel Colquhoun Grant, serving as his main link with the Spanish irregulars. The names recorded in the Irish College for the academic year 1807–08 were: Edmund Redmond, Francis Prendergast, Patrick Murphy, Maurice Parre, Patrick Burke, Denis Joseph O'Sullivan, Peter Ward, Peter Marum, John Maguire, William Hanegan, Francis Smith, Patrick Brady.[16]

Who actually took part in the campaign, and how many survived, is not known. Nor is it possible to say how many returned to Salamanca when the war ended five years later. Like many soldiers after the two World Wars of the twentieth century they may have been only too glad, when the time came, to take up the service of Christ. For the ordained there was much priestly work to be done amongst their numerous Catholic fellow-countrymen; Irish Catholics composed about 30 per cent of the Peninsular Army.

The Lisbon base

Lisbon became the main base for the Peninsular Army. Battle casualties and sickness created a demand for hospitals, and twenty were established in the Lisbon area. A Catholic chaplain to attend the sick and wounded Catholic soldiers was recruited from the English College, Lisbon. Although the students had been evacuated, several professors remained, and two, the Rev Edmund Winstanley and Rev Thomas Hurst, became officiating chaplains.

> Upwards of twenty hospitals were established in different parts of the city, and they were all kept constantly filled by the crowds of sick and wounded that daily poured in from the army. As many of the regiments were almost exclusively composed of Catholics from Ireland, a most laborious and extensive work was thus created. The task of administering the succours of religion to all these distressed objects was assigned to the Rev Edmund Winstanley who for this purpose was retained at the College and unremittingly continued to exert himself in the discharge of these severe duties until the close of the war. He was assisted in this charitable work by the Rev Thomas Hurst, who devoted to the hospitals or to the making of private or public exhortations, whatever time he could spare from his duties in the Academy.[17]

The friendship which developed between Wellington and Mgr Patrick Curtis and Fr James Doyle survived the war. Patrick Curtis became Archbishop of Armagh and Doyle became Bishop of Kildare and Leighlin, the redoubtable JKL. In the years before Catholic Emancipation, both advised Wellington upon the depth of Catholic feeling on the issue, 'much of it unpalatable'.[18]

Catholics in the post-Waterloo Army

In the post-Waterloo period the Army in general was grievously neglected. The spiritual welfare of soldiers, who were still regarded as the scum of the country, was overlooked just as much. The Chaplains' Department became so run-down that in 1845 four elderly commissioned chaplains and a number of officiating clergy were all that cared for religious practice in the entire Army.[19] During 1848, the Rev G. R. Gleig was appointed Chaplain-General, and during the thirty years of his appointment did much to improve matters for Anglicans. Nothing, however, was done for Presbyterians and Catholics until the outbreak of the Crimean War. Officially, there were no military chaplains for 'dissenters', regular or officiating. The Horse Guards, later the War Office, recognized officiating chaplains for Presbyterians in 1827, and for Catholics in 1836. Wesleyans applied for similar recognition in 1856 but had to wait until 1881 before it was granted.[20]

In the post-Waterloo era, the Army recruited heavily in Ireland. In the 1830s the Irish, and therefore Catholic, presence in the Army amounted to 42.2 per cent, but in 1840 this had fallen to 37.2 per cent [21] – probably a result of the Peninsular veterans taking their discharge on pension after thirty years' service.

Such was the concern felt about the spiritual welfare of Catholic seamen and soldiers that in 1842 the Rt Rev Thomas Griffiths, Vicar-Apostolic, issued a circular through the Catholic Institute instructing Catholics how to petition Members of Parliament about grievances. A draft of the petition to 'The Commons in Parliament Assembled' specifically draws attention to the grievances relating to the Royal Navy and the Army.

> It is probable that one fifth of the persons engaged as seamen and marines in the naval service of the country are Catholics: yet your petitioners have the melancholy duty to perform of calling the attention of this Honourable House to the astounding fact that no provision whatsoever is made for the spiritual instruction, or for administering the sacraments, or performing divine service, for Catholics …[22]

With respect to the Army, the petition refers to the high numbers of Catholics and shows the disparity in budgetary funding for religious worship: no allocation of funds was made for 'dissenters', Methodists and Presbyterians.

> That your petitioners further show that with respect to Her Majesty's army your petitioners are confident that full one-third of that army

consists of Catholics. Yet, although a sum of £12,000 is allocated by the army estimates for purposes of religion and divine service, yet not above £800 thereof, that is, less than one-fifteenth of the whole, is applied to Catholic purposes, so that great destitution of religious instruction and divine service pervades the British army.[23]

The Crimean War

The centuries-old struggle between Russia and Turkey was at its height in the middle of the nineteenth century, Britain siding with Turkey. Diplomatic incompetence led to war in 1854, and British and French armies were sent to the Crimea to capture and destroy Sebastopol, the great Russian naval base for the Black Sea.

Although the war proved once again the spirit and bravery of regimental officers and men, utter incompetence was exposed at command and staff levels.

War correspondents accompanied an army into the field for the first time. All of them, but notably William Russell of *The Times*, exposed the inefficiency within the Army, and the terrible suffering of the soldiers. Russell's despatches caused an outcry in Britain, forcing the Government to act to alleviate the suffering of the troops.

Amongst the measures taken was the despatch to the East of two parties of nurses, one of 38 under Florence Nightingale, and a second of 46 under Mary Stanley. Bishop Grant of Southwark was approached by the War Office and asked to provide nursing nuns and Catholic chaplains. As a result, ten nuns under Rev Mother Moore accompanied Miss Nightingale.[24] Dr Manning was later instrumental in sending fifteen nuns with Miss Stanley's group. The Rev Mother Bridgeman went with the latter. At Miss Nightingale's request, three additional nuns were later sent out directly to the Crimea.[25]

Following the outcry caused by Russell's despatches to *The Times*, the War Office approached Bishop Grant of Southwark, intent, as he wrote to Cardinal Wiseman, 'upon the means that are to be taken in order to give Catholics fair play'. He added 'Of course, I do not intend to undertake anything without the concurrence of the other bishops'.[26] During the absence in Rome of both Cardinal Wiseman and Bishop Grant for the definition of the dogma of the Immaculate Conception, the work connected with sending chaplains to the Crimea was conducted by Dr Manning.[27]

Ultimately, no fewer than 21 Catholic priests served in the Crimea, and of the twelve chaplains who died there, seven were Catholic. The priests sent to the Crimea were all vigorous men in their thirties and therefore able to stand the rigours of campaigning. A total of 28 nuns also served with the Army of the Crimea. Two died while nursing in hospitals, and were buried at Balaclava.[28]

India

The Crimean adventure was barely over when the outbreak of mutiny in the East India Company's Bengal Army necessitated the despatch of heavy reinforcements. Bishop Grant was again asked by the War Office to provide Catholic chaplains. The Army List of the Indian Army down to the First World War shows the entire ecclesiastical structure and establishment of the Anglican Church in India as though it were part of the Army, with the addition of a few Presbyterian ministers. No Catholics are listed. Catholic soldiers serving in India, with the East India Company's European regiments and British Army units, were entirely dependent upon missionaries who acted as officiating chaplains. One such was Fr Nicholas Barry, an Irish priest who left All Hallows College, Dublin, in October 1847, for Agra in Oudh province. He became a professor at, and rector of, Agra College until January 1853. In that year he was sent to open a new seminary at Mussaorie, Gwalior, in the Himalayas, becoming its first rector on 1 November 1853. He also became officiating chaplain to the troops in the area.[29] During the Mutiny he was attached to the hard-marching force under Sir Hugh Rose in Gwalior. Kipling probably based his Fr Victor of 'the Mavericks' in *Kim* on a priest such as Nicholas Barry. In 1881 there was in fact a Fr Victor in Lucknow, who briefed visitors on details of the defence of the Residency on a scale model.

> Fr Victor took me to see a model of the residency as it was before the Mutiny, which I wanted to complete my understanding of the events of 1857. Chatted on subjects of use and interest, and he gained on my affections as he went along, so that I was sorry to say good-bye.[30]

Doubtless there were many like Fr Victor throughout British India, ministering to the troops, and caring for their orphaned offspring, like Kipling's Kimball O'Hara.

The chaplains recruited and despatched to India by Bishop Grant were described in the bishop's correspondence as 'missionaries'. They served with the Field Force sent out under Sir Colin Campbell. Marching in Indian heat to relieve Cawnpore and Lucknow, the unacclimatized newcomers suffered severely. Fr Patrick Fairhurst died of sunstroke at Lucknow, one of two chaplains to die. The other was Fr Charles Morgan. The exact number of Catholic chaplains, officiating and full-time, who served with the Indian and British Armies in India is not known, however we do know that seven were sent out. That Catholic chaplains were paid at different rates than their Anglican colleagues only increased Bishop Grant's concern for 'fair play' in his negotiations with the War Office, especially as many chaplains were not paid until they returned to England.[31]

The establishment of permanent commissioned Catholic chaplains in the Army

Following years of careful negotiations it was finally agreed by the British Government in 1858 that Catholic chaplains should be maintained in peace as well as war. Such chaplains were all at the disposal of the Secretary of State for War, and had to be prepared to move at short notice as directed. Date of commissioning determined seniority, promotion was by seniority and time served in rank. Anglican and Presbyterian chaplains reported to the Chaplain-General, and delicate work was required to prevent Catholic chaplains coming under the same control. Eventually, Catholic chaplains were directed by the War Office to report directly, through their commanding officers, to the Under-Secretary of State for War while their ecclesiastical control was vested in the Bishop of Southwark. From the earliest days of the Royal Army Chaplains' Department (RAChD) Catholic chaplains were therefore directly under military authority, never under any spiritual authority other than their appointed bishop.

However, the Vatican's Congregation for Extraordinary Ecclesiastical Affairs decided against negotiating with the British Government for the appointment of a Vicar-Apostolic for the British Army. Instead, military chaplains were to obtain the necessary faculties from their local Ordinaries.[32] Stole fees, the payment to a priest for the services of baptism, marriage and burial, also came under examination. Bishop Grant considered them to be iniquitous, especially as Protestants were not asked to pay. Cardinal Cullen concurred, but said that Ecclesiastical Affairs must make the decision.

Agreement with Rome

Agreement with the Government, and commissioning priests chosen to be chaplains, was not the end of the matter. Rome, which had been consulted at every step, still had to give approval on 'extraordinary' faculties for priests and whether chaplains, in view of their salaried position, should be forbidden from taking stole fees from soldiers. Extraordinary faculties were granted by the circular of 26 April 1859; a ruling on stole fees was given by the Supreme Congregation of the Sacred Office on 21 June 1859:

> Having carefully considered such a proposal, it was decided that Bishops should urge the Military Chaplains and priests not to demand any tax from soldiers but to content themselves with any offering which might be given spontaneously, also that should Monsignor Grant answer the minister about this matter, he is to tell him that appropriate dispositions have already been made.

There followed a sting in the tail; a caution to Bishop Grant on the lack of zeal shown by priests to soldiers residing in their parishes.

> When approving this resolution His Holiness has deigned to order that from this S.C. of Propaganda, such instructions should be communicated to the present Bishop and that at the same time, he should be notified that it is known by the Holy See how those priests do not devote themselves with great zeal to the teaching and spiritual care of the military residing in their parishes. They should therefore be encouraged by their Bishops to fulfill to the letter the obligations of their sacred ministries.[33]

A Royal Warrant in 1858 fixed a new establishment for Anglican, Catholic and Presbyterian chaplains in the RAChD, four grades replacing the previous two of Chaplain and Assistant Chaplain. The grades adopted, the equivalent of Captain, Major, Lieutenant-Colonel and Colonel, are still in use today. Concern on the part of the War Office on matters of discipline and the removal of chaplains, other than by court-martial, was overcome when Bishop Grant told them a chaplain could not officiate without a licence from his Ordinary, which could be removed. With these matters settled, the War Office wrote to Bishop Grant:

General No 130   War Office.
                                                   Pall Mall S.W.

The Rt. Rev Bishop Grant.   21 June 1858

Sir,
    I am directed to acquaint you that Secretary Major General Peel is about to nominate sixteen Roman Catholic Clergymen as Acting Chaplains to the Forces. I am therefore to request the favour of your transmitting the names of such clergymen as you are prepared to recommend for the office of Assistant Chaplain, for consideration and approval of the Secretary of State.[34]

That same year sixteen Catholic priests were commissioned as full-time chaplains to the forces, and three full-time officiating chaplains appointed to the Royal Navy. Additionally, many missionaries or parochial clergy were appointed officiating chaplains to the forces, for which they received *per capita* allowances. In 1859 the acting chaplains became permanent commissioned officers on the same terms as their Protestant colleagues.

Despite the happy relationship between Grant and Cullen and their constant consultation, Irish bishops were unhappy. When four of the newly-commissioned chaplains were appointed to Ireland, the bishops there refused to grant faculties, and they had to be withdrawn.[35] Following correspondence between Dublin and Southwark it was agreed in 1863 that military chaplains would operate under the Bishop of Southwark throughout the British Empire, except in Ireland. There, Irish bishops would make arrangements for the military establishments in their dioceses, and Irish priests began an association with the British Army that has never faltered.

> The decree for the nomination of army and navy chaplains did not for some reason or other give satisfaction in Ireland, and its rejection came from a quarter where it was extremely painful for a Catholic Bishop to meet with opposition … He [Grant] set to work, however, at his old mission of pouring out oil upon the waters, and after a while they subsided, and there was peace once more between the sister arks.[36]

At this time the British Army had more troops stationed in Ireland than in India, over 50,000. Most were quartered in and around Dublin and the Curragh and in many parts of Munster, so they fell within the jurisdiction of the Archbishops of Dublin and Cashel. The appointment of chaplains to government positions in Ireland was a prerogative the Irish bishops demanded be reserved for themselves. They maintained that they wished to guard against the possibility of government appointees who would become 'yes men'.

The system of appointing chaplains

In a letter to an Irish candidate for chaplaincy, Fr James Daly, Bishop Grant set out the procedure which all prospective chaplains followed.

> According to the Circular of the Sacred Congregation, His Holiness wishes the first step to be the asking and obtaining the consent of your Ordinary, and with it the faculties which His Holiness has granted for Military Chaplains. When you forward a letter to me stating that your Ordinary has allowed you to become a Chaplain and to exercise the Papal faculties you must be so good as to say that you fully understand the duties of a military Chaplain and are prepared to perform them. Some of the duties are described in the enclosed printed paper and it is very important that you shall notice that you will be expected to go to any part of the world with the Troops at a moment's notice. It is further important that you should notice that when you go to any other diocese, you will have to obtain faculties from the local Bishop. If he refuses to grant them, the War Office will not be able to continue you in your appointment, as it does not wish to interfere in any way with our Ecclesiastical government or organisation. It is right therefore that you should take into account these risks when you make your application to the Primate; and in order that I may be justified in stating that I have made you fully aware of the nature of the appointment, then I write formally to the War Office on your behalf.[37]

One of Grant's first practical concerns was the consecration of Catholic marriages in the Army and their proper registration according to civil law. Grant arranged that what is now St Michael's at Aldershot should become virtually the Catholic parish church of the Army. Baptisms, confirmations and marriages of Catholic soldiers, and their families, are recorded there in a central archive, irrespective of what part of the world the sacrament actually takes place.

To add to the problems of 1857, war broke out with China. After some difficulties, the War Office accepted that a chaplain should accompany the force. Accordingly, Fr J. J. Mahé, a Westminster priest originally from Brittany, accompanied an expedition to Hong Kong.[38] Following his return to England, and to Bishop Grant's annoyance, Mahé entered into direct negotiations with the British Government on chaplaincy matters. It was an early challenge to Grant's authority and he acted swiftly: Mahé's faculties were withdrawn, and he was forthwith ordered to resign his commission.

Catholic chaplaincy and the development of the colonial Church

Because there were so few permanent chaplains in the colonies which later became the Dominions of Australia, Canada, New Zealand and South Africa, responsibility for the spiritual welfare of the troops rested with local Ordinaries, with local priests acting as officiating chaplains. In some cases, particularly in South Africa, the duties of these chaplains assisted in the spread of Christianity.

The colonial wars

Some of the hardest fighting in all colonial wars took place in New Zealand. Ensconced in extremely well-fortified villages, the Maori people defied imperial troops and local levies for years. In the earliest days of the conflict the Catholic troops of the 14th (West Yorkshire) and 18th (Royal Irish) Regiments were ministered to by French Marist missionaries, one of whom had the distinction of being mentioned in despatches.[39] Two of the newly commissioned regular army chaplains soon joined them, Frs John McSweeney and Lawrence Parsly. They were the first priests in a long procession of RAChD (RC) chaplains to go to war in British Army uniform.

Shortly after the end of the Maori Wars, the Louis Riel rebellion broke out in north-west Canada, to be put down by an expedition led by Garnet Wolseley. Two Canadian Catholic officiating chaplains took part: Fr F. X. Faguy attached to the Quebec Rifles, and Fr P. Provost with the Mount Royal Rifles.[40]

Chaplains in the outposts

In addition to those serving in the main bases within the British Isles and in New Zealand, the newly-commissioned chaplains were posted all over the Empire. Permanent chaplains were now stationed in Bermuda, St Helena, Mauritius, Halifax (Nova Scotia), and Malta. At these overseas garrisons and bases on the lines of communications, the Army had chaplains, and all the sacraments could be attended by both sailors and soldiers. For example, the North American Squadron alternated, summer and winter, between Halifax and Bermuda. At Halifax, an officer of the squadron had permission to march the Catholic ratings to Mass on a Sunday morning, either to the garrison church or to the cathedral:

> through the principal streets of the town, and the sight of the men marching under their youthful leader would create quite an interest.[41]

In addition to ministering to the garrison and fleet, the chaplains had other duties. Fr John Vertue received a special vote of thanks for gallantry during an outbreak of the dreaded 'yellow jack' in Barbados, West Indies[42] – he later became first Bishop of Portsmouth. A punitive expedition was mounted against Ashanti in 1895 under command of Sir Garnet Wolseley. Fr William Le Grave served as Catholic chaplain, later becoming a canon of Portsmouth diocese.[43] Another army chaplain elevated to the episcopate was Fr James Bellord, who started a new mission while attached to the Fareham Forts. He was only one of several chaplains who began missions in the south of England in the latter part of the nineteenth century.[44]

South Africa and northwards

Portuguese explorer settlements had existed in South Africa from Vasco da Gama onwards, but were suppressed upon the arrival of the Dutch. The creation of the Batavian Republic following the French Revolution brought religious toleration to the Cape Dutch. Three priests arrived from Holland to serve the scattered Catholic communities, and a room in Cape Castle was placed at their disposal for saying Mass for the Catholic troops of the garrison. But their mission ended with the arrival of the British in 1795. Because they served the garrison, they were expelled with the Dutch troops.[45]

Catholic missionaries eventually followed the British Army and a resident Bishop of the Cape of Good Hope was appointed: the Rt Rev R. P. Griffith, a Dominican. The castle was put at the disposal of the bishop because the major part of his congregation were Catholic soldiers. Realizing the potential of the mission, the bishop appealed for assistance. One of those who answered was a student of St Peter's College, Wexford, Thomas Murphy. On his arrival in Cape Town he was ordained by Bishop Griffith in a barrack room of Cape Castle, and shortly afterwards went to a frontier settlement, Grahamstown. There, in addition to his missionary work, he became officiating chaplain to the Inniskilling Fusiliers. Fr

Murphy and his white horse soon became familiar to and popular with the soldiers. When, in 1843, the regiment moved to Fort Napier (later Pietermaritzburg) in Natal, Fr Murphy accompanied them and founded another Catholic community.[46] In succeeding years settlements grew around what were predominantly Catholic garrisons.

When imperial troops were committed to action against the Zulus, South African priests served as officiating chaplains. One, Fr Andrew Walsh, accompanied the column composed mainly of the South Wales Borderers which met with disaster at Islandlhwana, and his death in action was reported. Shortly afterwards, during an Army memorial service for the dead of Islandlhwana, Fr Walsh appeared, dishevelled, but very much alive.[47] No longer threatened by Zulu power, the Boers of the Transvaal revolted in 1880. In an action at Bronkhorsepruit, the 2nd Connaught Rangers were ambushed by the Boers and suffered severely. Fr Meyer OMI had the sad duty of burying the dead and giving the last rites to the wounded and dying.[48]

Reinforcements were sent out and a regular army chaplain was despatched with the Natal Field Force. Fr Henry P. Kelly OFM had been commissioned chaplain on 11 January 1879, and he arrived in Natal in 1881.[49] It is possible, although not certain, that he may have been present at the Battle of Majuba. Bishop Jolivet of Natal was taken prisoner of war by the Boers but released shortly afterwards. During the siege of the British at Pretoria, the Loreto convent was for three months turned into a redoubt because of its position on the edge of town: the nuns, women and children 'packed like herrings in a barrel'.[50] Mother Jolivet, sister of the bishop, died in January 1881, and was buried in the grounds of the convent with full military honours.[51]

Fr H. S. Kerr SJ and two other Jesuits, Frs Prestage and Hartmann, accompanied the first pioneering expedition into what was to become Rhodesia. Mother Patrick, a Dominican sister of King William's Town, at the request of Cecil Rhodes and through the insistence of Bishop Ricards, also accompanied the first pioneer column to Matabeleland as a nurse. Her memory long remained bright in the minds of the Rhodesians and for many years on St Patrick's Day a service of commemoration took place at her grave in Salisbury (Harare).[52]

The Matabele War, 1896

In 1896 the Matabele rose in rebellion and about 200 white settlers were killed. Urgent appeals were sent and Lieutenant-Colonel H. C. Plumer (later Field-Marshal Lord Plumer of Messines) raised the Matabeleland Relief Force. A mounted force of 800 officers and men, it concentrated at Mafeking and included Fr M. Barthelemy SJ as its chaplain. In the course of its eight-month campaign, Fr Barthelemy accompanied the force until

peace was made between Cecil Rhodes and the Matabele chiefs. Among the
many letters of congratulations received by Herbert Plumer on the
disbandment of the force was one from the chaplain:

> One letter which touched him very much came from the Jesuit Father
> who had been with the Force during all their engagements. He writes: 'It
> is almost useless to tell you that I join heartily in all the congratulations
> you receive and will receive. Men more authorized to do so than I am
> praise your work; still, nobody perhaps knows better than I how much
> you deserve the love your men have for you.'[53]

Cyprus 1879–80

Fr Henry Schomberg Kerr SJ, a former commander Royal Navy, was the
first British Army Catholic chaplain to serve in Cyprus following the British
occupation of the island. Landing at Larnaca on 4 February 1879, he was
attached to the 20th Foot, the Lancashire Fusiliers, and travelled widely
over the island ministering to the various detachments at Nicosia, Mathiati
and Limassol (Polymedia Camp). In the summer of 1879 he rode a donkey
to the newly-organized camp at Troodos. He kept a journal for family
reading, and this gives fascinating glimpses of the work of a chaplain:

> Preparing for tomorrow's feast. Trying to stir up the British soldier to be
> equal to the occasion, who, for the most part, won't be stirred.
>   Sunday 29th, Feast of SS. Peter and Paul. Mass and service as usual;
> singing a trifle better. People are wonderfully shy in church. Meeting of
> Temperance Society as usual. In the evening established a Confraternity
> of the Sacred Heart in honour of the feast, some eight or nine making
> their consecration in my tent.[54]

Some things in the British Army never change:

> It is strange how hard it is to get hold of men. They always seem on duty,
> one day on guard, another fatigue, orderly man, cook's mate, guardroom
> – always some excuse. Any amount of red tape too. If the colonel,
> adjutant and quartermaster were not such good fellows, it would be very
> disagreeable getting anything done.[55]

Despite all the frustration and red tape, with the assistance of the
Commander Royal Engineers, Fr Kerr succeeded in having a sanctuary
built at the summer garrison camp on Mount Troodos.

> Very busy preparing to open sanctuary, about twenty men at work – all
> for love. Every one asked responds cheerfully – tailors, carpenters,
> armourers, and the like. It is a small place, but it has an eighteen-inch
> stone wall.
>   August 21st – I enclose a photograph of the sanctuary of Our Lady of
> Mount Troodos. A labour of love for the feast of the Assumption. It is
> complete and pretty in a rough way. It is lighted from above. There is a

good deal of detail for young eyes to make out. The altar and step are of white limestone from the ruins of St Epiphanius' Catholic Chapel. The altar-cloth was worked by the schoolmistress. Pictures and candles I brought from Naples, the damask-like curtains from Limassol.[56]

Shortly afterwards, on 12 May 1880, Fr Kerr left Cyprus on being appointed chaplain to the Marquis of Ripon, whom he joined at Port Said. Fr Kerr travelled to India with General Gordon, who at this time was Secretary to Lord Ripon. On arrival in India, Gordon resigned this most comfortable of posts, in order to return to the Sudan – and his heroic death.

Egypt and the Anglo-Egyptian Sudan

When British troops landed in Egypt in 1882, Fr Robert Brindle, attached to the Royal Irish Regiment, was present at the Battle of Tel el Kebir. He remained with the regiment on duty in Egypt and was part of the force formed in 1884 to relieve the besieged General Gordon in Khartoum.

Because of the Government's delay in mounting the expedition, the Nile was low and the cataracts exposed, causing the greatest difficulty in dragging the boats of the expedition upstream. Sir Garnet Wolseley offered a prize of £100 to the unit which arrived first with its stores intact. Fr Brindle captained the boat which flew the flag of H Company.

The future Field-Marshal Sir Evelyn Wood, a friend of Brindle, was part of the Camel Corps, and was encamped on the banks of the Nile when:

> I saw a little flotilla of boats flying the Royal Irish flag toiling up the river. Father Brindle got out when he pulled up to us, hot, tired and irritable, with his hands blistered and perspiration running down his face. Said I 'Father, what have you been doing?' 'Pulling stroke oar in order to encourage them'. 'Any result?' 'Devil a bit' was the reply. The Father was, however, unduly pessimistic, for the Royal Irish won Lord Wolseley's prize given to the battalion which had made the best time for the three or four hundred miles up the river, and also which brought up in good order the largest amount of public stores intact.[57]

In a race to try and get to Khartoum quickly, Wolseley sent his flotilla of steamers up the Nile with as many troops as he could cram on board. He also sent the Camel Corps across the Nubian Desert where the Nile makes its great bend in the Sudan. At Metemeh the Dervishes were repulsed, and having ascertained that Khartoum had fallen, the steamers floated down the Nile and the column retired across the desert. To reinforce that column on its retirement was important. Wolseley despatched the Royal Irish. Tall and bearded, disdaining to use his pony, Brindle led the way, always marching outside and in front of the regimental square. To all ranks he must have appeared like an Old Testament prophet leading his people through the wilderness.

His genial personality, his devotion to duty, his coolness in danger, his indifference to hardship, combined to give him a remarkable influence over the men, which he exerted invariably in the interest of the service.[58]

After some years doing garrison duty at Colchester and Aldershot, Fr Brindle returned to Egypt for Kitchener's reconquest of the Sudan (1896-98). During the advance to Omdurman he repeatedly distinguished himself; on one occasion by taking a gunboat into action, on another for ministering to the troops during a cholera outbreak. Present at the Battle of Atbara, he heard of a dying Catholic soldier in a camp about ten miles away and could not rest until he had attended to him.

> Brindle walked at night unarmed across the perilous desert of El Teb - infested by the enemy - administered the last rites to the dying soldier and stayed with him until the end. Then he tramped back across the desert to his own camp in time to say Mass next morning.[59]

Following the Battle of Omdurman and the taking of Khartoum, a memorial service was held for Gordon at the spot where he fell outside the palace. An eyewitness later described the scene:

> After the British and Egyptian flags had been run up on the roof of the palace there followed a dead hush while the four military chaplains - Catholic, Anglican, Presbyterian and Methodist - came slowly forward and ranged themselves with their backs to the palace, just before Kitchener. The Presbyterian read the fifteenth psalm, the Anglican led the rustling whisper of the Lord's Prayer. Snow-haired Father Brindle, best beloved of priests, laid his helmet at his feet and read a memorial prayer bare headed in the sun.[60]

Kitchener had Fr Brindle's prayer officially printed and distributed amongst the men.[61] Some years later, Kitchener wrote to Brindle after he had been elevated to the episcopate. It was a letter between good friends.

> My Dear Father,
> I like this form of address better than your exalted title of Bishop. I wonder you did not excommunicate the War Office and all its contents, including the staff that now rules there, perhaps you had not a bell, book and candle with you, and only murmured the formula...
> I often look back in memory of the old Soudan days when you used to lead the troops across the desert, and wish those days back again.
> I am shortly going back to Khartoum for the winter and to shoot up the White Nile.
> I was delighted to get your letter and to feel that you still have a kindly remembrance for your old friend,
>
> Kitchener[62]

Retiring from the Army on 12 March 1899 he was consecrated titular Bishop of Hermopolis and Auxiliary of Westminster, then appointed

Bishop of Nottingham on 6 December 1901. When Bishop Brindle died on 17 September 1916, he was buried with full military honours in the crypt of St Barnabas' Cathedral, Nottingham. It was the Army's final honour to a distinguished chaplain.[63]

Notes and references

1. Rt Rev Maurice Taylor, *The Scots College in Spain.*
2. Lt Col J. P. Riley, 'Coalitions – world wars: a study of 1813', unpublished.
3. *Canadian Dictionary of National Biography* (CDNB).
4. Ibid.
5. Jacques Pelletier and Rev Francis G. Morrisey OMI, *Le Vicariat Militaire du Canada* (Faculté de Droit Canonique, Université Saint-Paul, 1976).
6. CDNB.
7. Rawlinson MSS, War History Box, DAA.
8. News item, *Hampshire Chronicle* (12 January 1798).
9. Colin Johnston Robb, 'The story of the Royal South Down Militia', unpublished, Linen Hall Library, Belfast.
10. W. J. Fitz-Patrick, *The Life, Times, and Correspondence of the Rt Rev Dr Doyle* (Dublin, 1880).
11. Ibid., p. 28.
12. Ibid.
13. Ibid.
14. Ibid., p. 33.
15. Edward Gallagher, 'The Irish College, Salamanca under the rectorship of Patrick Curtis 1780-1817', thesis, St Patrick's College, Maynooth. After the Battle of Salamanca, Patrick Curtis was arrested and narrowly escaped being shot, presumably because 'He was operating a large espionage organization, consisting mainly of priests and *alcaldes*, linked by a system of "foot messengers" and based at the Irish College of the University (of Salamanca)': Jock Haswell, *The First Respectable Spy* (London, 1969), pp. 178-9.
16. D. J. O'Doherty, 'Students of the Irish College, Salamanca 1776-1837', *Archivium Hibernicum*, VI (1917).
17. The Very Rev Canon Croft, *Historical Account of Lisbon College* (Barnet, 1902), p. 115.
18. Charles Chevenix-Trench, *The Great Dan* (London, 1984), p. 146.
19. Sir John Smyth VC, *In this Sign Conquer: The Story of Army Chaplains* (London, 1968), pp. 56-7.
20. Ibid., pp. xviii-xix.
21. H. M. Hanham, 'Religion and nationality in the mid-Victorian Army' in M. R. D. Foot (ed.), *War and Society* (London, 1973), p. 165.
22. Document 1183, Ushaw College Archives.
23. Ibid.
24. Cecil Woodham-Smith, *Florence Nightingale* (London, 1950), pp. 183-5.
25. Sr Mary Aloysius, *Memories of the Crimea* (London, 1897).
26. Grace Ramsay, *Thomas Grant, First Bishop of Southwark* (London, 1874), p. 172.

27. Ibid.
28. Sr Mary Aloysius.
29. Obituary, SCD, p. 1899.
30. Hon Mrs Maxwell-Scott of Abbotsford, *Henry Schomberg Kerr, Sailor and Jesuit* (London, 1901), p. 218.
31. Rev Michael Clifton, *The Quiet Negotiator* (Liverpool), p. 115.
32. Archbishop Cullen Papers, 1852–57 – Sec 449/8 no. 45 (11 May 1856), ADA.
33. Chaplains papers, ASA.
34. Ibid.; see also Clifton, pp. 98–9.
35. Rawlinson MSS, War History Box, DAA.
    In March 1859 four of the newly commissioned chaplains were serving in India: Frs J. O'Dwyer, M. Cuffe, T. Molony and J. Browne. A War Office letter dated 28 March 1859 told Bishop Grant: 'I am to observe that as these Clergymen are in receipt of pay from the Government of India, no pay will be granted to them as Chaplains to the Forces until they commence their duties under this department.' WO letter, Clergy R.C. General no. 261, ASA.
36. Ramsay, pp. 180–1.
37. ASA.
38. Ramsay, p. 185.
39. J. Bryant Haigh, *Men of Faith and Courage: The Official History of New Zealand's Army Chaplains* (Auckland, 1983), p. 33.
40. Pelletier and Morrisey.
41. Maxwell-Scott, p. 34.
42. Brian Plumb, *Arundel to Zabi: A Biographical Dictionary of the Catholic Bishops of England and Wales 1623–1987* (Warrington, 1988).
43. G. Dwyer, *Diocese of Portsmouth, Past and Present* (Portsmouth, 1981), p. 57.
44. Plumb.
45. Rev J. E. Brady OMI, 'Soldiers in Christ', unpublished paper, Catholic History Bureau, Johannesburg, South Africa.
46. Ibid.
47. Ibid.
48. Ibid.
49. *The Army List* (London, HMSO, 1882).
50. Brady.
51. Ibid.
52. Ibid.
53. Gen Sir Charles Harington, *Plumer of Messines* (London, 1935), pp. 26–8.
54. Maxwell-Scott, p. 151.
55. Ibid., pp. 152–3.
56. Ibid., pp. 153–4.
57. Sir Evelyn Wood, *From Midshipman to Field Marshal* (London, 1906), pp. 173–4.
58. F. Le M. Gretton, *Campaigns and History of the Royal Irish Regiment, 1684–1902* (London, 1911), pp. 285 and 306.
59. Wood, pp. 173–4.
60. George Stevens, *With Kitchener to Khartoum* (London, 1898), p. 314.

61. Fr Gerard Hetterington, 'Bishop Brindle, DSO, 1837–1916', *The Lisbonian Magazine*, XXVIII, nos 1 and 2 (article in two parts), Part I, p. 22.
62. Stevens, p. 314.
63. Plumb.

2

The South African War

By the outbreak of the South African War, some sixty Catholic chaplains, including those temporary chaplains for the Crimean War and the Indian Mutiny, had served with the British Army throughout the world. During their service they had risen steadily in rank and, more importantly, in the esteem felt for them by the Army. What was said of one of them could equally apply to many, if not all.

> In this happy blending of the priest and officer in the Army, by ever keeping the priesthood in the front rank, but always sharing the hardships of the soldiers was ascribed the esteem and respect of every fellow-officer, of every superior and every man who served with him and under him.[1]

In March 1899 serving with the Army there were six chaplains 1st class (colonel), two 2nd class (lieutenant-colonel), three 3rd class (major), six 4th class (captain):

1st Class	*Station*
Rev R. Brindle	Egypt
Rev J. Bellord	Colchester
Rev T. Foran	Shorncliffe
Rev R. F. Collins	Gibraltar
Rev W. Le Grave	Bermuda
Rev T. Twomey	Aldershot
2nd Class	
Rev E. M. Morgan	Halifax, N.S.
Rev C. W. Keatinge	Egypt
3rd Class	
Rev W. B. L. Alexander	Dover

Rev E. Ryan   Aldershot
Rev L. J. Matthews   Egypt
4th Class
Rev Bickerstaffe-Drew   Malta
Rev W. Keatinge   Portsmouth
Rev R. H. Nash   Netley
Rev S. Rogers   Aldershot
Rev D. P. Lane   Home Service
Rev W. Forrest   Home Service

The South African War, 1899–1902

From the Crimean War to the outbreak of World War I, each chaplain was dealt with directly from the War Office, except for purely local matters, such as the arrangements of services. In these, chaplains dealt with local commanding officers and general officers commanding the station. Where more than one Catholic chaplain was serving at the same station, the senior of them was recognized as having a general responsibility for their work and, as a rule, all communication with the military authorities was conducted through him. There was no representation of the Royal Army Chaplains' Department on the headquarters staff of any Command, either in the United Kingdom or abroad.

The South African War was the first since the Crimea which led to difficulties for the RAChD, and particularly for Catholic chaplains, where the ecclesiastical machinery for the selection and recruitment was so distant from the War Office. There was the added difficulty of having no staff representative at either the War Office or Home Commands. Southwark therefore had little idea of the large scale of mobilization and expansion, where the troops would be accommodated, or what percentage of Catholics any temporary camp was likely to contain. The retirement of the Rev Robert Brindle from the Army in March 1899 and his elevation to become Auxiliary to the Archbishop of Westminster deprived Catholic chaplains of a figure capable of taking the reins of control. Indeed, at Westminster he was shortly in disagreement with Bishop Bourne over a chaplain for the Army garrison at Colchester, Essex.

All regular chaplains who could be spared were sent to South Africa as soon as possible: Frs Collins, Morgan, Alexander, Ryan, Matthews, William Keatinge. The Rev Thomas Foran, senior 1st class chaplain, was at Shorncliffe and not in good health. He was not considered fit enough even for Malta to relieve Fr Bickerstaffe-Drew for South Africa. Fr Charles Keatinge in Egypt could not be spared; however, to reinforce those already there, Fr Le Grave was ordered home from Bermuda and sent to the Cape. Upon the outbreak of war, eight South African officiating chaplains reported to the colours for full-time duty. The regular chaplains were replaced by officiating chaplains, and their pay increased from £130 a year to ten shillings *per diem*, without travelling expenses.

Yet even this considerable list of chaplains, in comparison with the previous number despatched with Field Forces, was insufficient to meet the requirements of the large numbers of Catholics involved. For the first time all the Irish infantry and cavalry regiments were deployed together in the same theatre of operations. Although at the beginning of the war only one battalion of each regiment was sent out, more followed. The size of Catholic units, and distances over which they were deployed, was too great for the available chaplains to minister to. In addition to the many Irish units, there were the English, Scottish and Welsh battalions with sizeable Catholic numbers.

An unprecedented situation developed when on arrival at Cape Town the Bishop refused to grant faculties to the chaplains. This meant that while they remained within the diocese of Cape Town, Army chaplains could not minister to the troops.

> And so the chaplains were put into an absurd position, by being inhibited in that diocese from doing the work which they were sent to carry out.[2]

The Army chaplains sent an urgent appeal to Rome and very quickly got a decision in their favour. The chaplains had been placed in this embarrassing position by what can only be explained by a lapse of communications between Southwark and the Colony.

In November 1914, writing from the Western Front to a fellow-chaplain in England, Fr Foran commented:

> This is so different from the South African War! No British Catholic soldier may have the least fear of living or dying without the sacraments.[3]

Implicit in this is the fear Catholic soldiers had in South Africa of death without the sacraments. The reaction to the news of the battles and casualties was concern for the dangerously wounded on hospital ships.

In the only recorded personal intervention of the Bishop of Southwark about the provision of chaplains for South Africa, Bishop Bourne sent a letter to the War Office dated 21 December 1899 expressing concern about Catholics dying at sea without the ministrations of a Catholic priest. He assured the Secretary of State 'I could provide as many as would be required'.[4] To this the War Office replied in early January:

> My Lord,
> I am directed by the Marquess of Lansdowne to acquaint you that your letter of 21st ultimo, respecting the religious ministrations to the sick and wounded Roman Catholic soldiers returning home from South Africa, has been very carefully considered. His Lordship fully appreciates the great importance of this question, but it is found that as yet the number of invalids sent home in any one ship is inconsiderable, and it may be taken

as fairly certain that the number of invalided Roman Catholic soldiers on board would not ordinarily exceed seven or eight. The medical authorities in South Africa would not put on board anyone whose death could be reasonably anticipated to take place during the homeward voyage which would occupy from 16 to 22 days according to the class of steamer.

The Secretary of State suggests, for your consideration, that the case might be met if the Senior Roman Catholic chaplain in South Africa were requested to provide that all Roman Catholic officers and men invalided home in a specially precarious state of health shall, as far as possible, be prepared by the appropriate religious ministrations before embarkation.[5]

Apart from this concern, and notwithstanding the news from the front, there appears to have been considerable complacency in London about the chaplaincy situation for soldiers in action on the battlefield, as the following letter from the War Office to Southwark shows:

Dear Canon Connelly,

Lord Lansdowne is prepared to accept the services of a priest as voluntary chaplain in South Africa, if the Bishop of Southwark cares to nominate one. Only one can be accepted: he will be provided with nothing but a free passage out, rations in the field, and free passage home if he stays in S Africa until the military authorities dispense with his services. He will, under the Army Act, be subject to military law and discipline, and must be prepared to serve under the R.C. Chaplain to whose Division or brigade he may be attached. He must be absolutely at the disposal of the military authorities, and will rank as 'Acting Chaplain (unpaid)'.

Please nominate officially without reference to any previous correspondence. If Father Watson or any of your other volunteers is not immediately available there is, of course, no need to hurry. It will be for you to decide in the meanwhile before you nominate how far you will make the Secretary of State's offer public.

This offer has been made to meet the views of those who urged that the clergy alone were allowed to take no part in helping. Three Church of England and one Church of Scotland clergymen are going on the above terms.

Lord Roberts has expressed himself as very well satisfied with the number of chaplains we have sent out. We are lucky so far not to have had any casualties among them, but we can hardly hope for immunity throughout.[6]

Despite such an unpromising offer, at least one priest, Fr Albert Knapp OP, volunteered as an unpaid chaplain and was accepted. A month after the War Office request, Southwark replied:

The Bishop has pleasure in recommending this priest as well suited for the duty. Southwark 12 Mar 1900.[7]

Many other priests also volunteered. One such was Fr Bradley OFM, of Clonmel. He wrote to Canon Connelly to say that he was expecting to receive from Rome his *exeat* and was anxious to become an Army or naval chaplain. However, perhaps impatient with the delay, Fr Bradley also enlisted the help of influential friends to solicit the War Office on his behalf. The result was unexpected.

> I am directed by the Bishop of Southwark in answer to your letter of the 29th Ultimo (posted on the 6th inst) to return the enclosure and to say that he has nothing to add to what he has already said to Fr Bradley in his letter of 24th Ultimo, unless it be to remark that Fr Bradley seems to misunderstand the whole position of things.
>
> In the first place the Bishop of Southwark has nothing whatever to do with the appointments of chaplains to the navy.
>
> Fr Bradley seems to think that by influence he will be able to induce the War Office to send in his name in such a way that the Bishop cannot refuse to nominate him. As you very justly remark, it has never been the practice of the War Office to interfere in any way with the Bishop's selection. Priests are recommended by the Bishop entirely on their merits after a period of probation, and any attempt to precipitate things, such as Fr Bradley seems to contemplate, is calculated rather to prejudice than to improve a candidate's chances of being selected.[8]

Nevertheless, as great numbers of troop reinforcements flowed into South Africa and news of the desperate plight of the wounded and dying on the various battlefields began to unfold, additional chaplains were requested and the pace quickened in London. Canon Connelly appears to have been ill, yet he was allowed to continue overseeing Army chaplains while living at Hove. Taking the distance involved and his state of health together, it can hardly have contributed to an efficient working arrangement for the religious benefit of troops at war.

> Dear Canon Connelly,
> I have telegraphed to Mr Hayward, asking him to be ready to start in about a week. Mr Le Grave is under orders also, making five priests in all.
>
> I am not quite certain yet whether we may want a sixth. Monsignor Bickerstaffe-Drew can I fear, hardly be spared from Malta, especially as Father Foran's health does not permit him to take up duty at that station. In case we require a sixth, is there anyone you would specially wish to send? What about Father Byrne, our Acting Chaplain at Gosport?
>
> In a few days we shall probably be asking you to nominate two Acting Chaplains for the summer manoeuvres on Salisbury Plain, starting about 7th May.[9]

The letter has a note upon it 'Two camps, 1 at Bulford Irish Militia Brigade near Amesbury. 2nd at Perham Down. About 3000 Catholics in all.'

The action taken upon receipt of this was to apply to the War Office requesting payment for the additional chaplains for Bulford and Perham Down. This was granted on 9 May 1900, for an acting chaplain at ten shillings *per diem*, with no travelling expenses. A priest was not immediately appointed. On 17 May 1900, Fr Connell at Woking wrote to Canon Connelly explaining that he had applied for additional help because he had four Irish regiments under canvas nearby. This was followed on 26 May 1900 by a letter from the General Officer Commanding Salisbury Plain District requesting an additional priest 'with the least possible delay'. Belated action appears to have been taken, for on 7 June Fr Connell again wrote to Canon Connelly, this time objecting to being curate to a newly-arrived priest.[10] There is nothing in the Southwark Archives to indicate what steps were taken for the spiritual welfare of the four Irish battalions while they waited, over a month, for a chaplain to be appointed. The intervention of the GOC Salisbury Plain is an indication of the concern felt by the battalion commanders (Protestant officers) for the spiritual welfare of their soldiers. This concern is confirmed by a letter from one battalion commander, Colonel J. Massy-Westropp, 5th Royal Munster Fusiliers, to Canon Connelly later the same year before the battalion departed from Bulford:

> We shall be leaving Salisbury Plain for Lydd, and as all my men are Roman Catholics we must have a priest with us. Father Partridge does a great deal of good in the Regiment and we have all a great regard for him and would be much obliged if you can see your way to grant the request.[11]

It would appear that the colonel's request was not acceded to, for on 22 October 1900, a letter to Canon Connelly says 'finding a place for Fr Partridge is rather difficult';[12] the suggestion is then made that he might go as chaplain on a hospital ship. What happened about a chaplain for the Munsters is not apparent in the chaplain's correspondence.

There is ample evidence at Southwark Archives that it was the action of the War Office, by its constant reminders, which led to the nomination of chaplains for appointments to temporary and regular commissions. Regrettably, there is nothing to suggest that in the chaplaincy section of Southwark there was any thought or idea of long-term, or even short-term, forward planning, as the following letter illustrates:

> The War Office, 27 Jan 1900.
> To The V. R. Mgr Canon Connelly, St George's Cathedral House.
> Sir, With reference to your letter of 18th January 1899, intimating that the Bishop of Southwark had nominated the Reverend D. P. Lane for duty as a Chaplain on probation to the Forces, I am now directed by the Marquess of Lansdowne to enquire whether the Bishop is prepared to recommend the clergyman in question for confirmation in his appointment.
> I am, Sir, Your obedient servant, E. Fleetwood Wilson.[13]

Temporary chaplains for South Africa

Between 1900 and the Peace of Vereeniging in 1902, which ended the South African War, no fewer than thirty more temporary chaplains were sent out.

The critical situation in South Africa and the demand for additional chaplains changed the minds of the War Office administrators about terms of service for temporary chaplains. Each prospective chaplain was now sent the following when his name was forwarded from Southwark:

> I am directed by the Secretary of State for War to inform you that conditionally upon your forwarding to this Office a formal undertaking to serve in South Africa for so long as your services are required in that country, and a certificate from a registered medical practitioner that you are in good health and fit for service in South Africa, he has appointed you to be an Acting Chaplain to the South African Field Force, with the pay and allowances of a Fourth Class Chaplain while so employed, from the date of your embarkation.
>
> On receipt of the above-mentioned undertaking and certificate, an advance of 40 days' pay at 10s a day and ninety-one days' field allowance at 3s. 6d. a day will be issued to you, and instructions forwarded respecting your passage. On arrival at Cape Town you are to report yourself to the General Officer Commanding.[14]

In addition to the above pay and allowances, for those chaplains allocated to hospital ships (who were not entitled to field allowance) there was a detention allowance of one pound per day whilst at Cape Town awaiting a homeward ship.[15]

There were some administrative distractions to the orderly working of the chaplains which might have been avoided by conscientiously adhering to the procedures set out by Bishop Grant over forty years before. Possibly, also, diocesan bishops, in their recommendations to Southwark, were not altogether accurate in assessing the qualities required for Army chaplaincy. Two priests were dismissed for drunkenness and the issue became public knowledge, to the embarrassment of Bishop Bourne and the Church. One temporary chaplain, Fr A. J. Manga CRP, who possibly joined from overseas, was sent to Aldershot. The Bishop of Portsmouth, learning that he had left his Order without the permission of his Superior, refused to have him work in Portsmouth diocese and insisted he be replaced.[16]

Upon the retirement of Fr Brindle in March 1899, his vacancy in the establishment was filled by the appointment of Fr Albert Boddington, a Westminster priest, to a chaplaincy 'on probation'.[17] He was appointed on 17 May 1899 and sent to the military garrison at Colchester. In April 1900, Fr Boddington was warned for South Africa, but a replacement for him at Colchester was not arranged. In desperation he appealed to the diocese, Westminster, explaining the situation and asking for a replacement:

Lonsdale, Maldon Rd, Colchester. 25 April 1900.

Dear Mgr Johnson,
I have been ordered to sail for South Africa on Saturday morning next and though I have tried to get a Father to take duty here I have so far been unable to get one. I have tried the Passionists, Highgate, the Redemptorists, Clapham, and Fr Kelly of Harwich.
    There are about 600 soldiers besides women and children who will be deprived of Mass etc. unless a Priest is sent for Sunday next.
    Trusting you will be able to send help.
    Yours very truly, Albert Boddington, CF[18]

The letter was sent from Westminster to Southwark, annotated by the Auxiliary Bishop: 'The diocese does not Supply for military stations. That is done through the Bishop of Southwark.✠ Rob Brindle.' At Southwark the letter was again annotated: 'Noted. 4 May 1900. Wrote to Bp Brindle. Bp of Southwark not responsible. J. C.'

Fr Boddington left for South Africa. What happened, if anything, to provide cover for the Catholics of Colchester is not stated. However, Fr Boddington fell ill in South Africa. Without finding a replacement, or obtaining permission, he returned to England. Meanwhile, the War Office machinery ground on and as Boddington's probationary year expired, they wanted to know about the Bishop of Southwark's nomination for his regular chaplaincy.[19] This was answered on 16 June 1900: 'Reference Reverend A. Boddington in South Africa. The Bishop has applied for a report and will let you hear from him as soon as it is received'; in the meantime he was 'Stood over for further consideration'.[20] We next hear about Fr Boddington in a letter from him dated 14 September 1900 to Bishop Bourne begging to be reinstated as CF in South Africa; and on 22 October 1900, Fr Boddington is reported as being on the sick list with 'debility'. Eventually Fr Boddington failed to obtain a nomination for a regular chaplaincy, and he disappeared completely from Church life in 1906.[21]

During the war, one officiating chaplain died at a home station, Fr J. W. Reeks, at Woolwich, and was immediately replaced by Fr J. Lonergan on War Office authority. It is pleasing to record that the War Office, in their letter of 20 September 1900 nominating the replacement, also observed the niceties: 'I am also to express Lord Lansdowne's condolences to the relatives of the deceased chaplain.'[22]

Priests at the front

Fr William Keatinge went from England to Durban with Buller's Natal Field Force. With Hart's Irish Brigade he accompanied the Force at the Battles of Colenso and Spion Kop and when, upon the relief of Ladysmith, the brigade was given the honour of entering first, he was with them.[23]

The temporary chaplains sent out to the Field Force came from the entire spectrum of the priesthood. Priests, regular and secular alike, answered the call. They were to have an impact on their new comrades, and enjoy, or not, adventures far out of the ordinary events of the past, in either presbytery or monastery. A few, through personal intemperance, brought discredit to the Church. One virtually deserted. The vast majority, however, upheld or indeed enhanced the reputation of Catholic chaplains.

One chaplain, Fr Simon Knapp OCD, may have wondered what to expect of his new brethren and flock, in the regiment to which he was posted – the 6th Inniskilling Dragoons, one of the many detached cavalry columns. But his own concern would have been nothing compared to the stir created by the signal notifying the regiment of his impending arrival:

> About this time the Inniskillings received an official notification that a Carmelite monk, Father Knapp, was to be attached to the regiment as chaplain. There was some consternation at the announcement, and anxious canvassing as to which of the squadron messes was to receive this unknown quantity, who sounded so little likely to adapt himself to the life of a cavalry regiment in the field. He fell, by lot or otherwise, to the headquarters mess of Allenby [later Field-Marshal Lord Allenby] and the regimental Staff, and proved to be not only 'quite the best specimen of Army Chaplain I've ever met', as Allenby wrote home, 'but a charming companion'.[24]

During Lord Roberts' advance to Pretoria, Fr Rockcliffe, serving in Pole-Carew's division, became the only chaplain to be wounded in South Africa, when he was hit by a shell splinter.[25] Elsewhere, while attached to 1st Royal Irish, Fr Alexander had a very narrow escape from death. The battalion was part of a detached column holding down a Boer force, while Roberts prepared his main army for the advance to Pretoria. The Royal Irish held an extended line in front of superior numbers at Colesberg, and they drew Boer artillery fire. The regimental historian explains that 'One of the shells fell in the tent occupied by the Roman Catholic Chaplain, Father Alexander, happily when he was not at home!'[26]

When the Royal Irish reached Bloemfontein, and in no way connected with his narrow escape, Fr Alexander left and was succeeded by Fr Bernard Rawlinson OSB, a temporary chaplain who had made a very good impression on a regular chaplain earlier: 'from what I have seen of Fr Rawlinson at three or four short interviews, he is a man out of the ordinary, a man of notable ability and commanding presence.'[27] Fr Rawlinson remained with the Royal Irish and was twice mentioned in despatches for his work in South Africa. These were not to be his last decorations for war service as an army chaplain: more were to follow in a greater war. Three other chaplains were decorated for service in South Africa: Frs Collins and Le Grave, both regular chaplains 1st Class, were awarded the Distinguished Service Order. The third, Fr William Keatinge, was promoted in the field and twice mentioned in despatches. Much more will later be heard of both Fr Keatinge and Fr Rawlinson.

Fr Peter Bradley, at last serving in the field, was at Morvals Point Hospital, Cape Colony. For his dedicated and conscientious work amongst the sick and wounded, Fr Bradley was given a testimonial by General D. Kelly-Kenny, GOC Lines of Communication, which he forwarded together with a letter applying for a regular army chaplaincy. As a result the War Office on 5 November 1900 wrote to Bishop Bourne saying that Lord Lansdowne and Lord Wolseley only required a nomination from the Bishop of Southwark for this to be granted. The nomination was duly given.[28]

Frs Morgan and Nash were stricken by fever in Kimberley.[29] Fr Walmsley contracted enteric fever at Pretoria and was invalided home. Fr Rockcliffe was invalided out of the Army, and of course lost his pay and emoluments, without any compensation. Moreover, he was for a time unable to work in his diocese because of his disability and received no stipend from the diocesan authorities. Considerable hardship resulted for both Fr Rockcliffe and his widowed mother whom he supported.[30]

Winston Churchill, then a correspondent with the *Morning Post* in South Africa, caused Lord Roberts' displeasure by criticizing an army chaplain's sermon just before the Battle of Vaal Kraantz.

> I attended a church parade this morning. What a chance this was for a man of great soul who feared God ... All around were men who within the week had been face to face with Death, and were going to face him again in a few hours. ... It was one of those occasions when a fine preacher might have given comfort and strength where both were sorely needed ... But the Church had her lamp untrimmed. A chaplain with a raucous voice discoursed on the details of 'The siege and surrender of Jericho'. The soldiers froze into apathy, and after a while the formal perfunctory service reached its welcome conclusion. ... I remembered the venerable figure and noble character of Father Brindle in the River War, and wondered whether Rome was again seizing the opportunity which Canterbury disdained – the opportunity of telling the glad tidings to soldiers about to die ...[31]

The call to arms resounded through the Empire, and colonial troops hurried to South Africa from all over the world. The newly-emerging, semi-independent, countries within the Empire, conscious of their new-found nationhood, sent mounted contingents. Fr Patrick Fagan OP was appointed chaplain to the second Australian contingent, which left Australia on 17 January 1900. Cardinal Moran of Sydney wrote to Cardinal Vaughan asking him to apply to the War Office on his behalf for official recognition for Fr Fagan. Cardinal Vaughan duly wrote to the War Office, 'Our Colonials are very proud of their present turnout and expect to do great things. They would be pleased to have their own chaplain who enters into their views.'[32] Three more Australian chaplains followed with the later contingents. The Canadian contingent also had a Catholic chaplain, Fr Peter O'Leary.[33] But, as would be expected, the South African clergy contributed significantly more, particularly in the besieged towns:

Cape Colony	Rev C. McCarthy, Rev J. O'Reilly
Natal	Rev Baudry, Rev Murray
Orange Free State	Rev Miller, Rev G. Ogle
Transvaal	Rev J. de Lacy, Rev J. McCarthy, Rev O'Donnell[34]

Mafeking, Ladysmith, Kimberley

The Sisters of Mercy who arrived in South Africa in 1897 at the invitation of Bishop A. Gaughren of Kimberley, 'the first Bishop of the Diamond Fields',[35] were sent to Mafeking to establish a convent and school, and within a short time were also involved in nursing the sick and wounded during the siege. At the end of the war, at the invitation of the War Office, two of the sisters went to London and were decorated by King Edward VII at Buckingham Palace. Shortly after the siege was lifted, one of the sisters wrote simply:

> We had many upsets during the siege, nevertheless, we managed to keep the rule, except that two mornings and one evening we could not say Office aloud in choir because the roar of the cannon was so deafening.[36]

Fr G. Ogle, a Londoner, was parish priest of Mafeking, and during the siege kept a 'Diary of the Siege' which is in the archives of the Catholic History Bureau in South Africa.[37]

Closely associated with the Boer War of course is the siege of Ladysmith. Bishop Jolivet of Natal had brought Augustinian sisters from his native Brittany in 1894, intending that they should staff a nursing home in Durban. Instead they were sent to Ladysmith. When war came, the sisters, along with the resident priest, Fr J. Seby OMI, became heavily involved in nursing the sick and wounded throughout the siege.[38]

Kimberley, the diamond city, was besieged longest and was not relieved until 15 January 1901. Bishop Anthony Gaughren remained throughout the siege and died shortly after its lifting. He was one of three Irish brothers who became priests and served in South Africa; one as a temporary army chaplain. Their sister, a nun, also served there. A photograph of a group of chaplains in Kimberley during the siege shows Fr O'Donnell, a South African priest, in clerical black with a broad-brimmed black hat. His only badge of military rank is a Red Cross armband. A few months after the siege was lifted the Sister Superior, Nazareth House, Kimberley, sent a long letter to the Mother General at Nazareth House, Hammersmith. It is particularly interesting to learn how the 'enemy' were treated exactly the same as friends.

> Nazareth House, Kimberley, April 5th (1901).
>
> We received your letter, also your parcels for the soldiers: they are fully appreciated by them. Just as I am writing they are carrying two men into ward. One poor young fellow died last night (the only death we have had). Dr Newman is one of the doctors in attendance here. He is a Catholic and knows our house in Ballarat. He is delighted that we are nursing, as some of the Australians are patients here. One of our Boer patients underwent a serious operation the other day. The doctors feared he would not pull through. He had a shell wound in the thigh, and they had to remove the injured bone. I am glad to say he is going on well. Mr Bagshawe is going on very well and the wound in the shoulder is healing. Lieutenant O'Malley (who was wounded at Paardeberg) is in the same ward with him. His friends may enquire about him. He, too, is going on well. I received your letter with £20 enclosed, for which I am most grateful. The first of it went to buy boots for some of our wounded soldiers who were returning to the front, as they had nothing but the tops of boots tied on with twine. Those who sent the money were blessed a thousand times for their thoughtful charity. As soon as one batch of wounded is better we get another. Two more Boer prisoners have been brought in badly wounded. I forgot to tell you before that we had amongst our patients Mr Wessells, one of the Boer Commandants at the siege. We are constantly having a change of doctors. Strange to say, they were all Catholics except one, and he, too, was exceptionally nice. It was most touching to see the gratitude of the poor soldiers for anything that is done for them. I feel we will have very little merit, as it is such a pleasure to help them – they are so good and grateful … A great number of the new patients are suffering from dysentery and fever. Father Morgan and Father Nash are laid up here unfit for duty. They asked for a military chaplain from Kimberley for the front. Father Goodfriend, a German priest, who arrived only a fortnight ago, has been taken suddenly ill and is with us.[39]

References

1. Portsmouth Diocesan Records on Brindle.
2. Rawlinson MSS, DAA.
3. Letter, Foran to Forrest (1914), ASA.
4. Letter, Bourne to WO (21 December 1899), ASA.
5. Letter, WO to Bourne, ASA.
6. Letter, WO to Connelly, ASA.
7. Letter, Connelly to WO, ASA.
8. Letter, Connelly to WO (dated 7 April 1900), ASA.
9. Letter, WO to Connelly (dated 21 April 1900), ASA.
10. Letter, ASA.

11. Letter (dated 4 September 1900), ASA.
12. ASA.
13. Letter, WO to Connelly, ASA.
14. WO, example, standard letter to prospective chaplains, ASA.
15. Ibid.
16. Undated letter, ASA.
17. Letter (dated 13 March 1899), ASA.
18. Letter, ASA.
19. Letter, WO Clg Gen 3527 (dated 1 June 1900), ASA.
20. ASA.
21. Charles FitzGerald-Lombard, Abbot of Downside, *English and Welsh Priests 1801–1914* (Downside, 1993), p. 17.
22. ASA.
23. Brian Plumb, *Arundel to Zabi: A Biographical Dictionary of the Catholic Bishops of England and Wales, 1623–1987* (Warrington, 1988).
24. A. P. Wavell, *Allenby* (London, 1940), p. 93.
25. *Daily Chronicle (13 December 1900)*.
26. F. Le Gretton, *Campaigns and History of the Royal Irish Regiment, 1684–1902* (London, 1911), p. 319.
27. ASA.
28. Ibid.
29. Sr M. St Austin, letter published in *Weekly Register* (4 May 1900).
30. Letter from Fr Francis Goldie SJ, explaining the circumstances, ASA.
31. Randolph S. Churchill, *Winston Churchill*, vol. I (London, 1966), p. 523.
32. Letters, AWA.
33. Jacques Pelletier and Rev Francis G. Morrisey OMI, *Le Vicariat Militaire du Canada* (Faculté de Droit Canonique, Université Saint-Paul, 1976), p. 2.
34. Rev J. E. Brady OMI, 'Soldiers in Christ', unpublished paper, Catholic History Bureau, Johannesburg.
35. Ibid.
36. Sr Austin.
37. Brady.
38. Ibid.
39. Sr Austin.

3

A new broom at Southwark

From the beginning of his episcopate at Southwark the future Cardinal Bourne made clear to the War Office his views about who should bear the cost of administering chaplains. Writing to the War Office on 28 September 1897, he told the Secretary of State:

> For upwards of forty years the Bishops of Southwark have acted as advisor to the War Office on any matter affecting the Roman Catholic chaplains to the forces and has carried out the extensive correspondence which this duty entails without cost to the country.[1]

'My secretary is fully occupied with my own correspondence', the Bishop wrote, therefore there had been created a separate department to administer to Army chaplains, entrusted to Canon Connelly who 'by doing the work is debarred from an appointment giving considerable income'. The letter ended: 'I find myself unable to draw upon the extremely limited resources'[2] of the diocese, and requested the sum of £80 per annum in defrayment. A modest sum in the circumstances. The War Office accepted the argument, but haggled over the amount, and suggested £50.[3]

To this Bishop Bourne replied personally and gave an example of the expenditure necessitated by the provision of one chaplain for Gibraltar. Two letters to the War Office, two letters to the chaplain, three letters to the replacement priest, two to the P & O shipping company, one to the Bishop of Gibraltar. Plus one telegram to Rev T. J. Harker at one shilling and two and a halfpence. Cab fare at six shillings for two interviews at the War Office and four at the P & O offices. 'One is liable to this sort of thing at any time.' At the end he declared:

> I doubt whether in any other department of the Service similar duties are discharged at the nominal remuneration of eighty pounds for which I asked.[4]

The War Office argued no further. Canon Connelly, however, was shortly moved by Bishop Bourne to Hove, near Brighton. From there he continued to administer the Roman Catholic Chaplains' Department for the armed forces. The distance between Hove and Whitehall could only have increased the administrative cost and diminished efficiency, as was clearly shown during the South African War when much of the correspondence dealing with the expansion of the Catholic chaplaincy had to be conducted by telegram. Usually this was between the War Office and Brighton, and between Brighton and prospective chaplains and dioceses in all parts of the United Kingdom, not to mention whatever liaison was necessary between the canon and his bishop.

One of Bishop Bourne's earliest discussions with Rome in connection with chaplaincy was the use of a church by the Army in Valletta, Malta. The resident chaplain wanted a garrison church, and there appear to have been a number of suitable spare churches. The chaplain, Fr Edward Ryan, wanted St James's church, but the Maltese hierarchy suggested St Mary Magdalen which, it was said, could be restored at small cost for the exclusive use of British troops. This had already been rejected as being in 'an extreme corner of Valletta and distant from troops'. Eventually the matter was resolved to Bishop Bourne's satisfaction while on a visit to Rome.

Towards the end of the South African War, Fr Ryan, now Senior Chaplain South Africa, informed Bishop Bourne about a War Office proposal to retain regular Army chaplains in South Africa after the war, to continue administering to Catholic troops. However, before agreeing, Bishop Bourne wrote to Fr Ryan saying that he wished to consult both the Congregation of Propaganda in Rome and the South African bishops about the proposed arrangement. For, he maintained, they may very likely prefer to do the work with their own local clergy as acting chaplains.

> I will write to Propaganda to ask them what they would wish. It is important that we at Southwark should not go beyond the instructions of Propaganda or enlarge the sphere of our military responsibility. It is understood that we recommend chaplains for Home Service and for active service in time of war, but not for an army of occupation. The local Ordinaries would in the ordinary course provide for this.[5]

Bishop Bourne's position as ecclesiastical superior of British Army Catholic chaplains entailed an appearance on the international Church scene. It was not a duty he shirked.

The major shortcoming in the creation of British Service Catholic chaplaincy was Rome's failure to grant authority over all service chaplains to one bishop, either Southwark or Westminster – or, alternatively, to create a Vicariate to the Services. Chaplains had several masters: their own bishop, the Bishop of Southwark who granted them faculties as chaplains, the local bishop of wherever they happened to be serving overseas, and the War Office. By the outbreak of the South African War the system had worked successfully for forty years, through the practical good sense of the chaplains themselves. Bishop Bourne determined upon changing it.

An undated handwritten paper in Southwark Archives, certainly written before the death of Queen Victoria in 1901 (because it refers to 'Queen's Regulations') recommends changes in the supervision of Army chaplains. The paper, which is not in the handwriting of Canon Connelly (but is possibly that of Dr Cahill[6]), outlines the disadvantages of the current control of Catholic Army chaplaincy:

> Disadvantages of present system.
> 1. Practically, Catholic chaplains have no superior, except the commanding officer, who cannot be expected to know whether or not an R.C. Chaplain performs his duties as a Catholic priest is bound to do.
> 2. The Bishop is responsible in conscience for every priest that he recommended as Chaplain to the War Office. At present he has no means of knowing whether a Chaplain does his duty, or how he does it.
> 3. Under the present system it would be quite possible for a chaplain never to hear a Confession, or administer any Sacrament to the living or dying, without in any way incurring censure from the military authorities. All that the Queen's Regulations oblige a Chaplain to do, is to perform some service for the troops each Sunday morning, to give an occasional voluntary service and to be able to sign his name as having visited Hospital and Prison occasionally.
> 4. A chaplain performs a small part of the essential duties of his priesthood, he fulfils all that any commanding officer will require of him; and there is at present no one to enquire how he fulfils the obligations of priest to his spiritual charge.
>
> The War Office contemplates this in suggesting that Chaplains (R.C.) should be subject (See blue note in Q. Reg) in matters ecclesiastical to their Bishops, but does not define anything on the subject.
>
> A Catholic Chaplain has less supervision than any other priest in England. He has to join while young, and once commissioned, goes on for life, unless there arises some gross scandal, such as would probably deprive any regimental officer of his commission.
>
> Advantages resulting from proposed changes.
> 1. The Church of England Chaplains can refer any matter to their Chaplain-General, with a certainty of his being able to settle any grievance. The Bishop of Southwark has no official position, and as a result, everything, even a complaint of an ecclesiastical nature, is referred to the military authorities.
> 2. A chaplain's work, even in England, deprives him of much of the help that other priests have in the society of their brethren; and therefore, having an ecclesiastical superior, to whom he would be immediately responsible by War Office Regulations, would make a far more efficient priest and chaplain.

3. Supervision is poor even for zealous men, and still more needful for others.

4. The Bishop ought to know, and so be able to approve or disapprove of all contemplated moves of chaplains. In practice the Chaplain-General moves the men of his department himself, and the arrangement works well.

5. The proposed change would save the military authorities unnecessary trouble. Quarterly reports of R.C. Chaplains would be sent in, not as now, only occasionally, but regularly, to the R.C. Bishop of Southwark, and the Roman Catholic Chaplains' Department would be placed on a far more satisfactory basis than is now the case.

Proposed change.
Changes to Queen's Regulations. That in the next Army Circular (A.C.I.), Section VII Para 266 should be amended to the following effect:
'That the Roman Catholic Bishop of Southwark shall stand in the same relation to R. Catholic Chaplains, as the Chaplain-General stands towards Chaplains of the Church of England.'

A memorandum within the paper recommends to the Bishop a new type of annual report form (C301), drawn up by him for, and printed by, the War Office, for RC Chaplains to submit regularly to the Bishop. The Bishop should get a copy of Instructions for the Guidance of Chaplains of the Church of England in their Ministrations to the Troops of 1 February 1878 and a later pamphlet by Dr Edgehill, an Anglican senior chaplain, issued in 1886.[7]

The remarks by the author of the paper concerning the want of supervision and lack of comradeship of his brethren, may be taken as true in respect of Catholic Army chaplains. It was also true of the few and isolated priests working to keep the faith alive throughout the British Isles in penal times, just as it was certainly true of many missionary priests in distant parts of the world at the time the paper was written, as it is today. That part about Army chaplains saying Mass only on Sunday, hearing no confessions and giving no sacraments other than at Mass, has a marginal line on the original document. It displays an ignorance of Catholic soldiers and their officers. If there were ever such a chaplain, his shortcomings would quickly be made known by them, and his removal would be certain. The suggestion that any chaplain would behave in this way, without quoting evidence of its occurrence, was surely taking the lowest possible denominator of priestly behaviour to support a hypothetical argument. But the major error of the paper was to ignore or overlook the failure of Rome to delegate complete ecclesiastical control of chaplains to a single authority. Bishop Bourne's later actions show that this particular failure was clearly seen by him.

At the Low Week meeting of bishops in 1901, item four on the agenda was military chaplains. The opening sentence stated:

> In order to secure ecclesiastical control over Military Chaplains, it was agreed that the Ordinary have power to inspect the performance of religious duties by Commissioned Chaplains stationed in his Diocese: and, if he thinks it needful, to report negligence or misconduct to the Bishop of Southwark, who shall be able to communicate with the War Office.[8]

At the same meeting the following year, 1902, Army chaplains were again on the agenda:

> After hearing the Bishop of Southwark, the bishops agreed that, on the occurrence of a vacancy among Commissioned Army Chaplains, each Diocese in turn should furnish a Priest. With reference to the supply of Chaplains for South Africa, His Eminence was requested to write to the Superiors of Regular bodies, urging them to furnish Priests when applied to by the Bishop of Southwark.[9]

On the evidence of available correspondence, the problems of Army Catholic chaplaincy during the South African War arose from lax control at Southwark. It had been engendered, in the main, by hiving off the responsibility for Catholic chaplains in the field from Southwark to Hove. Now, going to the opposite extreme, Bishop Bourne sought to centralize control at Southwark of all matters pertaining to Army Catholic chaplaincy. The regular Army chaplains, principally Fr Collins DSO[10] and Fr Morgan,[11] were opposed. In their view the solution was the creation of an *Episcopus Castrensis* (bishop of the camp, or forces) as existed in the armies of Catholic countries. He would be a bishop exercising central control over all chaplains for so long as they served, wherever they were sent by the requirements of the service. The experienced voices of chaplains were ignored. In 1903 Bishop Bourne went to Rome and remained there for four months, at the end of which time the Congregation of Propaganda accepted his proposal and appointed him Delegate of the Holy See for the British Army. The War Office, as they were bound to do, accepted this ruling. Later that same year, when Bishop Bourne was translated from Southwark to Westminster, responsibility for Army chaplaincy also moved across the Thames.[12]

Ecclesiastical responsibility for naval chaplains, as for the Army, had once rested only with Southwark because the three great naval dockyards of Chatham, Portsmouth and Devonport were in that diocese. However, when the diocese of Portsmouth was formed, taking over responsibility for the latter two, and with the rise in importance of Queenstown (Cobh), Queensferry and Rosyth, the Lords of the Admiralty in 1900 requested that Westminster, then the only archdiocese in England, should assume ecclesiastical control of naval Catholic chaplaincy. Cardinal Vaughan agreed.

The Admiralty had an ulterior motive. When the Royal Navy turned to

steam propulsion in the nineteenth century, a requirement arose for
stokers, traditional seamen refusing to do the work. The Navy turned to
Ireland and many Irish were enlisted through Queenstown. The Irish
hierarchy became interested in their welfare and Cardinal Logue took up
the cause. Logue's complaint about the neglect of the spiritual welfare of
sailors reached Parliament. The Admiralty riposted by having naval
Catholic ecclesiastical control placed under an English cardinal and
announced in Parliament that all matters dealing with Catholic chaplaincy
were to be dealt with through Westminster, and less stormy waters.[13]

Archbishop Bourne therefore became *de facto* ecclesiastical superior of
both Army and Navy chaplains, in addition to being Delegate of the Holy
See for the Army. The Congregation of Propaganda in 1906 confirmed
the Archbishop of Westminster as *pro tempore* ecclesiastical superior for
the Army, and created him Delegate of the Holy See for both Army and
Navy.[14] Jurisdiction over chaplains of regiments quartered in Ireland and
India was not included in the Holy See's regulation. Chaplains in those
countries continued to be subject to the jurisdiction of the local Ordinary,
in the same way as military chaplains in Australia, Canada and New
Zealand.

The Archbishop of Westminster had in effect become Bishop to the
Forces, in addition to his many other duties. On the outbreak of war in
1914, these duties were delegated to Mgr Manuel Bidwell, Vicar-General,
later Bishop.

The status of naval and Army Catholic chaplains was vastly different.
The former, unlike Anglican chaplains who were commissioned naval
officers and ranked as Chaplains RN, were 'full-time officiating chaplains'.
Without commissions they had little naval status, ranking as warrant
officers. They were not members of the wardroom, but, at sea, would have
to mess in the gunroom with midshipmen. They had no pension rights,
even if injured while on active service. In the Army, Catholic chaplains had
full equivalent status with their Protestant counterparts as commissioned
officers. Cardinal Bourne now sought, not to enhance the position of naval
Catholic chaplains as might be expected, but to reduce the Army Catholic
chaplains to the level of their naval colleagues.

The biographer of Cardinal Bourne, Oldmeadow, presents the Army
Catholic chaplains as:

> accustomed as they had been to live with practically no superior save the
> War Office and its nominees, they resented the Church's retrieval of them
> for purposes of ecclesiastical oversight and discipline.[15]

Oldmeadow ignores the truth. In the forty years following the institution of
Catholic chaplaincy, Army chaplains, by comparison with their numbers,
had contributed more bishops and canons to the English Church than any
other single section of the priesthood. In recalling this fact, the names of

Bishops Bellord, Brindle, Butt and Vertue spring instantly to mind. The courage of Catholic chaplains, their spiritual constancy, and robust influence for good, had utterly changed the view of a considerable section of the ruling Establishment towards the Catholic Church.

Oldmeadow makes no comparison between the Catholic chaplains and Anglican ones. However, such a comparison was made during a debate on Army chaplains at a Church of England Congress in the late nineteenth century by one of the principal speakers, the Rev Dr Edgehill (the same person mentioned in the paper to Bishop Bourne). He declared that 'the supervision of the Roman Catholic Church in the Army puts to shame that of the National Church'. Bishop G. R. Gleig, a former Chaplain-General for over thirty years (1848–78), who under Wellington had fought as a combatant officer, wrote in a long letter to *The Times*:

> The Roman Catholic Army chaplains are under the supervision of a special prelate. In my day the Bishop of Southwark was intrusted with this power. On his recommendation all appointments are made. From him each chaplain receives his faculties. Under his eye and by his instructions all spiritual functions are discharged, and a mandate from him severs at once the military priest from his flock, whether the Government be willing to lose his services or not. The case of Mr Mahé will at once occur to the memory of all who had any connection some 20 years ago with the church in the Army. By this same prelate, also, the soldiers and their families are confirmed, the soldiers' burying places are consecrated, and the soldiers' altars hallowed. The Roman Catholic soldiers have, in short, their spiritual head, whose word with them is law. And do not let me forget to add that in consequence of all this the Roman Catholic chaplains are confessedly most zealous in the discharge of their duties, and to the authorities at the War Office and the Horse Guards the least troublesome of all Army chaplains.[16]

Amongst the proposals was that of the requirement for a priest embarking as a military or naval chaplain to find his own replacement, and remunerate the locum from his service pay, for the duration of his chaplaincy.

> My Dear Archbishop.
> The suggestion requiring Volunteers of Military Chaplains to find substitutes for themselves during their absence seems to me to be a very happy one. If acted upon, it will remove difficulties which are not at all unlikely to occur under the existing arrangement. A Priest for instance who is not pleased with his present appointment may ask for permission to become a military or naval chaplain hoping – not without grounds – that if he succeeds in securing a commission, he will thereby be altogether released from his present uncongenial position. By requiring that he shall Supply his place, he will be given to understand in a very practical way, that he is still looked upon as the Priest of that place to which he is

naturally supposed to return when his term of military chaplaincy comes to an end. ...

They should in my opinion be allowed to go for not less than twelve months or until the end of the war. It would be scarcely fair to ask young Priests to throw up their present positions and to become Substitutes; and then, perhaps after a few months be left without any appointment.

I would say also that the Substitutes should occupy the same status as regards remuneration as the other young Priests who are now doing temporary duties in places vacated by those who have become Military Chaplains. These Military Chaplains are fairly well paid and can afford this amount.

I remain My dear Lord Archb.

Yours sincerely and respectfully

Terrence O'Donnell. Archiepiscopal Vicariate of Dublin, 47 Westland Row (Dublin)

12 Mar 1906.[17]

This suggestion, which serves only to illustrate the depth of change being contemplated at that time, obviously died quickly. Nothing further is heard about it.

While the debate on ecclesiastical control went on, the work of appointing chaplains, regular and officiating, continued. The priest appointed to minister to Woking and Pirbright, as officiating chaplain, apparently was too busy to care for both places, and Woking demanded a dedicated officiating chaplain. On 13 April 1905 the officer in charge of administration at headquarters, Aldershot Command, wrote to Southwark asking 'whether arrangements have yet been made with a view to the appointment of a Roman Catholic Priest to minister to the troops at Woking'.[18] The following day Southwark replied: 'his Lordship the Bishop of Southwark (Bp Amigo) directs me to say that he is unable to make any arrangement till his proposal with regard to the remuneration of such ministration receives the recognition of the War Office.'[19] The priorities of Southwark diocese had clearly undergone a drastic change since the days of Thomas Grant, when the spiritual welfare of the Catholic troops took precedence over all else.

There was to be another change of emphasis. At the instigation of Cardinal Bourne, the War Office, in 1909, began appointing temporary Catholic chaplains to the forces, the idea being to phase out regular Catholic chaplains in the British Army. The pay and terms of service of temporary chaplains was totally different to that of regular Army chaplains, and placed them at a grave disadvantage. Just before the outbreak of war the cause of Catholic chaplains was taken up by a senior Catholic officer, Colonel C. E. Pereira of the Guards (he later commanded the Guards Division in France). In a private letter to Cardinal Bourne, Pereira outlined the facts clearly and trenchantly. His opening paragraph no more than reiterated the advice given to Bishop Grant over fifty years before:

Catholic Chaplains in the Army.
Military and Ecclesiastical control.

One of the objections raised to a chaplain receiving a commission is that, should a chaplain through unworthy conduct become unfit to carry out his calling, there is no way of cancelling his commission except by a Court Martial. It is evident that before a chaplain can be tried by Court Martial he must have committed some offence against the Army Act; and there is no doubt that grave scandal would be given if a chaplain were tried by a Court Martial.

A commission however is held at His Majesty's pleasure, and at times the names of officers appear in the Gazette with the notice that their services 'are dispensed with'. This generally means that the officer in question has been removed from the Army without the option of resigning his commission; and he is turned out the Army as a mark of disgrace.

The general rule is that a Court Martial upon an officer is sometimes resorted to in cases of gross breach of discipline or of trust; but for lesser cases he is removed from the Army or permitted to resign; it follows therefore that the chance of a commissioned chaplain ever being tried by Court Martial is infinitesimal; and the Military authority is ample for removing a chaplain at any time and in such a way that all scandal can be avoided.

There is further control over a commissioned chaplain. Every year a confidential report is made on all officers, including chaplains. Every five years before attaining promotion entitling him to an increase of pay, a chaplain has to make an application through his military superiors and senior chaplain; and he only receives this promotion and increase of pay if they are satisfied that he is deserving of it. In case he is adversely reported upon, promotion is suspended until he receives a satisfactory report; or it may be refused altogether.

In addition to the above mentioned disciplinary control, purely military, but in which Ecclesiastical authority has its say, there is a purely Ecclesiastical power of suspension of faculties. Cannot an army chaplain's faculties be suspended for the same reasons as those of a secular priest?

It seems indeed that it is possible to exert far more control over an army chaplain than over a secular priest. Was there not a case some nine years ago, in the Aldershot Command, that illustrates the control of the Ecclesiastical authorities over the chaplains? The case referred to was that of a chaplain who had finished his probationary period yet whose commission was quashed through the adverse representations of the Ecclesiastical authorities.

It seems possible that sympathetic cooperation with Army chaplains would remove most of the difficulties that now exist. From a soldier's point of view one meets keen zealous men interested in the welfare of those under their charge; but one is aware that the career of military chaplains, whether commissioned or temporary, is hedged round with difficulties many of which it always seems might be made easier even if they could not be removed.

Review of the Working of the Temporary Appointments.

The following is a short review of the working of the new system as far as it concerns the temporary chaplains who are now serving. The names of four appear in the Army List of December 1913.

The senior appointment is that of Father Grobel. He has now been serving for four years, but under special circumstances; Firstly at Tientsin where he received a special rate of pay; secondly at Malta, the only commissioned or temporary chaplain's station where living is cheap: under these circumstances he could, no doubt, live in a way suitable to his position.

It is obvious to all serving officers how very important it is that army chaplains should be properly housed and clothed, as to be able to mix with officers on equal terms. If Catholic chaplains alone are unable to do this, Catholics in the army are placed in a very invidious position.

Father Moloney's case has already been mentioned in a previous letter, and his circumstances are unsuitable and uncomfortable.

The third temporary chaplain is Father O'Reilly. He is stationed at Deepcut, he can only afford to live in lodgings, and is over two miles from his church. At one time he was allowed transport but this has since been disallowed as, under the terms of his engagement, he is not entitled to it. If he held a commission he would be entitled to suitable quarters or lodging allowance, and would then be within a suitable distance of his church. As it is cheaper for the government to provide quarters than pay an allowance, quarters are usually provided except in new stations where they are eventually built.

The fourth temporary chaplain, Father Flynn, lives in a row of Workmen's cottages at Bordon, and he is lucky to have found accommodation within a mile and a half of his church. It is understood that the surroundings are respectable, and it is better than living in a public house, a fate which sometimes occurs to temporary chaplains. In Father Moloney's case, mentioned previously, a public house was the only available lodging he could get; but as a commissioned chaplain he would not have been in this position; as, had the military authorities provided lodgings, they would have been of a suitable nature and not in a public house; failing to have lodgings Father Moloney would have had lodging allowance. Lodging allowance at the lowest rate for a chaplaincy is three shillings a day or over fifty pounds a year, and it gives the commissioned chaplain, with pay of £182 a year and allowances, considerably more scope for finding suitable accommodation than there is in the case of a temporary chaplain with consolidated pay at the rate of £200.

Temporary chaplains finding their pay not equal to the demands made upon them have, at times, applied to the military authorities for lodging allowance, but as they are not entitled to it naturally the request has been refused.

Temporary chaplains are finding that under the present conditions they are unsuitably housed; and they live in penury and discomfort, and they cannot take that place to which their position entitles them.

If they do not already know it, the secular clergy will soon appreciate the fact that temporary army chaplaincies are positions to be avoided. One dreads to think of the only available priests that will be appointed in future to replace gradually our present excellent commissioned chaplains, men who are looked up to and respected by all ranks and all denominations.

Unless a change is speedily made in the system of appointing chaplains the outlook for Catholics in the Army will be most disheartening. Those Catholics are serving their country, and have every wish to uphold the honour of their religion, but they alone of all denominations meet with the greatest of difficulties in following their religion, *and these difficulties do not come from the military authorities.* (Authors' italics)

The Catholic officers who have interested themselves in this question, which they believe concerns so nearly the spiritual welfare of the men under them, have every confidence that it will receive full and sympathetic consideration.

Signed… C. E. Pereira 4th January 1913.[20]

This letter, in Westminster Archives, is annotated 'Asked him to see me'.

By the outbreak of war in 1914 four temporary chaplains had been appointed, and although vacancies occurred in the establishment before and during the war years, no further regular Army Catholic chaplains to the forces were appointed until afterwards. Added to the neglect of the regular Army was a failure to provide chaplains for the Territorial Force, although the opportunity had been presented in 1909. That year the Army Council authorized the attachment of Nonconformist chaplains to Welsh battalions of the reserve Army. Notwithstanding the precedent thus created, there was no move on the part of Westminster to apply for Catholic chaplains for service with the Territorial Force.

Those priests who had been gazetted temporary chaplains before the outbreak of war lost considerable seniority towards promotion, and therefore status vis-à-vis their Protestant colleagues, during the war years and afterwards. Until the changed circumstances of war altered their terms of service they suffered considerable hardship. Bourne's changes to the chaplaincy also had an effect which endured until the Second World War; after the war, due to lost seniority, no Catholic chaplain was qualified for a senior post anywhere.

On the outbreak of war the future of permanent regular Army Catholic chaplains was in the balance. The RC Chaplains' Department for the first time since 1858 was under-established, as the chaplains prepared to accompany the troops of the British Expeditionary Force to France in August 1914. To fill this establishment, two retired chaplains were re-employed and one was recalled from the Royal Army Reserve of Officers (RARO).[21] One, Fr Morgan, was reemployed despite his being '*persona non grata* with his Eminence'.[22] Despite a severe shortage of Catholic chaplains, Fr Collins, who had led opposition to the re-organization, was not re-employed.

During the war years the system of appointing only temporary chaplains continued. The dangers were as apparent to temporary chaplains as they had been to senior regular chaplains, in particular to one notable Westminster priest, Fr Francis Aveling. Dr Aveling, author of many philosophical works, was the President of the British Psychological Society and Rector of Westminster Cathedral Choir School. He became a temporary chaplain in May 1915; served on the Western Front, was mentioned in despatches, awarded the Military Cross and the Order of Christ (Portugal). Aveling applied for a permanent commission on 25 October 1915 through HQ BEF to Westminster. Bidwell wrote to the War Office, which, under the rules laid down by Cardinal Bourne, could not appoint him. On 25 May 1917, Aveling presented a case for permanent chaplaincy, citing the instance of two C of E chaplains being gazetted. In another letter to Mgr Bidwell, dated 6 June 1917, Aveling stressed the need to get the War Office to bring the Roman Catholic permanent chaplains' 'establishment up to strength ... as a matter of principle for Roman Catholic CFs'.[23]

As early as January 1916, before he left for Macedonia, Mgr Keatinge had warned about the failures of the system. In a letter to the War Office he outlined the difficulty over allowances of temporary commissioned officers, and wrote that Bourne was against permanent commissioned chaplains, and asked:

> Do you not think it would be a favourable time to drop back to the old system? ... This temporary...system cannot go on ... once the war is over, it will be hard to get chaplains, but I know several here who will gladly join ... as regular chaplains if conditions were more favourable.[24]

Regrettably the War Office did not consider it a 'favourable time'. As a result of loss of seniority since 1909, Bishop Keatinge could obtain no senior post for Roman Catholic chaplains in the post-war Army.[25]

References

1. Chaplains papers, ASA.
2. Ibid.
3. Ibid.
4. Ibid.
5. Ibid.
6. See Ernest Oldmeadow, *Francis Cardinal Bourne* (London, 1940), vol. I, pp. 196–202.
7. ASA.
8. AWA.

9. Ibid.
10. Fr R F. Collins, letter, *Catholic Herald* (5 December 1915).
11. Letter, Morgan to Bidwell, AWA.
12. Oldmeadow, pp. 196-202.
13. Hansard, 4th series (1901) 89, 1189-90.
14. Oldmeadow, pp. 196-202.
15. Ibid., p. 200.
16. Letter to *The Times*, extant copy in ASA, undated.
17. Archbishop Walsh Papers, ADA.
18. ASA.
19. Ibid.
20. AWA.
21. *Army List*, 1915.
22. AWA.
23. Correspondence, Aveling-Bidwell (1915-17), AWA.
24. Keatinge to Strange at WO (29 January 1916), Rawlinson MSS, DAA..
25. Keatinge correspondence, Rawlinson MSS, DAA.

4

Catholic naval chaplains ashore 1733–1918

Catholic chaplains to seamen 1733–1854

In his excellent history *Sea Chaplains*, the Rev G. Taylor charts well the early struggle of the Church to minister to Catholic seamen of the fleet who despite the penal laws against Catholics, volunteered to serve, or were pressed into serving, in the Royal Navy.

> From 1733 an R.C. priest had been stationed at Havant and in 1739 a mission was started at Gosport. As has been shown, a priest named Plunkett ministered in 1797 to Roman Catholic Marines who were under sentence of death for murder at Chatham; after requesting some remuneration for his services which possibly were unsolicited, he received 100 guineas from the Navy Board. At the same time the sum of twenty pounds was paid to Mr J. Marsland, who doubtless was a priest 'for his services as Roman Catholic minister at Haslar' from October 1797 to 31 March 1798. Likewise in 1799, a priest named Flynn also ministered to Roman Catholics, and an admiral wrote to the Board acknowledging his services. The payment to Plunkett was possibly the first overt instance in the Navy of the use of state funds for Roman Catholic ministrations. At about the same time three émigré French priests, named De La Rae, Salmon and Guilbert, built chapels close to the dockyards in all three naval ports.[1]

The considerable numbers of Catholics in the Navy during the Napoleonic wars can also be attested by the necessity to provide a Catholic chapel for naval pensioners in the Royal Naval Hospital, Greenwich, in 1846. Two hundred pounds, a very considerable sum at the time, was made available from hospital funds towards the cost. It was indeed sufficient to warrant the officiating chaplain at the time, Fr Richard North, recording his thanks to the hospital authority.[2]

Lord Nelson, son of a Norfolk rectory and England's greatest fighting admiral, is also known for his disregard for the conventions of his day. This was never more apparent than when he entertained the Cardinal Duke of York on board his flagship at Naples.

> It is a tradition in Nelson's family that when the victorious admiral came to Naples after the battle of the Nile, the Cardinal of York was entertained by him in his flagship, *Agamemnon*, and that the Cardinal presented to Nelson a silver mounted dirk and cane that had belonged to Prince Charles Edward. This the admiral gave to Lieutenant Suckling of the *Agamemnon* and it is now in the possession of Captain Suckling RN of Romsey.[3]

It is difficult to imagine what was considered worse by the Establishment in England, Nelson's entertaining Henry Stuart as the last of the Royal Stuart line, or as a prince of the Roman Catholic Church.

The rise of another Napoleon in France, first as President in 1848 then as Emperor in 1852, awoke in England xenophobic fears dormant since Waterloo. New fortifications were constructed for the protection of ports in southern England, and a ring of forts to protect London was planned. One such, Fort Halstead near Chislehurst, Kent, was built before the fear of invasion was replaced by the greater one of increased public expenditure. As in past ages, priority was given to the nation's first line of defence, the Royal Navy. However, an expansion of naval building and recruitment was opposed in Parliament by Catholic members, in a rare show of unanimity. Their opposition won a long overdue concession for Catholic seamen. The Sea Lords, for the first time, recognized in a small way the religious rights of Catholics by promulgating an Order in Council on 25 August 1852. In this the Admiralty directed that the chaplains of HMS *Victory* should

> not enforce the teaching of the Protestant Church of England catechism on boys serving on board that ship, who being of a different religious persuasion ought conscientiously object to receive Religious instruction in a creed at variance with their own. Their Lordships desire that this rule be made general throughout the service, but the captains and commanding officers of H.M. Ships are in all instances to satisfy themselves as to the validity of such objections. The printed form of 'List of Volunteers for H.M. Navy' containing a column headed 'Protestant or Catholic' has been recalled, and all officers entering volunteers for H.M. Navy are to enter all seamen and boys who may be duly qualified, without regard of any difference of a religious creed.[4]

Catholic chaplaincy in the Royal Navy 1855-1918

As a result of this Order, Bishop Grant wrote to Cardinal Wiseman:

> The Admiralty have issued an important order that Catholics are to be received equally with others into the navy and that the Faith of the boys in the navy is not to be tampered with.[5]

Although Bishop Grant successfully negotiated Catholic chaplains for the Army, Prison Service and Colonial Service, he failed with the Royal Navy. The Lords of the Admiralty were less sympathetic to the spiritual needs of 'dissenters' of any sort. In this their Lordships were supported by the Established Church. Nevertheless, thanks largely to Bishop Grant, in 1855 officiating civilian chaplains were appointed at three main dockyards, Chatham, Devonport and Portsmouth, at a salary of £120 per annum (Anglican chaplains received £220 per annum; the difference would seem to be the price paid for celibacy). Sunday Mass was said in hulks, to which Catholic sailors on board ships in port rowed themselves in organized parties under command of the senior Catholic officer or rating. Officiating chaplains were not allowed on board HM ships except in an emergency. The first appointed were Frs William Woollett at Portsmouth and Henry Clarke at Devonport. Fr Clarke had never recovered from the hardships of the Crimea and was in poor health; he was shortly succeeded by Fr Hubert A. Woollett. Fr J. Stourton was appointed to Chatham.

A further small advance was made in 1867 when a full-time chaplain, Fr Gauchi Azzopardi, was appointed at Malta. He died shortly afterwards and was succeeded by Fr Andrew Sceberras. A major breakthrough occurred when Fr Sceberras made a successful case for saying Mass in ships with Maltese sailors on board. Curiously, that same year, 1867, the Rev James Clark, a Westminster priest, was shown in the *English Catholic Directory* as being chaplain to the Peruvian frigate *Independence*.

Despite the success of Fr Sceberras, nearly ten years elapsed before positive action was taken to allow priestly ministration on a wider scale. Renewing their efforts, the English bishops requested the Admiralty to accord Catholic chaplains the same standing as their Anglican counterparts. In an unusual display of charity the Treasury acquiesced, pointing out that this was the case in the Army. Notwithstanding this ready concurrence, the Admiralty declined the bishops' request, but two years later allowed a minor concession.[6]

> On 6 June 1878 an Admiralty Board minute directed that when a large number of ships forming a squadron was sent away on any service that would keep them for a considerable time away from a port where the services of a Roman Catholic priest would be available, arrangements were to be made for a Roman Catholic priest to be attached to the staff of the Admiral in Command and to be under his orders, but this was not acted upon until 1887 when an English priest was taken with the Mediterranean Squadron.[7]

In 1887 Fr Thomas Kent was appointed full-time officiating chaplain and may have been the priest taken out with the Mediterranean Squadron in 1887. From this time all Catholic priests serving the Royal Navy became full-time officiating chaplains; but with warrant, not commissioned, status, which in their case was not pensionable. Moreover, Fr Kent had to wait until 2 August 1918 before he, and others who joined after him, were commissioned as acting Roman Catholic chaplains. Even so the aim of full equality with their Anglican counterparts was still a long way away.

The Royal Navy chaplains under Westminster

Because of the spread of naval bases outside the south of England, and the creation of the Portsmouth diocese, in 1900 the Lords of the Admiralty, in order to deal with only one bishop, asked Cardinal Vaughan, Archbishop of Westminster, to assume responsibility for their Catholic chaplains. He agreed, but seen against other factors, the Admiralty request takes on a new light. Cardinal Logue of Armagh had long been protesting against the poor facilities given to Catholic seamen to practise their faith. In 1900 the matter was raised on the floor of the House of Commons on his behalf. The request was rejected on the grounds that Catholic interests for the Royal Navy were now in the hands of the Archbishop of Westminster.[8]

Shortly after becoming Archbishop of Westminster and Apostolic Delegate for the Royal Navy, Cardinal Bourne, on 15 April 1907, sent to those bishops dealing with naval chaplains a number of blank forms for naval chaplains. This 'Report of the Chaplain to Catholics in the Royal Navy' was to be completed and returned to Westminster by 1 May 1907.[9]

It was a semi-annual report, requesting information about the chaplain, his faculties, salary, allowances, and his duties; when and where he said Mass, heard confessions, and visited hospitals, sick bays and naval barracks. It demanded figures about average attendances at: Mass, on Sunday and weekday; evening service on Sunday; catechism or instruction; number of communicants during half-year (each person to be counted once only); number receiving the last sacraments, and number of deaths during the half-year.

The form also asked 'Are the following Regulations and instructions observed?' and then quoted fully from King's Regulations and Admiralty Instructions: paragraph 707, dealing with the right of dissenters to absent themselves from Church of England religious services; paragraph 708, the right of dissenters to attend religious service ashore; and paragraph 709, provision of chaplains for the sick in hospitals, sick quarters and prisons.

To what purpose such information was intended, or used, by the Westminster authorities is not stated. There is no record of the returns being put to any practical use for furthering the case for the proper religious ministering to Catholic seamen in peace or war. Indeed, when the Royal Navy went to war in 1914, it had the most unsatisfactory sector of service Catholic chaplaincy.

World War I and the Royal Navy Catholic chaplains

On the outbreak of war the chaplains serving with the Royal Navy were:

Canon Peter Thomas Paul Kent, Plymouth
Mgr Canon Joseph Cassar, Malta
Rev Henry Russell, Portsmouth
Rev Hamilton Macdonald MA, Westminster
Canon Edward M. Bray DD, Salford.

In addition to the above, the Rev James O'Reilly was transferred from the Army to the Navy on the outbreak of war and sent north with the Grand Fleet, first to Queensferry and Rosyth, then to Scapa Flow where he remained until 1916 as senior Catholic chaplain. It is pitifully obvious that so few priests could not adequately attend to the spiritual needs of the Catholic seamen in the fleet in peacetime. To anticipate that they could do so in wartime was ludicrous. Yet, this is apparently what the Admiralty expected, and little appears to have been done urgently by the chaplains' ecclesiastical authority to persuade the Sea Lords otherwise. By the end of the year only a further seven priests had been appointed full-time officiating chaplains. Of these, two were dead before the end of the year.

Knowing that the ships of the Royal Navy totally lacked Catholic chaplains caused concern, not least amongst the seamen. Wartime added urgency to what some had been calling attention to for years. The *Irish Catholic* on 26 September 1914 reported that Mr William Redmond MP had written to the First Lord of the Admiralty about the provision of naval chaplains for Roman Catholics and that Mr Churchill had replied that the Admiralty were in contact with Cardinal Bourne.[10]

The press added its voice to the call for chaplains to serve afloat. The editor of *The Irish Catholic* wrote personally to the Admiralty upon the subject. They ignored his letters. The editor, William Dennehy, then sought to enlist the aid of Irish archbishops by writing to Archbishop Walsh of Dublin on 17 December 1914:

> You will see by an article in this week's *Irish Catholic* a copy of which I enclose, that the Admiralty have adopted a course which I have long expected they would eventually reply on. They have, apparently, decided to ignore my remonstrances on the subject of the absence of Catholic Chaplains in the Navy.
>
> I am conscious that my insignificance warrants this policy, but it occurs to me that some expression of opinion from our four Archbishops, approving of the action taken, would show that it is a Catholic demand they have to deal with.
>
> Under these circumstances, I venture to hope that your Grace may favour me with some statement of your views on the subject for publication, the more especially as the recent resolutions of the Bishops did not especially refer to the case of the sailors.[11]

The *Catholic Herald* also added its thunder on 26 December 1914. It pointed out that there were 233 Anglican chaplains to the Fleet afloat and only one Roman Catholic. The apparent lack of movement on the part of the Admiralty to rectify this was put down to bigotry, ignorance or stupidity.[12]

At least one English bishop, Bishop Hedley, had already written to Winston Churchill, the First Lord, about the shortage, but even amongst naval chaplains opinions were divided as to the best way to approach the problem of securing more chaplains for the Royal Navy. As Bishop Hedley wrote to Miss Pope on 18 February 1915:

> ... Adrian [Weld-Blundell OSB], who seems to be the Chief Naval Chaplain, evidently thinks such letters do more harm than good. I differ from him, and if he and the other Naval Chaplains (there are only five altogether) cannot do more than is being done at present for our Catholic sailors in the fleet some means ought to be found of enabling them to do it.[13]

On 22 January 1915, the *Catholic Herald* published an appeal by Irish bishops for naval chaplains. The Irish bishops voiced their fears that the seamen had the same requirements for chaplains as soldiers, yet sailors were denied them. The bishops proclaimed that '... as pastors of our brave men who are so heroic in the service of the state, we will not and cannot cease to cry out till their spiritual rights are duly protected'. In an editorial on 30 January 1915, the *Catholic Herald* supported the Irish bishops. However, in fairness, the difficulty of ministering to Catholic seamen on scattered ships was recognized.

The call of the Irish bishops was published even further afield. A letter dealing with Catholic chaplaincy matters written in emotive language was published in the Irish-American *New York Freeman's Journal*. Having admitted the advances made to satisfy the need for Catholic chaplains in the Army the letter continues:

> But all this time the Catholic sailors were utterly neglected. They had no chaplains, except the priests who lived at the various ports of call. Cardinal Logue had been protesting against the injustice and scandal for twenty years. No heed had been paid to his protests. But on January 19th 1915, the Irish Bishops held another meeting and made protests for the Catholic sailors.[14]

The letter raised such a storm in the United States that Cardinal Bourne wrote to Cardinal Farley of New York a letter which was also published by the *Freeman's Journal*. Cardinal Bourne stated:

> But as I have been dealing with these matters for many years past in my capacity of Ecclesiastical Superior of the commissioned Catholic Chaplains of the Army and Navy,[15] I am glad to testify publicly to the

courtesy and consideration with which my representations have at all times been received. During the war there has been constant, often daily, communications between this House and the Admiralty and the War Office, and every effort has been made to ensure to our Catholic soldiers and sailors the spiritual ministrations of which in these terrible days they stand in such urgent need.[16]

To the faithful of the Church serving afloat as seamen, the neglect to provide chaplains in their deadly peril was incomprehensible. Surely, it seemed to them, it would only require enlightenment at the highest level for their dire peril of loss of salvation to be rectified? Written on behalf of a group of such men, the following letter is to be found in Westminster Archives. In copperplate script, the appeal is compellingly poignant.

> HMS Tiger: June 27th 1915.
>
> My Lord Cardinal,
> I hope by the help of our blessed Lady that you will let us have a Chaplain in our Squadron. It is sometimes five weeks and we can not go to Holy Mass on Sunday, we did not go to Mass today and last Sunday only forty of us were allowed to go to Mass on the HMS New Zealand and that was the first time for five weeks. Fr Bradley is always staying on the HMS New Zealand. But he is not able to do the work on all the Ships of two squadrons. We commissioned the HMS Tiger Oct 8th (1914) we were four months and no Priest and no Mass. Two Priests came aboard at Newcastle on the 6th Feb and the 6th March and on the 17th April Fr Bradley came and stayed about 8 days. We are in harbour at Queens Ferry nearly all the time some times for five weeks at a time and then only going to sea for two or three days so it is not just that we should be depriving of what we hold and love most dear than life 'Our dear Lord said if we did not eat His Flesh and drink His Blood we could not live for ever'. To be in mortal sin we are dead we can not keep in His Grace without the Holy Eucharist for the only true and just God has said it. Need I say that two young Irishmen have not returned to the Ship from Ireland because there is no Mass, and the sin and insults to our dear Lord is terrible. So I beg of you for the love of our Lady of Sorrows to send a priest or see that we can go ashore to … Our Lord in the Sacrament of his love. I know that you will see it is very unjust keeping us from the Sacraments, there are over 200 Catholics on the Tiger alone. I humbly beg of you to grant my little request my Lord Cardinal Archbishop of Westminster.
> Asking your blessing, I am,
> Yours humbly in JMJ
> William Francis Jones. No 4 Mess, H.M.S. Tiger c/o G.P.O. London.
> P.S. The Tiger belongs to 1st Battle Cruiser Squadron and the new Zealand belongs to the 2nd Battle Cruiser Squadron. It is two much for one Priest to do the work on about 10 great battleships.[17]

It was a cry from the heart, which surely must have been contributed to by many of the Catholic lower deck of *Tiger*. But on its receipt at Westminster, instead of the tocsin ringing from its great campanile to resound throughout Westminster and Whitehall, it met with a typical bureaucratic response. On the letter is a note, obviously in connection with an enquiry to the Admiralty:

> Cardinal informed that Catholics on ships of the Battle Cruiser Squadron do not get opportunities of Mass and Sacraments would be glad to know whether this is so.[18]

It should hardly have been necessary for Westminster to write to the Admiralty for the information. The facts were already well known. There is no question but that bigotry against 'dissenters' persisted in the senior ranks of the Royal Navy long after it had been largely negated within the British Army. In the early years of World War I considerable disquiet was felt within influential Catholic circles, in both Great Britain and Ireland, about the paucity of Catholic chaplains in the Royal Navy. This was reflected by the campaign in the Catholic press. The Irish Parliamentary Party in the House of Commons vigorously articulated the widespread concern, and eventually forced the Admiralty to take action. A high-level conference took place in London during February 1915 between Church, Admiralty and Parliamentary representatives, attended by Cardinal Bourne, Mr W. S. Churchill MP (First Lord), Mr John Redmond MP, and Bishop Sheehan of Waterford, representing the Irish hierarchy. The success of the meeting was reported by the *Catholic Herald* on 27 February. A considerable increase in the number of Catholic naval chaplains followed.

Catholic chaplains on the outbreak of war ...	4
Appointed in 1914	8 (Two with the RN Division)
Appointed in 1915	17
Appointed in 1916	3
Appointed in 1917	Nil
Appointed in 1918	8[19]

By the end of the war there were 31 Catholic chaplains serving with the Fleet.

At the end of the war a report was submitted, on his own initiative, by the Rev Richard Carr of Liverpool diocese, a temporary naval chaplain, to the Westminster archdiocese. Carr lists the nine ships of his squadron, the number of days he spent in each, the number of Catholics in each ship, and the number who attended Mass, confession and Communion. Its figures and analysis are precisely those which would be readily understood by Whitehall bureaucrats. Had such detail been requested by Westminster on a wider scale much earlier in the war, and used urgently to justify additional naval chaplains, an increase could have been realized without the outcry which had arisen. The report also gives an interesting insight

into Christianity within the Royal Navy during 1914-18, as observed by a
Catholic priest. The analysis, its comments and damning conclusion, is
worth quoting in full. The term 'pre-Christian' is used by the reporter,
because, presumably, 'post-Christian' was at that time unimaginable.

> Analysis of Services and Sacraments to the 10th Cruiser Squadron. Based
> at Liverpool in the period Aug 1915-Sep 1916.
>
> One.
>
> A. Admiral kept me on shore for five and a half months. Result of my
> shore work - most unsatisfactory - the ships had come home to refit. The
> men had come home to enjoy themselves. Half crew was away on shore,
> other half hard at work on the ship and only waiting opportunity to slip
> ashore also. Officers were worried. Ships dirty. No place for religious
> services and no congregation.
> B. At sea after Jan 18 1916. Following table speaks for itself.
>
> | Ship | Days in ship | Nr Catholics | Confession | H.C. | Mass |
> |---|---|---|---|---|---|
> | *Almanzora* | 24 | 61 | 56 | 27 | 1 |
> | *Hildebrand* | 15 | 45 | 38 | 33 | 1 |
> | *Mantua* | 17 | 64 | 46 | 38 | 2 |
> | *Andes* | 29 | 55 | 52 | 53 | 2 |
> | *Teutonic* | 23 | 178 | 155 | 144 | 5 |
> | *Victorian* | 19 | 79 | 77 | 71 | 15 |
> | *Alsatian* (F) | 21 | 160 | 142 | 131 | 17 |
> | *Otway* | 6 | 56 | 29 | 25 | 4 |
> | *Virginian* | 19 | 63 | 57 | 59 | 4 |
>
> Your Lordship's notice specially directed to:
> 1. These men were nearly all Mercantile marine ratings.
> 2. They would not look at one when I was shore chaplain - now they
>   kept me up to the mark.
> 3. Their own pastors (when they were at home) had evidently not
>   neglected nor trained them badly.
> 4. Every possible help was given by all the officers, and with hearty good
>   will.
> 5. We went home every 7 weeks and many of the few who did not come
>   to sacraments on board may have taken opportunity of going to
>   sacraments in their own parish at home.
>
> Two.
>
> Service in Royal Navy - in Royal ships Sep 1916-May 1919. Chaplain
> attached to 1st Division, 1st Battle Squadron (*Royal Sovereign*) and did
> occasionally work in 2nd, 3rd, 4th Squadrons (Some 20 Battleships).
>
> Report. From Catholic point of view state of religion highly
> unsatisfactory. On every big ship there is a C of E chaplain. Prayers are
> said in public at divisions each morning and there are regular Sunday
> services. This sounds all right - but these religious observances are a
> matter of formality and routine and are so regarded by the crew. On

Sunday the Almighty takes a secondary place to ship and captain, captain's inspection occupies all minds. The tone of mind is, as far as expressed, latitudinarian in the extreme. All the external adjuncts of religion are, perhaps necessarily, most inadequate. The C of E chaplains are principally valued as school masters, decoding experts, censors of letters, or for their social qualities. Almost all the C of E chaplains (mostly temporary men) whom I met were earnest men and they deplored the situation.

Admiralty regulations on paper may appear admirable in provision for religion. But owing to (1) instability of the element on which ships live, weather etc, the carrying out of regulations is often difficult, and discretion of commanding officer can be much used in avoiding regulations. (2) These commanding officers joined when very young, have no grounding in religious doctrine, but a most absorbing interest in their ships, and the material efficiency of the ship is [the] main object to be provided for. Given a deeply religious commanding officer, then the regulations are sufficient to make a Protestant ship sufficiently religious as everything depends materially and religiously on the captain. But how often is such a captain to be found? All without exception of my Commanders, as men had my sincere admiration, but their administration produced a splendid paganism in Wardroom and left lower deck without anything splendid. In Wardroom I never heard a dirty word nor tale, during my close on 4 years of service. I never saw an officer drunk. The officers were gentlemen to a delightful extent, but pre-Christian – of course there were some fine Christians. What can be expected in the way of practical Catholicity, amidst such surroundings, in the men brought up in [the] Navy, and even in the men who for hostilities had joined temporarily?

It was most difficult for the RC Chaplain of a squadron even to get to know his flock. The flock was small – one tenth of crew on average. The individual Catholics (often one or two in a mess) did not like being visited and questioned before their mates, and were shy and reserved. The older men had never been accustomed to see a priest afloat, and had lost the desire to have him at hand, as it interfered with his previously formed habits. He did not want to attend prayers and sacraments, and feared ridicule. The new men soon took the tone of the older.

In three out of my five ships about fifty percent as far as I could judge, made annual Holy Communion – in other 2 ships things were slightly better.

Long established habits of neglect enchained them – but the years of the war were not long enough to remove the consequences of absence of chaplains afloat before 1914. There was a growing friendliness. In looking over lists of Marines it was appalling to see the number of names suggestive of Catholicity [Irish names] but the bearers of those names now Protestant. There was a marked improvement in the religious training of the Boys who joined in last year of the War and hence they withstood better the irreligious influences surrounding them. As to immorality. Of

course it existed in the ships – but I never came across cases of open vice
– though I had, at first hand, information of frightful 'carryings on' in
some ships. What one might call the 'academic view' of sexual relations
was very low, and I know on excellent authority that facilities to avoid evil
consequences to health on visiting brothels were supplied in some
medical departments. In spite of a few health lectures by the Surgeons,
there was not much effort made to protect Truth.

I conclude this Report with (1) a profession of undying devotion to the
Royal Navy. England loves the Navy, but it little knows what self-sacrifice,
endurance, fidelity to duty, cheerfulness amidst appalling surroundings
the naval man has displayed in this war. (2) I make the statement that no
lad from my parish will ever (whilst religion is as it is in the navy) with my
consent, join the Royal Navy. It will take years even with an adequate
supply of right sort of chaplains to make the Royal navy a fit place for
young Catholics. I who say this belong to an Association which has, with
satisfaction, sent hundreds of boys to the Mercantile Marine. Richard Carr
Late Roman Catholic Chaplain in [the] Grand Fleet.[20]

Fr Carr's report is too sincere and painstaking to be dismissed as one
reflecting the pessimistic view through the perspective of a very war-weary
priest. To broaden our horizon of Catholicism in the Royal Navy, and
balance the account, it is necessary to appreciate the views of a chaplain
elsewhere. Through notes from the log of another naval chaplain we can
see Catholic life aboard a ship of the Grand Fleet which had a Catholic
chaplain permanently attached to it.

We are now in the middle of Easter week, and during the past few days
my thoughts have often turned to Ushaw and the grand ceremonies in the
College Chapel. I dare say you have been wondering how we celebrate
Holy Week in my squadron. I manage to secure a lot of crosses made of
palm leaves, and on Palm Sunday gave them out to the officers and men.
The altar was draped in purple, and looked very proper. One of the
officers had arranged to read the Passion while I read it in Latin, but on
the day itself our time for Mass had to be shortened, so the Gospel was
not read in English. However, what with the abundance of purple, the
palms and a passion hymn, the men had sufficient to remind them of the
Holy Season. I was on the quarter-deck when those of the other ships
went down the gangway to their different picket boats and cutters,
already wearing their palm stuck in their cap ribbons. They kept them
there the whole day, much to the interest and, in a small degree to the
edification, of their messmates. Most of the palm crosses were afterwards
sent to wives and sweethearts, and those who had neither, kept them in
their 'ditty boxes', where they still lie – a reminder of the first time they
had received palms on board ship.

Holy Thursday was naturally a *dies non* as far as Church ceremonies
were concerned, but on Good Friday we had Sunday routine. This time
we were able to read the Passion and had the Rosary also and a few
hymns...

Then came the Sunday, and we erected our altar. The men think it is the finest in the Fleet, and I confess I agree with them. A portion of the band volunteered to accompany the hymns, so we even rise to the *O Salutaris* and *Tantum Ergo*. One of our hymns seems to be a great favourite. Perhaps the tune is catching. I hear it whistled on the mess-decks and hummed in the wardroom. The other day I went to the C. of E. chaplain's cabin and even he was whistling quietly to himself.

West country ships, i.e. ships commissioned at Devonport, usually carry the biggest number of Catholics, because they receive the majority of the men from Ireland. It is a pleasure to go along the mess-decks of such ships and to be greeted with 'Good evening, Father', and so forth. These Irishmen are very proud of the priest, and not ashamed to show it. We have night prayers down in the bowels of the ship every evening when in harbour, and the majority are very faithful in attending. They are also very fond of the Catholic papers. Some of these, viz. *The Irish Catholic* and *Fireside* come regularly, and are quickly snatched up. One good lady, who for years had taken a deep interest in the spiritual welfare of the sailors, sends every month a bundle of C.T.S. [Catholic Truth Society] pamphlets, *Messengers*, etc. They are all taken and read. This monthly parcel is always very welcome.[21]

The Admiralty, under a new First Sea Lord, Admiral Sir Rosslyn Wemyss, and with Admiral Sir David Beatty in command of the Grand Fleet, finally rectified the injustice and allowed the commissioning of 'dissenter' chaplains. On 2 August 1918 full-time naval officiating chaplains became 'Acting Roman Catholic Chaplains'. Further progress on the way to full parity with their Anglican colleagues was achieved in 1921 when 'Acting Chaplains' were gazetted as 'Temporary Chaplains'. It was not until 17 November 1943, however, by Order in Council and AFO 13/1944, that they became full 'Roman Catholic Chaplains, Royal Navy' at the same time as all other 'dissenter' naval chaplains.

Notes and references

1. G. Taylor, *Sea Chaplains* (London, 1978), p. 378.
2. Ibid. Fr North was the parish priest of Greenwich.
3. Alice Shiel, *Henry Stuart, Cardinal of York and His Times* (London, 1908), p. 285.
4. Michael Clifton, *The Quiet Negotiator* (Liverpool), p. 106.
5. ASA.
6. Taylor, p. 379.
7. Ibid.
8. Hansard, 4th series (1901) 89, 1189 90.
9. A specimen can be seen in ASA.
10. *The Irish Catholic*.
11. Ibid.
12. *Catholic Herald* (26 December 1914).

13. J. Anselm Wilson, *The Life of Bishop Hedley* (London, 1930), p. 363.
14. *New York Freeman's Journal.*
15. Naval Catholic chaplains were of course not commissioned at this stage of the war.
16. *New York Freeman's Journal* (26 August 1916).
17. AWA.
18. Ibid.
19. Taylor, pp. 544-6.
20. AWA.
21. Rev W. I. Meagher, 'Notes from the log of a naval chaplain', *Ushaw College Magazine*, vol. XXVI (July 1916), pp. 147-9.

5

Catholic naval chaplains with the Fleet 1914–1918

The English College, Lisbon, the Royal Family and the Royal Navy

Possibly the earliest, if not the only, connection between an English Catholic seminary, the Royal Family, and the Royal Navy, was that of the English College, Lisbon. In the post-Emancipation era, it became customary for the Procurator of the English College, acting as port chaplain, to visit Royal Navy ships when they were in the port of Lisbon. Until the 1950s there was also a parade from the visiting ships to the college for Sunday Mass. The college used to fly the White Ensign for the duration of Royal Navy presence in the Tagus. The privilege dated back to the second half of the nineteenth century, when the Prince of Wales – the future Edward VII – was with the Navy on a visit to Portugal. Fr Singleton, college Procurator, requested from the Prince the privilege of flying the White Ensign while the Navy was in the Tagus. The request was granted at once. From then on until the college closed in 1973, the White Ensign was flown from a mast at the college whenever a ship or ships of the Royal Navy were in port. A priest from the college on his visit to the ship(s) would be given a White Ensign to signify the official source of the privilege.

In the late 1950s, about three months before Queen Elizabeth II, accompanied by the Duke of Edinburgh, paid a state visit to Portugal, two naval officers made a courtesy call on the Rector of the English College, Mgr James Sullivan, and inspected the place from which the ensign was flown. On its arrival, the college chaplain duly went aboard the Royal Yacht *Britannia*, made the customary request, and received an enormous White Ensign. After the state visit was over and the ensign lowered for the last time, the flag became a college treasure, to be guarded and not to be flown. It is now in the Lisbon Room, Ushaw College, Durham.[1]

This story illustrates the changing circumstances of the relationship between the Royal Navy and the Catholic Church. But the road to achieving this happy state was at times a painful one for individual chaplains to travel.

Seagoing Catholic chaplains

Before World War I, although there were no seagoing Catholic naval chaplains, some nonetheless went to sea. One priest, Fr Edward Bray DD, later a canon of Salford, had been serving at Malta when the disastrous earthquake of 1908 occurred at Messina in Sicily. He accompanied the Royal Navy task force sent to give assistance to the victims. For his work Fr Bray was appointed, by the King of Italy, a Commander of the Order of the Crown of Italy.[2]

Full-time officiating chaplains lived ashore and could rarely 'get in among' Catholic seamen in their true environment. A prelate at distant Westminster could have little idea of the difficulties in ministering to a fleet of ships from a naval port. One of the first priests on record as reporting such difficulties was Dom Frederick Odo Weld-Blundell OSB. Fr Blundell, a monk of St Benedict's Abbey, Fort Augustus, had worked with the Royal Navy since 1905, ministering to seamen at Cromarty, Invergordon and Kirkwall. Off the Isle of Arran in 1908 Fr Blundell had the distinction of becoming the first priest to say Mass in a Royal Navy ship on home station since King James II's reign.[3]

Fr Blundell's letters at Westminster, written while still a part-time officiating chaplain, are the earliest letters of the war years to highlight problems and seek advice and assistance. Some of his requests were coldly received. One such, on 11 August 1914, was for Fr Blundell's faculties to include heresy and censures attached to illicit marriages. These, Mgr Bidwell informed him politely, 'are reserved for the Holy Father'.[4] In a letter written at Cromarty on 31 October 1914, Fr Blundell is more practical. He explains the extreme difficulties of ministering in circumstances where some forty to fifty ships called into harbour, coaled as quickly as possible and departed with the maximum speed. Blundell was making a case for relaxing certain rules, e.g. fasting before Communion, and for greater use of general Absolution. He tells the impossibility of even seeing all Catholics, on every ship, even without individual confession. Two weeks later, on 13 November 1914, now in HMS *Colossus*, of 1st Battle Squadron, Fr Blundell tells how in six weeks 1,500 men received Holy Communion after individual confessions. He writes of the Admiralty being against 'public services'; but Fr Blundell argued that 'public services' are not 'public' if they are for Roman Catholics only. Yet this was often ignored. The First Lord, Winston Churchill, wrote in rebuttal that there were four Catholic chaplains on board ships and that every facility was offered them; this was in contradiction to Admiralty policy of 'no public service'. Fr Blundell requested Cardinal Bourne to clarify the situation with the Admiralty. He pointed out that he had had requests from ships' captains to hold services on their vessels.[5]

Fr Alfred Adrian Weld-Blundell OSB, also of Fort Augustus and a brother of Odo, was another early wartime naval chaplain, who served with 2nd Battle-Cruiser Squadron, Grand Fleet, until the beginning of 1915.

Fr Thomas Bradley had first served with an Army battalion, the 7th Royal West Kent, at Purfleet. However, his Father Provincial wrote to the War Office to have Bradley returned to Orders duty in February 1915. The War Office wrote to Mgr Bidwell, who agreed on 27 February 1915 to replace Bradley with Fr W. Donlevy at Purfleet. Obviously having persuaded his Provincial to change his mind, Bradley appeared as an officiating chaplain with the Royal Navy, and on 25 February 1915, Fr Bradley replaced Fr Adrian Weld-Blundell as chaplain with 2nd Battle-Cruiser Squadron in *New Zealand*. In an undated letter to Mgr Bidwell, obviously shortly afterwards, Bradley writes of his arrangements with Fr Patrick Gibbons RAN, HMAS *Australia*, to share the ships and visit all RCs on board. He writes that some men, especially stokers, are unable to attend Mass or the Sacrament. He also seeks to obtain permission for naval chaplains to marry seamen in a diocese where the fleet is based. He also informs of his need to say two Masses on one day, and stresses the requirement for more RN chaplains.

In the new circumstances of chaplains at sea, it became painfully apparent to Catholic priests serving afloat how different their status was compared to Church of England chaplains, who ranked with other commissioned officers. Fr Bradley went further than any other naval chaplain explaining to Westminster the injustice of their position. Fr Bradley wrote of the 'sufferance' under which he laboured, and stressed the need to have Catholic chaplains on a secure commissioned basis. Although, he explained, he was not interested in pay, *per se*, Fr Bradley told how he was paid in a different way to officers and Anglican chaplains. He was not on the ship's books and therefore 'cannot purchase things from the paymaster's stores in my own name'. He pointed out that he would get no compensation if wounded or invalided out. Bradley also drew attention to the iniquity of the system whereby Catholic chaplains could not be awarded decorations reserved for officers – and gives an example. He writes that Admiral Beatty was in favour of commissioning Catholic chaplains and pointed out that Fr Patrick Gibbons held a commission in the Royal Australian Navy. Bradley concluded his letter:

> I think it is up to chaplains, who are making traditions and precedents, to make our own position as secure and as honourable as possible.[6]

Catholic naval chaplains in action

The first chaplain of any faith in all the British Services to die in World War I was Canon Robert Basil Gwydir OSB, of Douai Abbey and St David's Priory, Swansea.[7] Following his appointment as full-time officiating chaplain, Fr Gwydir worked at Rosyth and Queensferry, and at the end of October 1914, departed for Portsmouth in the Home Fleet hospital ship *Rohilla* loaded with sick and wounded seamen and marines. During a storm on 30 October the ship was wrecked off Whitby. Fr Gwydir remained on board with the wounded and drowned with them. By stark contrast, the C of E chaplain, the Rev Richard Allen, who may have been on the upper deck away from the ship's wards at the time, allowed himself to be rescued with many others. The Admiralty was unforgiving, and Allen was not appointed to another ship. He resigned his commission on 23 December 1914.[8]

The Dardanelles

Five Catholic naval chaplains served at the Dardanelles. Fr Alfred Adrian Weld-Blundell OSB had been transferred from the 2nd Battle-Cruiser Squadron to the Eastern Mediterranean Fleet, and with Fr Charles Ritchie CongOrat worked on warships; Fr Eric Green was attached to the RN Division; Fr Alfred Barry OSFC was attached to the Fleet Auxiliaries; and Fr Stephen Thornton was also with the RN Division, of which we shall hear more later.

Fr Eric Green, a Westminster priest accompanying the Royal Naval Division, took part in the ill-fated landings at Cape Helles. There Fr Green, in his ministrations to the marines and seamen who fought as infantry, had 'miraculous escapes from death by snipers and shell-fire'. Like all the other divisions at Gallipoli, the naval division also suffered heavily. The *Catholic Herald* in 1915 reported him working in 'intense heat amidst widespread sickness' ministering to over 2,000 wounded in an ambulance post in two days. Once again the absence of general Absolution is remarked upon (long after it was used in the Army). He is reported as giving Holy Communion to 3,000 communicants after individual confessions.[9]

In close support of the medical services at Gallipoli was a small fleet of hospital ships and fleet auxiliaries. The visiting hospital ships had Army chaplains on board who remained with the wounded for the duration of their evacuation to either Malta, Egypt or England. The naval chaplain remained on station. Fr Barry was appointed full-time officiating chaplain early in 1915, and was immediately drafted to work on auxiliary and hospital ships with the Eastern Mediterranean Squadron. In a letter dated 1 September 1915 to Mgr Bidwell, Fr Barry explained the difficulty of reaching hospital ships due to 'emergencies' which created a shortage of inter-ship boat transport. He also observed that 'there is a distinct tendency to regard a Catholic chaplain's work as an unnecessary nuisance'. Apparently having tried and failed to improve the situation locally, Barry asked that Cardinal Bourne apply pressure on the Admiralty to increase the number of chaplains and improve their terms of service. He stressed 'if sailors complain it is not the fault of Roman Catholic chaplains'.[10]

Nevertheless Fr Barry clearly concealed his worries and frustration, because according to a naval historian, at the Dardanelles Fr Barry became renowned as 'One of the most genial of all the Padres out in the east. His duty was to visit all HM ships and hospital ships in the eastern Mediterranean.'[11] Indeed, in the next three years, so great did his influence for good become that following his departure for England, the captain of HMS *Skirmisher*, his last ship, wrote to Mgr Bidwell:

> My Dear Monsignor, As the senior Catholic officer on this station I should like to write you a few words in appreciation of the services of Father A. Barry OSFC who has been our chaplain out here for last three years. Needless to say neither he, nor anybody else knows of my intention of writing. Fr Barry has in fact left for England, where no doubt he will be seeing you and I hope His Eminence. It is hard to find words to express the great love and admiration which all ranks and ratings feel for Father Barry. He has been untiring in his efforts for the welfare of us all and believe me his work has been far from easy entailing an immense amount of travelling often in very small and uncomfortable vessels. He has got on so well with *everybody* no easy matter I can assure you. I have been spoken to about him by my brother captains saying how much they like him and what good he has done, not only amongst those of his own faith, but universally. I am very diffident in thus specially praising a Priest which seems somewhat presumptuous on my part but a little praise from our superiors often helps us of the laity and if His Eminence could say a word or two to Father Barry, I, and I know everybody else out here, would be very grateful. All other officers – chaplains included, get reports etc. from their commanding officers expressing much the same as what I have written but I do not think our chaplains come under the same conditions. In fact I don't see who is going to write them!
>
> Please forgive me if I offend by this letter which is not meant in the least to disparage the work of others. Believe me, Yours very truly, Archibald Loshiane, Captain RN, HMS *Skirmisher*, June 15 1918.[12]

The Grand Fleet

At the end of 1915 a former student of Ushaw College wrote in the college magazine about his recent experience of joining a battleship of the Grand Fleet:

> To one who has been accustomed to a life on shore and the parochial work accompanying it, it is with strange and mixed feelings that he boards a battleship for the first time, knowing that it is to be his future home and that his work lies here and among other huge floating monsters he sees at anchor. Soon he begins to be surer of himself, and learns the routine and is able to distinguish between the different bugle calls from 'pipes out' after breakfast to sun down, when the white ensign is saluted and lowered for the night. He goes on a voyage of discovery

around the ship, and if he is lucky he finds a place - usually a medical distributing station - where he is able to say his daily Mass. He may have eight vessels or less under his charge; it all depends on the size of the squadron. If among his ships there are any from the West Country, he is certain to have a large congregation, because these take the majority of recruits from Ireland. As a matter of fact, most of the Catholic sailors are Irish. On the whole they are excellent and deeply religious men. Of course they have had to work out their salvation under very great disadvantages ... The sailor does not like a long 'service'. Neither would you if you had to kneel on a steel deck. He may be tough, but he is also human. But he dearly loves a hymn. All the more popular ones, such as *Sweet Sacrament Divine, Hail Queen of Heaven*, etc. are known by them all. Our singing at first was accompanied by a flute and violin, but this was not an unqualified success. Then the men in one ship bought a portable harmonium, which is quite good and serves well ... In another ship we engage the 'musician', who in piping times of peace plays the piano in the Royal Yacht ... One chaplain who has a big number to choose from has trained an excellent choir. They sing *Asperges*, and now he is teaching them the *Missa de Angelis*. He is fortunate enough, too, to have a space between decks set entirely apart for his own use. Here, with the help of his men, he has 'rigged up' a little permanent chapel. Against the bulkheads are little coloured prints of the Stations of the Cross. In this quiet spot his congregation can in their free time come and say their prayers or read the C.T.S. lives of the Saints. He hopes to be able to erect a little crib ... Not the easiest part of a priest's life here is the going from ship to ship in a 'choppy' sea to visit one's flock. When one is seated in the stern sheets of the picket boat the danger is over. But to jump on and off it when the boat is bobbing up and down like a cork and at the same time trying to smash the gangway into matchwood, requires a certain amount of agility ... The sailor is given plenty to do. On the whole he is a very happy and contented individual. But he must have a 'moan'. His complaints are two: First of all he wishes to see his home oftener ... His other complaint is that the Germans have not yet appeared. About that he feels very sore. He has brothers and friends in the trenches and knows what splendid work they are doing while to all appearances he is idle. It is no use telling him that if it were not for the Fleet the armies in France and elsewhere could never be re-inforced and provided for. He wants to fight. He is spoiling for it.[13]

The time was fast approaching when they would have their wish granted.

There were no fewer than six Catholic priests present at the Battle of Jutland: Frs Thomas Bradley, *Tiger*; William Driscoll, *Natal*; Patrick Gibbons, HMAS *Australia*; William Meagher, *Bellerophon*; Stewart Phelan OMI, *Black Prince*; and Anthony Pollen in *Warspite*. In the course of the battle HMS *Black Prince* was sunk and Fr Phelan was listed as missing presumed drowned. He became the second Catholic naval chaplain to die in the war.

Fr William Driscoll, of Plymouth, became a full-time officiating RC chaplain on 24 November 1914 and initially served with the Royal Naval Division at Blandford Camp after its return from Ostend and before it left for the Near East. Appointed into HMS *Natal,* he was in her when she was blown up at Jutland. Fortunately, he was rescued from the sea by HMS *Cochrane,* and was able to watch the remainder of the battle from her deck.

Fr Anthony Pollen in *Warspite* performed what was described as 'one of the finest deeds of the day'.[14] Fr Pollen, Catholic chaplain to the 5th Battle Squadron, threw himself into a cordite fire caused by enemy shell-fire without a thought for his own safety to rescue two seamen. He managed to drag them both out alive, becoming badly burned himself.[15] It was a deed which merited the Victoria Cross, but his commanding officer recommended Fr Pollen for the Distinguished Service Order. The Commander-in-Chief, Admiral Sir John Jellicoe, refused to support the recommendation for the DSO, on the grounds that Fr Pollen was not a commissioned officer:[16] he was awarded the lesser Distinguished Service Cross, which could be awarded to warrant officers. Jellicoe's decision was strictly in accordance with the rules and was probably recommended to him by his administrative staff although, as will be shown later, had he decided otherwise and allowed justice to prevail, an award of the DSO could have been made for this most gallant deed. Well might Fr Frederick Odo Weld-Blundell, writing to Mgr Bidwell, warn 'I trust that you will allow me to express the hope that our take of Jutland and other war medals will be carefully watched ...'[17]

The visit of Cardinal Bourne to the Fleet, August 1916

Possibly the greatest contribution made by Cardinal Bourne to the war effort was his visits and addresses to Catholics in the fighting services. When no Irish bishop had thought to visit and pray with either 10th or 16th Irish Divisions before they departed from Ireland, Cardinal Bourne addressed the 16th Division just before it embarked for France in December 1915. He also visited the troops just behind the front in France and Flanders. The only other Catholic bishop on record as visiting troops of the British Expeditionary Force was Archbishop Clune of Perth, representing Archbishop Carr of Melbourne, who was ill. In August 1916, just over two months after Jutland and for the first time since the Reformation, an English cardinal paid a visit to the Grand Fleet. Not since Admiral Nelson and Cardinal Stuart met well over a hundred years before had there been such an occasion. This time there is no doubt that the visit of a prince of the Church to the Navy was well received in England. Cardinal Bourne went to Scapa Flow on 5 August and stayed for three

days, before going on to visit other northern naval bases. He was welcomed
hospitably by Admiral Jellicoe and his staff, and visited many warships.

> He made particular point of acquainting himself with the different aspects
> of a sailor's life, visiting the men's quarters, examining the guns, visiting a
> turret, and having explained to him the mechanism for supplying
> ammunition and for firing it, thus grasping, in a practical manner, all the
> elements which composed the work and play of officers and men with the
> Grand Fleet.[18]

The cardinal also visited hospital ships where he 'was able to cheer the sick',
shore establishments, and he blessed the Catholic section of the naval war
cemetery. He confirmed many seamen, and spoke to thousands, on one
occasion alone addressing over 1,000 Catholic officers and ratings in an
anchored 'theatre ship' at Scapa Flow, and giving an inspiring address.

> It is the proud boast of the Navy to be 'always prepared'. You have to be
> ready at every moment for whatever may befall you. Make use of all the
> opportunities that you now enjoy of hearing Mass and approaching the
> Sacraments. Keep yourselves in God's friendship by frequent and earnest
> acts of sorrow for anything in your lives that may have been displeasing to
> Him, and thus be ever ready for the moment in which, perhaps quite
> suddenly, He may call you out of this life.
>   Never forget that it is God alone Who can grant us victory. Live in such
> a way that you may be ever worthy in God's sight of the victory that we so
> earnestly desire. Let there be nothing in your lives to render you or your
> country unworthy of this blessing of victory which we humbly beg from
> God, Who alone can bestow it upon us. As you look back hereafter upon
> these days spent in defence of King, and Country and Empire, be able to
> say that you are better men in God's sight because you have been
> privileged to take part in so great a cause. Avoid everything that might one
> day cast a shadow on your memory of these days.
>   There is no victory without sacrifice. The greatest victory that the world
> has ever seen, the First Easter Sunday, was preceded by the greatest
> sacrifice, that of Good Friday. Your lives are a daily sacrifice - of comfort,
> freedom, home and friends; you may be called to make the highest
> sacrifice, even that of your lives. Make every sacrifice, great and small, not
> grudging or grumblingly, not as a mere matter of routine which you
> would shirk if you could, but generously and wholeheartedly, offering all
> to God Himself in union with the sufferings of our Lord and Saviour Jesus
> Christ. Thus, by your daily sacrifices, you will gain the victory which
> without such sacrifices no man can win.[19]

On 12 August at a naval base 'elsewhere', the Cardinal again said Mass and
gave Holy Communion to a great number of men, after which he spoke of
related matters.

> His words were also concerning the arrangements made for the spiritual
> care of the Catholics of the navy, which have recently been so much

improved, so that now they have opportunities that before the war were
not available.[20]

The organizer of the cardinal's highly successful visit to the Fleet was Fr
James O'Reilly, senior chaplain at Scapa. He had been a naval chaplain on
fixed allowances at Gibraltar as early as 1907. Shortly after the cardinal's
visit O'Reilly was transferred to the Mediterranean Fleet as Principal
Catholic Chaplain. It was one of his letters to the Admiralty in 1918, after
Sir Rosslyn Wemyss had replaced Sir John Jellicoe as First Sea Lord, which
resulted in the removal of anomalies of treatment between C of E chaplains
and 'dissenters'.

> The accession to commissioned rank on a temporary basis as Acting
> Chaplain by these Roman Catholic civilian priests who had volunteered
> or had been requested to undertake wartime duty as chaplains, seems to
> have been due in the first place to action taken in 1918 by the senior
> among the Roman Catholic Chaplains in the Mediterranean, James
> O'Reilly.[21]

At the end of the war Fr O'Reilly was awarded the OBE for his
distinguished service, and continued to serve as naval chaplain.

The sinking of HMS *Vanguard* at Scapa Flow

In 1917, by some unexplained tragic accident, HMS *Vanguard* blew up and
sank with almost all hands. A Catholic chaplain, Fr W. I. Meagher, was in a
warship nearby and was an eyewitness to the disaster. He took part in the
memorial service which followed.

> On a sudden I came to my full senses: the hills and sheep were far away.
> The stillness was broken by a loud explosion as though a broadside of 15-
> inch guns had been fired. My first thoughts were that Zeppelins were
> attacking us and then that the aerial guns were at night practice.
> Immediately there was another heavy, dull report which, by its very
> sound betokened death and destruction. I thrust my head out of the
> scuttle, and as I looked the whole harbour was illuminated by a bright
> yellow flash – the flash of cordite – and in that instant a third and final
> explosion took place. By the light of the awful flame one saw that one of
> our great dreadnoughts was no more. A portion of the outline of the ship
> could be made out. The after-funnel and main-mast seemed to be leaning
> at an angle of 60 degrees. The flash died away on a sudden as quickly as
> does lightning. A great glow took its place for a moment; then it too,
> disappeared – and all that was left of H.M.S. *Vanguard* sank. Less than
> thirty seconds covered the whole of that terrible tragedy ...
>
> Two days later the funeral service was read over the watery grave. The
> Commander-in-Chief and all the Admirals were present on board the ship
> that lay next in line to the *Vanguard*, Catholic officers were there too. After
> the arrival of Admiral Beatty, massed bands played Chopin's Funeral

March. As the music ceased, all turned and faced the sea, as did the men of all the ships in this magnificent fleet. The 'Order of Burial' was then read by our Senior Chaplain. Two other chaplains were present, both sons of Ushaw, and a number of officers and men from the squadron. The Church of England were ranged up on one portion of the quarter-deck; we on the other. Between was the firing party. It was a sad, melancholy sight. All one could hear were the words recited by the priest. Apart from that the silence was profound. The day was one of clear sunshine … A firing party of fifty 'bluejackets' now saluted their dead comrades and fired three volleys over the grave. As the last salvo rapped out eight buglers from the top of a turret sounded that call - triumph and farewell - the 'Last Post'. The last prolonged wailing note died away; and the distant hills sent back a gentle echo.[22]

Naval chaplains in France with the BEF

Following the evacuation of Cape Helles in January 1916 the Royal Naval Division served for a time in Egypt before transferring to France. In the course of two years' service in France and Flanders the division took part in the Battles of First and Second Somme, Third and Fourth Ypres, and the advance to victory. On 13 November 1916, during the final action of the Battle of the Somme, the capture of Beaumont Hamel, the last bastion which had defied the British attack on 1 July, a Catholic priest with the division won renown. Fr Stephen Thornton, formerly a professor at St Peter's College, Glasgow, was now Catholic chaplain to the Army brigade in what was called the 63rd (RN) Division. Fr Thornton had served with the division in Gallipoli and in France was attached to 10th Dublins during the final action of the Battle of the Somme.

> Many of my readers will recall how a certain Roman Catholic priest won the DSO at Beaucourt. To see this venerable, whitehaired old man, spectacles on the end of his nose, his legs clothed in gumboots, stumbling through trenches waist-deep in mud to some point in the front line where the shelling was heaviest and hence all the casualties greatest, was always an example to all. His creed was that a man wants to see his priest *before* he is dead.[23]

Fr Thornton accompanied the RN Division during all its later battles. His award of the DSO was made through the recommendation of his divisional commander to HQ BEF. There, unlike in a naval flagship, it would not have been considered unusual, and Fr Thornton became the first naval chaplain to be awarded the DSO, gazetted on 31 January 1917.

Another naval chaplain who served in France was Fr John MacNeil, of Eriskay, South Uist, in the diocese of Argyll and the Isles. Fr MacNeil, a Gaelic speaker, was commissioned chaplain to the forces in the Army on 29 November 1914. He served in France with a battalion of the Cameron

Highlanders, was awarded the Military Cross and was mentioned in despatches. In successive battles the hard-fighting Camerons lost their Catholics as casualties. Then, feeling that he was not adequately employed, and hearing that his own Gaelic-speaking islandmen in the Navy were without a native-speaking priest, he resigned his Army commission on 25 March 1918 to transfer to the Royal Navy. Subsequently Fr MacNeil served with 4th Battle Squadron in HMS *Bellerophon*.[24]

After the Armistice the German High Seas Fleet surrendered to the Grand Fleet at Scapa Flow. Fr Bradley was with the fleet at the time and recorded that their main duties was guarding the interned German ships. There were no shore facilities for Catholic worship and Fr Bradley had to get around the ships and hospital ships in all weathers to minister to the sailors, including German sailors. Another priest then at Scapa, Fr Alfred Barry, in a letter to Westminster dated 4 December 1918, reported that he had requested permission to hold services on German ships. The request was denied for fear of a 'mutinous element in one ship taking the opportunity of expressing their views on another ship's company'. Fr Barry was only given permission to visit German Catholics in the hospital ships.[25]

During World War I, 40 Catholic chaplains served in the Royal Navy. One chaplain died on active service. Naval Catholic chaplains, like their Army brethren, served God and their flock in a most fitting and glorious way in terrible conditions.

Notes and references

1. Rt Rev Mgr James Sullivan JCD OBE, last Rector, the English College, Lisbon, conversations with T. Johnstone.
2. Portsmouth Diocesan Records.
3. G. Taylor, *Sea Chaplains* (London, 1978), p. 380.
4. AWA.
5. Ibid.
6. Ibid.
7. This unusual distinction for a 'Regular' is shown on two photographs of Dom Basil held at Douai.
8. Taylor, p. 340.
9. *Catholic Herald* (14 August 1915).
10. AWA.
11. Taylor, p. 349.
12. AWA.
13. Rev W. I. Meagher, 'College notes', *Ushaw College Magazine*, vol. XXV (December 1915), pp. 298–302.
14. Taylor, p. 357.
15. Ibid.
16. Letter, Fr Bradley to Mgr Bidwell, AWA.

17. Letter, Weld-Blundell to Bidwell, AWA.
18. 'The Cardinal Archbishop's visit to the Fleet, August, 1916', *Westminster Chronicle*, vol. X, no. 9 (1916).
19. Ibid.
20. Ibid.
21. Taylor, p. 381.
22. Rev W. I. Meagher, 'Things seen', *Ushaw College Magazine*, vol. XXVII (December 1917), pp. 185-7.
23. Quoted by Taylor, p. 350.
24. Obituary, SCD.
25 AWA.

6

The Royal Army Chaplains' Department with the BEF

The total strength of the RAChD in August 1914 was:

Anglican	89
Roman Catholic	17
Presbyterian	11
Total	117[1]

With its worldwide commitments, the Department could only deploy a fraction of this number with the British Expeditionary Force (BEF) which prepared to move to France following Britain's declaration of war on 4 August 1914. Catholic chaplains serving with the Army on 5 August 1914 included two re-employed retired chaplains and one recalled from the reserve of officers. Of the seventeen, six were serving overseas or were detached:

Rev Lewis Matthews	Chaplain 1st class, Gibraltar
Rev William Keatinge	Chaplain 1st class, Cairo
Rev Robert Nash	Chaplain 2nd class, South Africa
Rev Daniel Lane	Chaplain 2nd class, Malta
Rev John Moth	Chaplain 3rd class, South Africa
Rev James O'Reilly	Chaplain 4th class, attached to the Royal Navy[2]

One other chaplain was recalled from the reserve before the end of August, making a total of eighteen regular army chaplains. The widespread deployment of chaplains shown above meant that only eleven were available for immediate service with the British Expeditionary Force (BEF), some of whom had to remain at home stations until they could be replaced by temporary chaplains. In the event seven priests accompanied the BEF in August, others followed in September and October.

Rev Francis Bickerstaffe-Drew	Chaplain 1st class, Salisbury
Rev Stephen Rogers	Chaplain 2nd class, Aldershot and 1st Division
Rev William Forrest	Chaplain 3rd class, Shorncliffe and Base Area
Rev James Dey	Chaplain 3rd class, Aldershot and 2nd Division
Rev Peter Bradley	Chaplain 4th class, Netley and 6th Division
Rev James Dunphy	Chaplain 4th class, Tidworth and 3rd Division
Rev John Moloney	Chaplain 4th class, Aldershot and 27th Division
Rev William Flynn	Chaplain 4th class, 5th Division
Rev Emmanuel Morgan	Retired re-employed chaplain, Devonport
Rev John Hessenaur (later Carden)	Recalled to the active list on 5 August 1914, 2nd Royal Irish Fusiliers and 4th Division
Rev Edward Ryan	Retired re-employed chaplain, 1st Cavalry Division
Rev Peter Grobel	Recalled on 20 August 1914[3]

The senior 1st class chaplain, Rev L. J. Matthews, was nearly 60 and already close to death (he died in 1916). He was considered too old for active service and the Rev William Keatinge was recalled from Cairo to accompany the 3rd Division to France.

Two of the early temporary chaplains came from India with the Indian Corps. One of them, Fr Frederick Peal SJ, a spade-bearded missionary, had been an officiating chaplain at Jalapahur on the outbreak of war, and immediately volunteered for active service. Permission was granted by his Provincial Superior almost at once and Fr Peal received notification of this while at Darjeeling on 12 August 1914. He went to garrison headquarters and from there a wire was sent to the ADC to the C in C India. Back at Jalapahur on Saturday 15 August, Peal received a reply on the Feast of the Assumption, 'you have been appointed RC Chaplain to accompany 3rd (Lahore) Division, Expeditionary Force and should proceed to Bombay as early as possible and report to the Embarkation Officer who will arrange accommodation – Administration Division'.[4] He left that evening and on Monday, 17 August was at Calcutta. The Indian Corps arrived in France during the crisis of First Ypres. It was badly needed to strengthen the thin line at Neuve Chapelle, and soon Fr Peal had much work to do with his battalion, 1st Connaught Rangers.

On the outbreak of war Mgr Bickerstaffe-Drew had suggested that he might be better employed in England training and organizing new chaplains which the New Army expansion would necessitate. The War Office, however, probably in consultation with Westminster, considered the first priority was the Field Army and he was informed that 'the need of such chaplains at the front is even greater'.[5] Many chaplains won considerable honour in France during the war. None exceeded those already held by the Rt Rev Mgr Count Francis Browning Bickerstaffe-Drew; Chaplain to the Forces 1st Class (Colonel). A convert, son of a Church of England minister and grandson of a Church of Ireland minister, he was 56. He had already been appointed Private Chamberlain to Pope Leo XIII and awarded the Cross of Leo XIII. A Private Chamberlain to Pope Pius X since 1903, he had recently been created Domestic Prelate, a Knight of the Holy Sepulchre, Count and Protonotary Apostolic. In addition to these honours and awards, he was a Foreign Member and Delegate of the Société Archéologique de France.[6] Such was the variety of Mgr Bickerstaffe-Drew's accomplishments and positions that it is curious that his request to remain in England to assist with the organization and training of chaplains should not have been acted upon, especially in the light of the experience from the South African War. A senior chaplain, able to liaise directly with various branches of the War Office, HQ BEF and Home Command headquarters, would have been invaluable in advising on probable manning requirements, establishments and deployment, in addition to training and briefing chaplains before they embarked for France or elsewhere. Taking account of his obvious diplomatic skills and Army experience, this would have prevented many of the errors which occurred in the early months of the war, especially in dealing with the hierarchies of both sister islands of the United Kingdom. He was also at an age where he was past his best for active and demanding field operations.

The planned strength of the BEF was six infantry and one cavalry divisions. The allocation of Catholic chaplains was one to a division. Each division had approximately twenty major units ranging in strength from 500 to 1,000 men, often spread over a wide area, especially in mobile operations such as the battles of August–September 1914. With so few chaplains available to minister to their scattered flock, the nearness of battle brought anxiety to Catholic soldiers. Some, if we are to accept the following story, took unorthodox methods to ensure their spiritual salvation:

> We cannot vouch for the following story, but it is told by one of our 'old boys' who was at Mons, and was wounded in the course of the retreat: A party of Catholic soldiers of 'the Warwicks', finding themselves near an Irish regiment went in search of a priest. But in those days 'a padre' of the

right sort was a luxury, in many cases denied even to the sons of Erin. Undaunted and now joined by some Irishmen, they decided to capture one for themselves, and ended by stalking a French curé, who, struggling and loudly vociferating, was triumphantly carried off into the presence of the retailer of this story. Having deposited their burden upon the ground they made a formal request that the officer would be good enough to explain to the affrighted curé that they had no designs on his life, but wanted absolution. Absolution followed, and the curé recovering from his rough handling marched and ministered to his captors for many a long mile of the retreat.[7]

During the retreat from Mons one Anglican chaplain was captured, and Frs Keatinge and James Dey were nearly captured. As Dey later said, 'it was the finest retreat I had ever been on'.

The concentration of major Catholic units proved too much for the available Catholic chaplains to minister to effectively. There were eight Irish infantry battalions and three cavalry regiments with the initial Expeditionary Force of five divisions; all predominantly Catholic. In addition, some English and Scottish battalions had large Catholic minorities. From experience gained in South Africa, the chaplains attached themselves to the Field Ambulances to minister to the wounded. But in August and September 1914 infantry battalions sometimes wholly composed of Catholics suffered heavily, and the absence of a Catholic chaplain was keenly felt and remarked upon in letters home. The Munsters, rearguard to 1st Corps, held at bay an entire German corps at Etreux for over twelve hours and were annihilated. Much the same occurred to the other Catholic battalions until the front stabilized in November. So great was the shortage of priests that it was a German Catholic chaplain who read the service over 127 Munster dead at Etreux,[8] and succoured hundreds of wounded Munstermen. Catholic chaplains, of both sides, were to repeat this service for the 'enemy' many times in the course of the war.

In the course of the 'race to the sea', the attempt by both sides to find, and turn, the flank of the opposing army, a series of battles were fought during October and November 1914. The fate of Europe depended upon a tenuously held line from the Channel to the Swiss border, but the main German effort was directed against the British. On the front held by the BEF, now enlarged to four infantry and one cavalry corps, the British regulars fought with stubborn courage to halt repeated and massive German attacks. First at Bassée and then at Ypres, a single line of trenches – muddy ditches – was all that could be manned to hold the German flood. Without a properly constructed front-line system with support and communication trenches, it would have been foolhardy, or supremely courageous, to attempt to say Mass, especially as priests were so scarce. Nevertheless, aware of the effect of their example, priests attached to fighting units insisted upon taking the risks. Fr Peter Bradley, with 18 Field Ambulance, 6th Division, counted 70 shells exploding a minute. He had tried to say Mass in the trenches, but told that it was 'an experience I shall not try again'.[9] Fr Daniel Lane, nearly 50 years of age and recently recalled from Malta, was attached to a battalion of the Leinster Regiment, also with 6th Division. Despite his years, and his cloth, Fr Lane insisted on sharing the discomforts of the infantrymen. A letter to the *Catholic Herald* about Fr Lane tells how he '… sleeps standing up in the trenches with his blanket around him; he is a hero. Hardly recognisable as a priest – filthy, mudcovered, cold, frostbitten.'[10]

Shortly after his arrival in France Mgr Bickerstaffe-Drew was attached to a Field Ambulance, where his considerable labours among the shattered bodies of the wounded were on a more earthy level than his honours might suggest him capable. Nor did his work pass unnoticed:

> He has shown an amazing amount of energy for an elderly man, but several times I have seen him sitting with the driver of one of the ambulances, nodding his head, absolutely worn out for want of sleep owing to his labours amongst the wounded.[11]

So thinly spread were those few Catholic chaplains in a large mobile Army 'diocese' that, as a chaplain was to write many years later,

> We were a disorganised body, each playing his own lone hand. There was no definite public policy, no one to train us, no one to lead. Each had to learn his work by experience of his own failures.[12]

Each chaplain worked for God in isolation, as an individual missionary in the unit or formation to which he was attached. Since they were so few in numbers it is not surprising that it should appear to Catholics in fighting units that when under the stern trial of battle they saw too little of the chaplain.

As early as the Battle of the Aisne in September 1914 voices were already beginning to be heard complaining about the scarcity of chaplains.

> Regarding the want of Catholic Chaplains. A Chaplain writes from the Front, 'I have seen the wounded Irish Rifles and others, and they have not met a priest since they left home, or heard Mass on Sundays …' The arrangements are unsatisfactory and complaints are general.[13]

However, the labours of the comparatively few chaplains did not go unnoticed in the small professional army that was the BEF at this time.

> In the circumstances, it is remarkable that Catholicism should have held the position of respect which it did in those days, and it was in no small measure due to the courage and perseverance of Father Keatinge and his generation of Army Chaplains.[14]

Following the South African War, a committee had been set up by the

Government under Lord Esher to examine the lessons of that war and make recommendations. As a result of its report, considerable Army reorganization took place which affected all War Office operations and administration, with the exception of the Royal Army Chaplains' Department (RAChD). The lessons of expansion during the Boer War had not been learned. Nothing was done to improve liaison between chaplains and the rest of the Army. With the establishment of a British Expeditionary Force based in the United Kingdom, provision had been made for the attachment of a Principal Chaplain to its Headquarters. In the mobilization plan. However, he was located at Third Echelon head-quarters, far behind the lines at base, with no means to keep in touch with his chaplains in the forward areas. Moreover, as the number, and denominations, of chaplains greatly increased, it became impossible to supervise them effectively from the War Office.[15]

The five-division BEF of August 1914 grew by the end of the year into two separate Armies, each of three infantry corps and a cavalry corps. Furthermore, greater expansion was envisaged. It therefore became imperative to improve the organization, administration, and structure of all supporting Arms. Restructuring the RAChD with the BEF was part of this. In November 1914, the Adjutant-General, Sir Nevil Macready, began with the Catholics.

> He called Monsignor Keatinge, who was then at Ypres, into G.H.Q. and told him to draw up a scheme showing the minimum number of Catholic chaplains required for performing adequately the necessary spiritual ministrations to the Catholic Troops. Mgr Keatinge asked for four Chaplains per Division, i.e. one for each Brigade and one for Divisional Troops: also one Chaplain to each Irish Battalion, and of course, proper provision for Hospitals, Base Camps, etc. The Adjutant-General forwarded this demand to the War Office and recommended it, and it was granted.
>
> It is only right here to express a deep debt of gratitude to Sir Nevil Macready for his help to the Catholic Cause, not only on this occasion, but on many others, it was a great loss to that cause when he was taken away from France to become Adjutant-General at the War Office.[16]

At the same time, the Principal Chaplain to the BEF, Dr John M. Simms, an Irish Presbyterian, was given a staff to run his Chaplains' Branch, and brought forward to General Headquarters at St Omer. Mgr Keatinge was appointed Assistant Principal Chaplain.

Mgr Keatinge was the most distinguished priest of his generation of chaplains, amongst whom he was universally respected and was:

> an inspiration to all who saw him before the altar of God. I never saw anyone say Mass with greater devotion or with greater attention to rubrics. It mattered not whether he celebrated in Camp or in Cathedral. His prayerfulness would change the atmosphere of a canvas tent and

make it seem the House of God. This was a side of his character that may be overlooked. But those who knew him well, knew that his was a life founded on prayer.[17]

Amongst his friends he was noted for his sense of humour. A born raconteur, he was able to turn this to good account in moments of danger, or difficulty. In a sphere often charged with hostility, it was a characteristic which served him, and his flock, very well.

The Principal Chaplain's organization in France as created by the Adjutant-General in 1915 turned upon the Senior Chaplain to the division dealing directly with GHQ. It was essentially an administrative arrangement. Each Church retained ecclesiastic control of its own chaplains. Not all chaplains, or Churches, were in agreement with the new arrangements. To allay misgivings, on 30 May 1915 Dr Simms appointed four senior chaplains for the main denominations within the BEF:

Anglican:	Rev E. Macpherson
Presbyterian:	Rev W. Jaffray
Roman Catholic:	Rev W. Keatinge
Wesleyan:	Rev O. S. Watkins

In the same letter Dr Simms wrote:

> chaplains of all denominations will, under ordinary circumstances, refer questions in the first place to the chaplain of their own denomination of the highest standing in their division. Departmental matters will then be referred to the Principal Chaplain and denominational matters to the Senior Chaplain of their several denominations of the Army in the Field, who will then bring them to the notice of the Principal Chaplain for action when necessary.[18]

One of the most fortunate chaplains' appointments of those early war days was that of Fr B. S. Rawlinson OSB. He had been attached to the Royal Irish Regiment during the South African War, and it seemed natural that he should return to it when he again volunteered for active service in August 1914. The 2nd Bn Royal Irish Regiment was one of the two battalions most seriously engaged at Mons and was again severely mauled at Le Cateau. The 2nd Royal Irish again suffered heavily on the Marne and on the Aisne, and having been 'filled up' repeatedly by replacements from Ireland, the battalion was practically annihilated on the La Bassée front. The remnants of the battalion were then taken from the line and assembled at the headquarters, BEF, St Omer, as the headquarters guard and duties battalion. Fr Rawlinson, who had accompanied the battalion, was therefore ideally placed to make the same impact which had been remarked upon in an earlier war. He became assistant to the senior Catholic chaplain, and it was to Fr Rawlinson that Mgr Keatinge entrusted the day-to-day affairs of the office. Mgr Keatinge was then able to tour the front, visiting his

scattered chaplains, giving spiritual counsel, advice and what material aid
he could in the chaotic opening months of the war. From the letters of one
newly-commissioned chaplain we know he also visited the wounded in the
base hospitals. It is therefore obvious that he travelled widely. Fr
Rawlinson, with many changes of title, was to remain at GHQ BEF for
the duration of the war.

When Expeditionary Forces were mounted elsewhere, in Macedonia
and Egypt, principal chaplains were appointed, but no separate organization was provided. In those theatres, each principal chaplain dealt with the
chaplains of the various Churches in consultation with the senior chaplain
in the force of the Church concerned.

At the end of 1915 a British Expeditionary Force was sent to Salonika.
The first British division to arrive was 10th Irish, and early in 1916 the
27th Division, which contained four Irish battalions, was also despatched
to Salonika. In 1916 Mgr Keatinge was appointed principal chaplain to the
Macedonia Army, with the rank of Brigadier-General, presumably because
of this large concentration of Catholic battalions. It was the highest
position ever achieved by a Catholic priest in the Army to that time. To
replace Mgr Keatinge in France, Fr Rawlinson was promoted to chaplain
1st class and appointed assistant principal chaplain BEF. He also became
senior Catholic chaplain.

Dom Bernard Stephen Rawlinson was 50 years of age when he became
principal chaplain to the Catholics of the British Army in France. Educated
at Downside and Rome, he had been a Benedictine monk since 1884, and
ordained in 1892. His tall commanding presence had been first noted in
the Army during the South African War, when as acting chaplain to the
forces he had served with 1st Royal Irish Regiment, and had twice been
mentioned in despatches. Before he returned to Downside Abbey in 1920
many more honours would be bestowed upon him, but to him, the
greatest was the respect accorded him by the vast majority of his fellow-
chaplains, and the headquarters staff of the BEF.

Not all fears were allayed by the appointment of senior chaplains within
the BEF. Later in 1915, because of ecclesiastical pressure from Church
authorities in England who refused to participate in the new arrangement,
the Church of England chaplains were removed from the control of Dr
Simms and partially out of the Adjutant-General's control. An independent
section of the RAChD was created by the Church of England under a
separate principal chaplain who was called Deputy Chaplain-General
(DCG). Under this DCG, Assistant Chaplains-General were appointed to
the headquarters of each home command, and each Army of the BEF; and
senior chaplains were appointed to each divisional headquarters. The
Church of England had created an organization which was in effect a
separate chaplaincy organization parallel to that of the BEF. The change
was promulgated by the AG to the BEF in August 1915.

Reorganization of the Chaplains' Department.

The Right Reverend L.H. Gwynne, Bishop Suffragan in Khartoum, T.C.F, has been appointed to represent the Chaplain-General with the Army in the Field, with the rank as a local and temporary Major-General.

Dr Gwynne's duties will be those of a Principal Chaplain, but his sphere of administration will be limited to matters appertaining to the Chaplains' Department, connected with the Chaplains and troops of the Church of England. All matters affecting other denominations will remain, as heretofore, under the control of Dr Simms the Principal Chaplain. In effect the change means the establishment of a Deputy Chaplain-General to do duty as an additional Principal Chaplain but for Church of England Chaplains and troops only.

With regard to correspondence emanating from General Headquarters, in connection with the Chaplains' Department, all routine correspondence which deals with the posting, transfer or relief of Chaplains will be addressed to Headquarters of Formations, Corps, etc., from the office of the Deputy Chaplain-General or the Principal Chaplain.

All instructions affecting the discipline, organization, establishment, etc., of the Department will be issued from this office and correspondence arising therefrom should be addressed to the Adjutant-General, General Headquarters.

C.F.N. Macready, Lieut-General.
Adjutant-General, British Army in the Field.
General Headquarters 24th Aug 1915.[19]

The growth of the Army in France was such that by the latter part of 1916, the system of chaplains operating from division to GHQ proved unworkable. In December 1916, the Adjutant-General, Maj Gen G. H. Fownes, who had replaced General Macready upon the latter's appointment as Adjutant-General at the War Office, again reorganized the Chaplains' Branch. Senior chaplains were abolished and an organizational structure created to conform with the BEF's normal chain of command. By an agreement between the 'non-C of E' chaplains and the principal chaplain, BEF (Dr Simms), an assistant principal chaplain (APC) was appointed to each Army, or lines of communication base area; a deputy assistant principal chaplain (DAPC) appointed to each Corps HQ, and a senior chaplain to the forces (SCF) at each Division. Under this arrangement Fr J. Carden MC was appointed APC to First Army; Fr C. W. Smith DSO was appointed APC to Fourth Army (Fr Smith was also created a Domestic Prelate to the Pope to enhance his position).[20] Fr C. Moth, who had recently returned from the Near East, also became APC. Fr F. Woodlock MC became APC Boulogne base area. A high proportion of senior corps and divisional appointments went to Catholics, which can be seen by the significant numbers of Catholics who were Lieutenant-Colonels and Majors. In 1918, Mgr Bickerstaffe-Drew was appointed APC.

It is therefore clear that Catholic chaplains were appointed to a comparatively high number of senior RAChD staff appointments.[21]

Notwithstanding this, a senior regular Army RC chaplain, Fr E. M. Morgan CM (who in 1914 had been on the retired list), objected strongly to the abolition of the senior RC chaplain. Fr Morgan possibly remembered an old Army adage that there is nothing as permanent as a temporary measure. His fear was for the Catholic position in the Army after the war. He corresponded with the Adjutant-General and later had an interview with General Fownes to express misgivings about the abolition of the senior RC chaplain.

> By this arrangement Roman Catholics felt that they had a safeguard and a guarantee that their religious matters would be in the hands of a Senior Chaplain of their own faith. Thus suspicion and misgivings were allayed and a tolerable modus vivendi was created.

He went on to cite the example of the Church of England.

> As is well known, after the above system had been operating for a few months, the Church of England revolted and proclaimed its independence. Logically the R. Catholics should have done the same. We, however, remained in having confidence that good faith would be kept ... and that our 'Denominational' affairs would continue to be in the hands of a Senior Chaplain of our own denomination.
>
> Last December, however, was issued the new scheme reorganising the Chaplains' Department which abolishes the Office of Senior R. Catholic Chaplain. By this new arrangement it seems that the guarantee of our religious rights and privileges has been taken away and that a breach of good faith has been committed.
>
> May I, in conclusion, make two remarks. Nothing which I have said above refers *personally* to Dr Simms. I believe our Chaplains invariably receive nothing but kindness, sympathy and consideration from him. Finally, I wish to assure that I have no personal motive making the above appeal. I look upon the Office of Senior Chaplain as a very arduous and thankless one. I have no ambition whatever to obtain the appointment.[22]

General Fownes took strong exception to Fr Morgan's letter. He explained how the growth of the Armies in France had necessitated decentralization,

> which as far as the non-C. of E. chaplains were concerned this entailed the creation of the following appointments: A.P.Cs. with the Armies and Main Bases. D.P.C.s. with Corps. Senior Chaplains (non C. of E.). The above appointments are filled in such a manner that the various denominations receive proportional representation.[23]

He did, however, consent to having the Catholic assistant principal chaplain, Fr Bernard Rawlinson, nominated as 'the accredited adviser of Dr Simms on Roman Catholic matters'.[24]

Fr Morgan's fears were also expressed in a report to Cardinal Bourne in January 1917, and in a covering letter to Mgr Bidwell he said:

> I am sending a report to the Cardinal. I don't know whether he has returned yet to England. If he is still in Rome I should be glad if you would send it on to him. I have left the envelope open as I should like you to read it. I think it was a great pity we ever consented to take any part in the new arrangement. We had our chance when the C. of E. revolted. Now that the post of SCF(RC) is done away with the situation becomes impossible for us. There is no disguising the fact that under the new organisation we are legally under the direct personal control of a Presbyterian chaplain in ecclesiastical matters. To try to draw a distinction between matters of military discipline and a chaplain's religious duties is simply ridiculous. The two are practically identical. What will they say in Ireland to this arrangement when it gets to know? Long ago Keatinge was getting suspicious. He complained often that he was treated 'as a cipher'. At last Dr Simms determined to get rid of him. He went to the W.O. and told Sir R. Brade that K... was 'of no use' in France and that he didn't want him back. This I have on most certain evidence. Having got rid of Keatinge it became fairly easy to suppress his office.
>
> Because I sent a letter of protest to the Adjutant-General against these proceedings, Dr Simms has threatened to get rid of me. Probably he will go to Brade and tell him I am a troublesome person – which is quite true. I think he has an idea that the Cardinal might help him as he knows that I am not a persona grata with his Eminence.
>
> Do you think Westminster will do anything in this matter? If not I propose trying Ireland.[25]

Apparently receiving no support from Westminster, Fr Morgan wrote a long statement of the facts to Archbishop Walsh of Dublin, and appealed for support in his (Morgan's) efforts to reverse the decision and restore the senior Catholic chaplain:

> I have ventured to send you a long statement concerning the position of Catholics in the Army here in France. All the priests whom I have been able to consult on the subject agree with me in considering the state of things as most unsatisfactory from a Catholic standpoint and fraught with danger for the future. Hitherto the War Office has been most scrupulous in never interfering with the religious independence of Catholics, they would not even send an official notice to a Catholic priest through a Protestant chaplain however senior he might be.[26]

The secretary to Archbishop Walsh replied:

> His Grace wishes me to say that he has had no responsibility for the Army arrangements for Catholic Chaplains from the beginning and does not see that he could interfere in the matter now.[27]

Of course Fr Morgan was unaware of developments then taking shape in

Rome which would alter profoundly the Catholic chaplains' department of the British Army. By the time those changes took place, however, it would be of no concern to him. Shortly after his rebuff from Dublin Fr Morgan was sent home from France and again placed on the retired list.

Contrary to taking exception to the reorganization, Cardinal Bourne gave it his blessing by appointing Fr Rawlinson Vicar-General to the Armies in France. Later he endorsed his approval when, after a visit to the BEF, the Cardinal wrote to Dr Simms: 'I was able to see at close quarters the satisfactory results of the re-organization of the Chaplains' Department.'[28]

Far away in Macedonia the principal chaplain to the Salonika Army, Mgr William Keatinge, shared Fr Morgan's unhappiness at the Adjutant-General's abolition of the senior Catholic chaplain. In a letter to Fr Rawlinson he wrote:

> It ought to have been fought out. It is a very retrograde step, and will be difficult to make right after the war. The whole Catholic position seems to be merged into 'non C of E' which seems an absurd title, and rather brands us as Dissenters.[29]

In 1920, the War Office reorganized, yet again, the RAChD, and wanted to place a Catholic bishop under the Chaplain-General. On that occasion the case was 'fought out'. The story will be told later.

References

1. Statistics, p. 190.
2. *Army List*, 1915 (London, HMSO).
3. Ibid.
4. Fr Frederick Peal SJ, *War Jottings* (Calcutta, 1916).
5. AWA.
6. WW (1936).
7. 'Ampleforth at war', *Ampleforth Journal*, vol. 21, p. 221.
8. Tom Johnstone, *Orange, Green and Khaki* (Dublin, 1992), p. 33.
9. *Catholic Herald* (26 December 1914).
10. Ibid.
11. Ibid.
12. Brian Plumb, *Arundel to Zabi: A Biographical Dictionary of the Catholic Bishops of England and Wales 1623–1987* (Warrington, 1988).
13. *The Tablet* (26 September 1914).
14. Plumb.
15. Rawlinson MSS, War History Box.
16 Ibid.
17. Plumb.
18. Archbishop Walsh Papers, ADA.
19. Chaplains papers, AWA.
20. *Army List*, 1918 and 1919.
21. Archbishop Walsh Papers, ADA.

22. Ibid.
23. Ibid.
24. Ibid.
25. Letter, Morgan to Bidwell (January 1917), AWA.
26. Archbishop Walsh Papers, ADA.
27. Ibid.
28. Rawlinson MSS, War History Box, DAA.
29. Ibid.

7

The shortage of Army chaplains

Shortly after Britain's declaration of war on Germany, Mr Asquith appointed Lord Kitchener Secretary of State for War. At a meeting of Cabinet ministers, admirals and generals, Kitchener astounded all present by declaring that the nation must prepare for a war of at least three years, and he demanded an expansion of the Army to 70 divisions. The prestige of Kitchener was at its zenith, and the Government and Parliament accepted his proposed Army expansion without demur. Recruiting began at once for what was termed the New Armies. In marked contrast, manpower in the Navy, following mobilization, exceeded warship manning requirements, enabling the First Lord of the Admiralty to create an infantry formation, the Royal Naval Division, from surplus seamen and marines.

Commensurate with the flood of eager volunteers who answered Kitchener's call to arms was the torrent of letters to the archdiocese of Westminster from all sections of the Catholic priesthood throughout Great Britain and Ireland offering their services as chaplains to the forces. So great was the desire to take part in the national effort that some priests were not content with just one letter but almost immediately followed with others. One such priest was Fr John Gwynn SJ, a professor at Mungret College, Limerick.

> It occurred to me since I wrote to you this morning that you might have the opportunity of putting in a word for me with Lord Kitchener.
> I am sure that he would be the very first to admit that when so many Irish soldiers are going to the front and nearly all Catholics that some Chaplains should come from Ireland and that if twelve English Jesuits are chosen at least a few Irish Jesuits should get the chance.
> It might, I feel confident it would, influence him to tell him that my father was in the Army and fought at the Crimea, also that, as I told you in

my last letter, I have done a good deal of work with the Irish Guards, and other regiments, and that I speak French and German quite fluently.[1]

The *Catholic Herald*, a month after the declaration of war, reported that Mgr Bidwell, Secretary of the Army Chaplains' Department, was busy arranging for the rush of priests who had volunteered as chaplains to the forces.[2]

> Each applicant must have the leave of his bishop. There are no difficulties placed in the way of those willing to go, and several hundred priests have made application.[3]

Even when all due form was observed there was considerable delay before a volunteer was appointed. One priest, Fr Henry C. Day SJ, volunteered three days *before* the outbreak of war and was accepted three days later. He waited three months for his appointment and was then only commissioned by the intercession of Alderman McCabe, Lord Mayor of Manchester, with the GOC Western Command. He was appointed to 2nd South Midlands Mounted Division (Yeomanry). Fr Day left the Holy Name parish in November to join the division then training in Berkshire and was attached to the Derbyshire Yeomanry. 'Found a Catholic chapel in Inglewood House, the residence of the Walmesley family. Said one Mass there before the division left for the East Coast. A local Vicar offered the School for Mass.'[4] Brig Gen Paul Kenna VC DSO was his Brigade Commander. Kenna, a Stonyhurst man, had won his VC at Omdurman.

It was unfortunate for Army Catholics that the War Office was almost as slow as the Admiralty in realizing the importance of the chaplains issue. Although chaplains were commissioned and appointed to New Army divisions, to the old pre-war establishment, the War Office did nothing to increase the actual establishment. Here was the problem, possibly because no detailed case was put by either the BEF or the Catholic ecclesiastical authority of justifying an increase. Talking about 'more', of anything, is one thing. Arguing the case in writing for specific numbers, and presenting detailed justification for an increase, is, to any bureaucracy, what matters. It was an issue which ought, in the light of the South African experience, to have been argued long before the war to the Esher Committee, by the chaplains' ecclesiastical Superior, Cardinal Bourne. Unfortunately, at that time he had other designs towards Service chaplaincy.

As many of the mainly Catholic battalions were Irish, it was to be expected that those most interested in the campaign to increase military chaplains at the front should be the Irish Members of Parliament. The early insouciant attitude at the War Office to the issue was demonstrated in the House of Commons on 17 September when the Under Secretary for War, in reply to a question on the subject, stated that 'there were at present twelve Catholic Chaplains with the Expeditionary Force, and the Secretary for War did not at present see his way to send more ... In case of extreme necessity, French priests would no doubt be available.'[5]

Although the soldiers in the trenches may not have heard the Minister's announcement, or could have done little about it if they had, the Catholic press, Members of Parliament, and hierarchy took exception to the words, especially as anti-clericalism in France obstructed civilian hospital chaplains in their work. A vigorous press campaign began. First to respond was *The Tablet* which reported growing dissatisfaction among the Irish soldiers in the field.[6] In a written reply the War Office told the editor of *The Irish Catholic* that 'Ample provision is being made for Roman Catholic soldiers in the New Army'.[7] The editor's immediate reply could have been predicted: 'My concern was not so much about the New Army as such, but about the Catholic members of the Expeditionary Force.'[8] The War Office then fell back on the logistical position, maintaining that: 'Only a limited number of non-combatants can accompany the Army in the field, owing to demands on transports and equipment, etc. The number of Roman Catholic Chaplains attached to the Field Force is in more generous proportion than the numbers allowed to other communions.'[9] This latter remark was absolutely correct. The number of Catholic chaplains was indeed greater in proportion to other denominations, but by this time that was not the issue, and the editor defended his position stoutly. 'Once more we repeat our request for the appointment of a Catholic Chaplain to every regiment containing a certain proportion of Catholics in its ranks, and of an Irish priest as Chaplain to every Irish Regiment.'[10]

The British Catholic press entered the campaign on the same day as *The Irish Catholic* called for a priest in every battalion. *The Tablet*, evidently inspired, took up the call:

> Up to the present, only two additional priests have been appointed to serve with the troops at the Front. On the other hand, some twenty-five newly commissioned Catholic Chaplains are now doing excellent work with the regiments still with this country. About the necessity of having more Catholic Chaplains with the Army in France, there can be no doubt ... We know that urgent representations are being made in the highest quarters ... We may add that the responsibility for any delay there has been in sending an adequate number of Catholic Chaplains to the Front, rests entirely and solely with the War Office. The Cardinal Archbishop, who, as Delegate of the Holy See, is the Ecclesiastical Authority to whom application is made when it is desired to appoint additional Chaplains, has always, and from the first, been in a position to meet every possible demand.[11]

Lending their no little weight to the growing disquiet, the Irish bishops in conference voiced their displeasure at the delay in appointing additional priests at the front. Speaking at the annual meeting of the Irish bishops at Maynooth, Cardinal Logue told them:

> Even if conscience were not concerned, any one must see that no policy could be more short-sighted than to allow such difficulties as those of transport to stand in the way of a full and efficient number of Irish priests ministering to their wounded and dying countrymen on the field of battle … We must claim that, without further delay, our Catholics in the field be duly safeguarded in the most important of all their interests.[12]

At the end of their meeting, the bishops passed a resolution proclaiming that:

> All the information at our disposal forces upon us the very unwilling conviction that the supply of chaplains for the Irish Catholic soldiers at the front is lamentably inadequate … It is the spiritual wants of our people that made us protest. The dying Catholic is entitled to the last Sacraments, and he needs them. Neither his right nor his need is the less because he dies at war. Therefore we must claim that, without further delay, our Catholics in the field be duly safeguarded in the most important of all their interests. A far larger number of Irish Catholic chaplains is urgently needed. The increase is required most of all in the battlefield itself, but also very largely in the French Hospitals to which wounded Irish Catholic soldiers are conveyed.
>
> Moreover the regulations should enable the Catholic Chaplains to know the names of the wounded Catholics in hospital and should secure full freedom of communication with them and should altogether relieve wounded Irishmen from the toils of the miserable French device which requires in hospital the signature of a wounded man to a document printed in French before his Chaplain may attend him.[13]

The issue became so well known, and deserving, that Margot Asquith told Kitchener at a Prime Minister's reception in No. 10 Downing Street that he should 'give them their priests'.[14]

Eventually the Adjutant-General in France, as has been explained, took charge of the situation and a large increase in the establishment of Catholic chaplains was sanctioned by the War Office. In November an official at the War Office, probably reflecting the tone from France, wrote a generous-spirited letter to Mr John Redmond MP, leader of the Irish National Party. It was explained that a 100 per cent increase in the establishment had been approved and additional increases were promised should these prove necessary.

> Since the outbreak of the war, the approved establishment for Roman Catholic Chaplains has been one to every division sent abroad and three were allotted to the general hospitals.
>
> It was recently decided that every Irish Regiment and battalion predominantly Catholic should have a Chaplain attached to it. Consequently the number of such chaplains was increased from 14 to 30 to admit of this being done, and, in addition to this, four more were sent out on the requisition of the Principal Chaplain.

By an arrangement with Cardinal Bourne, eight of the additional sixteen priests were nominated by Cardinal Logue of Armagh. When the priests arrive at the base, the Principal Chaplain details them for duty wherever the need is most urgent.

It is hoped that the additions thus made will be found to meet the necessities of the case. If, as I think you feared, there should be found an insufficient number of chaplains in the hospitals at the base to undertake the work, and this is reported to me, I need hardly assure you that our sympathetic consideration would not be wanting.

As regards the New Army, the Roman Catholic appointments to the Irish Divisions are made by the General Officer Commanding in Chief, Irish Command, in consultation with Cardinal Logue.[15]

During November and December chaplains poured over to France and the beneficial effects were immediately felt.

When sufficient numbers of chaplains with the field armies allowed the attachment of chaplains to battalions, Catholic priests won considerable prestige among the fighting troops by being the first chaplains to accompany them actually into the line. Fr Francis Gleeson, chaplain to 2nd Munsters, in the first recorded instance of its kind went forward with his battalion in the counter-attack at Givenchy to restore the line on 21 December 1914. After the attack 'Stretcher parties, helped by the chaplain, Fr Gleeson, heroically scoured the fire-swept battlefield searching for the wounded'.[16]

Cardinal Logue was the first senior Catholic churchman to advocate sending chaplains into the line, to give wounded and dying soldiers the consolation of the Church in their last moments. Speaking at Dundalk in October the Cardinal repeated words he had spoken to the Irish bishops at their annual meeting at Maynooth:

What we want is that chaplains will be permitted to go to the Front – not merely to go to the French hospitals, but to go to the firing line, so that when the poor fellow drops he may have a priest beside him to give him the last consolations of religion.[17]

Evidently sniping at this suggestion, *The Tablet* commented:

Some disappointment is expressed in some quarters that the Catholic Chaplains cannot be in the Firing Line, instead of being kept with the ambulances, but is complaint reasonable? A Catholic Chaplain, who has been at the Front from the first, describes the situation in these words: 'Every man is in a hole dug out. Nothing can live outside, and when they do advance to take up another position, lots are killed and wounded. All non-combatants – doctors, Chaplains, Army Service people – are kept behind. Sunday is, of course, the same as any other day, fighting or marching. The men are day and night in the trenches. I don't see that the authorities are to blame. I do not see how they can give more facilities for Mass, etc.'[18]

It is apparent that at an early stage in the war, two camps appeared to be forming in the Catholic press on the chaplains issue, one side pressing the War Office in the matter, the other satisfied with the progress being achieved by the Westminster authorities.

In an editorial on 21 October the *Catholic Herald* made it clear that it was firmly behind the actions of the Irish bishops. Indeed, it went very far out of line by advocating that the Irish bishops should make representations to Rome immediately for ecclesiastical jurisdiction over Irish troops. Additionally, the editorial hinted at wider dissatisfaction on the administration and organization of Service Catholic chaplains:

> For the dissatisfaction with the present situation is only typical of what exists elsewhere ... As a large proportion of the Catholic troops are Irish therefore it seems absurd that the selection of chaplains for these Irish troops should be in the hands of Mgr Bidwell, whoever he may be, instead of being controlled by the Irish ecclesiastical authorities in so far as chaplains for the Irish troops are concerned. By all means let the ecclesiastical authorities in England deal with their own proper subjects, but it will be the fault of the Irish Bishops themselves if the present state of affairs is allowed to continue.[19]

A month later the *Catholic Herald* continued its personal attack on Mgr Bidwell, growing even more bitter.

> Although there are such enormous numbers of Irish soldiers in the English and Scotch [sic] regiments it is unlikely that many Irish chaplains have been appointed by Bidwell... in whose hands it would appear that, for some reason or another, nominations now rest.[20]

The same edition also reported extreme dissatisfaction in the selection process at Westminster, voiced by those priests who had already volunteered. It advised Catholic men contemplating entering the Army to 'join an Irish regiment'.[21] In its next issue, the *Catholic Herald* published a letter from Fr Collins, a 'much respected chaplain who had been awarded the DSO in South Africa', who had not been re-employed because of his opposition to the pre-war reorganization of Catholic chaplaincy. In his letter, Fr Collins castigated Cardinal Bourne for not exerting pressure on the War Office for more chaplains.[22]

On the other side of the fence *The Tablet* was firmly behind Westminster, mustering letters from a chaplain at the front to support the *status quo*:

> An English Jesuit with the Field Ambulance of the 3rd Corps of the 4th Division writes to us as follows: For the first three months of the war the supply of chaplains was inadequate. Now, thanks to the efforts of our Cardinal Archbishop, we are very well provided, at least in our division. Besides the senior chaplain, Fr Forrest, who worked himself to death with great zeal as long as he was alone, there are now two chaplains for the

Irish regiments in our division, and myself. We are gradually overtaking arrears, but we have met regiments that had not seen an English-speaking priest since the beginning of the war.[23]

Every brigade of the 2nd Division has a Catholic Chaplain, and this I consider as satisfactory as one can hope any arrangement can be. I see in some of the papers a demand for a regimental chaplain. My own experience satisfies me that a chaplain is better attached to a field ambulance, as when he becomes regimental, the three other regiments of his brigade see little of him.[24]

At the end of 1914 regular troops from overseas garrisons were formed into fresh divisions and sent to France. Some divisions had Irish Catholic units, others had English and Scottish battalions with significant Catholic numbers. Territorial battalions from Glasgow, Liverpool, Tyneside and other Catholic centres were also sent to France to fill the gaps in the original BEF. Meanwhile, the formation of the New Armies went ahead, creating its own demand for chaplains. By increasing the chaplains' establishment, the War Office released the flood-gates, and soon there were signs that the supply of chaplains might not match the demand, except by additional effort on the part of Westminster.

As early as November 1914 *The Tablet* had sounded a low-keyed appeal;

There are now more than sixty commissioned chaplains ministering to our Catholic soldiers, and of these nearly forty are for service at the Front... Although the list of priests who have already volunteered for service with the Army has by no means been exhausted, it is now possible to entertain fresh applications. All such applications must be made by letter to Mgr Bidwell (at Archbishop's House, Westminster) who will submit them to the Cardinal.[25]

Bishop Amigo, in a letter to Cardinal Logue, voiced his pessimism and provided ammunition for others to fire. Why he did not voice his concern to Westminster is open to speculation.

It will be a great pity if and when the government gives us the opportunity to provide for the spiritual welfare of the troops we shall let our soldiers be without chaplains. I thought Your Eminence should have this information as you are so interested in the Army and Navy.[26]

To this Cardinal Logue replied: 'There are plenty of good earnest priests in Ireland longing to go out and help our soldiers.'[27]

While all eyes of those involved in the chaplains issue were focused upon France, the growth of the New Armies had created a major secondary problem in many parts of England. The erection of vast new training camps, in places as far apart as Catterick, almost in Co. Durham, and Shoreham-by-Sea in Sussex, created fresh problems for Westminster. Often these camps were in parts of England devoid of either Catholic priest or chapel, such as Catterick. Or where there was a priest, the additional work was too much, as at Shoreham. There the priest-in-charge, Fr M. Flanagan, appealed to Southwark for help on 2 October.

> Your Lordship is doubtless aware that there are more than 20,000 troops in camp at Shoreham, among them, as far as we have at present ascertained, about 700 Catholics. I hear today that I have been appointed acting military chaplain. We have church parade on Sundays at 9 o'clock.
>
> As I cannot do this work single-handed I write to make this suggestion before proceeding further.
>
> Would Your Lordship permit me to ask Father Byrne, who is at Haywards Heath, if he would consent to come to help me with one of my Masses in the church on Sundays. The difficulty is that I believe he has not got faculties...[28]

Soldiers wrote to their own dioceses about the lack of priests or chaplains in their locality. These complaints were passed on to Westminster for action. Mgr Bidwell, writing to the Bishop of Northampton on 26 September 1914, dissociated Westminster from the problem and placed the responsibility for the lack of chaplains at these camps on local Ordinaries and commanding officers.

> My Dear Lord, The Cardinal is only responsible for supplying and appointing those chaplains who are to give their whole time to the troops, whether abroad or at home. There is no difficulty as to this. We have a long list of Volunteers, and appointments are made as soon as we are asked for them by the military authorities.
>
> The care of those troops at home who have no whole-time chaplains of their own rests with the local Ordinaries and the local Clergy. This is necessarily so, as the Cardinal has no jurisdiction over the local clergy.
>
> The War Office has given the Commanding Officers power to arrange for the appointment of Chaplains, but many of them have not done so yet, being presumably under the impression that the services of the local clergy meet the needs of the Catholics under their command. If the clergy would impress on the Commanding Officers that this is not so, it would be undoubtedly a great help. We are doing all we can from here, but we do not come into touch with the Commanding Officers until they apply, and what is wanted is precisely to get them to apply.
>
> The War Office cannot give us information as to the movements of troops! So we have no means of knowledge where they are, which makes it all the more important that they should have chaplains of their own, and that the local clergy should help us to have this done.[29]

In other places conflicting personalities, or duplication of effort created by divided responsibility, caused confusion. In the diocese of Nottingham military camps at Sleaford and Bulswater were without chaplains. The bishop insisted upon sending one of his priests to each place as an interim solution. Then the War Office appointed a commissioned chaplain to Sleaford:

> The Sleaford matter is settled I hope. The W.O. have asked for a
> Commissioned chaplain to be nominated and Fr. Strickland S.J. will be
> appointed. He is going down today. As you wished Fr. Mostyn to begin as
> an acting chaplain, he could not be nominated.
>
> As regards Bulswater, the present arrangement really does seem
> unsatisfactory, and it has occurred to me that perhaps you might tell off
> Fr. Mostyn as an acting chaplain there? If so he ought to be appointed
> nominally to help Fr. Mason ... If this arrangement is not possible, I will
> ask the W.O. whether they can give us a whole time chaplain at Bulswater,
> but I am afraid that they will simply refer the matter to the Brigadier
> General, so it would really be quicker for him to be attacked first, as you
> did the Sleaford people![30]

In places where the bishop did not intervene to help, Catholic troops took
to complaining to their parents who passed on the message. Mr J. R. Dillon
of Cricklewood wrote to Bishop Amigo, with evident impatience: 'My boy
is at Knapp Hill, could he have a chaplain. Is it possible to have a chaplain
at least for a time, at least until the war is over?'[31]

Correspondence from the Bishop of Southwark to Mgr Bidwell on 3
October 1916 makes clear, however, that not all the confusion rested with
either commanding officers or the War Office. It is apparent from Bishop
Amigo's letter that with a little reorganization in particular dioceses,
commissioned chaplains could have been released from home duties for
the front, or elsewhere where the need was greater.

> I am willing to let Fr. Edward Daly at present at Dartford go into the Army
> to help the poor soldiers. I recommend him especially as his people have
> always been connected with the Army and he will understand how to deal
> with soldiers.
>
> I did not know till I received your letter that the Cardinal had anything
> to do with the posting of the chaplains. Whenever Bishops or priests have
> found fault with the way in which some chaplains are appointed where
> they are not needed, I have said so far that it was the War Office which
> was to blame. In this Diocese in the past I mentioned to you how priests
> could easily do the military work at Redhill, Hayward's Heath,
> Crowborough and Ashford. Last Easter there were 70 Catholic soldiers
> at Sevenoaks and though Fr. Cunningham could easily look after them,
> there were two commissioned chaplains there as well.
>
> At present I could still supply for Shorncliffe, and set Fr. McKee free, by
> placing Fr. Lynch-Staunton there. When Mgr Keatinge came to me
> begging for chaplains for the dying soldiers in France, I wrote to Fr.
> Lynch-Staunton at once, but though he could do the work well at
> Shorncliffe, his stomach could not stand the campaign life. I can also
> dispense with a chaplain at Canterbury by putting an additional priest
> there. At Canterbury there is too much work for one priest but not
> enough for two, but if the 500 Catholic soldiers have to be looked after
> from the Mission I shall have no scruple about placing a young priest
> there under Fr. Sheppard.[32]

On 5 November 1914 Cardinal Bourne found it necessary to write to the bishops. He balanced his appeal for information with an element of self-satisfaction, and, undiplomatically, appeared to place Cardinal Logue in a position subordinate to himself on chaplaincy matters.

> You will do me a great service if you would kindly let me know of any camp, or position of camp situated in your Diocese where no Catholic chaplain has been appointed.
>
> You will, I am sure be glad to know that after repeated representations, in which I had to involve the influence of the Prime Minister, the War Office has at length consented to send to the Front a number of chaplains proportional to our needs. At my request Cardinal Logue will select a certain number of these additional chaplains from priests actually resident in Ireland.[33]

However, the issue of chaplains for the training establishments in England had still not been addressed. The shortage grew to the extent that Cardinal Bourne made an urgent personal appeal on 16 September 1915 to:

> all the Bishops of England, Ireland and Scotland for their kindly aid in meeting the demand for another large increase in the number of Chaplains for the Army and Navy. We already have 270 Priests giving their services as whole-time chaplains to the Military and Naval Forces.[34]

Despite this Bishop Amigo found it necessary in November 1915 to write again to Mgr Bidwell, laying the blame anywhere but on his doorstep.

> I hope it will not be thought any fault of ours that the soldiers will be deprived of any other spiritual benefits. It may be that another full-time chaplain is needed and that is why the soldiers complain to the Bishop of Salford.[35]

Notwithstanding these warnings and appeals, a report by a senior chaplain upon just one area of England, the camps on Salisbury Plain, made on 31 January 1916 highlighted again the very situation which had been complained of a year earlier. An experienced chaplain, Fr William Murphy, recently senior chaplain to 10th Irish Division, had returned to the UK and was for a very short time senior chaplain on Salisbury Plain (shortly afterwards, he was sent to Ireland as senior chaplain, Irish Command). Accompanied by Fr Sheehan, a brigade chaplain, shortly going to France, Fr Murphy inspected fifteen camps in the Tidworth area, and reported his findings to Cardinal Bourne on 31 January 1916:

> I have the honour to submit to your Eminence an account of a circuit of the Camps of my district, completed the 17th Jany, 1916. I do not consider myself free to enter into particulars in writing as to the number of men in these Camps. Neither can I call upon your Eminence as the two Chaplains resident here have gone to the front and I am, from the present, in sole charge. The situation is a very urgent one, however, and I must

even make this imperfect statement of the case in all haste. I visited nearly all the camps which are fifteen in number.

Camp 1. Has normal number of chaplains.

Camps 2, 3, 4 are of enormous importance with a hospital of 300 beds. No chaplains.

Camps 5, 6. Are of great population with a hospital. This Camp is served from a neighbouring city for Confessions on Saturdays and Mass on Sundays. The men are not, however, visited in barracks with the result that, after a considerable residence they do not know the whereabouts of the Church. The Church is a hut in the midst of countless other huts in a very sea of mud these winter months.

Camps 7, 8, 9. Large Camps with a large hospital. With the exception of five Sundays there has been no Mass since last August.

Camps 10, 11. Are numerically small. No Mass.

Camp 12. Has a large hospital and a huge Catholic strength. There is one priest. It is a physical impossibility for him to visit these troops. The roads are newly made and one sinks to the ankles in mud at this season.

Camp 13. A very large Artillery Camp. No chaplain.

Camp 15. I have not visited. It has a hospital, with a considerable number of troops, and I believe, no chaplain.

These bare statements show how inadequate the staff of chaplains is. I cannot just yet give your Eminence figures, as I explained; let me say however that the figures make the statement of the case appalling.[36]

Fr Murphy then presented figures and names from the nominal rolls of one camp to show that a majority had Irish names. Going further, he gave a breakdown of Catholics in a brigade embarking for France. It had no battalions from either Ireland or the Catholic heartland in the north of England, yet of the 530 Catholics in the brigade 258 were Irish.[37]

In what a receptive mood these men are for the Sacraments one instance will illustrate. Fr. Sheehan and I interrupted our tour of inspection to warn the men of Camp 5 about Confession. They were on the eve of going to the front. It was a very hurried visit we paid them, but they came to Confession in crowds that evening. In an experience of the Army of over 14 years I have never met men more anxious for the ministrations of their Church. It is painful to be challenged by these men in the different Camps, and not to be able to give even a promise of help... One witnesses distressing scenes at the front, but, I assure your Eminence, our utter helplessness to do our duty by these men makes this the saddest place I have ever worked in. In the past, the number of those who have been lost to the Church for lack of ministrations, is legion. What assurance is there that the present situation will not work out similarly?

Many of these men have long been strangers to the practice of their religion and are now willing, and even anxious, to resume it. They are ten, twenty, thirty years from the Sacraments, many of them, and, with past experience of the present war to guide us, are going to certain death without the ministrations of their Church...

> But why do I trouble your Eminence with this harrowing story? You
> know it only too well. You have had letters from men in these Camps
> craving for help. Help you could not give, and you passed them on to me. I
> could not help. The War Office has been importuning you to send even one
> Priest to an entire Division at Camp 2, and there is no Chaplain to send...
>
> If I may make bold to offer a suggestion, I would say, make our extreme
> spiritual destitution known to Cardinal Logue, and I have no doubt that
> his Eminence will ensure a generous response from the Irish Clergy. I
> believe that to make known the state of things is to remedy it.[38]

Shortly afterwards Cardinal Bourne wrote to Cardinal Logue, sending him
a copy of Murphy's report. However the Cardinal omitted to say why no
action had previously been taken to identify, and resolve, or mitigate, the
problem.

> I am sure that you will be interested in reading the enclosed copy of a
> letter which I have received from Fr Murphy... This letter shows how in
> spite of all our efforts, we are still in urgent need of more chaplains for the
> Army. There are some 400 chaplains at work including those from the
> colonies; of these England has provided more than 270 - my own
> Diocese has given 35 and we are really at the end of our resources. Can
> your Eminence in your charity obtain no more help from Ireland which
> so far has given no more than 60?[39]

Fr Murphy had also sent a copy of his report to the Archbishop of Dublin.
For the first time the Irish bishops were presented with an eye-witness
account by an experienced Irish chaplain whom they trusted, and the
word-picture he showed them was of a spiritual desert, in which Irish
Catholic soldiers were stranded. The vivid report, obviously coming from
the heart, made a profound impression. This was no mere unsubstantiated
appeal for 'more'; reasons for 'demanding more' were clearly to be seen.
Four Dublin priests were commissioned chaplains in as many weeks, and
all four were sent to the front. Cardinal Logue issued an appeal on 10
February 1916 for the younger clergy to volunteer for active service.
Within a month 36 Irish priests had been commissioned, in addition to the
82 who had gone previously from Ireland.[40]

On 30 June 1916 Bishop Browne of Cloyne published a resolution
passed at the recent general meeting of Irish bishops.

> Ordered: That the Bishops address their Clergy - each in his own Diocese
> during the coming Clerical Retreats on the pressing need for a supply of
> Army Chaplains, and encourage the younger priests to accept temporary
> employment as Army Chaplains at the Front where the want of priests is
> directly felt, as many hundreds of our Catholic soldiers are left in a state
> of spiritual destitution.[41]

Despite this order, for whatever reason, one diocese in Ireland, Limerick,
sent no priests into the Army or Navy although countless hundreds of men

from Limerick diocese were serving at the front. Despite the obvious political partisanship on the part of the bishop, one Limerick priest serving outside the diocese volunteered and went to the front,[42] and the Superiors of Limerick colleges of regular Orders, Jesuit, Franciscan, Redemptorist, allowed their priests to go. One Franciscan, who died while on service, was accorded a full military funeral in the city of Limerick.[43] A Jesuit from Mungret College was the first chaplain to be killed in action on the Western Front; and a Limerick-born priest was killed in action near Jerusalem.

Notwithstanding the huge increase in the establishment of Catholic chaplains authorized by the War Office, throughout the war there was a constant shortage. Well might Mgr William Keatinge write from Salonika, then sixteen Catholic chaplains under establishment, in 1916:

> How miserable our English (and Irish) bishops have failed, in this war, to rise to the occasion. They can't see beyond the petty wants of their diocese.[44]

In early 1916 a mischievous report was circulating in Rome about the inadequate numbers of army chaplains supplied by Ireland. Curiously, certain figures used by Cardinal Bourne in his letter, above, to Cardinal Logue were closely related to Roman rumour. To counter this Mgr M. O'Riordan of the Irish College, Rome, published a memorandum written in Italian:

> Regarding the Allocation of the Chaplaincies in the British Armed Forces. A rumour has got around here in Rome and in Great Britain, and lately also in Ireland, that at present there are in the British Army about 400 Catholic chaplains; that, of this total, England has given about 280 and is unable to supply more, though a larger number would be necessary; that a request to the Irish bishops that this shortfall be filled did not have any success; and that Ireland has given less than 60 chaplains.
> Such a reading of the situation is seriously incorrect.[45]

The paper, based upon Catholic Directories and Catholic Yearbooks, presented the Catholic population of Great Britain and Ireland, and its distribution in the three kingdoms, advancing the thesis that England had more secular priests per head of Catholic population than Ireland: Ireland 1–1,060; England 1–760. Adding regular clergy changed the totals to Ireland 1–894; England 1–484. The memorandum noted:

> The Catholics in Ireland are spread through the whole country, while the Catholics in England are mostly concentrated in the cities. Moreover in Ireland the Catholics assiduously attend the sacraments and the churches are extremely full for every Mass on feast days.[46]

The number of serving Catholic military chaplains given by Mgr O'Riordan, as coming from the directories, was 280, nearly correct. He also made telling points:

In this number are not included the 16 permanent military chaplains, nor those parish priests who give spiritual assistance (officiating chaplains) to those soldiers and sailors stationed in their jurisdiction.

If there is a lack of chaplains, this does not come from a numerical insufficiency of good chaplains but from an inadequate deployment of them. In reality they are poorly distributed.[47]

Had the Army Lists been available to Mgr O'Riordan he would have done better. By presenting precise total numbers of chaplains, showing those from England, Ireland, Scotland and Commonwealth countries, his thesis would have had added cogency. There was a further point he failed to use: the age of the respective clergy, and high numbers of young priests on loan to English, Scottish and Commonwealth dioceses until vacancies could be found for them, usually caused by death, in the home diocese. Many of these priests 'on loan' became chaplains and not a few died whilst serving.

Harmonious relations between the Catholic hierarchies of the sister-kingdoms were never so important for Catholics in the English-speaking world as they were in the years 1914–19. These were years of stupendous events in world history and enormous change in nations, and national attitudes. It was a time which demanded width of perspective and clarity of vision in leaders, both secular and religious. Considerable subsequent anguish amongst Catholics could have been averted had Westminster acted generously and far-sightedly at this crucial time, and acted in unison with mainstream Catholic opinion. By allowing the Irish hierarchy to appoint chaplains to the 50 or so Irish Catholic battalions in action or being formed in 1914–15, relations between Westminster and Armagh would not have been soured at a critical time in the history of both islands. As a consequence of this and other insensitivities which followed, Westminster had later to appeal repeatedly to Armagh for additional chaplains. These appeals came at a time when events in Ireland (the Easter Rising and its aftermath) required, in their view, a more cautious approach on the part of the Irish hierarchy than was necessary in 1914–16. As a consequence Catholic soldiers suffered spiritual want.

Westminster's efforts to avoid public disagreement with the War Office and Admiralty in 1914–15 upon the chaplains issue yielded little good-will in return. Failing to win the support of the British Government, Westminster was to lose a crucial argument in Rome during 1917, and because of that, lost control of all British Army chaplains in 1918.

In early 1917 a 'Memorial to the Irish Hierarchy re shortage of Catholic Army chaplains' was published. The document was signed by 120 Irish Catholic notables, representing the nobility and landowners, judiciary, law, medical profession, university professors, retired and serving Army and naval officers. Enclosed with the memorial were extracts from letters sent by relatives at the front.

The undersigned, many of whom have near relatives serving in the present war, desire respectfully to call your Lordship's attention to the pressing need for more Roman Catholic Chaplains on the various fronts. It will be remembered that at the beginning of the war, His Grace, Cardinal Logue and other members of the Irish Hierarchy publicly made strong representations to the War Office to permit a larger number of Catholic Chaplains to be attached to the army, and rightly complained that the spiritual needs of Catholic soldiers suffered, as compared with other denominations, owing to the small number of Catholic Chaplains then allowed. We understand that these difficulties have now been removed, that the number of Chaplains allowed has been greatly increased, and that the War Office will appoint the Chaplains if they come forward; but in fact they are not coming forward, and for a considerable time there has been a great deficiency in Catholic Clergymen offering themselves for these posts. Fr Murphy, R.C. Chaplain, called attention to this matter as far back as January, 1916.

The evidence brought to our notice from letters from the front and otherwise is overwhelming, that on all the fronts, in the trenches, at the hospitals, and at the bases, the spiritual needs of Catholic troops are not, and cannot be met with the present inadequate staff of Chaplains.

... We are powerless in this matter without the help of the Archbishops and Bishops, who alone can give the necessary encouragement and directions to the young and active Clergy at home.[48]

With the evidence of pressure from the front so clearly made manifest, the Irish bishops made their move in Rome. What came from it will be seen later.

Notes and references

1. Archbishop Walsh Papers, ADA.
2. *Catholic Herald* (4 September 1914).
3. Ibid.
4. Rev Henry C. Day SJ, *A Cavalry Chaplain* (London, 1922), pp. 56-7.
5. 'Catholic Army chaplains: a diary', *The Catholic Bulletin and Book Review*, vol. VII, no. 4 (April 1917).
6. *The Tablet* (26 September 1914).
7. *The Irish Catholic* (2 October 1914).
8. Ibid.
9. *The Irish Catholic* (6 October 1914).
10. *The Irish Catholic* (10 October 1914).
11. *The Tablet* (10 October 1914).
12. *Catholic Herald* (17 October 1914).
13. Ibid.
14. Margot Asquith, *The Autobiography* (London, 1922), pp. 363-4. Also D. Bennett, *Margot: A Life of the Countess of Oxford and Asquith* (London, 1984), pp. 236-7.

15. *New York Freeman's Journal* (24 November 1914).
16. Tom Johnstone, *Orange, Green and Khaki* (Dublin, 1992), p. 64.
17. *Catholic Herald* (21 October 1914).
18. *The Tablet* (7 November 1914).
19. *Catholic Herald* (21 October 1914).
20. *Catholic Herald* (21 November 1914).
21. Ibid.
22. *Catholic Herald* (5 December 1914).
23. *The Tablet* (26 December 1914).
24. Ibid.
25. *The Tablet* (21 November 1914).
26. ASA.
27. Ibid.
28. Archbishop Walsh Papers, ADA.
29. Quoted in *The Irish Catholic* (10 October 1914).
30. AWA.
31. ASA.
32. Ibid. However, recalling the letter from Fr M. Flanagan at Haywards Heath, prehaps Bishop Amigo was being too optimistic.
33. AWA.
34. Ibid.
35. ASA.
36. Archbishop Walsh Papers, ADA.
37. Ibid.
38. Ibid.
39. Cardinal Logue Papers, AAA.
40. Kelly, Bishop of Ross, letter, Archbishop Walsh Papers, ADA.
41. Archbishop Walsh Papers, ADA.
42. Kelly, Bishop of Ross, letter, Archbishop Walsh Papers, ADA.
43. Fr B. Egan OFM, article, *Limerick Association Year Book* (1982).
44. Mgr William Keatinge, letter to Fr B. Rawlinson (2 July 1917), Rawlinson MSS, DAA.
45. Mgr M. O'Riordan, *Appunti riguardanti la sistemazione delle cappellanie dell'armata britannica. Pro Memoria* (Rome: Tipogravia Pontificia nell' Istituto Pio IX, 1916), pp. 1-3.
46. Ibid., p. 4.
47. Ibid.
48. 'Memorial to the Irish Hierarchy re shortage of Catholic Army Chaplains', copy held by the authors.

8

The priests in the line 1914–1915

Priests commissioned as temporary chaplains to the forces entered the Army under contracts of usually one year. After this, the priest either extended for a further period, or terminated his contract and relinquished his commission. Most extended, but some relinquished their commissions for a variety of reasons. One missionary home from Borneo gave up his year's home leave to serve at the front, and then returned to his mission. Some were also solo priests-in-charge of missions in England, who had obtained locums whose term could not be extended to cover their absence. One left to undertake a lecture tour of the United States on behalf of the Foreign Office. Many were elderly men who were already in poor health before volunteering, and the strain of the trenches was too much for their physical constitution; although willing to continue, they had to leave for health reasons. A few had their commissions prematurely terminated for unsuitability.

The procedure established by Bishop Grant over 50 years before still applied. Each candidate had to apply to Westminster and send a recommendation from his bishop. His name was then forwarded to the War Office, who informed the priest directly of his commissioning date, and to where he was to report. The priest was granted a commissioning allowance to cover the cost of uniform. All entered the Army with the rank of captain, and pay and allowances commenced from the date a chaplain reported for duty, in uniform. Since Religious are not allowed money of their own, chaplains were expected to surrender surplus monies to their house or diocese. At least one Prior received statements of accounts from his priests actually in the trenches. He also had to explain to his Superior the different messing charges - in the line (bully beef stew, tea and hard-tack biscuits), and normal living in a regular Officers' Mess behind the front.

> It has just struck me that the balance in my name at McGrigor's must now
> be about £100 and I am writing to know whether you think it would be
> well to invest this ... Exchequer bonds may be withdrawn after six
> months: this might be an advantage to us. There the money is and it is for
> you to advise ... My pay comes to about £1 a day now, and I am spending
> very little, less than ever since I joined the 2nd echelon Mess where we
> live almost entirely on our rations.[1]

This priest, Fr Vincent Scully CRL, to save cost wrote his letters on the
back of the ones he received or on the envelope. He was from a poor priory
running missions in Cornwall, then the Catholic desert of England. The
average Sunday collection at Bodmin amounted to 13/6d – the equivalent
of about 67 new pence.[2] The remittance of the several priests from this
priory who became chaplains was essential to the success of their mission.
Fr Scully, in addition to being frugal and faithful, was courageous, and was
awarded the DSO in 1918.

On arrival at the base the chaplain, or since they usually reported in
groups, the chaplains, reported to the senior Catholic chaplain and were
assigned to various formations or units. Usually no indication could be
given as to where that unit or formation was located and the new arrival
reported to the RTO (Rail Transport Officer) for directions and transport.
Sometimes a chaplain would be unhappy with his appointment. One 53-
year-old priest, Fr Traill of Birmingham, was expecting to join a battalion
and was disappointed.

> I remember Fr. Traill, one of the oldest members of our party, coming out
> very distressed (from Fr. Rawlinson's office), because he was appointed to
> a base hospital, instead of up the line.[3]

Although a training pamphlet was later produced for RC chaplains, in the
early days of the war newly-commissioned chaplains received no training
whatsoever before joining their unit. Everything they learned about
military life and war was essentially acquired 'on the job'. However, after
the Germans in 1915 introduced gas to the horrors of war, 'gas training'
was introduced. It consisted in a demonstration of the care and
maintenance of a respirator (gas mask), adjusting, fitting and wearing
the mask. The final test was to wear the device in a gas-filled 'chamber'
which was often a tent.

> Our orders were to go to Amiens on the next day and report to the R.T.O.
> for further instructions. The following morning we all went to the Gas
> School to be instructed by an officer on how to put on our gas respirators,
> etc. We were put through the Gas Chamber and passed as 'knowing our
> job' when gas was about. This instruction lasted from 0915 to 1230.[4]

Often 'on the job training' was rushed, with one priest hurriedly handing
over to another. Among the gems one passed to another was: 'You won't

get anything in the Army unless you make a fight for it. You have to keep on worrying them. Remember you have as much right to be there as they have.'[5]

At other times the learning experience was in sad and dangerous circumstances.

> On Friday, August 18th, our men had succeeded in digging out the bodies of six of our men, and I went over the Redan to bury them. I have rarely seen anything quite so pathetic; the grave, dug in Flanders mud, was already filling with water; the poor bodies in their uniform as they had fallen, the utter desolation of everything all around made up a scene not easily forgotten. The adjutant and the burial party stood by; I had only just begun the burial office when a shell burst close by. 'Don't make the service too long, Father,' whispered my servant over my shoulder. Two or three more [shells] came over ere the ceremony was complete, and the burial party began hastily filling in the grave. 'You had better get across as soon as you can,' said the adjutant to me, after the ceremony was over; I again got across with nothing worse than some shrapnel bursting above me.[6]

What Fr Williamson had to 'get across' was a fire-swept section of the Ypres salient.

One of the reasons why Catholic chaplains were so well respected was their forthright sermons to the troops about personal behaviour, especially about the many temptations offered to young men in the rest areas behind the line. One former officer of the Connaught Rangers recalled how 50 years previously he had listened to the battalion chaplain, Fr McShane, laud the fact that 16th Irish Division had the lowest VD rate (0.1 per cent) of all divisions on the Western Front: 'we were always kept very far away from temptation.'[7] With the best intentions, confusion of understanding was sometimes edifying.

> The troops greatly appreciated the opportunities afforded them in this sanctuary, after all we had been through in the line. I spoke strongly on the importance of being grateful to God for their deliverance, and the necessity of avoiding excess in drink after the strain of the line. It so happened that, in spite of my exhortations, one or two cases of drunkenness occurred, so next Sunday morning I said 'Greatly as I regret it, I think it well to make a rule that no man shall drink more than two pints of beer a day, which I think is ample for anyone.'
>
> A few days later one of our soldiers came to me and said: 'Well, Father, I've always been a teetotaller, but since you told us we *must* drink two pints of beer a day, I've been doing it.' Which shows how one's best-intentioned efforts can be misconstrued.[8]

The life of a chaplain on active service

> I lived, of course, in almost entirely non-Catholic society. But I never met anything but courtesy and friendliness, and the comradeship of the various messes to which I belonged at different times or in which I was always made welcome is a memory I shall always treasure.[9]

Long-service officers of the professional Army, totally dedicated to the regiment, had much in common with a Catholic celibate priest. The cloistered male world of a battalion had many similarities with seminary or monastery. Priest and officer were motivated by a dedication of service, one to God, the other to Country, although this was always epitomized by 'the Regiment'. Both sincerely cared for the welfare of the soldiers, one spiritually, the other physically and, to an extent, morally, towards morale. The more thoughtful officers recognized the value of strong religious beliefs to regimental morale, especially in war.

In a close-knit community, sometimes cut off for extended periods from normal civilized social activity, good manners and courtesy was an essential harmonizing element. It was a society which would look critically at a chaplain of any faith, and if he were found wanting he would not be tolerated. Nearly a thousand Catholic priests served as chaplains during the Great War and only a handful failed the stern test of regimental society in action. Two chaplains, newly arrived in France, by the report of a fellow-priest, never got further than the Principal Chaplain's office at GHQ. Another lasted a month, and a third three months, before their engagements were 'terminated' without fuss or publicity, and they returned to their dioceses to face the wrath of the bishop. Towards the end of the war, the incidence of excessive drinking rose and a few more were sent home for this reason.

A Jesuit priest, Fr Henry Gill, was disappointed at being sent to a base hospital but made the best of things, as he reported to his Father Provincial:

> Medical department wonderfully well organised. It is certainly not the kind of life to select as an amusement. I hope however that one may go nearer the fighting line.[10]

When Mgr Keatinge visited that hospital, Fr Gill had an interview with him on the subject of appointments ('He didn't know I am a Jesuit'), and as a result was posted to 2nd Royal Irish Rifles and remained attached to the battalion until the end of the war.

> The Commanding Officer gives every encouragement, but between being in the trenches and sudden moves it is not always possible to hold Mass. Confessions in fields, roadside, generally in several inches of mud… Whole battalion have been to confession and Holy Communion in the last week to ten days. …. The advantage of being attached to a regiment is that I am able to be up this far… There are rumours of dispensation from

fasting before Communion for soldiers. But we in the Front Line who should be the first to hear of such things have heard nothing.[11]

The encouragement of the CO was probably because of the effect Fr Gill was having on his battalion, where military 'crime' had been greatly reduced due to the chaplain 'who moved about constantly among men'.

> I thought it worth the risk to pay a visit to the most advanced line of trenches in order that my influence with the men might be greater. I know that this had excellent results. When the chaplain knows at first hand the conditions under which the men live – and die, for several were killed soon after in the trenches I visited – he is better able to encourage the men to be patient.[12]

A company commander serving about this time in the same battalion as Fr Gill, whose responsibility it was to censor the letters of his soldiers, recorded in his diary the deep religious spirit amongst the men of his company.

> His letters [contain] questions as to the welfare of those at home, and prayers, so very often, prayers to God to take care of those they have left behind them. From ninety percent of the letters you would never discover the men were on active service. A strong religious strain runs through most of the letters, and I rather admire my old shell-backs for it.[13]

The chaplain's work in this particular vineyard evidently bore much fruit.

The size of the Catholic community served by a chaplain would vary. It would depend largely upon the recruiting area. In an Irish brigade there would be thousands, in others a few hundred. It could change overnight by the casualties of a single battle.

> The number of Catholics I had to serve was never very great – a few hundred at the best of times, often less than the hundred. But the labours were much the same whether they were few or many. Equally one had to follow the units about, keep finding them out in each new area, discover places and arrange times for Mass and Confessions, notify the orderly rooms and as many individuals as possible of the arrangements made; equally was it necessary to be in constant attendance at dressing-stations in times of battle. I have offered the Holy Sacrifice in many strange places – in huts, cellars, barns, in dug-outs, in the trenches, in the ruins of churches where rain and snow came through the missing parts of walls or roof, on a plough behind a haystack, on altars built of ration-boxes or shell-boxes, under camouflage in a gunpit, in the open-air in varying weathers. I did not often have big congregations – frequently just a score, or perhaps a dozen men – at other times, perhaps fifty, sixty or a hundred. But they were always congregations that stirred the heart, congregations of men in great need, kneeling in faith and hope and love before their Redeemer, men who believed in prayer, men who frequented the

> Sacraments with splendid eagerness, who did not heed publicity of place for their confessions, nor poverty of circumstance for their Masses and Communions, men who knew that death was around them and were striving to be ready for their Maker if He summoned them.[14]

The saddest ceremony next to a burial service is a memorial service immediately following a battle. The survivors, conscious of the recent loss of personal friends, are at their most bitterly critical. Never is a chaplain more exposed.

Fr Francis Gleeson was chaplain to the 2nd Munsters from November 1914 until 1918. In the spring of 1915 he watched his battalion grow again in numbers and spirit after the frightful losses of 1914 and the winter of 1914-15. In early May 1915 on the eve of the attack on Aubers Ridge, Fr Gleeson watched the battalion at rest before going into the line for an assault the following morning.

> I gazed out over the scene, there were hundreds of giant men sitting in the fresh grass under the shade of the thickly-blossomed fruit trees, praying, meditating, reading their prayer-books, saying their rosaries - silent, absorbed, reverential to a degree.[15]

Fr Gleeson accompanied the battalion, 800 strong, to the line.

> At a French wayside shrine Rickard halted the battalion and formed a hollow square before it... The chaplain raised his hand and intoned general absolution and all sang the *Te Deum*...[16]

In the subsequent attack the Munsters were annihilated. It was Fr Gleeson's sad duty to hold a memorial service.

> The roll-call of the Munsters on Monday was the saddest imaginable. In the field beside St Mary's (the little tent chapel Artillery chaps erected for us).[17]

A chaplain who served long with a predominantly Catholic infantry battalion could become emotionally involved with its welfare. When that battalion sustained repeated heavy casualties, the mental anguish of a chaplain was very great. He was, after all, closer to the dying and the dead than any other person in the unit, the medical officer being spared the burial. After the Battle of Loos, where the 2nd Munsters were again annihilated, Fr Gleeson wrote to the senior chaplain (RC) asking to be relieved.

> I am sorry to be leaving the dear old Munster lads, but I really can't stand it any longer. I do not like the life ... though I love the poor men ever so much ... will you please send me the papers regarding my discharge.[18]

Mgr Keatinge relieved Fr Gleeson with another chaplain, Fr O'Flynn, until Fr Gleeson overcame his grief and was able to 'soldier on' with the battalion, as he did until 1918.

Following the reorganization of the Chaplains' Department in France in

1915 and until the end of the war, a Catholic priest was assistant to the Assistant Principal Chaplain, and was chiefly responsible for the administration of Presbyterian, Wesleyan, United Board and Jewish chaplains. First was Bernard Rawlinson, then, on his promotion to succeed Mgr Keatinge, S. D. Young, both Benedictine monks of Downside Abbey.[19] It would therefore have been surprising had there not been a close relationship between Catholic and Protestant chaplains. The unifying effects of front-line service was remarked upon by a Protestant historian of the United Board. About a group of chaplains working together in France, the writer opines:

> Those six men represented several denominations, yet no stranger suddenly appearing in their midst could have determined, by any outward and visible sign, the denomination to which each belonged. Anglican, Presbyterian, United Board, Wesleyan and Catholic – they are dressed alike; for the most part they hold common rank; they confer together, they pray together, they work together. They respect each other, although some of them profoundly differ from each other. When the war is over and khaki is discarded in favour of ordinary clerical costume, they may, and probably will, unless a miracle occurs (which may God grant), renew their differences quite openly. But never again can they be *quite* the same men as they were before the war.[20]

Some chaplains had perhaps never met a Catholic priest, socially or otherwise, before the war. One Baptist related, almost in wonder, the helpfulness of a fellow-chaplain:

> One of the Free Church chaplains speaks of an incident which occurred at – [not given in a wartime publication]. He was enquiring about some of his boys when a Roman Catholic priest, fresh complexioned, and hearty, came forward and 'in a lovely Irish brogue he said: "Can I be of service to ye to show ye where your boys are? I know lots of Baptists and Congregationalists and others." Away we went, and from that day I have not wanted a friend. In the hospital, as we look at the men's discs, the padre will say "Bray, here's one of yours." He came over a distance of five miles to tell me a Baptist boy had been killed by a shell, and would I come and bury him.'[21]

A Wesleyan chaplain, Rev Richard Hall, recently of Chatham, writing about Fr Francis Bradley, maintained that

> A finer, better Christian young man he had never met. They slept together on the battlefield; they slept together in the same bed when they could get a bed in a cottage or a hospital. No distinction amongst chaplains to the forces. They work together and help one another.[22]

Catholic chaplains constantly shared the dangers of the fighting troops, to give Extreme Unction to the dying on the battlefield. Such was their commitment they won universal respect (from both troops and Army establishment) for their courage, endurance and leadership in addition to their priestly devotion. In an age of ecumenism, comparison may be invidious. At that time, however, there was a difference which was often remarked upon, and must therefore be mentioned, if only because for centuries Catholic priests had received a bad press in Great Britain.

> These Catholic priests impress one. Leeson (the RC padre) never dropped a word of religion in my hearing, but one felt a serenity and certitude streaming from him such as was not possessed by our bluff Anglicans. Already there was a growing dislike of these latter. They had nothing to offer but the consolation the next man could give you, and a less fortifying one. The Church of Rome sent a man into action mentally and spiritually cleaned. The Church of England could only offer you a cigarette. The Church of Rome, experienced in propaganda, sent its priests into the line. The Church of England forbade theirs forward of Brigade Headquarters, and though many, realizing the fatal blunder of such an order, came just the same, the publication of that injunction had its effect.[23]

The writer was referring to the Catholic sacramental system operating in this war as it had, historically, in all previous wars, but had largely gone unnoticed or unrecorded. Here is a compelling, unhistrionic description, by a wartime chaplain, of the application of one particular Catholic sacrament, Extreme Unction. The final comfort of its application to the dying soldier necessitated the priest's presence in the line, and he willingly administered it without thought of 'propaganda'.

> In the piteous work of clearing up the wreckage of battle Roman Catholic chaplains found they had a potent instrument in the Sacrament of Extreme Unction. Easy and quick to apply, this Sacrament could help men beyond the reach of human aid, and put to precious use the last, often agonizing moments of life. The physical alleviations which other chaplains - in default of more practical opportunities - busied themselves in applying were useless at this stage. But the Roman Catholic chaplain, not necessarily more patient, skilful, clerical, or courageous, could awake recognition in the last glimmer of consciousness and succour both soul and body in the extreme crisis.[24]

Extreme Unction could be spiritually, mentally, and physically traumatic for the chaplain. Fr Willie Doyle, in his last letter from the front before he was killed, described his work on Frezenberg Ridge of the Ypres salient during early August 1917:

> One man was the bravest I ever met. He was in dreadful agony, for both legs had been blown off at the knee. But never a complaint fell from his lips, even when they dressed his wounds, and he tried to make light of his injuries. 'Thank God, Father, I am able to stick it out to the end ... I am much better now and easier, ... God bless you' he said as I left him to

attend a dying man… Sitting a little way off I saw a hideous bleeding object, a man with his face smashed by a shell, with one if not both eyes torn out. He raised his head as I spoke. 'Is that the priest? Thank God, I am all right now.' I took his blood-covered hands in mine as I searched his face for some whole spot on which to anoint him. I think I know better now why Pilate said 'Behold the man' when he showed our Lord to the people. In the afternoon, while going my rounds, I was forced to take shelter in the dug-out…[25]

Fr Simon Knapp OCD volunteered at the start of the war, and had been appointed to the 8th Division being formed out of regular battalions returned from overseas garrisons. He served with 1st Royal Irish Rifles, just home from Aden. In South Africa Fr Knapp, then serving with the Inniskilling Dragoons, had won the respect and admiration of its commanding officer, renowned for his critical observation, the future Field-Marshal Lord Allenby. In the winter of early 1915 much the same admiration was evinced from the other extreme of the military rank, a rifleman (often as critically observant as a field-marshal), for his service in the trenches during the worst winter of the war.

> Our chaplain is not an Army chaplain, but a Volunteer who came from Winchester with us, and a regular saint. He is the Rev S. S. Knapp, and he is always in the trenches with the regiment. He has faced death at least forty times since we came out. No other clergyman have I seen in the front trenches but him - hearing confessions, with bullets, in showers like hailstones, passing over the heads of the penitents and confessor. This is what makes soldiers fight well and die calm.[26]

Admiration was not one-sided. The soldiers also impressed the chaplains. Fr Hubert Barnett went to France in 1915 with 28th Division, a division consisting of regular infantry battalions recently arrived from India. He was with them during the Second Battle of Ypres.

> The fighting here for the last few days has been terribly fierce. It is a ghastly thing to see the state of some of the poor fellows brought in. How the human body can stand such terrible rips and holes is a marvel to me. All the night through the doctors and bearers are collecting the wounded, bringing them in, washing, cutting and binding up the poor fellows. Then the chaplain goes to them and does all that is possible.
> All night I stay with my own ambulance, and the first thing in the morning I hurry off to the other ambulance's dressing station. They are about a mile away - rather nearer the firing line. If any R.C. is really badly hit an orderly is kept here ready to come over for me to administer the Last Sacraments. I just hurry off, stumbling along in the darkness, and administer the last rites. Poor fellows! They do appreciate the priest's visit. That morning is spent in arranging for funerals and in getting to the billets of troops before they go up to the trenches at night. The priest just goes amongst them, draws them aside in turn, and, as they stand, hears

their confessions. All around the men are gathering their sacks for sand bags, filling large empty biscuit tins with water to make tea in the trenches, replenishing their water bottles, getting their trench tools ready, packing their kits, oiling their feet, socks and boots with whale-oil to keep their feet warm in the trenches, laughing and smoking.

I have never appreciated Tommy as he is. I have never known him before. He is really a wonderful being. It makes one feel proud to belong to the same race. There is no showy parade of bravery, but an earnestness and lightheartedness that touches one. He is always ready to do his 'little bit', and to give his life in doing it. There is no joyous foolish rush to the trenches at night, but just a grave, quiet grim Tommy out to do his best. He does not like the scream of the shell nor the frightful noise of the explosion, but the sight of a comrade in danger or in need is enough for Tommy to make the greatest sacrifices to give his fellow soldier a moment's relief or the slightest help. The tales of the trenches are really very touching. My admiration for the average Tommy increases daily. Tommy is one of the very best![27]

Non-Catholic troops were not slow in observing and appreciating the spirituality, devotion and fortitude of these priests. During the war there were, according to *The Tablet* in 1918, 40,000 conversions to the Catholic faith in France alone. The number which followed after the war in consequence of war experience and priestly example are inestimable. One, Barclay Wilkie, late Royal Munster Fusiliers, was received into the Catholic Church in 1940. He wrote: 'my war time experience helped to set me on the right path.'[28]

The mother of an officer killed in action wrote to his chaplain, Fr P. Devas:

> He told me how he had attended Mass often as the CofE. Padres were not allowed up in the Front trenches and he could not have spoken more highly of any one than he did of the RC Padres. My father was a C.ofE. Padre in India. He and the RC Padre worked hand in hand in Afghanistan in 1879.[29]

Admiration came too for the robust stand Catholic chaplains made in their efforts to have the soldier attend the sacraments.

> The weather during my stay at Zelobes was extremely fine, so I was able to spend my day out visiting the various units of my brigade, and others in the neighbourhood. In my wanderings I called on a labour battalion, whose C.O. was not a lover of Padres. Without being in the least aware of it, I found I was the third Catholic Chaplain to call that day. 'What!' said the testy old gentleman, 'another of them? There's been two here to-day already.' 'Well,' I said, 'I am the third.' However, in spite of the unfavourable reception, he sent all the Catholics of his battalion to Mass on Sunday.[30]

In the vast logistics areas far behind the lines, there was considerable difficulty ministering to Catholics widely scattered at huge ammunition dumps, ordnance field parks, supply depots, engineering workshops, and all the other essential operations in the 'tail' of an Army at war. The operations of all activities were non-stop. The personnel, driven by the need to keep the front-line troops supplied, had little time for anything after long hours of work except rest. When sufficient chaplains arrived to permit appointing one to a base camp, it took considerable effort to break the mould of long-established work-practice. Fr Smith was sent to such an area to relieve Fr MacCabe CSSR, a chaplain who had served with an Inniskillings battalion for eighteen months before being transferred to a base area for a 'rest':

> When Fr. McCabe [sic] came he found that the men at the 'base-details' camp were *never* allowed to come to Mass on Sunday. He spoke to the C.O. about it, told him many of his men were Irishmen who had come to him bitterly complaining that they could never get to Mass: these men had been assured when they enlisted that they would be able to practise their religion; what did he think would be the effect on recruiting? The CO agreed to allow them to come to Mass every other Sunday.[31]

Having settled into his new appointment, Fr Smith paid a courtesy call on a neighbouring chaplain in a 'convalescent camp', a euphemism for a holding unit for returned wounded as yet unfit to fight but capable of 'fatigues', essential light manual work, in the base area.

> I called on Father Donlevy, our Senior Chaplain at the Convalescent Camp. While we were at tea in the Mess something was said about services, whereupon the Colonel said 'I don't know much about religion, but I understand that the R.C.s *must* go to Church every week.' Someone said 'Are you one?' 'No, I'm a Protestant.' Father Donlevy told me afterwards that after he had demanded that his men should be allowed to come to Mass, the other Chaplains began to make similar demands for theirs: the Colonel blurted out 'None of you fellows dared open his mouth till the R.C. Padre came here.'[32]

In the long-established base area three or four miles from the centre of Rouen, things were much better. Fr William Forrest had established a church in a large tent to serve the Catholics in his area. Other priests served the stationary hospitals in the area.

> I want to thank you for your kind and very prompt help regarding the Benediction set which arrived here safely some time ago. Now we have a very large store tent with wooden floor, an altar and altar-rail, a pulpit, two confessionals, a harmonium, a 'throne' for the Blessed Sacrament in-the-making, and stoves to heat up with – in fact our Canvas Cathedral is under way and soldiers come from the ends of the Earth (I mean the 6 square mile camp) to see and hear the wonderful things done and said there. The Benediction set you gave us a hand with was the crowning

glory! Now we have week-day Masses in three places in the camp, six Masses here every Sunday, Benediction at least once a week, Confessions at all times – in fact we only want a bishop's throne now and a Chapter and we are ready to stay here for the rest of our lives. In the town we have of course Mass every Sunday and week-day; and on Sunday in the workshops outside the town three or four miles, where there are neither churches nor Masses under ordinary conditions. In fact we are fairly set-up.

    This is so different from the South African war! No British Catholic soldier may have the least fear of living or dying without the Sacraments, and when enquiry is sometimes made in response to the letter of some responsible person at home to whom a soldier has written and told his tale of how he has seen neither priest nor sacrament for months, it is invariably found that he has lived almost next door to priest and church for months and never had the interest nor the care to put his head inside the door. These quasi-complaints are always – or nearly so – the cry of children looking for sympathy and pity, and you know what a baby the young soldier sometimes is. In fact up to now and for nearly a year we have had a practical sufficiency of chaplains – good men, nearly all of the right stamp, ready for hardships but glad of the easy spells when they can get it, putting God's work in the very front and paying little heed to anything else. The nearer the firing-line the better the work done, and the faith of the men and the prayerfulness of their lives is almost beyond all credit. The English soldier, as some one said, fights on his stomach. Well, perhaps, but there is no doubt that the Catholic one and most especially the Irish Catholic soldier fights from the fullness of his Faith, Confession and Communion: the grace of God: and though he knows it would be good for him, if necessary he is ready to forego everything else. The example of the practical religion of the Catholic officers and men leads almost the whole army; and I am sure there are thousands and thousands who have turned to God and his protective Providence for good through the wonderful faith of the Munsters, the Dublins, the Irish Fusiliers and the rest. Both for religion and as fighting-men they have done wonderful work.[33]

The respect accorded to Catholic chaplains was for their willingness to make a stand for what they believed to be right whether against officialdom who impeded their spiritual duty, or checking unseemly behaviour amongst the soldiers. It was to a large extent in the tradition of the old Irish *Soggart* (Father), best summed up in the words of Alfred Graves, 'checking the crazy ones, helping uneasy ones, lifting the lazy ones on with the stick'.[34]

    Father McCabe, whom I have been sent to assist, is a very zealous energetic man and at the same time a kind-mannered one. He is an elderly man, a Redemptorist... Up to the time of my arrival he had charge of the four large General Hospitals and two or three camps. Yet in the ones he has handed over to me I find he has given confession and communion to almost every Catholic.

He is up every morning before six and goes round the wards giving Communion: and then he gives Communion in the church tent at 6.30, goes out and comes back to say Mass at 8. At half-past four he hears confessions in the tent and at six gives Benediction in the church at Camiers.

On Saturday he took me to the camp at St. Cecile Plage, which I am to have charge of. Every man he meets on the road he stops and asks 'are you an R.C.?' If he says 'Yes,' 'Have you been to your duties lately?' Fr. McCabe asked each man if he had made his Easter duties, advised him to come to the 6 o'clock evening service and told him the time of Mass next Sunday. Most of the men showed goodwill; some of them were obviously very pleased. As we were coming away, some men a short way off were shouting at one another the British soldier's favourite obscene word. Fr McCabe called out to them sternly to 'stop that', and went up and spoke to them, after which they were silent. 'These Anglican fellows,' he said afterwards, 'daren't do that. They've no authority.' It was consoling to notice the difference between the manner of Catholics towards the priest to that of non-Catholics.[35]

The odd Catholic could also be difficult, especially in front of his friends.

One man in answer to the question 'Are you an R.C.?' said, 'No, I'm a Mahommedan.' He afterwards had to admit he was an R.C. Fr. McCabe took him outside the tent and rated him soundly. He excused himself by saying he did not know the priest was there, he thought it was only one of his comrades. He was a ruffianly-looking fellow. Afterwards when Fr. McCabe had gone I heard what sounded like a good deal of bad language coming from the tent, amidst the laughter of his companions.[36]

Alfred Graves' more famous son Robert Graves recorded in his memoirs of the war an anecdotal comparison between Catholic chaplains and others which, to be fair, is possibly apocryphal.

For Anglican regimental chaplains we had little respect. If they had shown one-tenth the courage, endurance, and other human qualities that the regimental doctors showed, we agreed, the British Expeditionary Force might well have started a religious revival. But they had not, being under orders to avoid getting mixed up with the fighting and to stay behind with the transport. Soldiers could hardly respect a chaplain who obeyed these orders, and yet not one in fifty seemed sorry to obey them. Occasionally, on a quiet day in a quiet sector, the chaplain would make a daring afternoon visit to the support line and distribute a few cigarettes, before hurrying back. But he was always much to the fore in rest-billets. Sometimes the colonel would summon him to come up with the rations and bury the day's dead; he would arrive, speak his lines, and shoot off again. The position was complicated by the respect that most commanding officers had for the cloth – though not all. The colonel in one battalion I served with got rid of four new Anglican chaplains in four months; finally he applied for a Roman Catholic, alleging a change of faith in the men under his command. For the Roman Catholic chaplains were not only permitted to visit posts of danger, but definitely enjoined to be wherever fighting was, so that they could give extreme unction to the dying. And we have never heard of one who failed to do all that was expected of him and more. Jovial Father Gleeson of the Munsters, when all the officers were killed or wounded at the first battle of Ypres, had stripped off his black badges and, taking command of the survivors, held the line.[37]

To their everlasting glory, many Anglican chaplains chose to disobey orders and accompany their battalion into the line as the award of three Victoria Crosses testifies. This aside, Graves was reflecting a widely held regard for Catholic chaplains within the British Expeditionary Force in France and Flanders. It was no mean achievement for the priest among the soldiers in battle.

*   *   *

It is worth recording the invaluable support given, to both troops and chaplains, by the Catholic Women's League (CWL) in the UK and in France and Flanders.

The 'Catholic Club' was founded and run in France by Mr Stephen Harding. The CWL, of which Mrs Fitzalan Hope was president, ran canteens in camps in England and France. Mrs Charlotte Blaynes was manageress of the clubs in France and Flanders. The CWL began work in the base areas in 1915 and by the end of the war they ran a total of thirteen centres, with another twelve smaller ones in the First Army sector, and one at Audruicq ammunition and railway depot. After the war two clubs were opened in the occupied zone of Germany. At each centre a room was provided for the camp chaplain. Mass was said every morning, and after the club was closed in the evening, prayers were said. Sometimes Communion services were held for troops going into the front line.[38]

One of the few wayside calvaries in England is near Studley Royal, Ripon. It was erected to commemorate the ladies of the CWL who ran a 'Hut' in a nearby camp. Here, in this camp, Wilfred Owen composed his poem 'The Send Off' before going to the front in 1918, for the last time.

> Shall they return to beating of great bells
> In wild train-loads?
> A few, a few, too few for drums and yells,
> May creep back, silent, to village wells,
> Up half-known roads.

References

1. Rev Vincent Scully CRL, letters, CRL Archives, Eltham.
2. Ibid.

3. Benedict Williamson, *'Happy Days' in France and Flanders* (London, 1921), p. 2.
4. Rev M. J. Flanagan, 'Our military chaplains', *St Francis Magazine* (1919).
5. Rev Lionel G. Smith, 'War journal, France and Belgium 1915-1917', AWA; Archives of St Edmund's College, series 12, 167A.
6. Williamson, p. 35.
7. Capt Desmond McWeeney, 'Fifteen days of the March Retreat', *The Ranger*, no. 76 (1968).
8. Williamson, p. 40.
9. Rev James B. Marshall MC, 21st Division, *St Francis Magazine* (1919).
10. Rev Henry Gill SJ, letters, JAD.
11. Ibid.
12. Gill, letter (11 March 1915), Rawlinson MSS, DAA.
13. Gerald Achilles Burgoyne, *The Burgoyne Diaries* (London, 1985), pp. 40-1.
14. Marshall.
15. Rev Francis Gleeson, Diary, Meagher Papers, ADA.
16. Tom Johnstone, *Orange, Green and Khaki* (Dublin, 1992), p. 82.
17. Gleeson.
18. Rev Francis Gleeson, letter (3 November 1915), Rawlinson MSS, DAA.
19. Rawlinson MSS, DAA.
20. Rev Frederick C. Spurr, *Some Chaplains in Khaki: An Account of the Work of Chaplains of the United Navy and Army Board* (London, 1916), p. 10.
21. Ibid.
22. *Catholic Herald* (24 April 1915).
23. Alan Wilkinson, *The Church of England and the First World War* (London, 1978), p. 111.
24. Rev T. A. Agius OSB, letter, Rawlinson MSS, DAA.
25. Professor Alfred O'Rahilly, *Father William Doyle S.J.* (London, 1930), p. 544.
26. Rfn S. O'Neill, 1st Royal Irish Rifles, letter, *Cork Examiner* (1915).
27. Fr Hubert Barnett OSB, 'Ampleforth at war', *Ampleforth Journal*, vol. 20.
28. Letters to Fr P. D. Devas OFM, IWM.
29. Ibid.
30. Williamson, pp. 17-18.
31. Smith, pp. 198-201.
32. Ibid.
33. Rev William Forrest, letter, ASA.
34. Alfred Perceval Graves, 'Father O'Flynn'.
35. Smith, pp. 198-201.
36. Ibid.
37. Robert Graves, *Goodbye to All That* (London, Penguin edn), pp. 242-3.
38. Brig Gen Sir John Edmonds, *Military Operations in France and Belgium: 1915* (London, HMSO), vol. II, p. 142.

9

Gallipoli

The landings

An amphibious assault landing on a defended beach, amongst other essentials, requires for success meticulous planning, good ship-to-shore communications between commanders and troops, and at least tactical surprise. At Gallipoli in April 1915 almost none of these essentials had been achieved when Australian, British, French, Irish and New Zealand troops stormed ashore upon widely separated beaches. One landing-place at Cape Helles, V Beach at Sedd-el-Bahr, was the scene of great slaughter, and the death of the first priest killed in action during the war.

A former collier, SS *River Clyde*, had been converted into an assault landing ship, and, in awareness of the nearness of Troy, was referred to at the time as a Trojan Horse. Into the ship two battalions were embarked, 1st Hampshires and 1st Munsters, with support troops. Fr T. A. Harker, chaplain to 1st Munsters, was an eyewitness and shortly afterwards wrote an account for his old College magazine:

> We ran in towards our bay surrounded by warships, which began a terrific bombardment, under cover of which we had our 'horse' run ashore, but unfortunately not near enough to disembark. We had lighters with us, but even with their assistance it was difficult to reach land. Men went out to fasten up the lighters, but were shot. The little bay was alive with troops, snipers and machine guns, while on both sides they had magnificent forts. About 6 in the morning we began to land, and for three hours we had immediate sights of deeds of heroism and of such a shambles as I hope never to see again. Men drowned, men dying without any hope of being assisted, and the only passage to the shore was over the bodies of living and dead. The enemy's machine guns had naturally the easiest job in the world to range themselves upon the landing spots.[1]

Another battalion, 1st Dublins, was taken ashore in ships' row-boats, about a platoon to a boat. They were towed by naval pinnaces until about one hundred yards from the shore, then tow-lines were cast off and sailors in the packed boats rowed ashore. Even the most skilfully crewed row-boat takes time to travel this distance; when machine-gun and rifle fire killed the rowers, it took an eternity.

> Meanwhile the little boats were trying to land, but just as they reached the shore they were met with a fusillade of rifles and machine guns, and the slaughter was appalling. Fr. Finn was in one of these first boats, and out of 45 in the boat 40 never reached the shore. He was hit in the boat and then four times more as he reached the shore and tried to crawl to shelter. He died after two hours' agony (R.I.P.). I buried him myself. The Turks were magnificently entrenched, and it was only by superhuman efforts and the terrific power of the Navy guns that they could be dislodged and finally dispersed. They are led by German officers, who are born soldiers, and undoubtedly they (Turks) are very brave. It is unfortunately true that many of our wounded have been bayonetted and outrageously treated. I need say no more.[2]

Fr William Finn of Middlesbrough insisted upon landing with the first assault wave despite appeals to remain in *River Clyde* at least until a beachhead had been secured. To all entreaty he replied 'The priest's place is beside the dying soldier'.[3] That night, when the Turkish fire subdued, a precarious beachhead was established and Fr Harker himself buried Fr Finn just off the beach. Accounts in newspapers at the time outraged the feelings Fr Harker had for William Finn, a fellow-Ushawman. With that indignation common to soldiers who have witnessed the death of friends in action towards unseemly exaggeration, Fr Harker wrote to Mgr Bidwell: 'The newspaper accounts and the stories told in a panegyric at Hull during Finn's requiem are a fake. Good zealous priest that he was, he needs no lies to endear his memory among the Dublins.'[4] An Anglican chaplain who was also present later wrote about the feelings of the troops towards Fr Finn: 'The men never forgot him and were never tired of speaking of him. I think they felt his death almost more than anything that happened in that terrible landing.'[5]

Nearly two years later, when the battalion had moved with its division to France and was on the Somme, Fr Harker, now the senior divisional chaplain, renewed the memory of Fr Finn in *Ushaw College Magazine*.

> I enclose a little ballad written by a Dub. on Father Finn. His memory is still green among his old regiment, though he was only a short time with them. Perhaps it might do for the magazine, though hardly a literary gem. It is, however, a very sincere tribute to a brave and saintly man.
>
>   The shells began to skip
>   As we started on our trip,
>   But the first to leave the ship
>   was Father Finn.

> With a smile upon his face,
> And a joke, he took his place,
> 'Now, boys, we'll have a race,'
> And I bet my boat'll win,'
> Said Father Finn.[6]

Fr Harker landed on the evening of the battle for V Beach to succour the wounded and dying and say Mass ashore for such survivors of the Dublins and Munsters as could attend. He was the first priest to say Mass at Cape Helles as the fighting raged around him.

> After a fortnight of warfare, weary days and sleepless nights we left the firing line (I say we because I stayed with the regiment) and came to the sea shore to rest ... I have some narrow escapes, but one in particular. The first Saturday night we were attacked by 18,000 Turks (the number we discovered from prisoners), and at one point just 30 yards to my left about 100 broke through. They bayonetted men on my immediate left and right and passed me within three yards, fortunately missing the doctor and myself. I had given up all hope, for I was unarmed not even having a stick. Generally speaking, however, one is nearly as safe in the trenches as further back, for shrapnel shell and bullets are bursting at every point, and by this means more are killed at a base than in the lines.[7]

The landing of the Australian and New Zealand Army Corps (ANZAC) at Ari Burnu took place as silently as possible in total darkness, and with great *élan* the troops rushed inland for the commanding heights. Only the presence of a Turkish reserve division commanded by the redoubtable Mustapha Kemal denied the Anzac troops victory. Severe fighting for these vital heights, which would have crowned the success of the landings, continued until the middle of August. With the Australians was Fr McAuliffe, an Australian priest of the Australian Imperial Force, who had the honour of saying the first Mass ashore on the Gallipoli peninsula. An extant photograph shows him in full vestments saying Mass before a small kneeling group of obviously devout men. It was said that his rubrics could not have been bettered in a cathedral.[8] A New Zealand priest, Fr Patrick Dore, served with the Auckland Mounted Rifles of the New Zealand Expeditionary Force. He was badly wounded at Anzac and awarded the Military Cross. Evacuated home, Fr Dore underwent a series of operations in New Zealand, and after much suffering finally died of his wounds, in the Mater Misericordiae Hospital, Auckland, on 15 July 1918.

A few days after the initial landing, elements of the Royal Naval Division landed in support of the Anzac troops. Accompanying them was Fr Eric Green, who has been mentioned earlier.

> Three days later, an hour or two after midnight, I landed at Gaba Tepe, in the dark and in the rain. We were packed on a lighter, like sardines. As one drew nearer to the shore bullets and shrapnel were falling all around.

On land there was still a scene of indescribable confusion. On the narrow strip of sandy, stony beach, not more than about thirty to forty feet wide at the foot of the cliffs, which rise above range, men were moving in every direction. Troops landing, troops marching west, troops marching east, men laden with rations, mules and horses packed with stores and water barrels and bearers coming down the cliffs with wounded and dying on stretchers.

Hugging the foot of the cliff I found my first quarters. Two ambulance stations had been contrived here, one belonging to an Australian division the other was to be ours, the Royal Naval Division ambulance. I say contrived, because it was a marvel how much had been squeezed in so small a space, when really there was no space at all.[9]

Because of Turkish dominance from the heights, most movement of troops, stores and supplies took place under cover of darkness. The flow of casualties therefore continued all night to the regimental aid posts and field ambulances.

Before half an hour was over my work began and it went on until 3 a.m. I had not one moment; one wounded and dying man following on after another. Just time, if he was conscious, to hear his confession and a muttered act of contrition, to give absolution, and the anointing, before a new man claimed attention. Poor fellow, with wounds of every description, all disfigured and defiled with blood, and clay and dirt, in many cases unrecognisable, often features blown away. But being suddenly, as it were, plunged into this valley of suffering and death; in the very thick of it, I hardly realised the terror of things; there was no time to think, but only to do and act in what way I could to give the help that I was there to give. Sights that at ordinary times would have unmanned anyone, were passed over with a businesslike indifference, all save the case of one poor lad; a Haileybury boy, hardly nineteen, who looked as though he might be asleep, but was moaning for his mother; he was shot near the heart and died before an hour was over. At 3 a.m., casualties, more or less, ceased coming in. I rolled myself up in my blanket and lay on the sand - next to a Protestant Padre.

The moon was brilliant, but I don't think I ever spent so cold a night before. It was not easy to get to sleep; the constant sound of the Turkish snipers came in waves from the cliffs overhead, now soft, now louder, and then firmly as though a whole Turkish horde were coming down from the slopes to overwhelm us. Just a few yards away a fire had been lighted, and the ambulance men, who were on duty all night, were making their tea; they were mostly Lancashire lads and how they talked and talked.

At 4.30 the din began again. I must have fallen asleep and I woke up in the greatest amazement I had ever felt. It was indescribable. The *Goeben* on the other side of the Peninsula had sent morning greetings, and shell after shell rushed through the air over our heads and fell in the sea just in front of us. The mighty, rushing noise as though it was carrying everything before it, the enormous volumes of water that rose like huge geysers from the sea, when the shell met the water. The whole sea round about was literally riddled with bullets and shrapnel so that the water looked as though it were torn by a storm of wind and hail.[10]

At the beginning of the campaign the evacuation of the wounded from Gallipoli lacked the organization and order of later days. There were too few ships, doctors and nurses and too many wounded. One hospital ship, without a chaplain, arrived in Egypt and was met at Alexandria by Fr Henry Day SJ.

> The scene was amongst the most heart-rending in all my experience. There on the decks, in the gangways, by the hatchway companions, on the stairs – everywhere – were to be seen the sick and the wounded, the dead and the dying, huddled in heaps together. For the most part they lay as they had been stricken on the field or fallen in the fight. The blood and mud of the battle was thick upon many. There were too few doctors and nurses to render more than 'first aid'. Some groaned, others asked help, calling in God's name for a ration or a 'fag'. There were some who were raving – cursing imaginary enemies, or laughing deliriously. Others on the contrary were all too silent, tired, weary, waiting for peace. One poor fellow – very young – dictated in whispers to a pal a letter for home …
>
> But the ship … God! What sights! What horrors! What a scene it recalls! Shall I ever forget it? Literally the Red Cross ship with its ghastly burden of mangled humanity appeared to be more like a phantom vessel emerging from Stygian darkness and regions of torturing horror than an English hospital ship carrying its precious freight of wounded men into a haven of healing and rest.[11]

On the night of 6–7 August 1915 Sir Ian Hamilton's great plan for the capture of the heights at Anzac was timed to coincide with a seaborne descent upon Suvla, a great bay just to the north of Anzac. At Suvla, 11th Northern Division landed first, two brigades of 10th Irish Division followed. There were many Catholics in both divisions. With them came their chaplains.

While the Australians created a diversion at Lone Pine, the main thrust against the ridges of the Sari Bair range was delivered by New Zealanders, Indians, 13th Western Division and 29 Brigade of 10th Division. Fr W. Leighton was attached to a Warwickshire battalion of 13th Division.

> Captain Leighton exposed himself freely in the discharge of his duties, and had some thrilling experiences, especially in the great attack on Hill 871, when he was the only one left in his regiment. He is proud of the fact that in the great attack on Chunuk Bair, the Warwickshires reached the crest of the hill and with the South Lancashires, stood it to the last.

In an account of the heroism of the Warwickshires, one of the New Zealanders wrote:

> I saw the Padre Leighton go out to a wounded Engineer lying out under
> fire, bandage him up, and place him in safety, and carried him to the
> Indian Hospital half-way down the Aghyl Dere. This man was a sport in
> all conscience and became a friend to all our boys in the gully. I saw him
> later wade through machine gun fire to attend a man of the Connaughts
> named Cullen, who lay mortally wounded in open ground.

About the losses to the Warwicks Fr Leighton says:

> ... I can bear very generous testimony to the way in which those gallant
> men went to their deaths. On the transport going out, an officer told me
> he had an idea I should be one of the officers left in the Warwicks. That
> prophecy has come true. You have heard of the thin red line. Well there
> was a thin khaki line at Chunuk Bair, a line of dead heroes, leading up the
> crest of the hill, men sitting dead, men lying dead, men standing against
> each other dead.[12]

The landing at Suvla saw heavy intermittent fighting from 7 to 12 August,
without the dominating inland ridges being captured. On 13 August the
two Irish brigades present at Suvla were concentrated for an attack on a
long whale-backed ridge, Kiretch Tepe Sirt. On the morning of 15 August,
Frs William Murphy and John Mulderry said Mass for the Irish in honour
of Our Lady's Assumption and gave general absolution before the attack to
take place that day. Two days later the battle ended with both brigades
shattered for little gain. For two days and nights both priests were hard
worked in the brigade field ambulances giving their final earthly
ministrations to many.

Fr John Moth became Principal Chaplain, and under him were the
brigade chaplains. In addition to those mentioned were Frs Michael
Carney, Richard Corcoran, Oswald Doland, Louis Herlihy, John Hogg,
Hugh Keegan and Thomas Rigby. When the attack was resumed at Suvla
and Anzac on 21 August all would have much work to do. At Anzac the
main objective was Hill 60. As part of this, the capture of the wells at Kabak
Kuyu was delegated to 5th Connaught Rangers. On the morning of their
successful attack Fr T. O'Connor said Mass and gave general absolution.
The whack of bullets overhead or striking the ground was a constant
reminder to the waiting Rangers of the ordeal to come.[13]

At Suvla the 29th Division had been brought from Helles, and 2nd
Mounted Division from Egypt to reinforce 11th Division for an attack on
Scimitar Hill. The main attack was delivered by 11th and 29th Divisions,
and the crest was carried at enormous cost. However, a well-timed Turkish
counterstroke restored the original situation. A most gallant attack was
then made by 2nd Mounted Division and although they too reached the
crest the attack was repulsed. With them were Fr Hugh Cameron, attached
to the Lovat Scouts of the Highland Mounted Brigade, Fr Arthur Day SJ
with the Sherwood Rangers Yeomanry and his brother Fr Henry Day SJ of

the Notts and Derby Yeomanry. Shortly after they arrived Fr H. Day observed a group of Yeomanry and Irish bathing together in Suvla Bay:

> In the water diving off the rocks were a number of the 10th (Irish) Division, as well as a crowd of Yeoboys. Though both were in similar undress attire, the two Divisions were easily distinguishable in the water. The Irish appeared older, and were much more demure in demeanour. They wore rosaries and medals. 'Your men', remarked my friend, 'are fond of decorations.' 'Yes' I said 'they are soldiers of Christ and Our Lady, as well as soldiers of the King.' He replied to the effect that he was pleased to see such faith in evidence in Gallipoli.[14]

The Yeomanry were ordered to advance from their concentration area on Lala Bay on the afternoon of 21 August, and to reach the start line at Chocolate Hill they had to march across the salt lake and flat Anafarta plain in full view of the enemy for a distance of about two miles. In open columns of squadrons the Yeomanry brigades advanced under Turkish observation and fire for the entire length of the march. With them went Arthur and Henry Day.

> It was no ordinary barrage which you might hope to win through quickly. It was a concentrated and enduring bombardment. There was small hope of escape. Step by step with our progress the shell-swept zone extended and advanced before us. Either the artillery shortened the range, or fresh batteries came into action. The guns roared defiance. The shells screamed death in the air. Through the corridor of fire the Division walked steadily forward.[15]

When Fr H. Day arrived at Chocolate Hill he heard his name called and much cheering. Lord Henry Bentinck shouted to Fr Day 'the men are cheering you'.[16] It was the soldier's accolade to one they called 'old Father Day'.[17]

The wounded were carried in to an aid post in the shelter of Chocolate Hill and while his regiment marched on to assault Scimitar Hill, Fr Day helped a wounded trooper to an aid post where he remained to help, and carry out his ministrations. In the next twelve hours Day assisted the hard-worked doctors treat over a thousand wounded, including giving the last rites to some 80 or 90 Catholics.[18] Meanwhile the attack was pressed home on Scimitar Hill.

A yeomanry trooper, writing with the restricted vision of one closely engaged in action, wrote from Suvla about his chaplain:

> In August we received the welcome order to proceed to the Dardenelles. We were issued with infantry kit and sailed from Alexandria, landed at Suvla Bay on the 18th Aug, under heavy Turkish gunfire. On the 21st we crossed the Salt Lake to Chocolate Hill under tremendous fire from the enemy artillery. That was our first real taste of war, and I shall never forget it, from thence onwards until November we lived almost constantly in the

trenches. We had a fine chaplain on the Peninsula, Fr. Day. At one time he was the only chaplain of any description on the front. Though there were others at the base. Fr. Day used to trudge the trenches all day long talking to the men and cheering the wounded, and he had to bury men of any denomination. We were unable to hear Mass whilst on the Peninsula as any grouping was promptly shelled by the enemy. We managed, however, to get confession in rather a queer manner as priest and penitent just sat down behind a bush in some quiet spot when it was dark.[19]

At the end of November a further terrible trial descended upon the unfortunate troops, when a great storm broke over all the Balkan countries, which lasted for three days, stretching as far south as the Gallipoli peninsula and the eastern Mediterranean. Behind the troops on Gallipoli was a large supporting fleet of merchant and naval ships, including many hospital ships. Fr Cosser, whose hospital ship took shelter off Imbros during the great storm, gives a description of both the storm and its effects on the infantrymen ashore.

It blew at least three hurricanes, it snowed and sleeted, and when it got tired of that, it rained; and all the time the cold was such as nothing could keep out. It was impossible to keep warm even on the ship, with the heating apparatus working ... After dark the sick began to arrive on lighters, and a pitiable sight they were. As we hung over the side of the ship, the first lighter arrived, coming suddenly under the flare of our lights. Some thirty men lay there, looking just like corpses, their pallor emphasized by the white glare of light thrown on them; and it seemed marvellous that so many could rise and make their way, unhelped, up the ladder.

Lighters arrived in steady succession till 3.30 a.m., by which time we had 750 sick men on board, nearly all suffering from frost-bite. Next day the work was resumed till we had picked up 1130 in all . As the ship was only meant to accommodate 750, it can be imagined that there was not much spare room. Meanwhile two other hospital ships were engaged in the same work; and yet, when all three had loaded up to their fullest capacity we were obliged to leave 1400 poor fellows on the beach. Many of the sick had been lying there for three days, with no shelter and no food; and they looked like it. The frost-bite too, in many cases, was really serious, not to be cured by a few hours' warmth and some good food. Half a dozen or more died of it during the first two days on board, and more had to have an arm or leg amputated. One poor man had to lose both his legs. But the great majority revived very quickly and were almost as fit as ever by the time they left the ship four days later. On our four days' trip to Malta, I and the priest attached to the ship were kept busy. We had nearly 200 Catholics on board, almost all of them delighted to see a priest and anxious to go to the Sacraments. And it was a curious experience hearing Confessions and giving Holy Communion in those crowded wards (they lay in bunks, three deep), without any privacy, not even the simple screen.[20]

The evacuation

Gallipoli, the most costly subsidiary operation of the war, was ended by evacuation at Anzac and Suvla in December, and Helles in January 1916. Unlike the landings, the evacuation was detailed and imaginative in planning, and meticulous in execution. It depended for success in deceiving the Turks into believing the Allies intended an attack, not a withdrawal. A Catholic priest on board the last hospital ship to leave penned a description of the evacuation of Anzac beach.

> So far the weather had been very favourable for our evacuation. During Monday and Tuesday nights thousands of troops had been got away without mishap. During the night-time the rifle fire increased in volume. Some bullets rang musically on the hills others cracked like whips, whined like puppies, twanged like harp strings, or made the sudden drone of bees in flight. Machine-guns made the sound like a boy rattling a stick along a fence, or like the crackling of a fire in the rush of a gale. All night long this metallic music shrieked until it was hushed by the heavy mutual bombardment in the morning.

At Mudros the patients were quickly unloaded to enable the hospital ship to return during the night.

> From what we heard the Turks may be awarded supreme honour for clean fighting. They *do* respect the Red Cross. We were lying all the time within range, not only of their batteries, but even their rifle fire, and any time, under plea of accident, they could have blown us to pieces. With all our green and red lights burning at night we present a well-defined target, but we trusted to their humanity, and our trust was not misplaced.
>
> On Friday, December 17th, we commenced throwing our patients overboard at 9 a.m. and finished by 1 p.m. Quick work getting off eight hundred patients in four hours when we had so many stretcher cases. By 6 p.m. the whole of the seven hundred and fifty-five cots were ready again for fresh patients, and we were well on our way to Imbros.
>
> It was all very exciting, because at any moment the plot might be discovered and the whole air electrified and the landscape ablaze with shot and shell. Our poor vessel would have been doomed in such a catastrophe, lying as she was amongst all these combatant vessels without any means of returning fire.
>
> Fortune, however, favoured the enterprise, and the boats soon began to draw off from the shore with their human freight. About 10.30 four trawlers set off from the pier drawing behind them a line of rowing boats filled with men. Not a single light was visible on any ship except ours: orders were given in a low tone, and the whole plan went ahead like clockwork, right under the nose of the enemy. Many of the lads had to wade out from the beach to the boat as the little pier could not accommodate the extra rush of passengers. Each transport when filled slipped away in the dark, and still the Turks slept in peace.

In his description of the evening of the final evacuation, Fr Gribben conjured up a vision of St Crispin's Day in 1415 at Agincourt: 'gentlemen in England now abed ...'

> At last the great day arrived Sunday, December 19th – and you can imagine our feelings when we thought that on the morrow our gallant little band ashore would be either safe or _____. The sea was again calm, and here was no suggestion of evil. All was favourable for the master-stroke. If only the people at home knew what was happening during those last eventful hours many a fervent prayer would have been uttered for our last line of defence at Anzac and Suvla.
>
> After breakfast the Turks started a violent bombardment of the whole beach but this was to be their last effective spasm. What ammunition Johnny wasted. We saw forty shrapnel shells fall just ahead of us on some dug-outs that had long since been vacated.
>
> About midday the 'white beetle' returned with a few bad cases resulting from the undermining of one of our saps early in the morning. The victims were chiefly Gurkhas, Sikhs, and a few Australians. One man died before reaching us, so we consigned him to a watery grave.
>
> During the course of the morning one of our aeroplanes made a very daring flight ... Not being able to spot any subs she flew over our positions on the beach and then rose above the Turkish trenches ... Just after lunch the gates of Imbros opened and there rushed forth murderous craft of every kind to deal a deadly blow. ...The Navy was out for a demonstration, and we must take the consequences arising from accidents, because we knew Johnny Turk was not sufficiently impregnated with German Kultur to sink us by design. On Port and Starboard side warships were to be seen creeping with such mathematical precision, as if the whole drama had been rehearsed for weeks ...
>
> At 4.30 we got the last of our sick and wounded from the beach clearing station, and at dusk, much to our disappointment, received orders to clear away. We concluded this meant dirty work in the night, and we were thoroughly disgusted at not being allowed to stay ...
>
> Back at Imbros all waited with feelings of anxiety mingled with hope about the fate of those they had left behind ...
>
> It is a dismal place unless the weather is bright and warm. We were thirsting for news of the fate of our comrades at Anzac and Suvla, and could hardly believe the good tidings when we heard they had all got away with but six casualties at Suvla and two at Anzac ... After lunch one hundred of the RAMC who have been the last to leave the shore, pulled up alongside of us singing, shouting, and playing ... We did not even rise to a cheer, because a chronic complaint cannot produce deep emotion, and into such a complaint has this ghastly war developed.[21]

References

1. Rev T. A. Harker, 'College notes', *Ushaw College Magazine*, vol. XXV (July 1915), pp. 182-4.
2. Ibid.
3. Rev O. Creighton, *With the Twenty-Ninth Division in Gallipoli* (London, 1916), p. 46.
4. Rev T. A. Harker, letter to Mgr M. Bidwell, AWA.
5. Creighton, p. 46.
6. Rev T. A. Harker, 'Notes from Ushaw at the front', *Ushaw College Magazine*, vol. XXVII (March 1917), pp. 98-100.
7. Harker, 'College notes'.
8. Chaplains' file box, Archdiocese of Melbourne Archives.
9. Lyn MacDonald, *Voices and Images of the Great War* (London, 1991), pp. 73-4.
10. Ibid.
11. Henry C. Day SJ, MC, *A Cavalry Chaplain* (London, 1922), pp. 56-7.
12. Tpr Charles Drake, Sherwood Rangers Yeo., *St Bede's Magazine* (July 1916).
13. Lt Col. H. F. H. Jourdain, *History of the Connaught Rangers* (3 vols; London, 1925-28), vol. III, p. 43.
14. Day, p. 129.
15. Ibid., p. 153.
16. Ibid., p. 135.
17. Ibid.
18. Ibid.
19. Drake.
20. Rev John Cosser, *St Francis Magazine*, Northampton diocese, War Memorial number (1919), p. 59.
21. Rev J. A. Gribben, 'The evacuation of Anzac', *Ushaw College Magazine*, vol. XXVI (July 1916), pp. 110ff.

10

The dying time on the Western Front: Part I

Loos 25 September–10 October 1915

The Battle of Loos was the British part of major Allied offensive to eliminate the great German salient occupying the industrial heartland of France. At the end of the battle Loos had been captured, but since the initial success was not exploited the result was just another fearsome salient for British infantrymen to hold under relentless German fire from three sides. To gain this salient, heavy casualties were suffered, including the first Catholic chaplain to die on the Western Front.

Fr Edmund Cullen CM was with 15th (Scottish) Division throughout the attack; he later described his experience and impressions of the battle:

> The battle commenced by a four days' bombardment, and a day and a night of intensive bombardment. During this – a gun about every 20 or 30 yards along, firing at points four to six miles away – I went along the artillery, hearing the men's confessions and giving Holy Communion. I rode up at midnight to our battery, with a Captain Kenny. When I got up the colonel had just been killed by a shell. The major, two captains, and sixteen men were Catholics, so I heard all their confessions in a little hole; it was most touching to see the major (the son of Lord Bellham), his two captains, and all the Catholic gunners kneeling on the ground behind their guns and receiving Holy Communion, and then making their thanksgiving aloud with me, at twelve o'clock at night.
>
> Next morning I went to another battery, and the major therein – Hanna, a relative of Hanna, K.C., an Irishman (Protestant) – told me that we, priests, were always after men. When I had finished the Catholics there, he brought me to his big guns and said, 'As we are both Irishmen we may as well celebrate our meeting by having a crack at the Huns.' So he fired two rounds in my honour ... Our Division (15th) has distinguished itself, and two young officers of my mess will get the Military Cross. But the casualties in officers were enormous ...[1]

In the initial assault the Scots edged too far south and missed several vital enemy positions, especially the Chalk Pits. Another, Hill 70, was by-passed and attacked later when the Germans had recovered. In its capture the Scots lost heavily.

> The battle of Hill 70 will never be forgotten by me as long as I live. The sights of horror are simply beyond description. Imagine a short road so strewn with dead and dying that those able to do so were kept very busy lifting the dead into a ditch to allow guns, ambulances, etc. to pass – and this amongst agonising groans all around – and you have some notion of many such scenes. The evening before the battle I went round hearing confessions and giving Holy Communion on the field or remains of houses along the line, and it was very sad to see these poor fellows laid out so soon, either dead, or horribly mutilated. I expected horrors and had already seen cases of shocking mutilations, but I never dreamt of anything like this. I had the consolation of attending about nineteen Germans, and felt so pleased to be able to hear their confession in their language, as they did not speak a word of French or English.[2]

Fr James Marshall of Northampton was chaplain to a brigade of 21st New Army Division of XI Corps. His report of the battle is, understandably, very brief:

> We arrived in France to take part in the battle of Loos. We made our way to the scene of action by a series of night marches, and by our final and terrible forced march on the day the attack was launched, September 25, 1915. I cannot enlarge here upon the grim experiences of our baptism of fire. Suffice it to say that the division arrived in the battle in a tired and hungry condition, fought for thirty-six hours with little food or water, lost half its effectives, and achieved just nothing at all, though the elated survivors wrote exuberant letters home saying how they had severely knocked the Hun and the war would soon be over. They continued to write in this strain after every engagement for the next three years.[3]

Fr Francis Woodlock SJ was one of two Jesuit brothers, who were both army chaplains. Attached to a 9th Scottish divisional casualty clearing station, his division's attack had been one of the most successful of the day. A gunner whose regiment supported the Scots reported on the Mass he attended on the day following the attack; the Mass was celebrated near the line by Fr Woodlock.

> I got to Mass again this morning. The service was held in a barn, not very far from our guns. Father Woodlock (the Divisional Chaplain) said Mass. Half the place had been blown away by shells. The altar was made on a little table at one end of the shed, and the place was crowded. All the artillery fellows from anywhere round were there, and some infantry straight out of the trenches, covered with mud, hadn't had a shave for days, and with full marching equipment on them after yesterday's attack. It was all very impressive. Everyone in the place went to Holy

Communion, and if the guns had opened fire while we were at Mass we would have had to get back. The colonel of the Argyle and Sutherland Infantry (Highlanders) served Mass and we sang hymns to Our Lady and meant them.[4]

The saddest report to be written after the battle, on 16 October, was that of Lord Desmond Fitzgerald, commanding the 1st Irish Guards, to Fr Delaney, the Irish Jesuit Provincial, concerning the death of Fr John Gwynn SJ. It is a concise account of what must have been a very grievous loss to the battalion, and contradicts lurid newspaper propagandist accounts, and artists' sketches, of Gwynn's death in action, which would have offended the battalion. It will be recalled from an earlier chapter how keen this son of a Crimean soldier had been to serve with the Irish Guards. Fr Gwynn had his wish, and he ministered to them nobly and had been wounded in March 1915. He recovered, and returned to serve with the battalion until his untimely death at Loos.

> Dear Rev Father Delaney,
>
> You will, of course, have heard by now of Father Gwynn's death, and I know full well that the universal sorrow felt by all ranks of this battalion will be shared by you and all the members of your University, who knew him so well.
>
> No words of mine could express or even give a faint idea of the amount of good he has done us all out here, or how bravely he has faced all dangers, and how cheerful and comforting he has always been. It is certainly no exaggeration to say that he was loved by every officer, N.C.O. and man in the battalion.
>
> The Irish Guards owe him a deep and lasting debt of gratitude, and as long as any of us are left who saw him out here we shall never forget his wonderful life, and shall strive to lead a better life by following his example.
>
> The unfortunate shell landed in the door of the Headquarters dug-out just as we had finished luncheon, on October 11th. Father Gwynn received one or two wounds in the leg, as well as a piece of shell in his back through his lung. He was immediately bound up and sent to hospital, but died from shock and injuries at 8 a.m. the next morning, October 12th. He was buried in the cemetery at Bethune, at 10 a.m. on October 18th. May his soul rest in peace. But, although he has been taken from us, he will still be helping us; and rather than grieve at our loss, we must rejoice at his happiness.[5]

During the battle six other Catholic chaplains were wounded: Frs A. Bouchier, P. Bradley, F. H. Drinkwater, A. J. Hicks-Gower, P. Looby, and J. P. Moloney. All returned to duty after recovery.[6]

During the rest of the winter of 1915–16 there were no further attacks, just the mincing grind of static trench-warfare. Its horror at least had the advantage of a set routine of duty in the line, and rest in the rear areas, however brief.

> The winter of 1915–16 was spent at Armentières. Five months we had here, and ever afterwards all ranks looked back on this as the happiest and 'cushiest' time we had in the line anywhere. It was the real 'old time' trench warfare, bristling with discomfort and sufficiently dangerous, it is true, but a routine a man could abide, with many compensations of humour and comradeship. And the line was only a couple of miles in front of the town where there were good billets, hundreds of civilians, estaminets, tea-shops, and a gay life, only occasionally interfered with by a bombardment that hurried a few soldiers and civilians, men and women, to their final judgement.[7]

Nevertheless, many still died or were wounded during this 'cushy' time. Among them was Fr R. Garrold, wounded on 21 January 1916.

There were also the casualties sustained during the realistic training which continued during the 'rest' periods out of the line. In the course of battalion training during the spring of 1916, Lord Desmond Fitzgerald, who had so recently reported the death of a battalion chaplain, was himself killed during a grenade-throwing exercise. Unfortunately, the chaplain who succeeded Fr Gwynn was involved in the accident.

> Father Lane-Fox, the late chaplain to the Irish Guards, lost his right eye and hand in a bombing accident. He was standing by the Colonel, Lord Desmond Fitzgerald, watching a bombing practice. The Colonel said 'Now, Padre, you have a try.' Lane-Fox took a bomb, pulled out the pin, and then, before the proper time, the bomb exploded in his hand, destroying his right eye and hand, killing Lord Desmond Fitzgerald and wounding or killing two officers and several men.[8]

Fr Richard Lane-Fox OSB had served with 2nd London Irish of 47th Division on the right of the Loos attack. There the London Irish had kicked and chased a football across no-man's-land in their dashing assault on the German positions. For his ministrations to the battalion in the field, Fr Lane-Fox was recommended for the Military Cross. The accidental grenade explosion, described in a letter from Mgr Keatinge to Fr Rawlinson as 'fooling around with bombs', placed the award in jeopardy. Eventually, however, the MC was gazetted. Fr Lane-Fox was later mentioned in despatches and recommended for the French *Médaille Militaire*.[9]

The heaviest German gas attack for a year took place in the Loos salient during 27–29 April 1916 on the front of 15th Scottish and 16th Irish Divisions. It was a particularly heavy concentration of gas which proved conclusively the inadequacy of the sack-type respirator. With 16th Division in the front line was Fr Willie Doyle. He had never tried on his helmet before the green gas cloud swept over the trenches, and he was unsure what to expect.

I had never tried the helmet on and did not know if it were in working order. In theory, with the helmet on I was absolutely safe, but it was an anxious moment waiting for the scorching test, and to make things more horrible, I was absolutely alone. But I had the companionship of One who sustained men in the hour of trial, and kneeling down I took the Pyx from my pocket and received the blessed Eucharist as Viaticum. I had not a moment to spare and had my helmet just fixed when I was buried in a thick green fog of poison gas.[10]

A little time later Fr Doyle carried to safety an unfortunate officer whose helmet had not worked properly.[11]

Fr J. J. Fitzgibbon SJ was one of those who volunteered early in 1916 shortly after Fr William Murphy's report upon the lack of spiritual facilities in training camps on Salisbury Plain. Within a week, he and three others left Ireland on a Friday and arrived at the front on Tuesday to serve as a supply priest to one who had already left a field ambulance, on leave. One of those who arrived with Fr Fitzgibbon was Fr Francis M. Browne, who went to the Irish Guards, and became one its most famous chaplains.[12] Following his death Fr Browne's photographic collection became world-famous.

Fr Fitzgibbon settled down quickly in his new role, and his energy and zeal were remarkable to the incumbent on his return from leave.

> When I arrived at the Ambulance I learnt to my surprise that another Chaplain had been sent to supply for me, an Irish Jesuit from Clongowes. He seems a most energetic man and has done a remarkable amount of work during the week he has been here. He managed to get about 200 men to Mass in the church at Méaulte on Sunday. He went beforehand to every billet in Méaulte, first one side of the road and then the other, routing up the Catholics and telling them the time of Mass on Sunday. He has visited the men in their Billets, after their return from the trenches, and during their tea-time, getting them to come to confession, hearing their confessions in the yards of the billets. He arranged a parade of the Borderers one evening at five in the Church; but, as he says, he 'doesn't believe in orders,' and so went round himself to all the billets beforehand to tell the men about it. Yesterday he went round the Gordons' trenches. I'm afraid there is no doubt it would be better for the men if he were to stop in my place. I consulted him about the advisability of my staying in Méaulte. On the whole he was against it. Also he does not think it worth while going into the trenches. The Catholics are in such a small proportion. In two or three hours' walking about you only meet four or five.[13]

It was not long before the organization and leadership of Fr Fitzgibbon was recognized, and he became senior chaplain to 4th Regular Division.

The Battle of the Somme, July–December 1916

Only one First World War battle has connotations more terrible than the Somme. But, because of the horrific casualties sustained on the first day of the battle, the Somme entered the British psyche like no other in that dreadful war. For five months the battle raged, moving from one sector to another with heightening intensity. In the opening phase of the offensive one priest was killed and another wounded.

5 July   Fr Donal O'Sullivan, killed in action at Bouzincourt.
24 July   Fr John Birch, seriously wounded at Thiepval.

Before the attack at Bouzincourt Fr Donal O'Sullivan, attached to 1st Royal Irish Rifles, was first denied permission to accompany the assault-waves. But he begged the commanding officer to be allowed to accompany the troops, saying that Catholic soldiers needed their chaplain at the hour of death. The CO relented. Four days later, on 5 July, O'Sullivan was killed by German shell-fire. After the war, the curé of Bouzincourt requested permission from Fr O'Sullivan's mother to re-bury him beside a newly erected calvary (to replace one destroyed in the war) near where Fr O'Sullivan was killed 'to do honour to Father O'Sullivan and for the edification of all pilgrims to the battlefields'.[14] But only one of the British war dead was ever allowed to be disinterred from a war cemetery for burial elsewhere – The Unknown Soldier.

At the height of the battle, near Thiepval, Fr James McShane, chaplain to a battalion of the Royal Fusiliers, was on the plateau at Thiepval with the remnants of his battalion, when groups of another battalion were seen falling back under shell-fire. Fr McShane rallied the men by his wit and chaff. Later the medical officer of the battalion which was falling back wrote of the incident: 'Near Crucifix Corner, before we turned left off the Longueval–Bouzincourt Road, the jovial RC Chaplain, McShane, chaffed and cheered us. He had assumed virtual command of the Royal Fusiliers.'[15]

One of the greatest fears of a chaplain was not death on the battlefield, but mutilation. This was because of the possibility of his being forbidden ever again to offer the sacrifice of Mass in public. On 24 July Fr John Birch, a Salford priest, was wounded and lost a leg. Happily, in this case, the wound did not prevent Fr Birch from becoming a canon of Salford.

One of the great landmarks of the Somme was a large calvary at the cross-roads near Thiepval. Naturally it became known as Crucifix Corner. It became the site of an advance dressing station where a battalion chaplain, Fr Philip Devas, positioned himself.

> My own Battalion made its first attack on, I think, the 21st July. The evening opened with a terrific bombardment, which went echoing and re-echoing over the desolate valleys and hills. All through the night I

remained in the Dressing Station, helping as far as I could. The place was a regular shambles, full of wounded, with stretcher cases lying in the open outside, and all through the night the stream of stricken humanity flowed unceasing under the gaunt outstretched arms of the great crucifix which marked the cross-roads where we worked.[16]

Beaumont Hamel

The Rev T. A. Harker became senior chaplain to 29th Division having been attached to 1st Dublins since the formation of the division in early 1915. A bad attack of enteritis at Cape Helles forced his evacuation to Malta. On his recovery he returned to 29th Division and was with them throughout the Somme campaign. 29th Regular Division had attacked Beaumont Hamel on 1 July and had been repulsed with heavy losses. Another of his articles for *Ushaw College Magazine* encapsulates a senior chaplain's work 'at rest' during the battle.

> The fine weather has been a godsend to us. The troops cannot always get to Mass in the mornings on account of fatigues, making roads, etc., so that, as I used to do at Gallipoli, we always have rosary and night prayers sitting in the open round my little tin hut. For the last two nights we have had Benediction also, and to hear the men singing both this service and the popular hymns is consoling. Beyond that one hears confessions any time during the day, and particularly in the evening and immediately after Benediction. I give Holy Communion to those who wish. I have several officers, who show a splendid example in this, and it pleases the men. From this you can gather that we are not in the line at the moment.
>
> One can easily be killed much further away from the line than we are in now. Guns nowadays are of such heavy calibre and high velocity that they can reach many miles behind the lines. As an example, I rode with my Colonel two miles to the rear of where we now are, and sat down to a cup of tea. Hardly had we started than a shell dropped over the house and a second one brought down the back premises of the house in which we were, the dust being scattered through all the rooms. Dressing stations and outposts have to be near the fighting lines, and as guns are everywhere about, it is not surprising that enemy shells drop into these Red Cross places by mistake.
>
> Fr. Healy was knocked out last week in one of them. We have received a circular recently telling us that priests are not to be hindered from any area of the fighting operations as long as they do not hamper work. It is left to the discretion of seniors to place them. For my part, I ask all my divisional chaplains not to be in the line at the actual moment of attack, but to visit the lines daily, and in a 'strafe' to take up assigned positions at aid posts and dressing stations. This seems to me the sanest plan, for they can hear all confessions, etc., before the affair and give a general absolution from time to time. A main Corps dressing station is an excellent place for giving the Sacraments, as they are all detained there

pending a re-examination of dressings. Many units are not served at all but it is unavoidable with so few priests. Priests are only attached to Brigades, and other units of the Division can only get to their duties by chance. I jog around on the horse and pick up stray men from other regiments, trench mortars, machine-guns, etc., and try to do a bit in this way. My own regiment is almost entirely Catholic, so I have good fortune, and, apart from the divisional work, an easy time.[17]

In August 1916 the main thrust of the battle moved southwards to Longueval, Guillemont, Ginchy and Combles. For over a month the battle raged and to reduce the final enemy strong point in the sector, the Quadrilateral, tanks were brought into action for the first time in support of the Guards Division.

Because they followed the battle closely, two more priests died and many were wounded.

19 Aug	Fr D. Doyle SJ	Died of wounds
1 Sep	Fr C. O'Connor	Wounded
3 Sep	Fr P. D. Devas OFM	Wounded
3 Sep	Fr P. M. Northcote	Wounded
4 Sep	Fr F. Stack	Wounded
17 Sep	Fr B. S. Wilson CSSp	Wounded
23 Sep	Fr F. M. Browne SJ	Slightly wounded
7 Oct	Fr J. J. Stratton	Wounded
17 Oct	Fr F. M. Browne SJ	Wounded
21 Nov	Fr F. Clune (AIF)	Wounded
24 Nov	Fr D. Guthrie OSB	Died of wounds
11 Dec	Fr M. Ryan	Wounded

Fr Wilson, attached to 44 Brigade of 15th Division was awarded the Military Cross for: 'Conspicuous gallantry and devotion to duty in action ... worked indefatigably tending the wounded, and aiding the stretcher-bearers under heavy fire. He has never spared himself in the trenches and has done all he could for the men.' Fr Wilson had 'brought in five wounded men from no-man's-land, the last one being shot off his back'.[18] After the war Fr Wilson was sent to the missions in East Africa where he became Vicar-Apostolic of Bagamoyo, Tanganyika in 1924. In 1934 Bishop Wilson was transferred to Sierra Leone as Vicar-Apostolic.

Strictly speaking not a battle casualty, because he died on a ferry taking him home on leave, Fr Cornelius McAuliffe OFM, a 4th Division chaplain, probably died of a heart attack following the strain of the trenches. His corpse was taken to his home city of Limerick and accorded one of the two full military funerals for a chaplain during the war. (The other was for Bishop Brindle that same year in Nottingham.)

> The coffin was borne on a gun-carriage to the Friary, Henry St. and escorted by soldiers bearing reversed arms. Colonel Sir Anthony Weldon

was the Officer in Charge. The cortege also included a contingent of the Royal Irish Constabulary. On reaching the Church trumpeters sounded the Last Post.[19]

Fr McAuliffe was under 30 years of age and very young for a Catholic chaplain. A fellow-chaplain in 4th Division wrote to the Father Prior:

> I knew his worth as a priest and friend. I worked with him in the same Division since his arrival in France and during his all too short life with us, he justly earned the highest esteem and love of everyone – officers and men – for his zealous work and priestly life.[20]

Fr J. Fitzgibbon, the senior divisional chaplain, wrote to the Franciscan Provincial: 'Personally, I have lost a great helper and a sincere friend and consequently I feel I should write a personal note to his people ... and tell them how highly his work was appreciated by both Officers and Men of all denominations.'[21]

The 2nd Leinsters was one of the most distinguished Catholic battalions to serve during World War I, from the Battle of the Aisne until it crossed the Rhine in December 1918; after the war the Prince of Wales was appointed its Colonel-in-Chief by King George V. The part played by its chaplains was duly recognized by the regiment. The regimental historian, a Leinster officer of English birth and not a Catholic, later wrote: 'throughout the Great War the Regiment was always fortunate in its chaplains.' About Fr James Leech, he wrote: 'The men, Catholic and Protestant, had an almost superstitious belief that in his company they were safe ... He was one of the most successful chaplains of the war, and was unbelievably popular with officers and men, Catholic and non-Catholic alike.'[22] An early Leinster chaplain was Fr Denis Doyle SJ. During one of the many attacks on Guillemont, Fr Doyle was mortally wounded while ministering to wounded Leinsters under fire.[23]

The 7th Battalion of the Leinster Regiment played an important part in the eventual capture of Guillemont by storming through the British barrage, catching the Germans, still sheltering in dug-outs, by surprise. The inspiration of their fearless courage may have derived in part from a sermon by their chaplain near Bernafay Wood just before the attack.

> The Padre, Father Wrafter MC, is spoken of with great affection and regard. At Guillemont, Fr. Wrafter held a service for 7th Leinsters on the bare side of a hill, ankle deep in mud. It was a deeply impressive sight and sent the men into action with a burning faith in the justice of their cause.[24]

Even without the chaplain being present the 2nd Leinsters had a deep religious faith, openly expressed.

> A rather wonderful thing happened this evening. The Germans were shelling us heavily. My company commander, with about five men and

myself, were grouped together in a certain part of the trench, and the shells were bursting on the parapet, when I asked my men if any of them would care to say the Rosary. They are simply delighted, so the captain gave it out. By the time we finished the shelling had ceased completely, so we have the Rosary every evening now, in or out of the trenches.[25]

Once again Fr Marshall succinctly, but cogently, summarized his division's part in a battle. His account gains much from its understatement.

We were moved to the Somme, and for three months were occupied with the elaborate work of preparing the great offensive that was opened against the enemy on July 1st, 1916. We were in and out of the desperate fighting that took place during that month, and never was there more cruel or heavier labour for the RAMC department. During August we had a quiet time at Arras, and in September we were back in the Somme battles. The battlefield by this time was churned up into a hideous morass, and we were in the midst of the ugliness of a devastated land littered with debris, broken implements of war, and corpses of men and beasts. It was a horrible time.[26]

The horror of the time, September to December 1916, is elaborated upon in an article by Fr T. Harker.

The last three months have been too much for most of us, and I don't except myself. The only strange part to me is that there is anyone left at all. The men have been really wonderful. Once they have got in the neighbourhood it is good-bye to roofs, floors and everything but Mother Earth. The slightest rain turns all this chalky surface to a horribly greasy mud, and when the extreme of comfort is reached in a bivouac you can guess what this means. To come out of trenches which are really holes, weary and broken, to a mud patch nearly breaks one's heart. Up in Ypres the men always come out to billets, here the billet from the trench is a distinction without a difference. Shells are plentiful no matter where they get, so it is a toss up which to prefer, and yet they remain as keen as mustard. Just before July I looked into a village from a hill just being inside the Boches lines, and yesterday I walked through the same village without knowing it – it was absolutely impossible to recognize it. There was a certain amount of shelling going on, but in spite of it a keenly contested football game proceeded, I daren't mention the combatants, but they were two battalions who a couple of days before made history.

I met also some Australians who had gone through Gallipoli, and they told me the latter was child's play compared to this. One said 'we didn't know what war was until we came here,' and I can well believe it.

A short time ago I met McShane; he's been privileged to have a permanent crowd under him, and they think the world of him. It is really a shame that he hasn't got something, but most of our people are that way, as it is merely the men who know them.[27]

Mass on active service

On active service Mass was perforce offered in a variety of strange places and situations, not always protected in bad weather, and sometimes with an element of danger. Fr James Bradley of Leeds, whom we have met earlier, described in his old school magazine some of the places where he offered up the Sacrifice in France.

> The sanctuary I had, the first Sunday with the Regiment, was a mere cart-shed of canvas. It sheltered my little altar, built of planks resting on two piles of empty boxes. There was room inside the shed for about a score of men in front and around me, while the rest of the congregation stood on the grass outside.
>
> The next place I said Mass was in a ruined village, behind the front line trenches. My own battalion was in the trenches, so that I had to do what I could for those in the 'support line.' They were out on 'working parties' till 4 a.m. I fixed Mass for them at 1 p.m. (a privilege granted to chaplains during the war). The chapel was a little room in the heart of a heap of rubbish. I placed the altar-stone on a piece of broken furniture (that looked like a harmonium or sideboard) propped up on bricks in a corner of the room, the altar cards, candles finding a convenient ledge on the top of the wainscoting. One note of interest may be added: the celebrant broke his fast that day at 2.30. The following week, I said Mass in a neighbouring village for some of my own men then out of the front line and 'in support.' My church was a slight improvement on the last. I had actually a table for my altar, and flowers on it. The little room belonged to the signallers who kindly lent it me. Two men, tired out with their work, were asleep in their bunk-like beds, and I said Mass and spoke to my men in a whisper so as not to disturb the sleepers.[28]

As time and experience progressed, Mass locations improved for Fr Bradley, but rarely could he find a church. Once he said Mass to a small congregation in the officers' mess of a Machine-Gun Company, and another time by a wayside calvary, which narrowly escaped being rained out. His most satisfying Mass was in a prisoner of war compound.

> We had been notified by our superior chaplain of the presence in that army area of Prisoners of War Camps, and bidden to do what we could when the opportunity arose, and a printed card in German and English for Confession was sent to us. I visited one of the camps, getting permission for Mass. There were more than two hundred Catholics in one camp and 180 in the second. My comrade (a neighbouring priest) said Mass in the former and I in the second camp, the place being nearest our men.
>
> The officer in command must have forgotten his promise to me, for nothing was ready when I landed at 6.30, and he could only allow me the half-hour from 6.30 to 7.0. Hasty preparations were made and a table set at one end of a hut in the middle of the compound (which was thick with

trampled mud). Then the 180 marched in and stood all the while, packed together in about what was sleeping accommodation for 30 men. A Pole served my Mass. Then facing the open door and the morning sun I offered up the Sacrifice that was the common link between us though we couldn't speak each other's tongues. I hope it was a ray of sunshine for them that day. I shall not forget my feelings. Our Lord's words came repeatedly to my mind, and though He will say them to others, this time they applied most touchingly to Himself as Visitant and Comforter - 'I was in prison and ye visited me.'[29]

Without a common language except perhaps Latin which none of the POWs could speak, Bradley sent for an interpreter; through him he apologized for not being able to say Mass for them the previous Sunday, and told them he had scapulars, badges and medals to give them. Afterwards the priest discovered that the interpreter, who wore the ribbon of the Iron Cross, was an atheist.

Sometimes, the soldiers attending Mass came from unlikely formations. One priest reported that at Mass near Crucifix Corner near Thiepval several men from 36th Ulster Division, reputedly all Protestant, attended Mass.

Whilst I was at Crucifix Corner I said Mass once or twice in the church at Aveluy. It was badly knocked about, though still serviceable in dry weather. Among my tiny congregation were some cyclists, detached from the 36th Division, who lived by the A.D.S. and acted as escort for the prisoners of war.[30]

Sometimes the unexplained moves of chaplains excited comments from well-wishers who were not aware of all the facts pertaining to particular cases. One such was Fr C. T. McGuinness CRL.

On Wednesday I went to Bethune and called on Fr McGuinness, who has taken Father Hanlon's place at the C.C.S. (casualty clearing station). He is an elderly man with grey hair and seemed low spirited. He did not want to leave his Division (the 25th), the move was quite a surprise to him. He says he thought of sending a wire of protest, but his successor arrived the same evening. His successor was an elderly man of 52, who in his turn was very sorry at having had to leave his C.C.S. The CofE Chaplain at No. 33 said Hanlon's move seemed to him very surprising and very injudicious. Hanlon was a delicate man, of consumptive tendencies, elderly, of studious and quiet tastes, very well suited to C.C.S. work and quite happy in it; and he is suddenly moved in the depth of winter to Brigade work, which requires different qualifications and of which he knows nothing. As he truly said, sociability and social qualities are an important matter at a C.C.S., where men have to spend so much time together.[31]

Neither the commentators above, nor Fr McGuinness, had knowledge of an exchange of letters between Prior McElroy CRL and Fr Bernard

Rawlinson in December 1916 and January 1917. The Prior was anxious about the 'indifferent health' of Fr McGuinness, chaplain to 75 Brigade. Fr McElroy explained that McGuinness had just recovered from bronchial pneumonia when he volunteered. 'I consented with considerable reluctance as I feared he is not strong enough for front line work in the winter. May I venture to suggest that, if possible, he be given a post at one of the bases?' Enclosed with the letter was a report from the doctor who had attended Fr McGuinness:[32]

> In reply to your letter of the 13th inst. I am quite in agreement with you that Fr. McGuinness is not fitted constitutionally for the severe exposure and vicissitudes of winter campaigning, and that hospital work would be much more suitable for him. I can only give this, however, as a friendly opinion, as I do not think I should be justified in writing anything officially as his former medical attendant. As this might be construed by Fr. McGuinness as an unwarrantable interference on my part with his private work in a national crisis. Where, after all, every man must judge for himself where is his duty. I am glad to think that so far Fr. McGuinness appears to have borne the stress and strain of work at the front wonderfully well and hope he will return eventually stronger and better physically than he was before.[33]

Fr Rawlinson replied to Fr McElroy on 5 January 1917 to the effect that he will consider giving Fr McGuinness less strenuous work but so far his health has been good. He added: 'You may count upon me, however, to give full weight to the report in your letter. I am always very grateful to get side-lights on chaplains out here from their superiors.'[34]

Fr McGuinness, in addition to being in delicate health, was also a very shy man. Once he found himself billeted in a French house still occupied by a woman who slept downstairs. Waking one night with a need to go to the toilet, which was downstairs, he made water out of a window. Unfortunately to his extreme embarrassment, and the amusement of fellow-chaplains, the water fell on to the tin roof of a shed.[35]

The stress of caring for battle casualties for long periods, without proper relief or rest, could do much to change the natural disposition of even the most gentle and kindly. One priest affected in this way during the Battle of the Somme was Fr John Gray of Selkirk.

> A quiet slow Scotchman [sic] and, it is easy to see, a very good kind strong man. He told me about his work on the Somme. He was four days and nights dressing wounded, without sleep and with the terrible din of guns going on all the time. At the end of it he was hysterical and cursed and swore at people (including a general and two Colonels who came and spoke to him), hardly knowing what he was saying. His feet came to hurt him so much that he took off his boots and worked in his bare feet, and in shirt and breeches.[36]

Fr Gray was later awarded the Military Cross for his caring work amongst the human wreckage of war.[37]

References

1. Fr Edmund Cullen CM, 'The Battle of Loos', *St Vincent's College Chronicle* (1916), pp. 18-20.
2. Ibid.
3. Rev James B. Marshall MC, 21st Division, *St Francis Magazine*, Northampton diocese, War Memorial number (1919), pp. 56-7.
4. Gnr Eddie Brown, RFA, 'Fr. Francis Woodlock', *St Bede's Magazine* (December 1915).
5. Lord Desmond Fitzgerald, letter to Fr Delaney SJ, 16 October 1915, Jesuit Necrology, Dublin.
6. Rawlinson MSS, DAA.
7. War Journal of Lionel G. Smith, France and Belgium 1915-17, AWA, Archives of St Edmund's College, series 12 167A, pp. 291-2.
8. Ibid.
9. Rawlinson MSS, DAA.
10. Alfred O'Rahilly, *Father William Doyle, S.J.* (London, 1939), p. 408.
11. Ibid.
12. Jesuit Necrology, JAD.
13. Smith, p. 57.
14. Curé of Bouzincourt, letter to Mrs O'Sullivan, mother of Fr Donal O'Sullivan. In possession of the O'Sullivan family, Ballydowney House, Killarney, Co. Kerry.
15. W. C. Dunn, *The War the Infantry Knew* (London, 1987), p. 234.
16. Fr Philip Dominic Devas OFM, *From Cloister to Camp* (London, 1919), p. 46.
17. Fr T. A. Harker, 'Notes from Ushaw at the front', *Ushaw College Magazine*, vol. XXVII (March 1917), pp. 98-100.
18. *London Gazette* (14 November 1916).
19. Rev Bartholomew Egan OFM, 'A West Limerick chaplain of World War I', *Limerick Association Year Book* (1982), pp. 33-7.
20. Ibid.
21. Ibid.
22. Lieut-Colonel F. E. Whitton, *The History of the Prince of Wales's Leinster Regiment* (Aldershot, 1926), vol. 2, p. 311.
23. Captain F. C. Hitchcock, *Stand-To: A Diary of the Trenches* (London, 1937), p. 144.
24. Whitton, vol. 2, p. 311.
25. Lt R. I. G. L. Stirling, 2nd Leinster Regiment, *St Vincent's College Chronicle* (1916), pp. 17-18.
26. Marshall, p. 57.
27. Harker.
28. James Bradley, 'Mass on active service', *St Bede's Magazine*, no. 6 (March 1918).
29. Ibid.

30. Devas, p. 48.
31. Smith, pp. 291–2.
32. Letter, Rev Prior McElroy CRL to Fr Rawlinson (16 December 1916), Rawlinson MSS, DAA.
33. Letter, Dr Hardwick to Fr McElroy (18 December 1916), Rawlinson MSS, DAA.
34. Letter, Fr Rawlinson to Fr McElroy (5 January 1917), Rawlinson MSS, DAA.
35. Fr A. Whitehead CRL, conversation with T. Johnstone.
36. Smith, p. 335.
37. Ibid.

11

Subsidiary operations

Macedonia 1915-18

Until September 1915 Serbia, although heavily outnumbered, had successfully held the Austrian Army, but that month the Germans launched a successful combined politico/military offensive to secure a land supply route to Turkey. As part of this, Bulgaria declared war on Serbia and German troops joined those of Austria in its Serbian operations. Serbia appealed for assistance and Russia pressed Britain and France to join in sending aid to Serbia. During early October a British division, 10th Irish, and a French division and a brigade were despatched from the Dardanelles to Salonika. The 10th Division was the first of many divisions which eventually formed what became known as the Salonika Army.

Although poorly equipped with mountain artillery and winter clothing, 10th Division entered Serbia, and a corner of Bulgaria, at the end of October. With the division went Frs Murphy, Mulderry and O'Connor, who were present when the division suffered severely in the great blizzard of November. Over a thousand casualties were evacuated with exposure and frost-bite. Shortly afterwards, in an effort to encircle the French higher up the Vardar valley, the Bulgarian Army struck 10th Division in overwhelming numbers at Kosturino. For three days the Irish managed to hold the line long enough to allow the French to retreat in good order, after which the Allies withdrew into Greek Macedonia.[1]

Fr Murphy, debilitated by his Gallipoli experience, and badly affected by the great storm, had to be evacuated to England. In January 1916 he was sent as senior chaplain to Salisbury Plain District where he conducted a survey into Catholic ministration to the troops in the area. His report to Cardinal Bourne on this eventually brought about far-reaching change. Just after the Easter Rebellion in Dublin that same year, Fr Murphy returned to the Curragh as senior chaplain Irish Command.

The Allies retired behind a strong and deep defensive position around Salonika until early summer 1916. When the British and French Salonika armies were strong enough, they re-occupied much of the territory they had abandoned. Mgr William Keatinge arrived following his appointment as Army Principal Chaplain. He had staff at Army Headquarters and worked through the Principal Chaplain of each denomination in co-operation with the Adjutant-General's branch. The Roman Catholic section was never up to establishment, and at one time was sixteen chaplains under-established. Many priests who served there became infected with malaria or other diseases, and were evacuated. A chronic shortage of Catholic chaplains at Salonika threw the burden of extra duty on the few.

Apart from the 10th, the 27th Division, with three regular Irish battalions, had most Catholics. Serving with them were Frs Joseph Reardon, Henry Bowes CSSR, and Francis Rusher. Reardon was attached to the 81st Field Ambulance and Bowes and Rusher to the 2nd Royal Irish Fusiliers and 1st Leinsters respectively. The 1st Royal Irish Regiment had no chaplain. Fr Henry Day, after service in Gallipoli, returned with his regiment to Egypt before going to Salonika in March 1916. On a visit to 27th Division the Irish Brigade attempted to poach him for the Royal Irish Regiment, without success.

> The next day, Friday the 17th, Feast of St Patrick, and the Irish units held sports in the afternoon, which I attended. On Sunday the 19th, I said Mass in my tent for the Yeomanry, and on the following Tuesday, at Fr. Bowes' request, I held a voluntary service for the Royal Irish. Having heard Confessions in their camp the previous evening, the early morning Mass and Communion were both well attended. The same afternoon I lunched at the headquarters of the Royal Irish Fusiliers, where I first made acquaintance with Lieut. McCarthy-O'Leary, the Adjutant. He was a son of Colonel McCarthy-O'Leary, the hero of Spion Kop, whom I had met years before. The O.C. of the battalion, Lieutenant-Colonel Orpen-Palmer, invited me to dine on the following Thursday. This invitation I gladly accepted, but I was obliged to decline later, on account of a telephone message from the Brigade, instructing me to proceed to Stavaros the same day.[2]

Fr Day was sent to 78 Brigade of 26th Division and attached to 7th Royal Berkshire Regiment, a regiment in which his grandfather had fought under Wellington. His initial reception by the commanding officer, a regular officer, was chilly, because he 'had not much use for Padres in camp, and regarded their presence somewhat in the light of a kill-joy, and showed marked coolness the first evening at mess. Fortunately, however, the unpleasantness did not last.'[3] It would appear that Fr Day was unlike the chaplains the commanding officer had previously known.

Fr Benedict Howard SMA served with the Highland Light Infantry in 28th Division. It is recounted by the archivist of his Order that in the years after the war Fr Howard 'always had a Requiem Mass with Absolutions, on Armistice Day, for those who had fallen in the two World Wars, complete with catafalque and his helmet on top of it'.[4] Also with 28th Division was Fr Charles Heurtley of Birmingham Oratory, attached to 1st King's Own Yorkshire Light Infantry. 'Tall and imposing; active, amiable and zealous; his physical and spiritual qualities endeared him to all. For those who know "Fr Charles" it will be enough to say that he was esteemed and popular amongst the troops.'[5]

It was usual in British Army mess life in the promotion of harmony and good manners, to avoid controversial or sensitive topics of conversation. However, in the New Army which sprang into being in 1914 this convention was not as rigidly observed as it had been with the old professional army. Fr Hugh Mulhall SJ, after attachment to 5th East Lancashires, served with 43rd General Hospital, Salonika. In the mess and in his general dealings with the officers, many of them doctors and surgeons, Fr Mulhall produced a deep impression. Whenever in group discussion a point of morals or a question of belief was mentioned, he would be asked for his opinion. His views were always received with respect, if not with agreement; he would give the Catholic position clearly and cogently. He undoubtedly exercised a great influence. 'The four or five years which he spent as chaplain were the most active and pleasant of his life and gave him a stock of memories and stories which he never forgot.'[6]

After the Serbian winter campaign of 1915 there were few pitched battles; one in 1916 and another in 1917. The greatest fight became the battle against the malarial mosquito which caused casualties out of all proportion to the size of the Army.

> One day I was very near the front on the Struma river, but could not catch any Bulgars for your museum. Mosquitoes and flies I could have caught in plenty, but I took up arms against these malaria pests. Of late they have been a greater menace to our men than the enemy, and the casualties caused by their big advance may not be published.[7]

However, when fighting was in the offing the irrepressible Fr Day was in the wings waiting to share the danger with the attacking troops, sometimes against orders. When ordered specifically by his brigade commander to remain at the advance dressing station during the action of 28th Division in the Monastir offensive, Fr Day was crestfallen but hopeful.

> I was to attend the wounded at the ADS in Christmas Ravine, and on no account to join the firing-line. Argument was of little avail, and the only concession I could obtain was that I might ask his leave to go forward in the morning if the battle continued. I communicated the general's decision to Col. Dene of the Berkshires, who sympathized with me, and promised to speak on my behalf if an opportunity occurred. The next day, Sunday the 22nd, after saying Mass for the few troops who could attend, I

began my visit to the front cases and trenches, in order to give the
Catholics who wished, an opportunity of making confessions before
going into what promised to be a heavy and dangerous engagement. It
took me the best part of two days to get round, and the tour was not
devoid of thrills.[8]

Day's desire to accompany his battalion in the attack was motivated, as he
explained, by

my knowledge that the path of our advance was also the sole way
whereby all the wounded would start to return. The worst cases could
only be attended on the spot. From past experience I also felt that the
voluntary presence of non-combatant in the danger zone was a useful
example and likely to encourage the men.[9]

Fr Day accompanied the Berkshires to a point 200 yards from the Bulgar
trenches on Petit Couronne. 'Our boys did all they could – all that was
asked of them. They stormed the trenches, took the hill, and laid down
their lives for England.'[10] But like all frontal attacks the cost was heavy.

Lying and sitting, in all kinds of positions, were rows upon rows of dead
and dying. Many of the wounded were horribly mangled. Some obviously
insensible to pain, while others were suffering agonies. Amongst the
wounded officers – and few escaped – was the CO, Lt.-Col. A.P. Dene, his
right arm was shattered and he had a second minor wound. He was still
carrying on. 'Stick it, Berkshires, and show them what you're made of!'

Fr. Day, although over fifty years of age, carried a wounded man on his
back down to a dressing station. Unfortunately as he trudged along the
man was wounded a second time and died later.[11]

Fr Patrick J. Dore OFM also distinguished himself during the Monastir
offensive and for his consistent devoted and distinguished services in the
field was awarded the Military Cross.

Fr Jeremiah Piggott, Cloyne and SSC, was awarded the MC and
mentioned in despatches. In later life when asked about his awards he
always replied that he had been the champion sprinter at college. After
demobilization he had an even more adventurous life. He joined the
Maynooth Mission to China, and from 1922 to 1939 was Vicar-General of
Hanyang diocese. Fr Piggott was on holiday when war was declared. He
immediately volunteered as chaplain. The Army turned him down on age
grounds (great amusement back in China), but he was accepted by the
RAF.[12]

In October 1918 the Allied armies in Macedonia were at last victorious,
more by staying-power than by battle, and marched into Bulgaria, Serbia
and Turkey. Fr Peter Harrington SMA, who in early 1917 had returned
from missionary duty in Liberia to become a chaplain in Salonika, went to
Istanbul with the force that later became the 'Army of the Black Sea'.[13]

Other priests who served with the Salonika Army were the Reverends Michael Carney, Oswald Doland, Louis Herlihy, John Hogg, Hugh Keegan, John Moth and Thomas Rigby.

German South West Africa

In 1910 the Union of South Africa had been formed by Cape Colony, Natal, Transvaal and the Orange Free State. After the outbreak of war came the recall to France and Germany of all nationals with army reserve commitments. This also applied to priests; many French missionary priests were recalled and shortly afterwards found themselves in uniform, not as chaplains but as soldiers. One German, Fr J. B. Schmidt, became chaplain to British prisoners in Ruhrleben. Eleven priests from the South African dioceses became officiating chaplains or full-time chaplains to the South African forces. Frs M. Costello, B. W. Glynn, and P. J. Walsh were commissioned chaplains and served on the Western Front; Fr Walsh was awarded the Military Cross. Two served in East Africa, the others served either in German South West Africa, or within the Union.[14] The absence of these priests denuded the mission stations, and urgent appeals were sent to Ireland for replacements, so Religious Orders, particularly the Holy Ghost Fathers,[15] sent young priests as their replacements.

General Louis Botha led the Expeditionary Force which invaded German South West Africa. Within six months, January to July 1915, the South Africans overcame all resistance in the territory, and the conquest was officially declared complete on 9 July 1915. In the course of the short campaign five South African priests served as officiating chaplains in the Force: Frs Ford, A. Lanfuet, John J. O'Riley (later Bishop in Cape Town), T. Ryan OMI, and Van Hecke OMI.[16]

German East Africa

The conquest of German East Africa was more difficult than that of South West Africa. Throughout the campaign there both German and British commanders employed mainly native troops commanded by white officers. British contingents arrived from the Gold Coast, India, Mauritius, South Africa, and the West Indies, in addition to many battalions of King's African Rifles from Rhodesia, Kenya and Uganda. A high proportion of these troops were Catholics.

The Principal Chaplain for the area was Fr James Dey DSO, a regular Army chaplain. In all only twelve commissioned chaplains served an area about the size of Europe: Frs A. Allchin, E. H. Collins OP, OBE, J. W. Cosser, W. J. Flynn, M. J. Galvin, J. L. N. Herlihy (after service in Salonika), J. Mulderry (after service in Gallipoli and Salonika), J. A. Wall, and two South African chaplains, J. F. O'Brien and O. O'Leary OMI. Fr Bernard

Carey accompanied the West Indies Regiment from Trinidad. Although
having its share of hardships, sickness, and privation, the East African
campaign was without the slaughter of the Western Front or Gallipoli and
without the plagues of Macedonia. Some of the chaplains remembered and
could reminisce about their experiences until they died many years later.
One such was Fr Collins OP. His army experiences supplied 'material for
all his future conversations; he lived with soldiers in England, France and
Africa; he hunted lions and other wild animals in Africa, and he would
relate, in his own inimitable way, the many hairbreadth escapes from
dangers'.[17]

Most priests served the troops on trek throughout much of the territory
of what is now Tanzania, northern Mozambique, and Malawi; a vast
territory about the size of Europe. Their story is possibly best epitomized
by that of one chaplain: Fr J. W. Cosser.

> My parish is extensive. I have this small Mohammedan town of Kilwa as
> my H.Q., with a large Stationary Hospital to which I am attached. From
> there to the port (Kilwa itself has no harbour), a matter of seventeen
> miles, there are small camps here and there, with quite a large one at the
> port; they are all in my parish. The fighting line, which is now seventy
> miles inland, and all the Lines of Communication Camps between are
> also without a priest, and so must be visited periodically.[18]

Towards the end of January 1917 Fr Cosser went on safari around his
scattered parish and at the same time visited the front line. It was his first
visit. His ideas concerning transport and supplies were rather haphazard,
and he set out badly advised and with little preparation. His servant, Ali,
was 'quite useless'. His baggage was in three sections consisting of his altar-
bag, bedding, food. Thus ill-equipped he set off on a Saturday afternoon on
a 72-mile trek. Fortunately he attached himself to a supply convoy of
wagons drawn by mules going to Mitoli, about 30 miles further inland. On
the first day they travelled from 5 p.m. until 8 p.m., and covered three-and-
a-half miles.

> The next morning we left at 4 a.m., and did twelve miles, after which we
> out-spanned and rested during the heat of the day. At this halt I found a
> camp of Indian pioneers, whose business was to repair the road, and
> among them seven Catholics. I was more fortunate, in finding three of
> them who knew a little English and were glad to go to confession.[19]

Late the following evening the convoy reached Mitoli where Fr Cosser met
an old doctor friend who offered hospitality. There was no transport going
on to the front, 42 miles further on, so he resorted to the age-old ploy of
badgering anyone who would listen.

> I spent three days in worrying everybody in the place, from the Post
> Commandant downwards, and was eventually rewarded by getting a lift

ten miles in the general's motor car. We were dropped at a tiny little post, containing one officer and a handful of men; but the officer was a Sahib, made himself thoroughly agreeable and gave me an excellent dinner. He could not put me up because there was nowhere to be put up; but I slept quite comfortable in the open under a tree, with my mosquito-net hung round me, suspended from a branch.[20]

Eventually Fr Cosser reached the front, just after a battle had been fought.

Fr Cosser learned very quickly. While at the front he succeeded in having three 'large and cheerful' African bearers attached to him as personal attendants. When he returned to Kilwa on foot, his bearers accompanied him carrying his kit. From that time until he left East Africa they accompanied him on all future expeditions, and he became 'a self-contained unit'. His main difficulties serving his scattered parish were over.

Fr Bernard Carey CSSp had a difference of opinion with the commanding officer of the West Indies Regiment on matters of discipline, and when Carey was rude, the CO 'gave him his marching orders'. Carey had a chequered clerical career before and after his short Army service, February to December 1916. He had been unhappy at his first mission post and asked for *exeat*, which was granted. After seven years he applied to rejoin, and was accepted following a probationary period. He was sent to Zanzibar, but the Vicar-Apostolic sent him home because of the intemperance of his sermons. After a short period in Ireland he went to the USA as a roving preacher, whence he went to Trinidad, and into the Army. After he 'relinquished his commission', Fr Carey returned to the USA, where he wrote a book about his Army chaplaincy before returning to Port of Spain, Trinidad.[21]

Mesopotamia

The Mesopotamia campaign, under the control of the India Office, was possibly the worst-run British campaign of World War I. Service in Mesopotamia (christened 'Messpot' by the troops) is not referred to with any pleasure in extant documents.

One chaplain wrote that 'The Mesopotamian Desert is the lid over the Purgatorial Fires'.[22]

Fr J. P. Moloney OBE, MC, who had been commissioned a temporary chaplain before the war, was still a 'temporary commissioned officer'. Upon his recovery from wounds received at Loos, he was appointed Senior Chaplain (RC), Mesopotamia. In relation to the size of the force, he had the extraordinarily high number of 57 chaplains who served under him during the campaign. This can only be accounted for by the high casualty rate from disease. Two chaplains died of illness during the war, and one by a tragic accident afterwards.

Fr Jeremiah Hartigan SJ was attached to the Argyll and Sutherland

Highlanders. He died of jaundice before Kut el Amara on 16 July 1916. Fr
Hartigan had been awarded a doctorate in Eastern languages at Beirut
University in the Lebanon, and before this he had taught Greek and Latin
at Clongowes Wood College. Apart from the natural sadness upon the
early death of a priest of great promise, the loss of such a highly-qualified
linguist was keenly felt by his Society.[23]

Fr Charles Watson CSSR was something of a horticulture expert and
was engaged in his hobby when overcome by sunstroke. He was taken to
hospital where he was anointed by a fellow-chaplain. Having failed to
respond to medical treatment Fr Watson died on 22 July 1918, and was
buried in the military cemetery at Nasiriyah.

The third fatal casualty in Mesopotamia was Fr Isidore J. O'Meehan.
Although nearing 50 years of age, Fr O'Meehan volunteered for active
service and was commissioned chaplain to the forces on 4 June 1915. After
service in France he was sent to Mesopotamia and was attached to a
casualty clearing station. He died from an accidental gunshot wound at
Kut el Amara on 19 December 1919.

Many priests had seen active service in either France, Gallipoli or
Salonika before being moved to Mesopotamia. A high percentage
terminated their contracts during service in Mesopotamia, usually on
grounds of ill-health. Some, however, remained there until 1920. Few ever
forgot the experience. One, Fr Philip Moore of Ossory, wore on his death
bed the chasuble he had used on service.[24]

Some priests also had highly interesting experiences before arriving in
Messpot. Fr Bernard Farrell of Meath diocese had served in Dublin during
the Easter Rebellion and had attended wounded troops in a dressing
station situated within the precincts of Trinity College. There he 'had the
unique distinction of being the first priest since the reign of James II to
celebrate Mass in Trinity College, Dublin, on 30 April 1916'.[25]

Another Irish priest, Fr James McRory, who had been wounded at
Passchendaele before being sent to Mesopotamia, appeared never to have
recovered from his war service experience. His diary,[26] which is really a
collection of hearsay gossip, consists of highly intemperate, racially
inspired observations on, and criticism of, senior chaplains, bishops and
a cardinal (apart from 'cabbage-headed generals'), none of whom he ever
met. Historically it is worthless except as a sad study of how a mind can be
warped by wounds or campaigning hardship.

So great was the heat of the Mesopotamian desert in summer that Fr
Montgomery CRL narrowly escaped death when he lost his way in the
desert and was overcome by heatstroke while walking, 'only a few miles',
from 27 Casualty Clearing Station, where he worked, to another camp.[27]

Perhaps the following pithy conversation between a newly-arrived
chaplain, Fr Claude Warren OBE, Leeds diocese, serving at 31 Stationary
Hospital, and Fr Moloney OBE, MC, the Principal RC Chaplain, is a

suitable note on which to end this stark sketch of Catholic chaplaincy in Mesopotamia:

M. Are you an Order man?
I.   Yes, the Order of St Peter.
M. I thought so. You are looking ill. Have you a temperature?
I.   Yes, 105 just now.
M. What is it, malaria?
I.   No, sandfly.
M. You didn't say Mass?
I.   Yes, 6 a.m. at the Rest Camp.
M. You shouldn't. Why didn't you let me know?
I.   No good. It would be impossible to do it from Baghdad.
M. Report sick at once.
I.   No, there are seven doctors here as anxious to keep me out as myself.
M. I'll come to see you tomorrow.
I.   Don't come except I send. I'll be all right.
M. By the way, isn't Shaw around here?
I.   Yes, he is my nearest neighbour. 150 miles south.
M. Well I can see you are bad. I hope you will soon be better again. Bye bye.
I.   Good bye and many thanks.
That was my first introduction to M.[28]

Well might Fr Warren write 'If the expression "of awesome wonder", is to pray, then I have prayed'.[29]

Sinai and the Holy Land

In 1869, with the opening of the Suez Canal, Lower Egypt became strategically important to the lines of communication of the British Empire. The Suez Canal, and Empire communications, were threatened when Turkey entered the war on the side of Germany in 1914. Britain took direct action to protect what was seen as an Empire lifeline: on 17 December 1914, Egypt, technically part of the Turkish Empire, was declared a British Protectorate.

During January 1915 a Turkish force laboured across Sinai, and on 2 February attacked British defensive positions on the Suez Canal and were routed. In 1916 the Turks again attacked the British positions and were defeated at Romani. The Egyptian Expeditionary Force (EEF) pursued the Turks along the coast, building a railway behind them, until repulsed at Gaza. The Gaza position was again unsuccessfully attacked on 27 March 1917. Following this reversal, General Sir Edmund Allenby was appointed C in C EEF and moved his headquarters into Sinai, to prepare a Christmas present for the British Empire: Jerusalem.

Allenby had served in two Irish cavalry regiments; and in South Africa, while commanding a column of Inniskilling Dragoons had Fr Simon Knapp OCD as regimental chaplain – his high regard for him has been described in an earlier chapter. A deeply religious man who knew his Bible well, Allenby cared much for the Holy Land and its antiquities. This last is amply manifested by his orders prohibiting careless or wanton damage to historic buildings or the felling of ancient trees.[30]

The Third Battle of Gaza was fought between 31 October and 10 November 1917. Allenby's three corps successfully drove the Turks from all their positions at, and between, Gaza and Beersheba, and drove them back on the coastal plain. He then switched XXI Corps, commanded by Sir Edward Bulfin (Stonyhurst and TCD), into the Judean Hills. It fell to a unit of 60th London Division (Sir John Shea) of XXI Corps, to accept the surrender of Jerusalem the Golden on 8 December 1917.

Fr George Griffin, a Salford priest, who had served in France and Flanders with a Lincoln battalion, was chaplain to a battalion of the Royal Welch Fusiliers. Later he was to write:

> A battlefield isn't a very pleasant sight after such a combat; some of our dead were horribly mutilated. The task of burying the dead was no small one. The hot sun puffed up the bodies making them unidentifiable; it was a real hardship for the chaplain to get to the disc which everyone wore around his neck, and the stench which arose from the corpses, and hung around the valley where they were buried, made life hardly worth living. The Protestant Chaplain went sick the first night and I had to bury the lot – nearly 200 of our own men. I have never chewed tobacco except on that occasion, and for three days and nights I was kept busy; what meals I had consisted of dog biscuit, strong tea, and broken cigar.

Fr Griffin was mentioned in despatches.[31]

On 26 December the Turks began a powerful counter-offensive opposite the London Division, directly in front of Jerusalem. On their right was the 53rd Welsh and on their left the 74th Dismounted Yeomanry. On the far left was the 10th Irish. Two Irish chaplains who were present at the time had very different lives, and deaths.

Fr Bernard Kavanagh CSSR, Limerick-born but long in London, was just over 53 years of age when he went forward to attend a wounded soldier during the advance on Jerusalem of 60th Division. A Turkish sniper mortally wounded the chaplain as he ministered to the soldier. Fr Kavanagh died of his wounds on 21 November and is buried in the Commonwealth War Graves Cemetery on Mount Olivet.[32]

Fr George Clenaghan, an Ulsterman, at 28 years of age was young to be a Catholic chaplain in World War I. He served with the Connaught Rangers, and lived to become, at 93, the oldest canon, and priest, of the diocese of Down and Connor. Upon his death on 30 September 1981 a newspaper obituary notice read:

His experience at the front provided him with a host of anecdotes that he often used both in preaching and in general conversation. Despite the suffering and slaughter, he carried away warm and consoling impressions of the fine comradeship of the Irish soldiers and their calm faith in the face of death. On his return home he travelled widely throughout Ireland to visit and console the relatives of many of the men killed at the front.[33]

Each priest in his own way had won immortality at the capture of the Holy City.

Following the capture and defence of Jerusalem against a Turkish counter-offensive in December 1917, the idea of an Army Catholic Congress in Jerusalem was conceived by Major General Western, the Deputy Adjutant-General, HQ EEF, and Fr Felix Couturier OP, assistant to the Principal Chaplain, EEF. Fr Couturier was afterwards Visitor-Apostolic in Egypt, then Bishop of Alexandria in Canada. Both were stationed at GHQ, then located near Ludd (or Lydda), between Jaffa and Jerusalem. For operational reasons the congress, or pilgrimage, had to be postponed several times. Eventually, just weeks before Allenby launched his army into the twin battles of Nablus/Megiddo, the pilgrimage took place on the feast of the Assumption, 15 August 1918. Samaria and Galilee were still held by the Turks, the Nablus front was only ten miles distant, and the boom of guns could be heard at night. All around Jerusalem, those not on pilgrimage were engaged in feverish preparation for the coming offensive.[34]

Local arrangements were in the hands of the two chaplains stationed at Jerusalem, Canon A. Sibley and Fr A. J. Parisotti, with the assistance of a Catholic officer from the Military Governor's staff. Because it was a military parade, Colonel Byrne of the Rifle Brigade was officer commanding troops. On the day before the pilgrimage, Fr Felix Couturier arrived in his car from GHQ. In all there were about twenty chaplains and 100 officers, including General Western, assembled waiting for the troops to arrive.

Selected Catholic troops from all the Allied formations and contingents in Palestine and Egypt attended. Furthest to travel were those from Egypt; many came from Alexandria, Cairo and Upper Egypt. They travelled by special train and after a long and exhausting journey across Sinai arrived at Jerusalem on the afternoon of 14 August, 'dead-beat but full of enthusiasm'.[35] In all, over 1,500 assembled and were quartered in camps around Jerusalem. Mass was said in the camps at 06.30 the following morning, and it is reported that nearly all the pilgrims attended the sacraments.[36]

The parade assembled by the Jaffa Gate through which General Allenby had walked as a pilgrim only eight months before. The Military Governor of Jerusalem with his staff were waiting at the gate to welcome the procession.

Down the steep hill from the gate into the Valley of Hinnom, and thence up the Mount of Evil Counsel on the other side, on the road to Bethlehem, as far as the eye could see, stretched the long ranks of soldier pilgrims, two deep, marshalled by Fr. Parisotti on his white charger, and commanded by Colonel Byrne of the Rifle Brigade. There were men from almost every unit of His Majesty's Forces in the E.E.F. – English, Scots, Irish, Australians, New Zealanders, Canadians, South Africans, British West Indians, and even some Catholic natives from the Indian Army.

At our head went the great silver crucifix from St Stephen's carried by a sergeant-major, while a Dominican lay-brother escorted us as guide. We all recited the Rosary going through the streets, led by the chaplains, who were distributed down the ranks, to the amazement of the people of Jerusalem, who said that they never knew before that British soldiers could pray!

I saw sights at Jerusalem that had never been seen since the days of the Crusaders, saw the victors prostrating themselves, as their forefathers had done centuries ago, before the Tomb of Christ, long processions of Catholic soldiers making the Stations of the Cross along the Via Dolorosa, British Tommies on guard at the doors of the Holy Sepulchre, and in the very cave where Christ was born for us at Bethlehem.[37]

Only a small part of the procession could enter the Holy Sepulchre at one time, therefore five divisions were formed and individual chaplains took charge of a division and led it inside.

All were deeply conscious of the historic significance of the occasion, that they were the inheritors of the cross from the Crusaders. Only one Crusader tomb remained at the door of the sanctuary of the Holy Sepulchre, that of Sir Philip D'Aubeny, who had signed Magna Carta and died in 1236 after fourteen years in the Holy Land. It was over his emblazoned tombstone that the pilgrims walked in prayer. Within the basilica the pilgrims were met by the Franciscan guardians, with cope, incense and holy water, who conducted the procession to the rotunda, and as they entered the Franciscan friars burst exultantly into the *Te Deum*.[38] It was a moment that none present would forget.

The first part of the procession filed into the Greek choir, facing the Sepulchre, and filled the rotunda surrounding the Tomb. All knelt, and Fr Bede Camm OSB led the devotions. Having spoken a few words of explanation about the holy place, all recited 'three Paters and Aves and the Act of Contrition, ending with the prayer of the Angelus, "that by His Cross and Passion, we may be brought to the glory of His Resurrection"'.[39]

After the prayers all rose and, still led by the cross, filed out by another aisle while the next division entered. During the intervals of change-over, the friars sang the *Te Deum*, as the rotunda emptied and was filled again. All passed and could see the Column of Flagellation because, in honour of the occasion, the Franciscans had it exposed.

Leaving the Basilica, the procession turned north-eastwards, and passed along the Via Dolorosa, under the arch of Ecce Homo, to St Stephen's Gate. 'A steep road leads down the hill to a bridge over the brook, and we see in front of us the Tomb of the Blessed Virgin and the Garden of Gethsemane, on the lower slopes of the Mount of Olives.'[40]

As it was the feast of the Assumption, it had been planned that the pilgrims should render their devotions at the empty tomb of Our Lady in a subterranean church. Unfortunately the church, which was under the control of the Armenian Church and Greek Orthodox Church, was found to be locked, despite prior notice of the pilgrimage. Within an hour the heads of both Churches were summoned to the office of the Military Governor to explain why offence was offered in such a way to soldiers, by which time the pilgrimage had moved on. Passing by Gethsemane, they mounted the hill once more to St Stephen's Gate, the old name for which was The Gate of the Lady Mary. There they halted at the nearby church of St Anne, an ancient crusader church, part of the White Fathers' establishment which they had restored. The crypt of the church is cut into the rock. Local tradition has it that Our Blessed Lady was born here.

This was the place selected as the place where the pilgrims would hear Mass offered by Mgr Felsinger, the patriarchal vicar: the Latin Patriarch, Mgr Camiss, was held prisoner at Nazareth by the Turks.

> It was an inspiring sight that met one's eyes as one looked round. The big church was literally packed with men. The General and the officers had seats in the nave, but the choir, sanctuary, nave, aisles were thronged with men, some sitting on the ground, others standing pressed together so closely that the priest had the greatest difficulty in getting to the altar. All carried their mess-tins and haversacks, for they were to lunch in the grounds after the Mass. I shall never forget facing that great throng of bronzed men who had been through so many dangers, endured so many hardships in order to deliver Jerusalem from the Infidel, and had now come on Mary's crowning day to render thanks to God at the Tombs of Jesus and His Mother.
>
> It was wonderful to hear them sing the familiar hymns during the Mass that followed. I have never heard anything like that 'Faith of our Fathers' shouted from fifteen hundred lusty throats, and it was even more wonderful to kneel in the hush and the stillness that fell on that great crowd when the bell rang out and the Host was raised. I don't wonder that the celebrant, Austrian though he was, burst into tears and could hardly go on with the Mass. He told us afterwards that he had never been so moved in his life, and he wrote a detailed account of the Pilgrimage to Rome, which (as I found later on) had delighted the Holy Father, and done good in many ways there. Indeed, it was difficult enough to refrain from tears.[41]

After a sandwich lunch and a rest the pilgrimage restarted. Forming up in the courtyard of St Anne's the procession moved to Antonia and began the

Stations of the Cross along the Via Dolorosa. This was one of the most impressive parts of the programme. The Stations were preached by one of the chaplains, the soldiers 'trudged along the cobblestones of the Sorrowful Way, kneeling humbly in the dust at every sacred spot, kissing the very ground, and singing between the Stations the verses of Stabat Mater'.[42] The Way of the Cross lasted two hours and ended at Calvary and the Holy Sepulchre, where Fr Parisotti OSB preached the sermon.

On emerging from the basilica, the pilgrimage wound its way to the Damascus Gate to the basilica of St Stephen. There, the Franciscan Custos of the Holy Land offered Benediction of the Blessed Sacrament and gave the papal blessing which had been asked for, and granted, by telegraph from Rome. Canon Sibley OSB played the organ, and the pilgrims sang old familiar hymns, ending with 'Faith of our Fathers'.

The following morning a Requiem Mass was offered for *all* who had fallen in the war. The Mass was said by the assistant Principal Chaplain, Fr Couturier, and General Western served. That afternoon the pilgrims returned to their war duties. Some of them, after a 36-hour journey and a strenuous 48 hours, began another train journey of 36 hours back to their units.

At the military debriefing which followed the pilgrimage, it was found that no one had misbehaved in any way. The organizers were overjoyed to find: 'there had not been a single case out of all the fifteen hundred men to claim the attention of the Provost-Marshal. Everyone had behaved splendidly, there had been no straggling, no drunkenness, no trouble of any kind. The Catholics of the E.E.F. had proved themselves to be worthy of the privilege which had been so generously given them.'[43]

Notes and references

1. Captain C. Falls, *Military Operations: Macedonia* (London, 1930).
2. Henry C. Day SJ, MC, *Macedonian Memories* (London, 1930), pp. 66–7.
3. Ibid.
4. SMA Necrology, Servite Archives, Begbroke.
5. Day, pp. 66–7.
6. Jesuit Necrology, JAD.
7. Rev J. A. Gribben, *Ushaw College Magazine* (December 1916), p. 256.
8. Day, p. 128.
9. Ibid.
10. Ibid.
11. Ibid., p. 130.
12. Fr Michael Healy SSC, conversations with Tom Johnstone. In 1946 Fr Piggott led a group of missionaries to take over a new Columban mission in Huchow, China. While there they were overrun by Communist armies in 1949. Most of the group were imprisoned until expelled in 1952, but four Columban priests were kept imprisoned until 1953. In bad times Fr Piggott would say to his

guards 'Good night, nurse'. After China service, he served in Japan (1953-61) and the Philippines (1961-75). He returned to Ireland in 1976 to celebrate his diamond jubilee; while there, he was knocked down by a car in Navan and died on 12 May 1976.

13. SMA Necrology, Servite Archives.
14. Rev B. E. Brady, 'Soldiers in Christ', Catholic History Bureau, Linden, Johannesburg.
15. Fr S. Farragher CSSp, correspondence with T. Johnstone.
16. Brady.
17. Rev Raymund M. Dowdall OP, DCL, *Memories of More Recent Irish Dominicans* (Dublin, 1951).
18. Rev J. W. Cosser, 'Campaigning in East Africa', *St Francis Magazine*, Northampton diocese, War Memorial number (1919), pp. 60-1.
19. Ibid.
20. Ibid.
21. Correspondence in AWA; CSSp Necrology.
22. Rev C. E. Warren, 'Extracts from my War Diary', IWM, London.
23. JAD.
24. *St Kieran's College Record* (1962), p. 88.
25. Meath Diocesan Necrology.
26. Rev James McRory, Diary, Public Record Office of Northern Ireland, Belfast.
27. Rev L. E. Montgomery CRL, Diary, IWM, London.
28. Warren.
29. Ibid.
30. Sir A. P. Wavell, *Allenby* (London, 1940), pp. 203-4.
31. Rev T. G. Griffin, *Ushaw College Magazine*, vol. XXXII (December 1922), pp. 166-78.
32. CSSR Archives, St Mary's, Clapham, London.
33. Obituary, *Irish News* (30 September 1981).
34. Rev Bede Camm OSB, *Pilgrim Paths in Latin Lands* (London, 1923), pp. 254-5.
35. Ibid.
36. Ibid., pp. 260-4.
37. Ibid.
38. Ibid.
39. Ibid.
40. Ibid.
41. Ibid.
42. Ibid.
43. Ibid.

12

The dying time on the Western Front: Part II

With the death in hospital of Peter Grobel on 1 January, the year 1917 began badly for chaplains. As the year, and the war, progressed, the intensification of battle on the Western Front brought more death and injury than had been thought possible at any time in the previous two-and-a-half years. Fr Grobel of Salford had been a naval chaplain during the Boxer Rebellion and was present at the capture of Tientsin and the relief of the Legations at Peking. One of the temporary commissioned chaplains on a three-year engagement from 1910, he had been released then recalled on 20 August 1914. He had served in France ever since and had been mentioned in despatches.

The first major Allied offensive of 1917 began in April on the Arras sector. Well aware of Allied intentions, if not the actual plan, the Germans began a strategic withdrawal on 25 February which ended on 5 April with them firmly fixed in the Hindenburg Line.

The British offensive opened brilliantly. The Germans were completely surprised when the assault troops left their shelters and stormed forward in a blinding snowstorm. The German lines were broken into, much ground was captured including Vimy Ridge; many prisoners and 247 guns were taken. Had the battle been halted at this stage it would have been counted a resounding success. Once again, however, GHQ intervened. At Haig's insistence the battle was resumed in May, and failed.

On 9 April, the first morning of the offensive, Fr R. H. J. Steuart SJ, attached to a battalion of Highland Light Infantry (HLI), accompanied the battalion medical officer and his team of orderlies close behind the assault companies.

> One of our companies found itself confronted by two 77mm batteries whose fire had been worrying us for some time past. The company commander made up his mind to silence them, snatching up a rifle and

> calling to his men, in the Glasgow phrase, to 'Ca' the feet from the
> beggars' charged the first battery, which was firing point blank at them,
> shot the commander, killed or captured the gunners, and then, turning
> half-right, treated the second battery in the same way.[1]

The medical officer and RAP, consisting of a sergeant and three orderlies,
established a temporary aid post in a dug-out on the captured position. An
unwounded German was taken prisoner in the dug-out, and his captors
saw evidence of loot from French houses being parcelled to be sent back to
Germany. As for the prisoner himself: 'The worst that a prisoner had to fear
from them was a dose of chaff, not usually couched in the language of Mrs
Grundy but still immeasurably removed from the "Hymn of Hate".'[2]

The attack of the 15th Division continued. The HLI advanced swiftly,
but for every yard captured the 15th Division lost heavily and suffered the
heaviest British losses, 6,313[3] in total, giving RAPs such as that of the HLI
heavy work.

> Here we established ourselves and were immediately overwhelmed with
> work … It began to snow again heavily. We were only three, coping with
> a tremendous flow of more or less seriously wounded from all units, and
> it was impossible to give them all immediate attention, much less shelter.
> To our great regret many died from exposure as they lay there. Imagine it!
> Men with ghastly wounds – with shattered limbs, or grisly rents in their
> tortured bodies, fainting with shock or hunger, lay silently with hardly a
> moan waiting their turn while the snow whirled about them and chilled
> them to the marrow.[4]

The chaplain did what he could to erect a shelter over the wounded, while
the medical orderlies relieved the waiting wounded in another, homely
way:

> The M.O. in particular worked like the hero he is and before long the
> quite wonderful medical orderlies of our battalion were supplying the
> poor suffering fellows with hot strong tea. It must have been nectar to
> them.[5]

All chaplains who went forward with the assault troops on 9 April suffered
the same hardships and shared the same danger. Fr Henry Collins, a
Westminster priest, was attached to 9th Black Watch during the attack.
Like Fr Steuart he accompanied the attacking companies as they went over
the top, and was killed. On the same day Frs A. Bouchier and C. P. Wright
were wounded.

Fr Marshall, still with 21st Division, was opposite part of the German
front which retired to the Hindenburg Line:

> We next journeyed towards that part of the line South of Arras and were
> preparing to take part in a new big push there, when the German changed
> our plans by making his great retirement. We were called upon to follow

him up and we did, through all the villages that he had destroyed and the country that he had laid waste. We marvelled at the devilish industry which did not forget to cut down so much as a currant bush. We had some rough experiences living amongst all this devastation during very severe weather, there being heavy snows right on into April.

We took our part in the successful battle of Arras and the capture of a large part of that amazing stronghold known as the Hindenburg line. In several months we were engaged in a good deal of fighting just North of that storm-centre Bullecourt.[6]

In addition to leaving a deserted wilderness across which the British struggled to keep in contact with the enemy, the Germans had left behind hundreds of booby-traps for the unwary. Hidden mines timed to explode long after the Germans had retired were placed under obvious headquarter sites. In one of these delayed explosions Fr Matthew Burdess was killed: 'On the night of 17 April, with the colonel and four other officers, he went to take some rest in a cellar in a village recently captured. Between three and four in the morning, a concealed mine exploded, and all six officers were killed.'[7]

Barely a week later, on St George's Day, Fr James Leeson serving with 13th Royal Fusiliers was killed. As the battle stretched further than had been originally planned, Frs T. Healy and J. J. Nevin were wounded. As a result of his wound, Fr Nevin had to have one leg amputated. When he recovered, he continued serving, at a convalescent centre in Lourdes.

The line at Arras had barely quieted when the front of Second Army just south of Ypres literally erupted, with the detonation of a million pounds of high explosives in nineteen great mines, under the German positions on Messines Ridge. On 7 June, advancing through falling debris and choking fumes, the assault division overwhelmed German resistance. In a classic siege operation with limited objectives, a hitherto impregnable position was captured in three days. But it was not without its casualties and as they had advanced with the infantry chaplains bore their share. Fr J. J. McMenamin, a City of Auckland priest with the New Zealand Division, was killed. Frs W. Fitzmaurice and J. McHardy were wounded; however, both recovered and were able to return to the front in time for the battles of 1918 when they would again be desperately needed.

The Third Battle of Ypres, a series of operations between July and November 1917, is usually called Passchendaele after two actions fought for the dominating ridge close to that village. If any evidence is required as to the horror of Passchendaele, an appropriate name, it is to be found at Tyne Cot cemetery in the Ypres salient. There, over 11,000 simple headstones, laid almost side by side, bear mute testament to military folly.

The progress of the battle can be charted by the dates on which chaplains died, were wounded, or gassed.

Preparatory bombardments	8 Jul	Fr E. Legros,	wounded
and counter bombardments	11 Jul	Fr M. Maguire,	wounded
	23 Jul	Fr R. Adamson,	gassed
	29 Jul	Fr G. Gallagher,	gassed
Battle of Pilkem Ridge	1 Aug	Fr S. Knapp,	died of wounds
	1 Aug	Fr I. McCann,	wounded
Battle of Langemarck	16 Aug	Fr J. Howard,	wounded
	17 Aug	Fr W. J. Doyle,	killed
Counter bombardment fire	26 Aug	Fr M. Gordon,	killed
Battle of Polygon Wood	5 Sep	Fr J.J. Fitzgibbon,	gassed
	6 Sep	Fr J.J. O'Gorman (Canada),	wounded
	26 Sep	Fr T. A. Agius,	wounded
	2 Oct	Fr J. McIlvaine,	gassed
	2 Oct	Fr J. Evans,	wounded
Battle of Broodseinde	4 Oct	Fr S. Clarke,	killed
Battle of Peolcappel	9 Oct	Fr F. M. Browne,	wounded
Battle of Passchendaele I	11 Oct	Fr M. Bergin (Australia),	killed
	13 Oct	Fr J. J. MacNeil,	wounded
Battle of Passchendaele II	21 Oct	Fr J. McRory,	wounded
	26 Oct	Fr P. Looby,	killed
	26 Oct	Fr J. R. Davey,	wounded
	28 Oct	Fr G. L. Smith,	wounded
	23 Nov	Fr V. J. Scully,	wounded
	27 Nov	Fr R. J. Monteith,	killed
	30 Nov	Fr C. P. Wright,	gassed[8]

Fr Knapp, for his service with 1st Irish Guards, was awarded the DSO, MC and two MIDs. He had been with a front-line battalion constantly since 1914. The denial of the Victoria Cross to another Catholic chaplain has been adversely commented upon by Professor O'Rahilly. But if ever a British soldier deserved the highest award for gallantry, it was Fr Simon Knapp. The place in battle of the followers of St Ignatius, St Francis Xavier, and St Philip Neri, all warriors, is readily understandable. But how a gentle Carmelite monk, such as Fr Knapp, could adapt himself in two wars to both cavalry and infantry units in the field, and distinguish himself in each, is incredible. After the war the Irish Guards commissioned a memorial window to Fr Knapp, and it was erected in the Carmelite church, Kensington. Sadly this stained glass window was destroyed in 1944 during the German flying-bomb bombardment.

Fr Rawlinson, in a letter to the Father Prior, Carmelite church, Kensington, said: 'No words can express what a loss he is to the Chaplains' Dept., or how highly he was thought of by the whole of the

Guards Division ... He is the greatest loss we could have sustained.'[9] There is no doubt that had he lived, the Victoria Cross could not have been denied Fr Knapp; the Guards Division would have seen to that. This is possibly what Fr Rawlinson meant by 'greatest loss'.

Fr Stephen Clarke, of Kilmore, was attached to the 7th Lancashire Fusiliers when killed on 4 October 1917 and his death could be announced at once. However, like many of the dead of Passchendaele, Fr Patrick Looby was first described as missing in action, and only later, when accounts were collated from survivors of the battle, was he declared on War Office authority to have died in action. It is not only infantrymen who die in battle. All arms and services on the Western Front were in mortal danger, and this applied equally to their attached personnel. Fr Robert Monteith SJ was attached to 70 Brigade, Royal Field Artillery in close support, when he was mortally wounded on 27 November, exactly seven months from his commissioning. He died later that same day.

Fr Michael Bergin, who served and died with the Australian Imperial Force, had an unusual distinction. An Irish Jesuit working in Syria, he had been interned by the Turks. Becoming ill with smallpox, he was released and went to Egypt. Hearing of the shortage of Catholic chaplains with the AIF, he had attached himself to the Australian Light Horse near Cairo. Accompanying them to Gallipoli, he was actually commissioned on the Anzac beach.

> He was killed near Zonnebeke, N.E. of Ypres on 11th Oct. Our battalion was in the front line, and as was his usual custom, he went up to find out if there was anything he could do for the men. On the way to the front a piece of shell caught him in the chest, killing him instantly.[10]

His name is on the magnificent Australian War Memorial at Canberra, although he never set foot on Australian soil.

Long-range counter-battery, or interdiction, fire accounted for many lives. Michael Gordon of Glasgow was killed by a shell that hit his billet in Coxyde. So respected was Fr Gordon, that there was 'a large and representative attendance at the solemn Requiem Mass in the Parish Church on Thursday morning. Most of the Catholic Army chaplains in the neighbourhood and representatives from various denominations, several Belgian generals and a number of British Staff officers attended to pay homage to the memory of a brave and devoted priest.'[11]

Fr John Howard CSSR, a priest 'very Irish in attitudes',[12] according to the necrology of his Order, 'was in attendance in the advance dressing post. The dugout becoming flooded, its occupants were compelled to continue their services in the open. Being thus exposed, they were in terrible danger and casualties soon resulted. The RC chaplain was among the number, a bullet passing through his thigh.'[13]

Fr John MacNeil, a Gaelic-speaker from the Hebrides, was attached to

5th Camerons and had already won the Military Cross and been mentioned in despatches before his battalion went into action at Third Ypres. On 13 October during the attack of 9th Division on Passchendaele Ridge he earned a Bar to the MC

> for conspicuous gallantry and devotion to duty, in going out in front of our lines under intense machine-gun fire to dress the wounded and bring them in; he saved many lives, and only gave up when wounded in the lung, left leg and right arm.[14]

The value of the priest in the line had by 1917 been realized by military authority. Fr Benedict Williamson OSB had hurried back from a court of enquiry into the burning of a farm billet so as to offer general Communion to the Catholics of his brigade before they went into the line. On arriving back at brigade headquarters, he found that the brigade commander had already made arrangements for the service.

> The day was raw and cold, and General Lewis, with the kindness and thoughtfulness so characteristic of him, had the large hut he was using cleared and a table prepared for Holy Communion, so that the troops might all shelter inside. Night was coming on when all had assembled. The shed was packed, and the congregation sang the Benediction service and some of the favourite hymns with great fervour. I spoke a few words exhorting them to entire confidence in Almighty God and entire conformity to His Holy Will, whatever that will might be, and then Holy Communion followed. So great was the pack that the men could not move up, so I had to make my way line by line and fracture the hosts several times that all might be able to receive. That for some was the last time I was to see them alive, and there was a great sense of solemnity over us all, as we knew how desperate was the struggle into which we were going; so that the hymn after Holy Communion, 'Soul of my Saviour', was singularly appropriate. The moment of silence while the blessing of Our Lord was bestowed was only broken by the half-suppressed sobs of some of the younger boys. All pressed round me as we went out, to express their grateful gladness at being able to be strengthened for the conflict by the Bread of the Strong.[15]

While his 'boys' were in the line, Fr Williamson brought the Host up to them. In one of his journeys he was accompanied by the brigade Presbyterian chaplain, Padre Watt, up the infamous Menin Road towards Passchendaele Ridge; actually a shell-torn track between piles of rubble.

> We passed on up the road, with its press of moving limbers, guns, pack-animals and men all pressing relentlessly forward like a great machine. Piled up on either side of the road or trampled underfoot were the carcasses of decaying mules and horses, streaking the mud with red, the bodies of men, slain as they went up, smashed and overturned limbers, and all the wreckage that marked the roads of the Ypres sector, shells

occasionally bursting in the desolate war-torn country on either side, the unceasing sound of shells passing overhead; by the roadside at one point lay horse and rider, just as they had fallen the night before, half buried in the mud and slime, trampled down by the ceaseless forward movement that never seemed to stay by day or night.[16]

Going from one battalion position to another, rifle platoon, machine-gun section or mortar battery, on a pathway formed by great teak planks of timber, was the only way to traverse the liquid mud. The planks were covered with mud and slush making them slippery for the unwary. Arriving at each position, the two chaplains served the soldiers, Catholic and Protestant, side by side in a small dimly-lit captured German pill-box.

> I gave Holy Communion to our boys, and Padre Watt spoke a few words to the others, and after a short rest we clambered out once more into the open. We next made our way to the line of little concrete pill-boxes where our trench mortar battery was established … In one of these small pill-boxes, as they were well named, our Catholic boys assembled. The building was so low that we could not stand upright. By the light of a solitary candle, all crouching down, we sang 'Faith of Our Fathers', 'Sweet Sacrament Divine', and 'Soul of My Saviour', and then after Benediction all the boys received Holy Communion. Shorn of every outward sign of solemnity, yet I scarcely remember a service more impressive than this, in that cramped underground vault, with the voices of the singers within punctuated with the crash of shells without.[17]

Long after the war, the memory of those who fought in it was undimmed, and time distilled the experience. Many ex-service men travelled far to attend the funerals of those they revered. One old soldier said of Fr Francis Donohoe SJ at the time of his burial, 'They never made enough VCs to give that man, he earned them a dozen times. Once, against orders, he brought in a dying man from no-man's-land.'[18]

One of several priests recommended for the VC was Fr Luke Bellanti, who had taught at Stonyhurst. One of his former pupils, Air Vice-Marshal J. C. Nealy, who had served as an infantry officer in the same battalion, wrote about him on 2 April 1953 shortly after Fr Bellanti's death: 'Fr Bellanti would crawl into no-man's-land to succour the dying and was recommended for a Victoria Cross: but as the unit had just received a VC, he was awarded an MC instead.'[19]

Much was written at the time of the battle, and shortly after the war, about the death in action of Fr William (Willie) Doyle SJ, who was serving with 16th Irish Division at the Battle of Langemarck, not least in the excellent biography by Professor Alfred O'Rahilly. Fr Doyle's life and death has been the inspiration of many, and some miraculous cures have been attributed to him. His divisional commander recommended Fr Doyle for the Victoria Cross. That he did not receive this has been the subject of comment. Professor O'Rahilly asserted that 'the triple disqualification of being an Irishman, a Catholic and a Jesuit proved insuperable'.[20]

It has recently been alleged, however, that 'it was the padre's clerical superiors who successfully blocked all attempts to confer the nation's highest honour on "Willie" Doyle'.[21]

This charge is based on a letter from Charles Doyle, Fr Doyle's brother, to the rector of Ratcliffe College, where both Charles and Willie were educated. In his letter, Charles Doyle claimed that 'the padre's clerical superiors' had prevented the award.[22] It is difficult to accept this theory. Cardinal Bourne and his Vicar-General, Dom Bernard Rawlinson, had never interfered with previous awards to priests for gallantry. Moreover, when a clerical superior to one chaplain requested, unsuccessfully, for an award to his priest, Fr Rawlinson told him that recommendations for awards were entirely the responsibility of 'commanding officers and the military authorities'.[23] Cardinal Bourne and Dom Bernard were very well aware, as were others, of the prestige attached to the Victoria Cross and the significance of its award to a Catholic priest. It is highly unlikely that they, the 'clerical superiors', would have prevented any chaplain being awarded the nation's highest honour for gallantry. Whatever the truth, it will never now be discovered. It is interesting, nonetheless, taking account of relative military achievement and losses of each division, to compare Victoria Crosses awarded to 16th Irish Division, and 36th Ulster Division.[24] Having carefully examined the circumstances of each award and the numbers involved, it is difficult not to accept that there was discrimination against 16th Division. Fr Doyle may have been a victim.

No battle fought on the Western Front opened with greater promise of success for the British Army than the First Battle of Cambrai. The British assault in November 1917, led for the first time in history by massed tanks, was everywhere successful. The Hindenburg Line was broken into and for a time it seemed Cambrai would be captured: lack of sufficient reserves on the spot denied the local commander the victory. In the race to rush reserves to the scene, the Germans won. Their subsequent successful counter-attack dampened initial euphoria.

During the German counterstroke on 30 November, many British positions were overrun and Fr C. C. Pike OP was captured. He was, however, released on 22 February the following year.

Fr Francis Browne had been twice wounded serving with the Irish Guards during the Somme battle, and was again wounded at Passchendaele where he had displayed his customary back-stiffening zeal from the pulpit:

> We were in a church somewhere in Belgium and Fr. Browne was in the pulpit. Shells began to fall all around. We began to look around and up at the roof already with many holes in it. Fr. Browne thundered out: 'What's

wrong? Why don't you listen? Which are you more afraid of – God or the Germans.[25]

The only failed attack on Day One of the offensive was opposite Bourlon. It was a failure the Guards Division had to rectify at heavy cost, but too late to redeem the initial loss of time. During a German counter-attack at Bourlon Wood Fr Browne was in the front line, and on witnessing a local German breakthrough hurried to battalion headquarters with the information. But for all his experience with the battalion he had not quite grasped accurate weapon terminology: 'Yes, yes, they are coming through the woods with bayonets fixed to their Lewis-guns.'[26]

Fr Browne made his own comment on the battle in which his battalion, 2nd Irish Guards, lost 90 officers and men dead and over 300 wounded:[27]

> It was one of the saddest sights I have ever seen. Imagine a fairly dark night, a deep sunken road lined with tiny excavations, some of them covered with oil sheets, and in the middle the wreck of our Battalion. I cannot tell you how many we were when we started nor how many when we ended, for it would be a crime against interfering DORA [Defence of the Realm Act].[28]

It was the mournful duty of chaplains to attend military executions. In the British Army sentence of death was normally carried out only for murder. However, as World War I progressed so little was the psychology of battle-fatigue and battle-stress understood that sometimes chronically sick men were taken for cowards. Medical staff at the front could usually detect genuine cases of shell-shock, and treat them. However, there existed a fear at higher staff levels that the incidence of 'malingering', 'shirking', or cowardice would spread like a contagious disease. To counter this, GHQ issued strict guidelines on punishment of those found guilty of desertion, or cowardice in the face of the enemy. No compassion could mitigate these orders, which were designed *pour encourager les autres*. Sometimes there were miraculous cures to shell-shock victims.

> What I think was a genuine case of shell-shock being cured by a subsequent shock occurred whilst we were here (at Thiepval). A man in a complete state of collapse, unable either to walk or speak, was sent off by motor ambulance on a stretcher with several other wounded. As the car crossed the bridge over the Ancre, a red-hot fragment of bursting shell struck the petrol tank and set it alight. In an instant the whole car, with its dry canvas sheeting, was a mass of flames. The shell-shock case was out of the car in a moment, and rendered the driver the greatest assistance in getting the other wounded safely away.[29]

When a sentence of death passed by court-martial had been confirmed by GHQ and promulgated, the sentence was carried out as quickly and humanely as possible in the circumstances. A chaplain was in attendance with the soldier under sentence until the moment of death early next morning. One priest, Fr R. H. J. Steuart, described an execution he attended in his spiritual capacity:

> He spoke of himself with curious detachment, as of one who had lived long ago. After the intimate revelations of himself of which I had been the recipient, I understood him well enough to know that this was neither artificial nor the result of natural obtuseness. He had faced and, after the first great agony, had fought down the terror that confronted him. He received the Sacraments that gave peace and security to his soul, and he was man enough to make little after that of the swift death that awaited his body. The impression that he made upon me was of a man who looked upon himself as no longer of the world of living men. I thought that in the intervals of silence I detected on his face an absent, tense, almost impatient expression, such as a man might wear who is trying to catch a faint, far-away sound.[30]

The priest remained with the prisoner throughout the night, lying on a bed in the same cell. The soldier lay down after midnight with his rosary twined around his wrist. The priest lay awake throughout the night, but the prisoner, who was to die at six o'clock, never stirred. Fr Steuart called him shortly after five, and he dressed in silence, with no sign of agitation, taking great care with the windings of his long puttees. He renewed his confession and received Communion for the last time.

Breakfast was brought in and he ate, then smoked, but refused the customary drink of rum. Priest and soldier talked quietly until the sergeant of the guard warned the time was near.[31]

> He then handed me a letter for his wife, and asked me particularly to remember that to the best of his belief he had no debts, and that he bore no grudge to anyone. I knew to what he referred.[32]

Just before six o'clock the Assistant Provost Marshal (APM), medical officer, three military police and the man's own company sergeant-major entered; the soldier rose and saluted. The sergeant-major formally identified the soldier under sentence, and the procedure of execution began.

> The policemen tied a bandage over his eyes and fastened his hands behind him, the medical officer pinned a small square of lint over his heart, to serve as a mark for the firing party.
>
> Then, with the A.P.M. leading, we went out ... I can vouch he never faltered nor trembled.
>
> Within the square he was bound securely to the post, and I had time to hear him make his last act of contrition and give him Absolution once more, to put the crucifix to his steady lips, to press his hand in good-bye and to get 'God bless you, Father,' from him, before the A.P.M. motioned to me to stand aside.

At a sign from the A.P.M., the firing party, which up till then had stood with their backs to the condemned man, faced about to him. At a second sign they took aim; at a third they fired: and the bound figure crumpled and slid down as far as the ropes would let him go. Instantly the officer in command called his men to attention, formed fours and marched them off; and the medical officer, stepping forward to examine the body, reported five bullets through the heart.

The cemetery lay a few hundred yards away; and in less than a quarter of an hour from the time that the dead man and I had sat talking together in the hut, the earth had been pressed down over him in his grave, and I was signing the label for the identifying peg at his head.

He had paid the just penalty of his offence; but I ask no better than that I may meet my death, when I must, as gallantly as did that Deserter.[33]

References

1. R. H. J. Steuart, *March Kind Comrade* (London, 1931), pp. 118-19.
2. Ibid.
3. Brig Gen Sir John Edmonds, *Military Operations France and Belgium: 1917*, vol. I (London: HMSO), p. 559.
4. Steuart, p. 131.
5. Ibid.
6. Rev J. B. Marshall, *St Francis Magazine*, War Memorial number (1919), p. 57.
7. *Northern Catholic Calendar* (1917), pp. 107-8.
8. Rawlinson MSS, War Casualties Box, DAA.
9. Letter, Rawlinson to Father Prior, ibid.
10. Lt Col Christie, 51st Bn AIF, letter, JAD.
11. Benedict Williamson, *'Happy Days' in France and Flanders* (London, 1921), p. 43.
12. CSSR Necrology.
13. *Dundee and District Catholic Year Book* (1918), p. 125.
14. *London Gazette* (23 April 1918).
15. Williamson, pp. 50-1.
16. Ibid.
17. Ibid.
18. English Jesuit Necrology.
19. Ibid.
20. Professor Alfred O'Rahilly, *Father William Doyle, S.J.* (London, 1939), p. 555.
21. N. Cave, *Battleground Europe (A Guide to Battlefields in France and Flanders)* (Barnsley, 1990), p. 128.
22. Br Nigel Cave IC, Ratcliffe College, Leicester, conversation with T. Johnstone.
23. Rawlinson MSS, DAA.
24. Tom Johnstone, *Orange, Green and Khaki* (Dublin, 1992).
25. Lord Nugent, 'Obituary', *Irish Guards Association Journal*; quoted in Irish Jesuit Necrology.
26. Ibid.
27. Rawlinson MSS, DAA.

28. Johnstone, p. 314.
29. Fr Philip Dominic Devas OFM, *From Cloister to Camp* (London, 1919), p. 47.
30. Steuart, pp. 100–3.
31. Ibid.
32. Ibid.
33. Ibid.

13

The dying time on the Western Front: Part III

At the beginning of 1918 the Catholic chaplains' department on the Western Front was about 90 under-establishment. The burden of work was further increased when the British Government insisted that the BEF assume an additional 28 miles of front from the French. In preparation for the expected German spring offensive frantic efforts were made to improve the poor defences the French left behind. Before these preparations were completed, on 21 March 1918, St Benedict's Day, the blow fell on Fifth Army, beginning with a bombardment the intensity of which was far greater than anything previously experienced.

> About 5 a.m., the roll of the artillery, which had been moderate during the night, became very intense; the crash and rush of shells became blended in one grand ceaseless tempest of sound, which continued without diminution till late in the afternoon ... Overhead the rush of thousands of shells of every calibre, with the crash of their bursting on either side, produced an intense volume of noise such as I had never heard before. It was no ordinary barrage, and we realised that the great attack had begun.[1]

From 21 March until 3 April a furious battle raged on the front of Third and Fifth Armies. On the opening day the British lost heavily in men and matériel, but the Germans also suffered heavy losses, now and in their second attack on 9 April, and failed in their attempt to drive the BEF into the sea.

Certain British divisions which had been hard hit in April were, in May, moved for a rest to the Chemin des Dames on the Aisne where the Germans again struck on 27 May against the French who retreated twenty kilometres in a single day, a record for the war. Once again these unfortunate British divisions were caught up in a massive German attack.

In all of these fierce battles, as might be expected, the chaplains suffered heavily.

21 Mar	Fr P. Casey,	prisoner of war
21 Mar	Fr M. J. Flanagan,	gassed
22 Mar	Fr A. M. Bouchier,	wounded, second time
22 Mar	Fr T. F. Duggan,	prisoner of war
22 Mar	Fr W. Fitzmaurice,	prisoner of war
24 Mar	Fr G. Galbraith,	gassed
1 Apr	Fr T. J. Molloy,	wounded
2 Apr	Fr R. B. Milroy,	wounded
9 Apr	Fr J. J. McDonnell,	killed
9 Apr	Fr J. Shine,	mortally wounded
21 Apr	Fr J. Shine,	died of wounds
15 Apr	Fr T. Bull,	wounded
Apr	Fr F. M. Browne,	wounded, third time
12 May	Fr J. Thompson,	wounded
27 May	Fr R. H. J. Steuart,	gassed
27 May	Fr J. Nolan,	prisoner of war
29 May	Fr C. Whitefoord,	mortally wounded
30 May	Fr C. Whitefoord,	died of wounds
30 May	Fr T. L. Baines,	mortally wounded
31 May	Fr T. L. Baines,	died of wounds[2]

On 9 April at Givency the 55th Machine-gun Battalion was the rock on which the German attack against the Lancastrians foundered. Its chaplain, Fr McDonnell CM, was killed on the opening day of the attack attending the wounded under fire. On the same day but in another place, Messines Ridge, Fr J. Shine was mortally wounded, described as 'Perhaps the tallest priest in Scotland, he was a commanding personality';[3] he too was attending the wounded. The death of non-combatants fearlessly doing their duty could not help but inspire the defence. Significantly, they fell at places which were held fast. During the magnificent defence of Hazebrouck, Fr Francis Browne with the Guards Division was once again wounded.

Fr Charles Whitefoord (Rugby and Merton) was described in a letter of recommendation by a canon of Shrewsbury as 'a pukka gentleman, whose only fault is that he is likely to lose his temper if called a Parson'.[4] He was attached to 6th London Regiment when wounded on 29 May 1918 during the last great German drive, and died of wounds on 30 May 1918.

One priest, Fr Joseph Woodlock SJ, a nephew of the poet 'Fr Prout', was cut off and reported missing in action. He managed to evade captivity but afterwards refused to talk about his experiences behind enemy lines.[5] Chaplains made prisoner of war were usually those who faithfully stayed with the wounded in their care who, in the circumstances of the great numbers of casualties and the speed of withdrawal, could not be evacuated before being overrun.

A long retreat before a victorious enemy is the most difficult, demanding and exhausting of military operations. It brings out the best, and worst, of everyone engaged in it. In March 1918 a party of exhausted army nurses entered a crowded camp at Amiens and were met by Fr Michael Cullen. When Fr Cullen died at the Hospital of St John of God, Scorton, north Yorkshire in 1940, one of those nurses took the trouble to write about him. 'He insisted we stayed in his room, which he surrendered to us. In that crowded camp he was absolutely worshipped.'[6]

It would not be in keeping with the spirit of the British soldier if he ever lost his sense of humour, even in desperate moments. Fr Philip Stack OP 'amused his brethren for many years and in particular he had many amusing incidents to recall about the Allied retreat from Vimy Ridge'.[7]

In September 1918, 21st Division, like many others, was back in the very trenches it had been driven from in March. Fr Marshall had been with his division since Loos, and had been present in every major engagement of the war since being awarded the MC and MID. In mid-September 1918, an Oxford graduate, he was appointed Oxford University chaplain. He had, however, one pilgrimage to make before he left for home.

> My last act before leaving the Western Front was to make a pilgrimage with a handful of men to Lourdes. How that blessed place appealed to those men! It was an exquisite and stirring finale.[8]

Meanwhile, in Germany, four priests found themselves prisoners of war. Frs Casey and Fitzmaurice SJ were held at Holzminden, and Fr Duggan at Mainz; it is not known where Fr Nolan was held. Frs Casey and Duggan wrote to Cardinal Bourne to pursue their release by giving proof of their priesthood and faculties,[9] Fr Duggan being particularly upset by not being able to minister to fellow-POWs. Fr Duggan volunteered for service again on the outbreak of World War II, during which he was awarded an MC and OBE. After war service a second time Fr Duggan now sought action in the mission field and went to Peru to take part in the fight against the poverty of its people. He died in Lima on 17 December 1961 aged 71.[10]

Fr Fitzmaurice had received the MC for service at Messines Ridge in 1917, and was mentioned in despatches; he was also recommended for the French *Légion d'Honneur* for 'constant bravery and endurance',[11] but received instead the *Croix de Guerre avec Palme*. During his time in a prison camp when he received a Red Cross parcel he gave the biscuits it contained to German children. Fr Fitzmaurice was present at the Battle of Langemarck with 16th Division; on bleak Frezenberg Ridge he heard the confession of Fr Willie Doyle fifteen minutes before Fr Willie was blown to pieces.[12]

Fr Henry Gill, who had taken part in the great retreat with 36th Division, was that unusual priest, a Master of Science. He had worked at the Cavendish Laboratory, Cambridge. A chaplain since 1914, he had been in every battle on the Western Front, and had the DSO, MC, and was twice mentioned in despatches. He was a respected senior chaplain in 36th Ulster Division, which was not renowned for its Roman Catholicism. Fr Gill was also recommended for the French decoration, *Récompense Militaire*: 'Served continuously in the line since November 1914. Displayed conspicuous bravery and devotion to duty.'[13] 'He seemed like a lost soul whenever you met him, but he was always there when wanted, and was afraid of no man.'[14] 'But his vitality had been much lessened by his experiences of the war years.'[15] Fr Gill spent the last thirteen years of his life as Father Minister and spiritual father to the Leeson Street Jesuit community in Dublin.

The losses of chaplains during the spring offensive, coming on top of under-establishment, increased the strain on the remaining chaplains. Fr Rawlinson was understandably delighted when he learned that the ex-POW priests could return to duty when they were released.[16] The losses by death, wounding and gassing continued through the summer and autumn of 1918 during the advance to victory, almost to the eve of the Armistice.

16 Jun	Fr O. F. Dudley,	wounded
26 Jul	Fr W. Moran,	wounded
17 Aug	Fr A. A. Geoghegan,	wounded
15 Sep	Fr W. J. Brown,	wounded
18 Sep	Fr N. H. Brown,	wounded
18 Sep	Fr J. J. Fitzgibbon,	killed
5 Oct	Fr F. H. Drinkwater,	gassed, and temporarily blinded
12 Oct	Fr D. Roche,	gassed
31 Oct	Fr W. P. Montagu,	died of wounds
1 Nov	Fr G. McBrearty,	wounded
4 Nov	Fr H. C. Day,	wounded
7 Nov	Fr B. Duggan,	wounded[17]

Such was the high regard in which Fr John Fitzgibbon was held amongst chaplains that Fr Rawlinson the Vicar-General read his burial service.

> Father Fitzgibbon had blessed a grave and read the Burial Service over one of our boys about 2 p.m. on Wednesday last, and was talking to a German Catholic prisoner of war in the cemetery, when a shell landed in our midst, and the Father fell forward. One of our boys rushed to his help, but had only raised him to his knees when another shell burst in on them, forcing him to drop his burden and fall on his face to avoid being killed himself. A few minutes later Father Fitzgibbon's dead body was removed, and was buried next day.[18]

He was the second son of John Fitzgibbon, Nationalist MP for South Mayo. Mr Fitzgibbon's eldest son had been killed in 1915 while serving with 10th Irish Division at Gallipoli.

Fr John Delaney, of Salford, had joined 2nd Dublins after Fr Casey had been captured on 21 March on the heights above Ste Emilie. During the advance to victory the 2nd Dublins was in one of the divisions which spearheaded the advance. At the end of the war the commanding officer of his battalion took the trouble to write a letter of appreciation to Fr Rawlinson about Fr Delaney, who by this time had been awarded the MC and mentioned in despatches.

> He was with me from Sep 1918 to June 1919. He greatly distinguished himself by his fearless conduct under fire, especially in the big fight at Le Cateau, October 1918, where he won the Military Cross. Even when the battalion came out of the fight, he spent days afterwards searching for the missing under heavy shell fire, and was rewarded by finding and burying our dead. He took the greatest interest in the men, and the fact that there was practically no crime and such a good tone in the Battalion, I put down entirely to his individual care and interest with the men.[19]

The end of the war

Although soldiers are happy to take part in staged triumphalist celebrations of military victory, usually arranged by politicians, it is rare to find it expressed on the battlefield.

> Next morning, the historic day on which the armistice was signed, opened cold and brilliantly fine. I went across the road and said Mass early at the Ursuline convent, and then went back to the White Chateau at Froyennes, to bury our poor boys killed in the last fight of the war. It was strangely pathetic and moving to look at the white upturned faces that one had seen in full vigour of life so short a while before. Some artillerymen helped to carry them to the grave which the men of the 15th battalion had dug for them the night before. I then set off along the road after the brigade. Everywhere people were out, overjoyed at their deliverance. Some handed flowers to the boys as they passed, others hand out coffee. Everywhere the note of joy, gladness, and relief at the great deliverance filled the hearts of the people. Along the road streamed back the men and boys who had been carried away prisoners by the enemy, and abandoned in his retreat. They carried flags, sang the 'Marseillaise', and toiled along determined not to rest until they reached their home at Lille. They were of every age, from mere children to old men, just able to struggle along, but all were glad the enemy was crushed, the net was broken and they were delivered. 'You are our deliverers, you are our saviours.'
>
> That night a solemn hush seemed to fall upon all. The great and overwhelming triumph caused no such hysterical and foolish outburst as

that which disfigured the night at home, and utterly disgusted all the Front who heard of it.

The men who had been through all the cruel reality of war only felt a strange sense of solemnity, and their minds turned back to their comrades who had fallen; indeed, when we reflected on the tremendous price that had been paid to win peace, none of us could spend these hours in senseless and noisy rejoicings.[20]

In the peace which followed, reaction to the war was varied, most wanting to forget completely a traumatic experience which seldom, if ever, had been endured before. Writing shortly after the war about the officers and men he had served with on the Western Front, and although giving just praise, one chaplain is not uncritical. These are, however, essentially the words of a loving pastor.

How wonderful they always were, patient, plodding, so often soaked in rain, trudging from one cheerless abode to another, facing gaily the rising of each hopeless dawn, living out so often the brief months of a hard life, and cheerfully closing it in blood. Their language, which shocked so many, was as meaningless and harmless as it was too often filthy, and their very blasphemies were pathetic. And what conditions they so often lived in. A good billet was a barn with straw, that was luxury; a bad billet, a bad line of trenches, no pen can describe, just as no mind can conceive, without having seen them, what such places can be like.

The officers - they were of course of all sorts - but how few and far between were the really unpleasant ones. One of the great joys of Army life was the welcome one might always expect from them. If one was stranded anywhere, or called in for a meal or for information at any Officers' Mess, one was always sure of a greeting. The Army was like some vast brotherhood: friendly hospitality one could meet with almost everywhere, and no matter what a man's belief or profession or antecedents, life in their company was almost wholly pleasant. Of course, in religious matters, the prevailing ignorance not simply of Catholicism, which one might expect, but of Christianity and religion in general, I can only describe as abysmal beyond all conception. Of course there were marked exceptions, but that was the general impression one got.[21]

It would be extremely surprising if the Church itself had no real casualties apart from the gassed, wounded and killed; casualties of battle. One priest lost his faith, and had to be sent home from France.[22] He died shortly after the end of the war, reconciled to the Church. Two priests left the Church and married. One, having been granted *exeat*, obtained a commission in the Royal Naval Air Service and was married in 1917, in what was described by the archivist of his Order as 'the society wedding of the year'.[23] The other priest was demobilized in India, and when granted *exeat* married in a Mesopotamia register office.[24] Far worse were the three priests who having been released from the Army were never heard of again.

*   *   *

In a letter to all Catholic chaplains in France and Belgium written shortly after the end of the war, Fr Rawlinson thanked them for their loyalty and willingness in a job which was 'almost unbearable at times'. He praised their efforts, ministrations, and heroism. Yet ...

> Whilst the work of the Catholic chaplains has been most faithfully performed, it has been seriously hampered by the shortage of priests in the field. Roughly speaking, during the whole campaign three priests have had to do the work of four. The day the Armistice was signed, out of 407 that was allowed by Establishment, and therefore considered necessary by the military authorities, there were only 312, leaving a deficit of 95.[25]

At the beginning of the war the strength of the RAChD was:

Anglican	89
Roman Catholic	17
Presbyterian	11
Total	117

During the course of the war a total of 810 Catholic chaplains served in the armed forces, 780 in the Army and 30 in the Royal Navy. This includes the regular chaplains serving on 5 August 1914. Thirty-six were killed in action, died of wounds or died on service. A further two died shortly after the end of the war while still serving; and some twenty died within four years because of their war service. At the end of the war the strength of the RAChD and the deployment of chaplains by theatre was as follows:[26]

	Home	BEF	MEF	Salonika	Mesopotamia and India (including hospital ships)	East Africa	Italy	Misc. Areas	Total
Church of England	709	878	134	93	62	30	58	21	1,985
Presbyterian	75	161	19	22	11	–	8	6	302
Roman Catholic	78*	389#	54	45	38	2	32	13	651
Wesleyan	60	127	20	14	17	–	12	6	256
United Board	60	126	19	13	15	1	12	4	250
Welsh Calvinist	4	5	1						10
Jewish	4	8	3	1					16
Salvation Army		4	1						5
Total	990	1,698	251	188	143	33	122	50	3,475

*Mainly invalided from the front; 'England is full of Crocks.'[27]
#The difference between the figure given in Fr Rawlinson's letter and those in 'Stats' can be explained in that 'casualties' were held on strength of the original field formation for an extended period of time.

The Principal Chaplains' Department at HQ BEF was far from being the sinecure which might be imagined from the writings of one chaplain.[28]

Under Dr Simms, a few Catholic priests administered all the chaplains of the BEF except those of the Church of England. The extent of Catholic involvement at the PC's Department was revealed when Abbot Butler of Downside in February 1918 requested the release of one of his priests, Fr S. D. Young. In his reply Fr Rawlinson explained that Fr Young was the assistant to the Principal CF and the Senior Catholic Chaplain, and he was responsible for the administration of Presbyterian, Wesleyan, Non-conformists and Jews, in addition to Roman Catholics – 800 chaplains in total. Fr Rawlinson stressed that:

> He is the only one who understands anything about it, besides myself … Maj. Gen. Simms relies heavily on him … and would put every difficulty in the way of his going … That the whole of the Principal Chaplain's Department is being run by Downside would perhaps be also of some consideration to you.[29]

The Chaplains' Department, in addition to dealing with the obvious administration of chaplains, also corresponded with the relatives of Catholic soldiers and chaplains who were serving, or had served, with the BEF. These were essentially in the nature of replies to queries regarding the state of grace at the time of death of loved ones. It was a task which required considerable sympathetic tact and understanding. Sometimes it also meant further correspondence with chaplains in the line asking for details. These enquiries added to the burden of those already busy, yet the evidence is that wherever possible, information was passed back to relatives. Fr Young asked Fr Hessenaur (Carden), to find a Maltese gunner 'on the French front, 28th Siege Battery RGA'. Hessenaur found him! Other letters asked CFs to 'take special care of' or 'special interest in' men. Other letters were from anxious relatives enquiring about chaplains, their state of health and locations. Some relatives even expressed concern that their loved ones were buried by a non-Catholic chaplain, or that men were incorrectly labelled.[30] All were faithfully answered with due consideration for the concern of the relatives. It was an essential service which must have brought considerable comfort to the bereaved. Yet it could only have been an onerous task, which, in addition to biblical patience, wisdom, and commonsense, required profound sympathetic understanding of human nature. In this collection of letters, all these qualities are amply evinced.

The Tablet estimated in 1918 that 40,000 had converted to the Catholic faith on the Western Front. One priest, John Myerscough SJ, is reported to have baptized a convert with water from a steel helmet and later gave the same man his first Holy Communion in a shell-hole. Fr Myerscough was going on leave but missed his transport because he came under fire. 'My heart was in my boots, going across open ground, with no cover. On reaching Marcoing I missed my connection.' While returning to his unit, he came across a wounded RFA gunner he had been instructing. A few days later he baptized the gunner, and gave him the last sacrament.[31]

Only one Trappist monk appears to have served as a chaplain in the British forces, Bruno Murphy. A former regular soldier with the Royal Irish Regiment, Fr Murphy had served in Egypt and the Sudan with his regiment. Possibly he was on the Nile Expedition to relieve General Gordon and was inspired by Fr Brindle, his regimental chaplain. After army service he became a Trappist monk and was ordained at Roscrea in 1907. Commissioned 5 September 1915, he served in France until demobilization on 3 February 1920. Perhaps understandably, after war service he did not return to his monastery. Instead, he was accepted by the Aberdeen diocese in 1927.[32]

It would be difficult to find a more remarkable Catholic family on the Western Front than that of the Devases. Charles Stanton Devas was distinguished for becoming a Catholic while a schoolboy at Eton. He later went to Balliol, married, and had nine children. One became a nun, three were priests: Francis SJ, Raymund OP and Philip OFM. All three became army chaplains. Two other sons went into the Army; one was killed. Between them, the five brothers were awarded three OBEs, one DSO and two MCs.[33]

Fr G. Galbraith, of Glasgow, marched with 15th Scottish Division to serve with the occupation forces in the Ruhr, and had the distinction of preaching in Cologne Cathedral. While acting as an officiating chaplain during World War II, for his services to Allied troops he was decorated with the Polish Order of the Golden Fleece and the French *Légion d'Honneur*.[34]

Following service in Salonika where he was awarded the MC, Fr Rupert Roche OP became Catholic chaplain to the Murmansk expedition. He was captured by the Russians and only escaped the firing squad by the intercession of a Polish Catholic officer. The Foreign Office had reported him dead when he returned to read his own obituary.

> Teaching, however, was not to be his career in the Dominican Order, for within a year of his return [from active service], he received an invitation to join an Expeditionary Force to protect White Russia during the Bolshevick revolution. While there, Fr. Roche with a group of men became separated from the main body of the Force, and were promptly surrounded by the Bolshevicks, who arrested them and put them into prison. Some of his captors were Catholics and he told them that he was a priest. The news reached the commanding officer who happened to be a Polish Catholic. The officer told Fr. Roche that he would release him because he was a priest. As far as it is known, the others with him were shot.
>
> Since he did not return with the Expeditionary Force, the Foreign Office posted him as missing. Some months later the Irish Dominican Province presumed him to be dead, and so a solemn Requiem Mass was celebrated in Tallaght for the repose of his soul.[35]

Notes and references

1. Benedict Williamson, *'Happy Days' in France and Flanders* (London, 1920), pp. 97-8.
2. Rawlinson MSS, Box 3231, vii A 3f, DAA.
3. *Glasgow Observer* (4 May 1918), p. 3; quoted by Rev Canon Bernard J. Canning, *Irish Born Secular Priests in Scotland 1829-1979* (Dundee, 1980).
4. Rawlinson MSS, Box 3231, vii A 3f, DAA.
5. English Jesuit Necrology.
6. Ibid.
7. Raymund M. Dowdall OP, DCL, *Memories of Still More Recent Irish Dominicans 1950-1960* (Dublin, 1961), p. 75.
8. Rev J. B. Marshall, *St Francis Magazine*, War Memorial number (1919).
9. Rawlinson MSS, Box 3231, vii A 3f, DAA.
10. English Jesuit Necrology.
11. Rawlinson MSS, Box 3231, vii A 3f, DAA.
12. JAD.
13. Rawlinson MSS, Box 3231, vii A 3f, DAA.
14. Ibid.
15. JAD.
16. Letter from Lt Col K. C. Weldon, 2nd Royal Dublin Fusiliers, Rawlinson MSS, Box 3231, vii A 3f, DAA.
17. Ibid.
18. JAD.
19. Letter, Rawlinson MSS, Box 3231, vii A 3f, DAA.
20. Fr Philip Dominic Devas OFM, *From Cloister to Camp* (London, 1919), pp. 197-9.
21. Ibid.
22. Rawlinson MSS, Box 3231, vii A 3f, DAA.
23. CSSR Archives.
24. Keatinge correspondence, Rawlinson MSS, Box 3231, vii A 3f, DAA.
25. Letter (3 December 1918), Rawlinson MSS, Box 3273, vii A 3j, DAA.
26. *Statistics of the War Effort of the British Empire* (London, 1922), p. 190.
27. Letter, WO to Fr Rawlinson, Rawlinson MSS, Box 3231, vii A 3f, DAA. At this time so greatly was the shortage of Catholic chaplains felt that some conscription of priests was under consideration in 1918.
28. James McRory, *Diary*, Public Record Office of Northern Ireland, Belfast. A moderate example of the diary's intemperate contents is:

   Mgr Keatinge had four priests idling their time at St. Omer, and an hour would take them in the chaplain's car to the firing line, but it was more comfortable and safer to be living in a swell French house than going over the front line. Fr. Rawlinson OSB, was ADC to Mgr. Keatinge, neither of them did any spiritual duties. There was another priest who was called a secretary to Mgr Keatinge, who had no duty at all.

29. Letter (27 February 1918), Rawlinson MSS, Box 3231, vii A 3f, DAA.
30. General letters of enquiry, ibid.
31. English Jesuit Necrology.

32. Canning.
33. WW (1936); English Jesuit Necrology.
34. SCD (1961), Obituaries, pp. 311–14.
35. Dowdall, pp. 45–6.

14

An Episcopus Castrensis *for the British Army*

During World War I Ireland provided 72 front line infantry battalions and many more training and garrison ones. Of these, 59 were mainly Catholic, regular Army or New Army battalions. Three divisions were raised in Ireland, two mainly Catholic, one mainly Protestant. The Irish position in relation to the war effort, shortly after the passing of the Home Rule Bill, was summarized in the *All Hallows Journal* of 1914. In addition to a positional statement, it is a prayer of hope for the future, soon to be dashed.

> As a nation we cannot stand alone. Our island is small and poor, and has no army or navy to defend an independent existence. Hence by a free act we have, for the first time in our history, chosen to be part of the British Empire. We have done so, not through any sense of gratitude, but in a spirit of courageous hope. The democracy of England has extended to us the hand of amity, and we have accepted it. They, on their side, promise to let us have our own customs, habits, and local laws, our own racial and religious characteristics; and we, on our side, consent to become willing members of the Empire. History has taught them and us many lessons. They have begun to realize that government tends to despotism unless checked by powerful institutions and that the co-existence of several diverse nationalities under the same government is one of the best securities of liberty and civilization. We on our side, have begun to recognize, in spite of bitter experience of feudalism and ascendancy, that within the British Constitution there is, both in theory and in practice, more regard for true liberty, more respect for individual, social, and racial freedom than in France or Germany, not to speak of other Continental countries.[1]

These words articulated the thoughts and ideas of many Irishmen who enlisted during the First World War. Although enlistment in the Army caused divisions in the Irish hierarchy,[2] every regular Order and almost every diocese sent chaplains to minister to the Catholic troops. However, it soon became apparent to the Irish bishops, as well as their English colleagues, that all was not well in the operation of the Catholic chaplains' department at Westminster.

As early as January 1915 the Irish bishops had come to the conclusion that the solution to the problem of the provision of chaplains for the Irish regiments was to have Cardinal Logue, and his successors, made Ordinary for Irish garrisons and Irish regular regiments in peace, and for those divisions and other units raised in Ireland in war. A case to achieve this was therefore prepared for presentation to Rome. In a letter to Archbishop Walsh dated 12 July 1915, Cardinal Logue wrote:

> I received from Dr. Sheehan for signature the document to be sent to Rome regarding the appointment of chaplains. I signed it, but I advised him to hold it over till the October meeting for more careful consideration. The suggestions put forward could not easily be carried out in peacetime. This I think would interfere with the success of the other protest which has gone direct to the Pope. If the two documents came together it would look as if the Irish bishops had made a set upon the Archbishop of Westminster and would create prejudice. The protest already sent forward is the really important thing.[3]

In a letter to the Holy See dated 30 June 1915, Cardinal Logue made three specific requests:

> and most humbly beg that Your Holiness deem it worthy
> 1. to appoint the Archbishop of Armagh ... as Ordinary of the military and navy chaplains of this kingdom in equal charge and jurisdiction with the Archbishop of Westminster.
> 2. to offer these two Ordinaries the opportunity to appoint a Senior Chaplain of the Navy and Army as is the case for Protestants in England and Catholics in Italy, Austria and other nations.
> 3. to make sure that only Irish priests are appointed chaplains to brigades and regiments which are made up of Irish for the most part.[4]

The letter asserted that 'Ministers of the Crown complain that no opportunity is given them of judging what indeed Catholics need. And recently ... when a question of the greatest importance to Catholic sailors came up, the Minister for the Navy decreed that it was necessary for him to summon a delegate from the Irish bishops to talk over plans with the Archbishop of Westminster.'[5] This refers to the successful meeting in February 1915 between Winston Churchill, Cardinal Bourne, the Bishop of Waterford and John Redmond which arranged a considerable increase in the establishment of Catholic chaplains for the Royal Navy.

As a result of this letter the Holy See, in August 1915, communicated to the Foreign Office a new arrangement for the supervision of the Catholic chaplains in the British Army and Navy, and this was communicated to Cardinal Bourne by the War Office. Cardinal Bourne went to Rome and on 12 December 1915 was able to write confidently to Sir Henry Howard:

> I have now been able to discuss fully with all here in Rome ... the project submitted to Your Excellency last August by the Cardinal Secretary of State with a view to a new arrangement for the ecclesiastical supervision of the Catholic Chaplains in the British Army and Navy. I am able to assure Yr. Ex. that it is not now intended to proceed further with that project.[6]

However, the British Government gave no formal answer to the Holy See on the matter. At a meeting on 14 July 1916 between Bishop Amigo and Sir Reginald Brade, Under Secretary of State at the War Office, Brade explained that this was because the Government had been told the Holy See were not proceeding with the matter of a new arrangement. Amigo asked Brade to have a formal reply sent to Rome 'which would bring about further communications from the Vatican'. To this Sir Reginald replied: 'From the War Office point of view the present arrangement was satisfactory enough and that they did not like to say that it was unsatisfactory and thus offend the Westminster Authorities.'[7] Whereupon Bishop Amigo:

> pointed out to him that Cardinal Bourne only had the nominations for Commissions and not the appointment of chaplains to different stations (postings), and that he had nothing whatever to do with the officiating chaplains. He (Brade) had understood up to now that Westminster had everything in his hands and that from a departmental side it was much better to work through one channel. This is just what the Holy See would like to have.[8]

Following the failure of their first attempt at reforming the Catholic chaplaincy administration, a meeting of a special deputation of Irish bishops was held on 10 February 1916; afterwards Cardinal Logue sent a further letter to the Holy Father:

> For a long time there has been consideration almost every year in the assembly of Irish bishops about the shortage of priests in the British Army and Navy. What particularly concerned us about this serious matter was the number of Irish Catholics in both forces diligently serving the British King without the spiritual help they deserve ... We have publicly complained on many occasions about the shortage of chaplains especially in the Navy ... With the help of Irish Members of Parliament ... a supply of chaplains was restored far more generously, though as far as the Navy is concerned there is still much left to be desired.[9]

The point of the letter was that 'the existing state of affairs ... seems to demand the Irish Hierarchy to appoint a Senior Chaplain and other

chaplains for Irish soldiers and sailors under the authority and control of
the Apostolic See ... more of our priests, especially suited to the work of a
chaplain, would join up if the nomination of senior chaplains should
concern the bishops of Ireland.'[10] The document then suggested that if this
could not be done, the administration and 'whole question of chaplains ...
be committed to an assembly of bishops partly from Great Britain partly
from Ireland. Perhaps two Irish and two British Archbishops could
compose the assembly. In individual cases the one who presides would be
president following the rules of ecclesiastical precedence.'[11]

At the beginning of 1917, when the students of Catholic seminaries of
Great Britain were about to be conscripted for military service, Cardinal
Bourne again went to Rome to resist efforts to remove Catholic chaplains
from his sole control. In a letter to Mgr Bidwell on 5 February 1917, the
Cardinal outlined the position.

> The situation is this: It is admitted on all hands – that the Curia of
> Westminster has done its work well, and that England has done her part
> nobly in providing Catholic chaplains. But that Ireland has done very
> badly owing, it is alleged, to dislike of Westminster control. And that to
> make Ireland do her duty, Westminster must be set aside, and a Chaplain-
> General appointed if the Government will accept this solution.[12]

Cardinal Bourne's answer was, he explained, what amounted to an
adoption of the formula presented to the Vatican by Cardinal Logue in
1915: 'That the only true method is to throw the whole responsibility on
the Irish Episcopate by giving to Cardinal Logue (with power to name a
Vicar) a position in Ireland analogous to mine in England. Thus in time of
peace, he would be responsible for the camps in Ireland, and in time of
war, would provide and control chaplains attached to regiments raised at
Depôts in Ireland. ... Result would be Westminster remains unchanged, as
defined by Propaganda decree ..., Armagh gets Home Rule with full
responsibility for Ireland.'[13]

His Eminence then asked Mgr Bidwell to ascertain 'confidentially' from
Lord Derby if the War Office would recognize Cardinal Logue in the way
suggested and give his (Logue's) representative a place on committee.[14]
Because letters between Westminster and Rome at this time took seven
days in transit, the letter ended with a request to Mgr Bidwell to wire the
reply.[15]

However, the Sacred Consistorial Congregation were awaiting a reply
from the Foreign Office, London, to their proposals communicated in
August 1916. And for the reasons Brade gave to Amigo, London, with
masterly diplomatic wit, kept silent.

Torn between wanting to return to London and knowing that he dare
not leave Rome with the chaplains' issue unresolved, the Cardinal wrote
again on 13 February demanding 'when will the Foreign Office wake up?

... The Consistorial will not decide the Chaplains question until F.O. answers. If they could be induced to say that they have confidence in me and my proposals, while willing to accept any reasonable suggestion of the Holy See, or any other diplomatic phrase it would help enormously.'[16]

Given the time taken for the letter of 5 February to reach London, Mgr Bidwell's reply to Cardinal Bourne, dated 19 February 1917, could not be regarded as slow. But it was like the curate's egg. Lord Derby proposed to write to Cardinal Logue 'with reference to the nomination of Irish chaplains. Lord Derby's object was to obtain more nominations as soon as possible and he proposed to refer to the conversation I had with him the other day. Sir Reginald asked for my observations. I saw him subsequently and explained that I did not think your proposal had been approved yet by the Holy See and that until it was approved a letter on the lines suggested could hardly be sent to Cardinal Logue.'[17] To answer Brade as he did, and then, while undoubtedly knowing it would hardly please the Cardinal, tell him what had taken place, Mgr Manuel Bidwell displayed all the moral courage, honesty and truthfulness one would expect of a Catholic prelate. The letter ended: 'I reminded him that my interviews on the subject with Lord Derby and himself were merely to ascertain privately whether they would have any objection to the scheme suggested. I said that if he liked I would write to your Eminence to say that Lord Derby would wish to write to Card. Logue as soon as the proposal had received the approval of the Holy See. He asked me to do this.'[18]

However, Bidwell's efforts in London and his reply to Bourne made absolutely no difference to the situation in Rome. In a letter of 24 February, His Eminence explained how he saw the matter: 'The absence of reply from F.O. may make no matter after all. Cardinal Gasparri interprets prolonged silence as meaning unwillingness to accept any change but reluctance to say so. I have of course explained fully the attitude of W.O., - plan proposed is being communicated Cardinal Logue and I must await his reply.'[19] However, this was not Rome's view, as was made clear to Cardinal Bourne later, when the Holy See announced the appointment of an *Episcopus Castrensis.*

At a time of great sensitivity in the relationship between Armagh and Westminster, and spiritual peril for hundreds of thousands of Catholic soldiers, *The Tablet* published tabulated figures on the origin of Catholic chaplains serving with the British and Dominion forces. With questionable coincidence, on 16 January 1917, it printed a review of a pamphlet entitled *Catholics of the British Empire and the War*, and commented that 'in the pamphlet there is full recognition of what the Admiralty and the War Office have done to meet the spiritual needs of Catholics in the Army and Navy. To-day there are 486 Catholic chaplains with the Fleet and the Army, and soon there will be 600. At present the chaplains are thus distributed:

Army		Navy	
British	372	British	30
Canadian	36	Australian	1
Anzac	32	Total	31
India	5		
South Africa	2		
Trinidad	1		
Malta	5		
South America	1		
Newfoundland	1		
Total	455[20]		

At the end of 1916 there were in fact 95 Irish diocesan priests (counting a few CFs on loan to missions in England and Scotland), and 46 from regular Orders in Ireland, serving as chaplains, as well as those from Irish dioceses serving with Dominion and Colonial forces. As was to be expected the table of figures was republished in Ireland with ironic comment.[21] The printing of these figures, which were clearly designed for consumption in Rome, was extremely mischievous, coming as it did at a delicate time in British/Irish relations. The War Office, knowing the truth, and aware of the delicacy of the matter, would not have been best pleased.

Meanwhile, the *Catholic Times* published a paragraph 'Purporting to emanate from its Roman correspondent',[22] to the effect that Cardinal Bourne was in Rome to resist the wishes of the Irish bishops in regard to the military chaplains. In a letter to Cardinal Logue, written in Rome on St Patrick's Day 1917, Cardinal Bourne rejected this 'mischievous paragraph'.[23] At the same time he outlined much of what was to follow, possibly expecting Cardinal Logue to resist the Roman plan.

> I trust that no such idea has entered your Eminence's mind or that of any of the Irish Bishops for it is the direct opposite of the truth. On the contrary I have been fighting your battle as well as ours.[24]

Tracing the history of Propaganda's circular of 15 May 1906, which excluded Ireland and India from Westminster control, His Eminence continued:

> When the Consistorial first realised that Ireland was unprovided for, it did not know of the existence of the decree for England, and proposed to imitate the example followed in Italy at the outbreak of the war here i.e. to name an *Episcopus Castrensis* quite independent of the hierarchy, either of Ireland or England. Without consulting me in any way such a proposal was actually made through diplomatic channels, to our Government at home. The project was to impose an *Episcopus Castrensis* upon us, chosen by the Holy See without consultation with either Hierarchy: and it was very nearly carried into effect. Had the War office not informed me I should not have known what was taking place. Happily the War office,

not being at all satisfied with having an Anglican Chaplain General and not desiring to multiply such offices, showed no readiness to accept such a scheme, and gave me full information.[25]

The fear of the Cardinal about such an appointment was that

It would mean the presence in our midst of a prelate, independent of the two hierarchies, in permanent official relation with the government. In times of peace he would have little to do. Unless extraordinarily prudent and discreet he, or his successors, might easily become a source of extreme embarrassment to the Bishops both in Ireland and England. He would be a *prelato aulico* and the existence of such in Austria, Germany and Spain in connection with the Army has often given rise to difficulty. I urged, therefore, that instead of abrogating the Propaganda Decree it should be completed by giving to your Eminence in Ireland (with power to appoint a Vicar) a position analogous to mine in England.[26]

Cardinal Logue replied on 27 March, and with gentle dryness showed he had observed more in English newspapers than Cardinal Bourne had mentioned. Moreover, he expressed that his real priorities were to obtain a sufficiency of chaplains for the front, while at the same time observing to Cardinal Bourne the harm the table of chaplains printed in *The Tablet* may have done to that objective.

I have received Your Eminence's letter dated from Rome on St Patrick's Day. I have delayed my reply till the time when I thought Your Eminence would arrive at home.

I do not see that the chaplain question and the arrangements regarding it are so pressing as to put Your Eminence to any inconvenience after your long absence and fatiguing journey. There will be a meeting of the Episcopal Standing Committee in Dublin on the Tuesday of Low Week. I shall submit the letter of Your Eminence to the Bishops, and shall communicate to you the views which they may express on the matter. I think this will be the most convenient course for all parties.

The matter really pressing at present is to get a sufficient number of chaplains to attend to the poor fellows at the front, especially now operations have become so intense. I published a fresh appeal in the *Irish Catholic* last week. What effect it may have I don't know yet. I fear the sources in Ireland are nearly dried up. I have [never] known such a dearth of Priests as exists in many Irish Dioceses. I infer, from a Roman Correspondent which I have seen, that the impression is to them that Ireland has sent no chaplains to the front. This is likely to be strengthened by a publication which I am told has lately appeared in *The Tablet*, giving the chaplains from the several countries without a word about Ireland. I fear such things will interfere with my efforts to get chaplains.[27]

The appeal for chaplains to which Cardinal Logue referred was published, together with Lord Derby's letter, on 21 March 1917. Lord Derby had written that he was anxious to secure the help of the Irish episcopate 'towards a fuller provision of spiritual ministration to the troops of the Catholic Church, and I should be very much obliged if you would undertake the responsibility for providing the authorised numbers of Catholic Commissioned Chaplains required for the Regiments the Depots of which are in Ireland'.[28] Cardinal Logue added his own spirited appeal; aimed not only at the intended chaplains, but at parish priests and bishops throughout Ireland.

> No one knows better than I do that it is not from want of zeal nor from the want of the spirit of self-sacrifice on the part of our priests that this want has arisen. I am well aware that they would be prepared to sacrifice not only their ease and convenience, but their lives, to come to the aid of souls in such extreme need. The fact is - a fact which the present circumstances have brought prominently to light - there is a great scarcity of priests in Ireland. In ordinary times there are barely enough, in most dioceses, to meet parochial wants. But it is a question whether parochial claims should not be sacrificed in order to come to the aid of brave men who are in momentary danger of death. Our people at home may be inconvenienced by having their opportunities for spiritual ministration lessened; but they certainly shall not be in such danger of passing out of life without the Sacraments as the soldiers engaged at several fronts.[29]

That the chaplains issue caused a rift between Armagh and Westminster there can be no doubt. Nevertheless, relations between the Cardinal Archbishops, Logue and Bourne, on the evidence of their correspondence on the subject, remained, as one would expect, polite. Only in one letter, from Cardinal Logue to Cardinal Bourne, quoted above, is there a hint of irritation. Following Cardinal Logue's appeal, despite the pessimism he expressed to Cardinal Bourne, a further 56 priests from Ireland volunteered as chaplains in 1917 and 1918.

Mgr Keatinge, who knew nothing of these matters, received a letter from the Sacred Consistorial Congregation in November 1917 informing him that he had been chosen for the position of *Episcopus Castrensis* to the British Army, and that he was appointed titular Bishop of Metellopolis.[30] When the Royal Air Force was created in 1918, the episcopal boundaries of the new bishop were extended to the chaplains of that force. However, the Royal Navy adhered firmly to its moorings at Westminster.

Upon the appointment of Bishop Keatinge, Mgr Bidwell, who was Cardinal Bourne's choice to be *Episcopus Castrensis*, became titular Bishop of Miletopolis and Auxiliary Bishop of Westminster. He was consecrated in Westminster Cathedral, by Cardinal Bourne, on 8 December 1917. In 1918, the King honoured him with the CBE for his services to the chaplains' department.

In the meantime the War Office was slow to relieve Mgr Keatinge in Macedonia, and the bishop-elect did not leave Salonika till 30 January

1918. He arrived in Rome early in February and was consecrated bishop by Cardinal de Lai in the chapel of the Venerable English College on 25 February 1918.[31] Bishop Keatinge arrived in England on 8 March, and assumed his duties at once. His position as regards the War Office was settled later by a letter from the Army Council:

> You will have the office and title of Principal Roman Catholic Chaplain with responsibility for the ecclesiastical supervision of Roman Catholic Chaplaincy services, etc.[32]

The problems Bishop Keatinge inherited were considerable. On the Western Front alone the Catholic chaplains' department was 71 priests (over 20 per cent) under strength.[33] He found that there were two priests dead, fourteen wounded or gassed and at least four prisoners of war (one was on his way home); plus two 'going home' for disciplinary reasons. Morale among chaplains was not high, because they were overstretched and overworked. There were also a few unsatisfactory chaplains who had to be dealt with administratively (retired without recourse to court martial).[34] 'I have found out already that some bishops are not, to put it mildly, "business-like".'[35] Nevertheless, there were hopeful signs of reinforcements; Keatinge had 'seen the Archbishop of Liverpool who promised more priests as a result of Autumn moves'.[36]

Because of these casualties, battle and administrative, by October 1918 the shortage against establishment had risen to 91, without including the newly formed Royal Air Force which accounted for another fourteen. In a letter to Bishop Keatinge, Fr Rawlinson wrote that more men would lift morale, adding: 'We are the only denomination that is not fully up to strength.'[37] Rawlinson then urged Keatinge to write to the Catholic press giving details of shortages and their effects.[38]

Amongst other headaches, the problem arose of thousands of Chinese labourers imported for construction work behind the lines, some of whom might be Catholic and ought not to be neglected spiritually. Fr Van Dyke, a Chinese-speaking priest, was to visit 'our Chinese units in the British zone' to find out how many were Catholics.[39] There were also two Maltese priests attached to British troops on the advice of Cardinal Bourne whom Fr Rawlinson found unsuitable to work with British troops because of lack of understanding; and an Irish priest who came into conflict with the military authorities because of 'no tact!'[40] He resigned shortly after the Armistice.

The peace brought more, not fewer, problems. Every Provincial and bishop expected his priests back home almost at once. Most pressing were the Fathers Provincial of the Benedictines and Jesuits. The Jesuits had given more than a quarter of all Catholic Army chaplains, and no Order (or diocese) had suffered heavier casualties. To the Provincial of the Society, Fr John Wright SJ, Fr Rawlinson wrote:

If there is one thing that is quite certain, it is that the greatest consideration is due to the English Province of the Society for the magnificent way in which they have responded to the needs of the Army. Without their help it would have been impossible to carry on at all and they have certainly done their share to bring about the glorious victory we have gained. Words will always fail me when I refer to the work of the Society during the war.[41]

The Royal Army Chaplains' Department (RC)

On 1 October 1920, the RAChD was reorganized. The arrangement thus made laid down that all of the denominations should be co-ordinated under the Chaplain-General, who was a member of the Church of England, and that there should be under him a deputy Chaplain-General, who would belong to another religious denomination. Bishop Keatinge refused to come into this scheme although great pressure was brought to induce him to do so. Since 1858 Catholic chaplains had been directly under the Secretary of State for War through the Adjutant-General, the normal Army chain of command. Keatinge felt it was quite impossible for him to change this, and place himself and his chaplains under the orders for administration or for any other purpose of clergy of another denomination. After interviews and correspondence with the Under-Secretary of State for War he received a letter, stating the following terms:

> As the accredited representative of your church, you will be consulted by the Secretary, War Office, or an official under him, on important administrative orders which will be issued by the Secretary, War Office, in the name of the Army Council. You will exercise supervision over Roman Catholic Chaplains in ecclesiastical matters and will hold the title of Principal Roman Catholic Chaplain with your present grading and rank of Chaplain (1st. Class).
>
> In the various commands the Senior Roman Catholic Chaplains would deal direct with the G.O.C. or his lay staff officer, and in stations where there is only one R.C. Chaplain, he should have direct access to the G.O.C. or his lay staff officer, and be under him. That is to say, that in no case will R.C. Chaplains be under a Chaplain of any other Denomination either for administration or other purposes.[42]

Catholic chaplains therefore continued to come directly under the Adjutant-General in accordance with the arrangements made with Bishop Grant. In the modern British Army chaplains of all denominations come under the control of, and are administered by, the Adjutant-General's Branch, exactly as Catholic chaplains have since the Crimean War. 'From then on, we began to be organised. He taught us our duties, he helped us in our difficulties, he fought our battles and he gave us an *esprit de corps*. Now he is gone. But his work will live. He welded our different elements into one body with one consistent policy. It is now no longer individual missionaries but a Diocese that works for God, and the difference is immense.'[43]

In 1924 the number of Catholic chaplains had shrunk to nineteen. Considering the reduction of army strength to below the 1914 levels, and the disbanding of ten southern Irish Catholic regular infantry battalions, this was a fair proportion. In many small military stations at home and throughout the world, civilian officiating chaplains continued the work of ministering to the troops where Army chaplains could not. In that year, Bishop Keatinge, under King's Regulations, was due to retire from the Royal Army Chaplains' Department. Such was his prestige, and the great respect in which he was held, the Under Secretary of State requested him to continue, as a retired officer, the work of Army Bishop.[44] Bishop Keatinge died in office on 21 February 1934.

> His life work was the spiritual welfare of the British Soldier. When he joined the Army, he found Catholicism unorganised and chaotic, while of spiritual life among Catholic officers or men, except in a few cases, there was none. He fought a lone hand, unaided by anyone, and was often opposed where he had the right to expect assistance. But his courage and fair dealing won him respect everywhere. He never compromised the Catholic position and knew how to refuse the kingdoms of the earth, rather than betray the flock committed to his care. In the end, the very people whom he opposed could not but recognise his sense of honour and they honoured him.[45]

References

1. 'Some aspects of the war', *All Hallows Journal* (Dublin, 1914), pp. 90–1.
2. Patrick K. Callan, 'Ambivalence towards the Saxon shilling: the attitudes of the Catholic Church in Ireland towards enlistment during the First World War', *Archivium Hibernicum*.
3. Letter, Logue to Walsh (12 July 1916), Cardinal Logue Papers, AAA.
4. Letter, Logue to Pope Benedict XV (30 June 1915), Cardinal Logue Papers, AAA.
5. Ibid.
6. Letter (dated 12 December 1915), Bourne to Howard, Chaplains correspondence, AWA.
7. Letter (14 July 1916), Amigo to Logue, Chaplains correspondence, ASA.
8. Ibid.
9. Letter, Logue to Pope Benedict XV (February 1916), Cardinal Logue Papers, AAA.
10. Ibid.
11. Ibid.
12. Letter, Bourne to Bidwell (5 February 1917), Chaplains correspondence, AWA.
13. Ibid.

14. Ibid.
15. Ibid.
16. Letter, Bourne to Bidwell (13 February 1917), Chaplains correspondence, AWA.
17. Letter, Bidwell to Bourne (19 February 1917), Chaplains correspondence, AWA.
18. Ibid.
19. Letter, Bourne to Bidwell (24 February 1917), Chaplains correspondence, AWA.
20. *The Tablet* (16 January 1917).
21. 'Catholic Army Chaplains: a diary', *The Catholic Bulletin and Book Review*, vol. VII, no 4 (April 1917), p. 257.
22. Letter, Bourne to Logue (17 March 1917), Chaplains correspondence, AWA.
23. Ibid.
24. Ibid.
25. Ibid.
26. Ibid.
27. Letter, Logue to Bourne (27 March 1917), Cardinal Logue Papers, AAA.
28. *The Irish Catholic* (21 March 1917).
29. Ibid.
30. Keatinge's correspondence (April 1918-November 1919), Rawlinson MSS, Box 3231, vii A 3f, DAA.
31. Rawlinson MSS, War History Box, DAA.
32. Ibid.
33. Ibid.
34. Ibid.
35. Letter, Keatinge to Rawlinson (24 September 1918), Rawlinson MSS, Box 3231, vii A 3f, DAA.
36. Ibid.
37. Letter, Rawlinson to Keatinge (4 October 1918), Rawlinson MSS, Box 3231, vii A 3f, DAA.
38. Ibid.
39. Letter, Rawlinson to Keatinge (24 May 1918), Rawlinson MSS, Box 3231, vii A 3f, DAA.
40. Ibid.
41. Letter, Rawlinson to Wright, in reply to his of 9 November 1918, Rawlinson MSS, DAA.
42. Letter, WO to Keatinge, Rawlinson MSS, Box 3231, vii A 3f, DAA.
43. Mgr Mullins, quoted by Brian Plumb, *Arundel to Zabi: A Biographical Dictionary of the Catholic Bishops of England and Wales 1623-1987* (Warrington, 1988)..
44. Ibid.
45. Ibid.

15

Peace and the Phoney War 1927–1940

Such was the temper of the country in the years between 1927 and 1937, that when the Army estimates for 1931 were introduced into the House of Commons, a motion was made to abolish the Chaplains' Department. Dr A. C. E. Jarvis, the Anglican Chaplain-General, defended the armed forces against the charge of fostering war and denounced 'the attempts to discredit religion in the army'.[1] Four days later, at the 1931 Spring Assembly of the Congregational Union of England and Wales, Dr F. W. Norwood called for the abolition of Army chaplains. 'He sought to get the Assembly to decide that in future it would refuse to nominate Chaplains to the Forces unless on an entirely voluntary basis, on the ground that a chaplaincy implied "general consent to the war system", and put the Churches in an anomalous position.' The motion was held in abeyance for one year.[2]

Nor was support for military chaplains wholehearted in the Catholic Church. The previous year Bishop Keatinge had sought an interview with Bishop Amigo of Southwark, to request a Southwark priest for a naval chaplaincy. His experience led him to write what can only be described as an astonishing communication between bishops.

> ... it seems incredible that you could not see me for a few minutes in the last three weeks, or even in the near future, even granting you were busy. I don't think any other bishop would test a brother bishop like that. However, my Lord, you can rest assured of one thing, and that is, I shall not trouble you again for an interview.[3]

Paradoxically, as the British Army retrenched, because of the technical advances made during the Great War of 1914-18, modern warfare became more complex, in armoured mobility, aircraft support and radio communications. Close co-operation between all arms of the Army and

the RAF, controlled by the use of radio, had contributed greatly to the
major British advances during the last hundred days of the First World
War. The major lesson of this vital period of the war had been learned
mainly by the vanquished. With great dedication and zeal, they prepared
for the next round aided by Hitler. The victors, rendered impotent by
Government policy, could only watch until almost too late for adequate
preparation.

In 1936 the threat posed by Hitler's Germany to the stability of Europe
could no longer be ignored by the Government, and measures were
reluctantly taken to improve national defences. The Army expanded; the
3rd Division which had been reduced to a cadre was reconstituted with
reservists; the number of Territorial Divisions was doubled, and an anti-
aircraft Army Corps was created. In the RAF new fighter squadrons were
formed and the aircraft building programme was accelerated; and vitally,
an early warning system organized. In conjunction with the rapid build-up
of armed strength, the Chaplains' Branch expanded. In the 1920s and early
1930s there was only one Catholic chaplain serving with the Territorial
Army, from 1936 onwards there was a steady increase in numbers.[4] The
lessons of chaplain shortages in 1914 had been well learned by the new
forces Ordinary. However, his fellow-bishops were less easily persuaded of
the national danger. This was especially the case with the Royal Air Force.[5]

Catholic chaplaincy on the outbreak of war

The working life of Mgr James Dey, apart from seven years at Oscott, was
given to the services. He had gone to war with the BEF in 1914, had been
awarded a DSO in France, and succeeded as Catholic Ordinary to the
Army and RAF in April 1935, about fourteen months after Bishop
Keatinge's death. At the luncheon following his consecration as *Episcopus
Castrensis*, he made plain to his fellow-bishops the extent of his feelings for
his life's work.

> In his own inimitable and pawky way he chaffed his brother bishops there
> assembled and compared his happy lot with their less fortunate one; he
> had no Chapter to be a check upon him, no devout females to worry him,
> no financial magnates to embarrass him. It was great fun listening to him
> but through all the persiflage there sounded a note of noble tribute to the
> army. My flock, he said, are not concerned with markets and money-
> making, they are self-dedicated to service – the service of their country.[6]

Cardinal Bourne died within a few months of Keatinge and was succeeded
by Cardinal Hinsley, who continued the special relationship with the Royal
Navy, but with a difference which will be told later. Cardinal Bourne had
continued to neglect both naval chaplains and the spiritual welfare of
Catholic seamen right up to his death. Cardinal Hinsley had memories of

those dreadful days and his approach to service chaplaincy was less authoritarian and more spiritual than his predecessor's.

> Hinsley's interest in the ethical and political considerations of national policy in wartime extended to the spiritual provision for Catholic servicemen. At variance with his own bench of bishops, Cardinal Bourne had opposed the Holy See's appointment of a military bishop, or *episcopus castrensis*, in October 1917, thus demonstrating his reluctance to devolve any of his tightly cherished authority as Archbishop of Westminster. The Holy See patiently awaited a chance to resolve this situation, well aware, as was the Admiralty, that the naval chaplains were never ecclesiastically visited nor the port chapels inspected. Bishop Keatinge, the first military bishop, and Cardinal Bourne died within months of each other, and Hinsley, anxious to delegate and ferociously opposed to the current slackness of [naval] chaplaincy discipline and administration, gratefully received Mgr James Dey as the military bishop ...[7]

Bishop Dey had many difficulties to overcome. Starved of funds by the Air Ministry and War Office, who had higher priorities in the financially straitened circumstances imposed by the Government, he was almost ostracized by his fellow-bishops, and was not allowed to attend the Bishops' Conference except when service chaplaincies were discussed.

Dey's pleas for more chaplains in the growing emergency had met stiff opposition, and as late as April 1939 the bishops, blind to the lessons of twenty years before, passed the resolution 'that the Religious Orders be approached and asked to be prepared to supply Chaplains for the Reserve'.[8] Bishop Dey did indeed approach the Jesuits and the Benedictines, and they gave him the priests he needed – for the moment. But in the emergencies of total war more and more priests were demanded, and some of the bishops were found wanting in caring for their spiritual children in uniform.

Army Catholic chaplaincy

With the vast expansion of the forces in World War II, it again became important to establish that Catholic chaplaincy services in the Army and RAF were administered separately from the Chaplain-General's Branch. It was established that Catholic chaplains were responsible to the Under Secretary of State at the War Office and the Under Secretary of State at the Air Ministry in consultation with the Bishop in Ordinary. The Admiralty continued to deal with Westminster on matters pertaining to Catholic chaplains in the Royal Navy.

In 1939 the number of Catholic chaplains with the services was: RN twelve; Army eighteen; RAF ten. The Territorial Army had been totally neglected by the hierarchy throughout the 1920s and early 1930s – only one Catholic chaplain served during 1924–34; from 1935 there was a slow build-up until on the outbreak of war there were 26 priests serving with the reserve Army. Of the 287 chaplains to the forces serving in the Regular Army and Territorial Army on the outbreak of war, 54 were Catholic.[9]

Mgr J. M. Coghlan was Principal Chaplain (RC) Army on the outbreak of war. He was appointed Vicar-General for the Army in 1940, and retained both posts until the end of the war. Following the precedent set by Mgr Keatinge in World War I, when the BEF went to France at the end of September 1939, Mgr Coghlan positioned himself, with an assistant, at HQ BEF in France, leaving Bishop Dey to control chaplains from London.

Bishop Dey, who as a chaplain in 1914–18 was renowned for his mordant wit, had much to contend with from his fellow-bishops in the early years of the war. Despite his earlier reluctance to accept 'friars', once the war started, he found them available and eminently suitable. Many secular priests were willing to volunteer, in the middle of the war, but some bishops were still reluctant to release them to serve in the forces. Southwark was a notorious example. At the end of 1942 of 435 secular priests available in the diocese only seven were chaplains. By comparison, Brentwood, a much smaller diocese with 99 priests, provided five.[10] However, Archbishop Amigo pointed out that Southwark was in the front line, and he provided 50 officiating chaplains if the Home Front was included.[11] Bishop Dey had made clear his views about officiating chaplains in war-time to Archbishop Amigo in a letter eighteen months previously. 'I am prepared to admit that very often when the priest is genuinely interested in the military men and completely sympathetic with them, and when he is an exceptionally energetic and devoted pastor of souls he can be moderately successful in his military work, provided he has easy access to them. But he cannot get this access in war time unless he is in uniform and he cannot be in uniform unless he is a regular chaplain.'[12]

In August 1942, Bishop Dey, obviously losing patience, went public with the 'straightforward incisiveness and directness'[13] for which he was known. In an open letter, copies of which were sent to all bishops, Rome and *The Tablet*, he denounced Archbishop Amigo's attitude to the provision of chaplains to the Forces as 'outrageous' and drew his attention to its significance.

> By refusing to allow Southwark clergy to minister to Southwark men and women in the forces, 1) you place under a virtual interdict all Catholic men and women who are your subjects and who are loyally risking their lives in defence of their religion, their country and their freedom. 2) You throw an unfair burden on all your brother bishops, whose priests will have to undertake the care of your unjustly forsaken people in addition to their own proper responsibilities. Your failure to fulfil your just obligations will make an undue call on their Christian charity in order that your shortcomings shall be made good. 3) You stultify the action of the Holy See, which as a result of the sad experience in the last war,

established the appointment of an *Episcopus Castrensis* precisely to secure for Catholic soldiers what you are now deliberately taking away from them i.e. a ready access to the Sacraments.

In 1938 the Government was asked to release Church students from the obligations of compulsory military service. One of the reasons you brought forward in favour of the privilege was that unless they were released there would be fewer priests in the country, and in case of war it would not be possible to give the army the military chaplains it might require. The Government gave what you asked for; do you not think that you are in honour bound to keep your side of the bargain?[14]

In early 1943, Cardinal Hinsley wrote to the bishops of England and Wales giving a breakdown of numbers of serving chaplains by diocese, and what the numbers would be if 10 per cent of the known strength of priests became chaplains. The dioceses of Westminster, Cardiff, Hexham, Lancaster, Menevia, and Middlesbrough exceeded the ratio. Most of the larger dioceses were below, particularly Leeds and Liverpool; Southwark was far below.

Of the 680 serving chaplains, 238 were from religious Orders in Great Britain; 259 from England and Wales; 22 from Scotland; Ireland, secular and religious, and overseas, provided 161.

The Cardinal's letter warned that 'many more chaplains are needed now' and told the bishops that the matter 'must certainly be raised at the Low Week Meeting'.[15] Such was the shortage of chaplains in the Army, that when two chaplains fell ill just before D-Day, finding replacements completely occupied the staff chaplain (RC) of 21st Army Group throughout 5 June 1944.[16]

A chaplain's introduction to the Army in 1939

A typical example of the recruitment, and introduction, to service life was that of a Benedictine monk of Fort Augustus, near Inverness. His experience was not remarkable and could be multiplied by every newly-recruited chaplain. Following the declaration of war, Fr Denys Rutledge sought permission from his Superior to offer his services as chaplain to the forces, which was granted. The War Office sent him an application form, and Fr Rutledge was instructed to have a medical examination. He was accepted as Temporary Chaplain 4th Class (Captain) and instructed to report to HQ Scottish Command, Edinburgh. He was informed that his pay would be fifteen shillings *per diem*, he was to provide his own uniform and equipment (a uniform allowance was provided). He also had to provide himself with a portable Mass kit, which could be purchased from Burns, Oates and Washbourne. The War Office made a special allowance to RC chaplains to cover this latter.[17] (Later in the war, an altar cloth was provided, with a piece of altar stone sewn into it.) Fr Rutledge reported on

9 October 1939 to Edinburgh as instructed, and met several other newly-commissioned chaplains. However, information about his future movements was not immediately available.[18]

> At the same moment there arrives the senior chaplain who has the task of posting us. A veteran of the Royal Flying Corps of the First World War, appearing now with wings and major's crown, he is, like the rest of us, a 'new boy' to the Royal Army Chaplains' Department and knows no more than we do of the dispositions of Scottish Command, the location of its forces and the pastoral needs of its units. He asks us to report at 15.00. In the meantime he will settle into his office and try to come to grips with the situation.[19]

On the following day, 10 October, Fr Rutledge reported to 6th Cameronians (Scottish Rifles), at Hawick. His Army service, pay and allowances, began on that day. It was an unlikely regiment for a Catholic to be posted to, descended as it was from a body of armed men raised to resist the imposition of the Episcopal Church on Scotland by King Charles II. 'An ancient regiment of Covenanters, bearing the Bible ceremoniously at the head of the column, carrying their rifles to Kirk and throwing out a protective cordon round the building in case of a surprise attack by the wicked Episcopalians, would not be the most likely choice of residence for a Catholic chaplain but he has no choice ... My reception is polite and friendly, but rather less than enthusiastic.'[20]

It was a Territorial Army unit of long standing and a Presbyterian chaplain had served with the battalion since before the war. He, naturally, was well entrenched, having a firm grasp of the regimental history, traditions, customs and personalities. However, a local priest, who had been a World War I chaplain, and had previously acted as officiating chaplain to the battalion, gave Fr Rutledge very useful information and advice from his own service experiences. He then comments in his diary upon the lack of training, or briefings, given to chaplains, not realizing that it had been to prevent this situation that Bishop Dey had been appealing, unheard, since long before the commencement of the war, for chaplains.

> It seems remarkable that there should have been no ecclesiastical equivalent of the Military Staff College, something on a very modest scale, where, for at least a few days, one might have learned the basic formation of an army, the organization of the medical services, the customs and traditions of an officers' mess, and even just how, when, whom and where to salute, instead of being thrown in at the deep end and left to sink or swim.[21]

The chaplains at war – France 1939–40

The War Office decided in 1939 to unify the Chaplains' Department of the BEF, and Mgr Coghlan was appointed assistant Deputy Chaplain-General.

The DC-G to the BEF was an Anglican. It was a return to the unified system of 1915–18 which in 1915 the Anglicans had withdrawn from, and against which Bishop Keatinge had fought in 1920. Mgr Coghlan together with a Staff Chaplain, Fr Basil McCreton, with the rest of the Chaplains' Department, were part of the rear element of BEF Headquarters stationed near Arras. Throughout the bitter winter of 1939–40 the troops toiled at improving the defences, and carried out open warfare training when they could.

Rarely was an overseas command fully up to establishment in Catholic chaplains, but the front always had first priority. Being only one to a brigade of three fighting units, based upon the experience of the First World War, in action the chaplain usually positioned himself at a section of the Field Ambulance which received wounded from battalion regimental aid posts (RAPs). Where there was an Irish battalion, or a majority of Catholics in one battalion, the chaplain might position himself at the RAP of that battalion. More usually in battle he was at an Advance Dressing Station or a Main Dressing Station. Naturally, before the battle he would have toured all the battalions in the brigade to minister the sacraments to the troops. But always the chaplain had to be prepared to go forward to minister the last sacraments to those in need of them. Usually he had a good working relationship with stretcher-bearers and medical orderlies, who kept him informed of any Catholic in need of his comfort.[22] Chaplains of all denominations were positioned with Casualty Clearing Stations and Field Ambulances, a mobile hospital unit.

Every casualty passed through a Casualty Clearing Station (CCS); on arrival an envelope was given to him which eventually contained all his medical records and moved with him through the medical system until his discharge. In addition to his regimental particulars: number, rank, name and unit, it also showed his religious denomination. 'It was the privilege of a Catholic Chaplain to mark an abbreviated sign under the name showing what sacraments had been administered to the patient while in his care.'[23]

Chaplains who buried soldiers usually wrote to the next of kin. 'Whenever I conducted a simple burial service, I always wrote to the next of kin to let them know that I had conducted the funeral, and to console them with the news whenever possible, that the soldier had received, thank God, the last rites of the Church. Such letters were always highly appreciated by the families concerned, and their letters of thanks were often very touching and really edifying.'[24]

Mgr Coghlan's deployment list for chaplains as the BEF prepared to embark for France showed many vacancies. Of 58 establishment posts, only 23 were filled, by either regular chaplains or reserve chaplains from first and second line reinforcements. A further seven names were 'pencilled in', leaving 28 posts in rear echelons, base hospitals and hospital ships, unfilled. In the circumstances, it was impossible to detach any chaplains to the UK bases to provide training for newly-commissioned chaplains, although in early March 1940, when he could be spared, Fr Stapleton was posted from GHQ Staff to UK, as a senior chaplains' staff officer.

However, progress was made and on 2 March 1940, Mgr Coghlan was able to report to Bishop Dey that all posts in the BEF were filled with 76 priests to whom he had presented the '*Pagella* of Faculties' – the instrument of authority as a Catholic chaplain. He then suggested to the bishop, 'if your Lordship has not already done so may I suggest it is now urgent to have Chaplaincy Services arranged for British prisoners of war in Germany. The Foreign Office is, I think, the proper channel.'[25] In view of what was about to happen in France, it was a timely reminder.

Since the Crimea, Catholic chaplains serving troops in the field were markedly different from all other service chaplains in religious essentials, their spirituality and devotion to sacramental duties. To minister the three essential sacraments, sacramental confession, Holy Communion and Extreme Unction, and to bring these, especially the last, into the front line, the priest took great risks to personal safety. Their example in this during World War I profoundly influenced many Anglicans, causing considerable debate during the 1920s on the nature of the sacraments. As a result of this, during World War II and thereafter, outward differences between Anglican and Catholic chaplains were markedly less. Moreover, in the course of the war, some Anglican priests and Protestant pastors attended Mass on occasion; especially Midnight Mass at Christmas.

The retreat to Dunkirk

When the rear HQ BEF in the Arras area was threatened by the German breakthrough and was ordered to withdraw to Boulogne on 15 May 1940, Mgr Coghlan and Fr McCreton were driven on roads crowded with refugees, often attacked by German aircraft. For almost a week they moved from place to place in this chaos of crowded roads under air attack. On the way they visited military hospitals, giving spiritual comfort where they could. Eventually, they arrived at Boulogne; here Rear Army HQ was established until 23/24 May when it was evacuated to England, leaving Mgr Coghlan and his staff behind.

In the movement of troops by rail, one chaplain, Fr Gerard Lake SJ, was wounded at Amiens by enemy aircraft attacking the railway.

Following the evacuation of rear HQ BEF, it was to Bergues that Mgr Coghlan's party was ordered to move. On arriving there they attached themselves to an Advance Dressing Station, helping the medical officers attending the wounded, and burying the dead. They were joined by a party of Belgian and French nuns, some of whom were trained nurses. Included in the wounded was a German from an armoured unit; 'Very smart soldier and well dressed; left arm smashed to bits.'[26] He had been brought in by French soldiers.

No matter how well conducted, the fog of war is never denser than in a fighting withdrawal. Up to 28 May, refugees, headquarters echelons, and service troops had withdrawn through their positions; on this day, fighting troops of the divisions began to fall back; the experienced chaplains then knew it was nearly time to go. Amongst the troops were their chaplains and Fr McCreton saw Frs Hobson-Matthews (1st Divisional Artillery), Ford (53 AA Regt), Withers (144 Brigade) and McNulty (7th Royal Warwicks). Seeing this withdrawal it was deemed advisable to evacuate the nuns to Dunkirk. Bergues came under enemy shell-fire on the 29th and engineer demolition parties began destroying everything of value including the railway station. A heavy pall of smoke lay over Dunkirk and soon smoke began to arise also from Bergues. That night, 29/30 May, a message was received ordering evacuation.

> At Ypres gate midnight. Giddins drove Mgr Coghlan and self in Humber. Main road to Dunkirk impassable so convoy, including 500 men on foot, took devious track much pot-holed with half-broken bridges. Heavy gunfire audible on both sides of gap, fields flooded by French. No lights allowed or smoking. Moved very slowly; everyone much keyed up. May 30th arrived beaches at dawn. Deserted car on dunes, surprised at number of troops on beaches.[27]

They tried but failed to embark at Dunkirk's docks; there were too many wrecks in the harbour and German planes overhead to allow this. They could see ships standing three miles off-shore firing at the attacking planes: 'terrific A.A. fire and tracers from destroyers'.[28] The chaplains' party decided to take their chances on the open beaches where a few days earlier Fr G. Hobson-Matthews OSB was killed, the first British chaplain to die in action in the Second World War. One of the armada of little ships spotted their party, but was unable to take all. The chaplains waited for the next and were eventually taken aboard an already overloaded cutter which took them to HMS *Impulsive*. In the embarkation *Impulsive* was damaged and had to limp to Dover but arrived safely that night. For his bravery and devotion to duty in the course of the retreat and evacuation, Fr McCreton was awarded the Military Cross. Another priest who was awarded a Military Cross was Fr T. Duggan for his sterling service with 151 Brigade. Later he was relieved by Fr Nesbitt of Lancaster and sent as SCF to Northern Ireland. There, the influence of this Nationalist Irish priest did much to counter the anti-British views of the Rt Rev Neil Farren, Bishop of Derry, who refused to become Vicar-Delegate to British Troops in Northern Ireland,[29] but willingly accepted that responsibility for American troops when they arrived in Northern Ireland.

The defence of Calais

The magnificently stubborn defence of Calais against overwhelming odds was the most forlorn and gallant of all British actions in France during May 1940. Undoubtedly, if Calais had fallen earlier than it did, the evacuation of the BEF from Dunkirk would not have been possible. During the bitter house-to-house fighting, Fr Vincent Gallagher SJ was wounded and captured. For some time nothing was heard about him, and the War Office reported him 'Missing, presumed killed'. Fr Gallagher spent the next four years in prison camps. 'He could have returned to this country in 1943 when there was an exchange of prisoners, but he chose to stay behind in order to let a married man go in his place.'[30]

St Valéry-en-Caux

The 51st Highland Division had been on its way back from a training period on a sector of the Maginot Line in the Saar region, when the German breakthrough occurred. They became cut off from the main BEF and trapped at St Valéry without hope of evacuation. Exhausted, short of rations and ammunition, after a resistance of several days the division was forced to surrender. Over ten thousand Scots marched into captivity. Attached to the Cameron Highlanders was Fr Kenneth Grant (later Bishop of Argyll and the Isles), a six-foot-one Highlander. As for tens of thousands of captured British soldiers, two weeks of marching through France, Belgium and Holland followed, short of rations and hungry most of the time. They were imprisoned in various camps in Bavaria and as the years wore on and hope of victory and release faded, Fr Grant's spiritual and temporal leadership saved many, even from suicide. During the long periods of great hardship the soft Highland brogue would speak encouragingly.

> 'Lift up your eyes to the hills,' he would say, pointing to the Alps, and then he would talk of the hills and glens of home which they would surely soon see again. He won the confidence of his captors, and thus won some measure of relief for his comrades. He kept bees, and lectured on their care, and on other subjects, he organised language classes, Gaelic and others. He persuaded many to use every spare moment of their time gainfully, making time pass more easily until victory brought release.[31]

Fr W. Scanlan, of Salford, had not been in France long when he was hurried back to the coast again, accompanied by his batman/driver. After three days on the beaches he spotted a small boat drifting off shore. He decided to swim to it, row it back and pick up some more people for evacuation when the next large vessel appeared. Handing his pyx to his batman, he explained that it contained the Hosts, asked him to take care of it; immediately on landing he was to go to the nearest Catholic church and hand it to a priest there, with the explanation that Fr Scanlan gave it to him.

> Bill swam out, and had only strength to pull himself aboard the boat, in which he flopped down unconscious. When he came to he found himself on board a naval vessel under the care of a doctor.
>
> After demobilization (in October 1945), he was a guest of the Sisters of St Joseph, near Altrincham; there also was Bishop King of Portsmouth. In the course of the meal the Bishop told of his experiences as a parish priest in Portsmouth during the war. Among them an anecdote about 1940, when a soldier appeared on a Saturday evening carrying a pyx given to him by a chaplain on the Dunkirk beaches. The Bishop concluded 'I often think what happened to that chaplain?' The reply came instantly 'He is at this table with you, my Lord'. To the delight of the other guests present, both then filled in the gaps of the story.[32]

The heaviest single loss of life during the evacuation from Dunkirk occurred when the hospital ship *Lancastria* was sunk by German aircraft. Fr Wilfred Murray CSSR was a much stronger swimmer than Fr Scanlan. He needed to be, to survive the sinking of *Lancastria* in which he was chaplain. However, not only did he save himself, but two others as well.

> A very gentle, lovable person. During the evacuation (from Dunkirk) he was on the *Lancastria* when it was sunk by a German bomb.
>
> A strong swimmer, Wilf saved one man from drowning, and helped another to stay afloat till they were picked up.[33]

The second BEF

It is remarkably little known that a second BEF to France was mounted in June 1940 shortly after the evacuation of the first BEF, with much loss of men and matériel, from Dunkirk. Mainly composed of the 52nd (Lowland) Division, its sojourn in France was short-lived. This second BEF could, however, have resulted in the complete loss of the Lowland Division which, on top of the loss of the Highland Division, would have been a major disaster for Scotland. Two of the Catholic chaplains with 52nd Division were Fr Patrick McNally and Fr Denys Rutledge. The latter accompanied 6th Cameronians to France and just before the battalion departed, it was reviewed by the King. Fr Rutledge commented in his diary: 'He looks very worried, as well he may considering what is happening at Dunkirk ...'[34]

On 11 June 1940 the battalion crossed to France. Brigade HQ was established at St Omer, but within days orders were received for immediate withdrawal. A long drive in convoy through the night took the troops to Cherbourg; on the way orders were given to dump all baggage. 'During the hours of daylight on the way here one has noted the roadsides littered for mile on mile with baggage and equipment of every kind, most notably officers' valises burst open, the contents strewn in the ditches. A retreating army is a sorry sight.' On the outskirts of Cherbourg the battalion dismounted from their vehicles and marched the last nine miles. Fr Rutledge marched with them. Arriving at Cherbourg he found warehouses full of army supplies which were to be set on fire to deny them to the enemy. Vehicles were sent on to the jetty. He noted that 'No attempt is made to marshal troops in the proper formations, they are shepherded aboard as they arrive ...'[35]

His vessel sailed without the battalion headquarters. Fr McNally was evacuated through St Malo at about the same time.

In the shake-up, within both the Government and the Services, which followed the disasters in Norway and France, it was found necessary to reverse the experiment of a unified Chaplains' Department. Within weeks of his return to England Mgr Coghlan was installed at the War Office as Principal Chaplain (RC)

> directly responsible to the Under Secretary of State, for the organization and administration of Catholic chaplaincy services in the British Army at home and abroad, and as Bishop Dey's representative in this and ecclesiastical affairs.[36]

As the war spread further afield and intensified, and the pressure of work upon the Principal Chaplain increased, he found it necessary to take an assistant, Fr E. J. Warner SJ, who remained in post until 1947.[37]

For a long period after Dunkirk the United Kingdom was under threat of invasion by the German Army, bombed by the German Air Force, and its life-line with the world was almost cut by U-boat attacks on its merchant marine. Yet, the sense of humour, of all the peoples of these islands, which has sustained soldiers and sailors in many grim moments, was undiminished. Fr Fergus Cronin SJ was working in a military hospital in the Faroes, when asked by a bombardier (with an injured hand) serving in 11th (Ulster Battery) RA to write a letter for him: 'Saying, "if my mother knew that this was written by a Parish Priest, she would burn it before she read it". I said that if he liked I could get the Protestant Chaplain to do it for him, to be told: "what have I got to do with a so-and-so Englishman? After all, blood is thicker than water".'[38]

Whatever happened to Original Sin?

Notes and references

1. *Daily Telegraph* (9 May 1931).
2. Ibid. (13 May 1931).

3. Rev Michael Clifton, *Amigo: Friend of the Poor* (Leominster, 1987), p. 158.
4. *Army List* for 1931–40.
5. Of the 229 wartime RAF CF, 35 were from English or Scottish dioceses. All the others were from religious Orders or Irish dioceses, plus a few from Australia, India and the United States. RAF Chaplains List - COA.
6. Rev Gosling SJ, panegyric, ABA.
7. Thomas Moloney, *Westminster, Whitehall and the Vatican* (London, 1985), pp. 144–5.
8. *Acta* of the Bishops' Conference (18–19 April 1939), item IV.
9. *Army Lists; Air Force Lists;* G. Taylor, *Sea Chaplains* (London, 1978), p. 545.
10. ECD (1942).
11. Letter, Amigo to Dey (5 November 1941), ASA.
12. Letter, Dey to Amigo (11 July 1940), ASA.
13. Gosling.
14. Letter, Dey to Amigo (5 August 1942), ASA.
15. Letter, ASA.
16. Rev J. W. Jones, Notes, RCCA.
17. Fr W. C. Hayes OSB, letter to the Abbot of Downside (9 December 1939), DAA.
18. Dom Denys Rutledge OSB, 'Padre's progress: diary of an unknown British Army chaplain in the Second World War', unpublished, pp. 2–4.
19. Ibid., p. 5.
20. Ibid., pp. 5–6.
21. Ibid., p. 7.
22. Rev Martin Dempsey (ed.), *The Priest Among the Soldiers* (London, 1947), p. 95.
23. Rev E. J. Swift SJ, 'In and around Belsen', *Letters and Notices* (Journal of the Society of Jesus), vol. 90, no. 399 (1990), p. 130.
24. Ibid., p. 131.
25. Letter, Coghlan to Dey (2 March 1940), RCCA.
26. Dempsey, p. 26.
27. Ibid., p. 27.
28. Ibid.
29. Canon Bernard J. Canning, 'Scotland's wartime spiritual contribution', *Scottish Catholic Observer* (5 August 1994).
30. Rev Vincent Gallagher SJ, *Letters and Notices*, vol. 68, no. 30 (1963), pp. 65–9.
31. 'Scottish Obituaries' (1960).
32. Memoir, RCCA.
33. Obituary, CSSR Necrology.
34. Rutledge, p. 25.
35. Ibid., p. 31.
36. Dempsey, p. 3.
37. Ibid.
38. Rev Fergus Cronin SJ, 'A bed of roses', *Interfuse* (Journal of the Irish Province of the Society of Jesus), no. 41 (1986), p. 53.

16

The Middle East, North Africa and southern Europe, 1940–1943

The Middle East

The vastness of Middle East Command which at one time stretched from Macedonia to Kenya and from Tunis to Tehran presented problems unique to the senior Catholic chaplain, Mgr Joseph Stapleton. He had been an army chaplain since May 1916 and had served in France and Flanders including all the battles from the Somme to Third Ypres. After the war he went to the Rhine Army with the occupation forces and was in East Prussia and Silesia during 1919–22. Long service in Egypt, Palestine and the Sudan in the 1920s and 1930s made him eminently suitable for his appointment as Senior Chaplain (RC), Middle East Command in 1940.[1]

His priestly jurisdiction included Egypt, the Western Desert, Palestine, Syria, Cyprus, the Red Sea littoral, the Sudan, Eritrea and for a time Iraq and Iran. Across this vast area was scattered the British Army, soon to be reinforced by Australians, New Zealanders, French, Poles and many others. In 1940 the number of chaplains ministering to the troops was 'under thirty' and rose to 154 in 1943. There was a distinct difference between ministering in the forward areas and in the rear areas, which called for his judgement in selecting the postings of newly-arrived chaplains.

Rear areas

The large base areas of the Middle East were concentrated in Egypt, mainly at Alexandria; Gizeh, near Cairo; Tel el Kebir; and in the Suez Canal Zone between Port Said and Suez, especially around Ismailia. A report from a chaplain in one of these areas to his old college magazine best describes the work.

Actually this is a base hospital,... a fair size camp which has its own Catholic church. The church is small, but good and well furnished, and I was able to carry out on a minor scale the Holy Week ceremonies, finishing up by singing Mass on Sunday. Not so bad for the Army – the choir were pretty good at plain chant.

The only trouble is that I have to make shots at speaking about five languages. Still, all the words you need in the equivalent English are Yes and No, Mass, Confessions, Confiteor, Sins, Are you sorry? (a pair of rosary beads to indicate penance), Act of Contrition. It is possible to manage quite well with that much ... I am lucky compared with some, and I must say that on the whole I am enjoying life. It is certainly a much quieter life here than that to which I grew accustomed in England. No bombs, no real black-out, although our turn may come.[2]

The infantry brigade chaplain

Very different was the work of a chaplain near the front line. Every brigade had a chaplain for each of the main Christian denominations. Usually he was attached to a major unit, a regiment or battalion, and became part of that unit's welfare team. The Catholic chaplain, on the other hand, unlike his many Protestant colleagues, was responsible for all the Catholics in a brigade. Without a nearby civilian Catholic church and priest to help, he alone had to minister to all the units, and not just brigade headquarters or the unit he was attached to. Tactical dispersal in the vast space of the desert, a roadless waste, increased the difficulties, which at times were compounded by adverse climatic conditions. An isolated instance illustrates how misunderstanding could arise. An over-zealous staff officer, possibly in field security or intelligence, reported a Catholic chaplain to Headquarters Middle East Forces 'as he gave evidence of having "fifth-columnist" tendencies: he was known to be frequently away on unknown missions to go as much as 100 miles to visit distant units: he spoke foreign languages'. The priest was recalled to Cairo, where investigation revealed the truth, and the misunderstanding.[3] The priest returned to duty; history does not record the name of the embarrassed staff officer. Once in action, however, the chaplain generally attached himself to the advance dressing station, working close to the surgical teams.

North Africa

In 1940 the fall of France allowed the Italian army to concentrate in Cyrenaica, and cross the Egyptian border. The much smaller British Western Desert Force occupied defensive positions inside the Egyptian frontier at Mersa Matruh. The Italians progressed slowly across the frontier, halted in front of the British, and then moved into defended 'boxes'. In early December 1940 the British struck with lightning swiftness and caught the Italians completely by surprise. General O'Connor instantly turned his limited-objective operation into a major offensive and routed the Italians; Sidi Barrani and Sollum were quickly captured. Switching his 4th Indian Division for the fresh and very aggressive 6th Australian Division while on the move, British armour and Australian infantry captured Bardia, and shortly afterwards, Tobruk. During the attack on Tobruk, Australian infantry noticed Italian wounded being ministered to by what they quickly realized were chaplains, and to their credit directed their fire away from the kneeling figures.[4]

During the disastrous British intervention in Greece, Fr John Berry CSSR was attached to a hospital unit in Greece in 1941 which was overrun by the Germans. The British and Commonwealth prisoners were herded into railway box-cars, where they were shut in, and not allowed to leave them for over a week. Fr James Knowles, of Middlesbrough, had better fortune with his unit, and after the evacuation he was 'mentioned in despatches'.

The desert chaplain

In military history the infantry have been described as the queen of the battlefield. During the desert war the armoured formations were undoubtedly the ace of trumps. The work of the chaplain in an armoured brigade was relatively easier than with an infantry brigade. The brigade consisted of three armoured regiments which were generally deployed with one in the line, one in support and one in reserve in a harbour area, resting and refitting. The first two were ministered to by attending to their wounded at an advance dressing station. In addition, because of their concentration, he could also effectively minister to the regiment in harbour. Here it was always possible for the chaplain to get the Catholics together, hear confessions, say Mass and give Holy Communion.[5]

One of the most gruesome tasks of a chaplain attached to an armoured formation was removing dead bodies from a knocked-out tank for burial; especially from one that had 'brewed-up' – burst into flames. As one chaplain put it simply: 'Much less did I like trying to get dead bodies out of knocked out tanks and burying them. Still it had to be done.'[6]

While ministering in an advance dressing station one priest was at first shy of joining the medical team as they attended to a seriously wounded victim. But he quickly discovered that medical staff, who at other times might be somewhat irreligious, expected the chaplain to be involved, and were somewhat scandalized if the patient was not ministered to.

> This applied too, generally, to non-Catholic wounded, when one tried to help them as they were about to meet the Creator. At first, I was nervous and hesitant. One could not even be sure that they believed in God, or

wished to hear about Him. And yet, I found that at such moments there were few who did not feel the need of Him. I remember on one occasion suggesting to one poor lad, whose face was one great wound, that he should say some prayer, and his whispered reply - 'I don't know how - help me say some'.[7]

The siege of Tobruk

The first siege of Tobruk was notable for the aggressive nature of its defence. In one company attack the 2/43 Australian Infantry Battalion lost 106 out of its strength of 129 when the Australians charged into a minefield. To retrieve the wounded, the battalion chaplain, Fr T. Gard, advanced with an NCO under a flag of truce. They made contact with the local German commander, who allowed them to evacuate the dead and wounded; and also brought out some wounded they had treated, and some dead from close to the German position.

> They brought four wounded and let the truck come up to take them away. Then they carried out the bodies of fifteen dead and helped us with those in the minefield. I told the doctor we were four short and he replied that three of our wounded had been taken away in ambulances earlier that morning: another badly wounded, had chosen to stay because his brother had been taken prisoner ... He saluted me and I saluted him.[8]

Following the German breakthrough at El Agheila, Tobruk was invested on 1 April 1941 and withstood an eight months' siege before it was relieved in December 1941. An Italian priest who had remained at his post in Tobruk continued to say Mass in his church. However his Mass was now attended by Allied troops, until it was struck by a shell from a long-range gun known as 'Bardia Bill'.

> Early in the siege about 200 men were at Mass being said by a captured Italian padre. During the service a shell from 'Bardia Bill' landed right on the back wall of the church. Bricks and mortar flew everywhere. But a statue of Our Lady of Lourdes situated near the point of impact escaped unscathed. And none of the worshippers was hurt. In fact, neither they nor the padre moved outside until the service was over. Thereafter, General Morshead decreed that church services must be held in the open.
> Attendances at Mass in Tobruk varied, sometimes one or two would be able to attend; other days up to 30.[9]

After the advance which relieved Tobruk the British suffered another reverse of fortunes, and Tobruk was invested yet again on 14 June 1942. It was now held by British and South African troops under a South African, General Klopper. When the Germans attacked with a preponderance of armour under cover of a heavy artillery and aerial bombardment the almost open town fell in just under a week, on 20 June. A battalion of the Cameron

Highlanders was the last to surrender; they then 'marched into captivity in perfect order, led by their Colonel and to the sound of their pipes'.[10]

During the German counter-offensive Fr Denis Bankes was wounded and taken prisoner. During the same action Fr D. P. Angold OSB had been involved in a tense action in which German and British tanks had been exchanging fire over his truck. Following this he was a German prisoner for five minutes. 'When the German officer who captured him discovered that he was a chaplain he confiscated his watch and told him to get into his own truck and drive in front of him. Fr Angold's driver moved ahead with alacrity, did a quick detour and found his way safely back to Tobruk.'[11]

Fr George Forster had but recently arrived in Egypt and was attached to the Sherwood Foresters. On the morning of the German attack, Fr Forster started Mass at 0645. 'Accompanied only by my faithful server ... I was reciting the Roman Canon, when the desert exploded as if struck by a thousand thunderbolts. Batteries of German and Italian guns poured salvoes of shells into the Tobruk defences. Then came waves of dive-bombing Stukas ... I felt very conspicuous in my white alb and gold chasuble and I was very frightened. I glanced round for a little reassurance but the server had wisely disappeared. I finished Mass with what I hope was decent haste, unvested and packed up the altar in record time ...'[12] Fr Forster spent the next three years in captivity. Also taken prisoner were Fr Edward Hodgson and Fr Edward Gibson CSSR.

El Alamein

When the great artillery barrage which opened the battle began two Australian priests were standing in the darkness admiring the spectacular illumination of the gun flashes. One said to the other: 'What a glorious sight! I've never seen the like of it before.' To which a voice from the darkness replied: 'If you don't bloody well get into a slit trench you'll never see the like of it again.'[13]

A British tank battalion, the 40th, was supporting the Australian attack, but ran into a German minefield and suffered heavy casualties. The chaplain, Fr Hayes OSB, in a letter to his Abbot, told him:

> I am fit and well. We were in the forefront of the battle and for us it lasted the first fortnight – then it got too fast for us and we are now having a wee bit rest before presumably going forward. I avoided trouble during the battle although I can't say I much enjoyed the night bombing. Much less did I like trying to get dead bodies out of knocked out tanks and burying them. Still it had to be done.[14]

With 51st Highland Division was Fr George Conlon. He had served as a combatant officer in World War I, and had volunteered immediately war was declared. A letter written by a soldier of the division to a Glasgow paper, shortly after the war ended, shows the depth of feeling there existed in the ranks of the division towards their chaplain. 'How well we recall the days below a blazing sun in the unfriendly desert when Father Conlon erected an altar and we gathered around him to hear Mass. We remember it all and our hearts fill with gratitude and justifiable pride to God's servant, our chaplain, as they did when we witnessed his courage, devotion and example in the grim moments of actual combat.'[15]

After the Battle of El Alamein, there was a Requiem Mass at the cemetery. Notice of the Mass had been sent out to units at short notice, it was a voluntary service, with no compulsion to attend. 'But the spontaneous response of the men provided an edifying spectacle when about 2,000 of them gathered to pray for the repose of the souls of their dead comrades.'[16]

Ministering to prisoners of war

> Things are looking up. The Italians are very funny when they are being brought in. Quite cheerful and very happy to be in a cage. They wave their hands to you. The Gerry is quite different, sullen and very proud – some of them in tears. One lot of Italians sent in had waited patiently for three hours before they were finally taken away – no one had any time to spare for them and they made several attempts to get captured but no one seemed to want them. Train loads have gone back.[17]

There were well over 100,000 Italian prisoners of war in the Middle East. Most were Catholic, and there were few Italian chaplains to minister to them. In the desert the British chaplains did what they could. Fr James Adamson OSB had been a regular officer of the South Lancashire Regiment in World War I. After the Great War he resigned his commission and became one of the many former soldiers to enter the priesthood. 'If you come back from a war minus an arm, a leg or an eye, you attract sympathy', he wrote, 'but if you come back physically intact but mentally scarred, few people discern your affliction.'[18]

Posted to the Middle East, Fr Adamson served in the Western Desert during General O'Connor's first offensive where tens of thousands of Italian prisoners were taken. It was Easter 1941 and several thousand young Italians wished to fulfil their Easter duties. Learning of this, Fr Adamson obtained a tin of army biscuits and broke them into fragments, and drove in his three-quarter-ton truck to the prisoner-of-war encampment – an open space in the desert, surrounded by barbed wire. There he said Mass on the tailboard of his vehicle, and consecrated the biscuit. Then, through a public address system he had connected, he announced, through an interpreter: '... "I'm going to recite the Ten Commandments – one by one. If you have broken any of them tell God you're sorry and I'll give you all absolution." And so the Mass was celebrated and three or four thousand young men discharged their Easter duties.'[19]

Following the conquest of Cyrenaica, as a result of German propaganda the Italian settlers fled, leaving the Catholic clergy isolated and religious places deserted. Bedouin tribesmen began despoiling and pillaging churches. The British military authorities responded by taking two Italian bishops, 36 clergy and 47 nuns on to army ration strength. 'Meanwhile the chaplains had visited the outlying churches and removed all the plate and valuables to the vaults of the cathedrals in Derna and Benghazi and afterwards at their request all those buildings were securely bricked-up by the Royal Engineers.'

When Tripoli, the capital of Libya, was eventually captured in 1943 the massed pipes and drums of the 51st Division led a victory parade through the city. Afterwards a High Mass of Thanksgiving was said in Tripoli Cathedral. The Cathedral was filled to overflowing with 3,000 Catholic troops of which over 1,000 received Holy Communion. It had an edifying effect on the Italian population, and not least on the Italian clergy. 'The Bishop of Tripoli quickly sized-up the situation and published a pastoral letter which helped in a marked degree in bringing about the submission of his diocesans and their full acquiescence in all orders issued. The Nazi propaganda had overreached itself. News travels fast ... it had a considerable effect on the Italian mainland and helped to bring about the capitulation of Italy which followed some months later.'[20]

Operation Torch

Operation Torch was the Anglo-American descent upon Algiers at the end of 1942. Possibly the best known chaplain in the British 1st Army was Fr 'Dolly' Brookes, 1st Irish Guards serving with 24th Guards Brigade.

Fr Rudesind Brookes, better known in his battalion as Fr 'Dolly' Brookes, had been a regular officer in World War I, serving in 2nd Irish Guards under the then Lt Col Harold Alexander; they remained firm friends throughout their lives. Like many former soldiers he entered the Church after the war. On becoming a chaplain with the Irish Guards, his former service with the regiment naturally endeared him to 'the Micks'. Shortly after he joined, 24th Guards Brigade embarked for North Africa. Not unnaturally, the chaplain of a Catholic battalion bound for active service was kept busy in his professional capacity:

> Unlike the other officers whose heaviest task was a little censorship, I was very heavily employed. There is nothing like the prospect of action for concentrating the mind: and this was reflected in the large attendances at my daily Mass and still more by the endless queues for confession. Some put it off to the last moment; but I reckon that by the time we reached Algiers I had shriven a very high proportion of both officers and men![21]

The battalion arrived in Algeria shortly before St Patrick's Day. On the previous day, the Anglican brigade chaplain, not being aware of the custom of the regiment, made a decided *faux pas*. Possibly knowing that the commanding officer, Lt Col A. Montagu-Douglas-Scott, was Anglican he enquired of him what arrangements were being made for non-Catholics. The instant reply was icy: 'I would like you to know that I command a Catholic Regiment and on St Patrick's Day we all go to Mass.'[22]

The Battle of the Bou

During the battle to break into the Tunisian plain, 24th Brigade was involved in a brigade attack on Bou Assoud.

During the battalion's approach march to the start-line, Fr Brookes stood conspicuously on the side of the road during a halt. Seeing him there, soldiers slipped out of the ranks for what was to be his final blessing.

> As I stood there, first one soldier, then another, then another slipped out of the ranks and knelt in front of me for my blessing before returning quietly to their places. Very many of these brave Irish lads were to die in the battle so soon to come; and for me it was one of the most moving experiences of the whole War, reminding me of what I had heard of the Regiment kneeling to be blessed before battle in 1914.
>
> ... The carnage was terrible; but fortunately night fell and under cover of darkness our men managed to climb on to the Bou and clear it of the enemy.[23]

Armoured formations exploited the infantry success and a week later Tunis was captured. After the Battle of the Bou, the survivors of the Irish Guards gathered on 'Hill 212' to hear Mass said by Fr Brookes.

Following the capitulation of the last German forces in North Africa, Fr Bernard Benson, attached to 1st Airborne Division, was able to arrange for the restoration to captured German priests of their rank and duties as captain-chaplains, thus allowing them to minister freely to the German Catholic soldiers.

Shortly after his return to Australia in 1942, one 'Digger' was able to write with feeling about a priest he had come to know well in the desert. Let his words speak for many.

> Those Middle East days are not so far behind that my imagination turns interludes to mere romantic fiction. I still see them as composed mostly of discomfort, petty anger over petty muddles, sore-throated thirst, sharp, mean twinges of fright, and boredom; above all perhaps of boredom. But odd hours with the padre on the way to the desert form a picture that is different. He could bring grace to a bleak wadi when he celebrated Mass at dawn with a solitary trooper attending, or to a hut full of rowdy men when he sat talking among them. He gave a pattern to the untidy

trivialities that are war, and to have glimpsed a pattern in those wastes is to have brought something of value from the desert.[24]

The work of the chaplain in the Western Desert demanded 'great zeal, high physical endurance, courage and initiative'.[25] In the North African Allied armies none of these high qualities were found wanting in any of the priests who ministered to them. Moreover, the priests themselves were not specially selected and trained Army chaplains. They were men who until recently had been engaged in the quiet, sedentary life of parish or monastery, an occupation ill-suited to equip anyone with the robustness necessary to endure the physical strain and mental anguish of modern war. Unlike the soldiers drawn from civilian life to serve their country, the priest in battledress was completely untrained for battle. It is to their everlasting credit that in the crucible of battle they passed a chaplain's supreme test – unflinching ministers of God among soldiers at the hour of death.

Invasion of Sicily, July 1943

On 4 July 1943, before embarking with the Hampshires, Fr Rutledge, now a typical brigade chaplain, visited the major units of the brigade, the Devons and Dorsets, on board other ships of the convoy. There being no time for Mass, he gave general Absolution and Communion. In addition to the Hampshires there were African troops on board his ship, a labour force of Basuto tribesmen. He discovered that many were Catholics and ministered to them for the duration of the voyage, and also baptized the catechumens amongst them. He then had what he describes as a little problem. It is one which experienced chaplains are very aware of. The call of religion comes strongest to soldiers when facing imminent battle. 'I realise that I may not have enough altar breads to last until I can find a new supply in Sicily. I have been using an exceptionally large number since we have been on the way, embarked and waiting for several days, larger than expected with no possibility of obtaining more.'[26]

Having ascertained that the flour he used was pure wheaten, Fr Rutledge asked the ship's baker to bake some very thin discs of flour and water. These provided Fr Rutledge with several sections, each a good yard long. When these were broken into small fragments they were suitable for Communion, and he considered there was enough to last until he found proper altar breads. On the day before the landings at Pachino, southern Sicily, Fr Rutledge said Mass at 0630; he had 150 in his congregation at Mass.[27]

When the first assault-wave went in Fr Rutledge was not allowed to embark, going instead with the second wave. As often happens in war, this met stiffer opposition from an alerted enemy. 'One landing craft only yards away receives a direct hit as I step ashore and goes up in flames.'[28] All day in the July sun Fr Rutledge toiled throughout the brigade landing area

under shell-fire, visiting the regimental aid posts of the Devons and
Dorsets, the brigade advance dressing stations, and the main dressing
station, before rejoining the Hampshires in the evening. His brigade met
fierce resistance at Caltagirone, and suffered heavy casualties. This had a
direct bearing on his pastoral care, and his altar breads.

> There have been so many casualties that I have had to celebrate Mass four
> times on the side of the road in order to replenish my stock of
> consecrated hosts as viaticum for the men. Each time I am reasonably
> certain that I shall not need more, yet I do. Only in such an emergency
> may one celebrate so many times and at any hour of the day. At one point
> I am fortunate enough to meet a group of reinforcements, young fellows
> just arrived and being sent immediately into action. I am able to gather
> together the Catholics among them and give absolution and holy
> communion. For some it is to be their first and last battle.[29]

A few days later he records what he describes as a typical 'warm' night.

> The Devons are to put in an attack on a German strong point during the
> night. Accordingly I move in with the medical team. The attack is not
> successful and the RAP team never even succeeds in reaching the point
> where it is intended to set up business. We are pinned down by heavy
> mortar fire from 2330–0330 … There is no cover and all we can do is to
> become as flat as possible on the ground. It is clear that we are under
> enemy observation. At dawn when we retire I am able to count nine shell
> craters all within yards of me.[30]

In the assault on Sicily, Fr D. F. Hourigan SC parachuted in with 1st Para
Brigade. In the days that followed, the paratroopers were involved in heavy
fighting in the face of determined German resistance; Fr Hourigan, being
with the forward elements, was naturally in constant danger. On the
evening of 10 July he was caught in German fire and killed. 'His knowledge
of the Italian language was of great value and it is known that he kept right
up with the advanced troops, using his knowledge in the interest of
humanity whenever possible.'[31] A curious insight into inter-faith relations,
which does not reflect well on the religious tolerance of some Christians,
was given in a letter written to the Father Provincial after Fr Hourigan's
death by a Jewish chaplain, 'who said that alone out of all the officers
Father Hourigan treated him with friendliness and with many acts of co-
operation and kindness, which had left an indelible impression upon his
mind'.[32] Fr Bernard Benson replaced Fr Hourigan. Later with the
paratroopers he too gained immortality.

When the enemy had been cleared out of Sicily, a Benedictine chaplain
serving with a Light Field Ambulance wrote to his Father Abbot, roundly
denouncing the clergy of Sicily.

> Meanwhile the show is over and quiet has descended on Sicily. The people
> are quite glad to see us - it means the end of the war for them. But the

Sicilian clergy could do with a Reformation – they are rather addicted to Fascism. A reform of the Italian clergy seems necessary. They embarrass us.[33]

Fr W. Hayes was perhaps hasty in his judgement. He overlooked the struggle between the clergy and the Mafia, and that the Fascists, alone of all governments in Italy in modern times, succeeded in its suppression. The Allies, unwittingly, used the Mafia in the newly-formed civilian administration. The result is that the evil, once essentially Sicilian, is now international.

Italy 1943–45

After the landings at Salerno, 1st Guards Brigade arrived with 46th Division. Attached to the brigade was Fr George Forbes OSB. Fr Forbes had trained at RMC Sandhurst and was commissioned into the Grenadier Guards before resigning and becoming a monk of Ampleforth in late 1923. Fr Forbes again received the King's commission in September 1940, as a chaplain. After service in Army hospitals, in March 1943 his dearest wish was fulfilled when he succeeded in serving again with the Guards, 1st Guards Brigade, during the final battles of the North Africa campaign. While the Guards rebuilt their strength in North Africa, Fr Forbes, anxious to serve in the front line, managed to have an attachment at the Pachino bridgehead in Sicily before his landing in Italy. Following almost immediately upon landing, the Guards were involved in a bitter battle to establish a bridgehead across the river Garigliano. Then, despite adverse weather conditions, the Guards continued the attack for the high ground on Monte Ornito. 'In really bad weather it took as long as thirteen hours to get a (wounded) case to a wheeled vehicle in this sector.' His account, written long afterwards, is full of praise of others but 'revealing little about himself.'[34] However, the recommendation written by the commanding officer of 2nd Coldstream Guards for an award of the Military Cross to Fr Forbes, which was gazetted on 29 June 1944, is more revealing.

> This officer was with my Bn when occupying positions in contact with the enemy in the vicinity of Mt. Ornito from 8 to 20 Feb. During this period the Bn was constantly subjected to artillery, mortar and small arms fire and was attacked frequently. The conduct of this officer was beyond praise throughout. He showed a complete and utter disregard for his personal safety, and was always to be found where the battle was fiercest or the shelling most intense, giving courage to the wounded and dying, and inspiring the remainder by his complete contempt of danger. He frequently organised and accompanied parties to go forward from our position in order to bring in wounded. He was an inspiration to the whole battalion, and I am not skilled enough with a pen adequately to describe his conduct.

The Brigade commander supported the recommendation, adding:

> The same facts concerning this officer's conduct have been told to me by both the Welsh and Grenadiers, as a result of his visits to them. He has indeed been an inspiration to all ranks.[35]

A chaplain attached to a regular battalion was rarely far from the front line. Fr Patrick Bluett, of Middlesbrough, attached to 2nd Royal Scots Fusiliers in 17th Infantry Brigade was one. In the line close to Minturno, north of Naples, he met Corporal Vincent Vokes, an Intelligence Corps Catholic attached to the Fusiliers. Vokes, on Observation Post duty, was trying to locate an enemy self-propelled gun which had been giving trouble, and was watching the ground through binoculars. 'Can I have a look?' asked the chaplain. 'Certainly, Father', was the reply. After a little, without lowering the glasses, Fr Bluett spoke: 'There's a house down there flying the Italian flag back to front.' Handing the glasses back to Vokes, Fr Bluett pointed out the position of the house. Fixing the house, Vokes identified the 88 mm gun of a Tiger tank. The crew had secreted the tank in a house, with the gun poking through a window, and flying the Italian flag to conceal the muzzle brake. The quick eye of the priest had penetrated the error with the flag. As Vokes telephoned the target co-ordinates to a battery position, he told the priest: 'You had better go back now Father, there's going to be killing here.' The priest, realizing he had unwittingly involved himself in action against the enemy, left.[36] Not far from Alfedena, he joined one of the forward companies of the Fusiliers and heard that another company was cut off in the town, having suffered casualties who could not be evacuated until night because of fire-swept open country. Aware of the danger Fr Bluett nevertheless realized he might be needed, and went forward in his vehicle. The enemy opened up with shell and machine-gun fire. Having ministered to the casualties he returned the same way. The citation for the Military Cross he was subsequently awarded stated that 'his disregard for danger had a most invigorating effect on the company'.[37]

Anzio, 1944

The landing at Anzio in January 1944 was intended to create havoc behind the German lines, capture Rome, and possibly bring an early end to the war in Italy. Two of the best known chaplains to serve in it were Frs Brookes and Cavanagh, both serving with 1st Division.

Chaplains are not exempt from reading their daily Divine Office, in peace or war. Battalion chaplains in action found it necessary to fulfil the obligation whenever the opportunity was presented, whatever the circumstances. In the forward positions at Anzio there was little cover. But one of the best remembered is a railway embankment held at one time by 1st Irish Guards. During a lull in the course of one of the most intense enemy bombardments of the campaign, Fr Brookes decided it was an opportunity not to be wasted. Rising from a dug-out, he walked up and down the railway line, in customary fashion, absorbedly reading his breviary. His coolness under fire could not fail to have an effect upon the Guardsmen; it certainly earned him a mention in the battalion war diary.[38] So heavy were the casualties suffered by the battalion, that when relieved, after six weeks, their numbers were reduced from 1,080 to 267.

Fr Cavanagh was less fortunate; there was no relief for him. He remained in Anzio until the bridgehead was relieved following the break of the German winter line. By then the strain showed. 'I met Father Cavanagh the other week in Naples at a Day Retreat. He had just come back from Anzio ... Looks very weary, and was rather depressed.'[39] Even shipping off-shore at Anzio was not safe, and the hospital ship *St David* was sunk by enemy action. Fr Patrick Bluett, mentioned earlier, was lucky not to be killed when he received serious chest wounds at Anzio.

St Benedict's monastery, Cassino

In the winter of 1943-44, Monte Cassino formed the pivot of the German winter line. Flanked by formidable natural obstacles it dominated the Allied positions in the Liri valley, and halted their advance. The monastery was bombed by Allied planes and destroyed in February 1944. General Alexander told his friend Fr Brookes that 'Giving the order to bomb the abbey had been the most difficult decision he had ever had to make, but that he had finally decided that men's lives must come before stones however holy'.[40] It has to be borne in mind that General Alexander was cousin to Fr Bernard Rawlinson OSB, V-G to the BEF 1915-19. He most certainly would not have taken the decision lightly.

Several chaplains have written that they witnessed German war matériel in the ruins of the abbey after the battle. However, the Germans claimed that they did not move into the sacred precincts until after it had been bombed. Certainly the ruins of the building afforded much better defensive positions than a standing building could possibly have done. In the fighting to take the monastery ruin Fr Joseph Wakefield of Nottingham distinguished himself and was mentioned in despatches.[41]

Fr Reginald Moore CSSR was awarded the Military Cross, because, according to himself, 'There was a wounded man near our front lines, screaming in agony. The CO said someone would have to go out and bring him in, so I thought, "Golly! I'd better do it. So I did. Simple as that." ' His obituary gently commented: 'Perhaps Rex didn't know the meaning of fear, but I doubt it.'[42]

Visitors to Rome

Rome fell in June 1944 to General Mark Clark's American Fifth Army. By ignoring the agreed plan of operations and snatching a moment of glory, Clark allowed the German defenders to slip away. However, before the Eternal City was liberated, Fr Ambrose Conlon, of Achonry, made some hair-raising journeys through the German lines with food for Jewish refugee children hiding in convents within Rome. In recognition of this he was later honoured by being made a Papal Prelate by Pope Pius XII.[43]

Mgr John Clarke, of Liverpool, was SRC (RC) at HQ Central Mediterranean Forces. Upon the retirement of Mgr Coghlan in October 1945, Mgr Clarke was destined to become his successor. With him at the headquarters was Fr H. Alban Boultwood OSB, who, with a group of Catholic soldiers at GHQ Italy, began publication of *The Sword*, a monthly publication of Catholic Action.[44]

Rome had been cut off from a major part of the Catholic world for four years and many visitors flowed in. Military, political and church leaders, of all denominations, flocked to St Peter's. One of the eminent visitors who had a private audience with the Pope was the Chief of the Imperial General Staff, Field-Marshal Sir Alan Brooke, a Northern Irish Protestant. He had a misfortune while touring new excavations in the foundations of St Peter's which tore his Achilles tendon and calf. He was in agony; however, not wishing to miss the audience with Pope Pius XII, he duly arrived in the audience chamber at the appointed hour. It was a long and painful walk through corridors and many chambers with the Swiss Guard; his batman had a soldier's remedy handy, medicinal brandy.

> I am afraid that I must have created a very poor impression on the Pope! My leg was hurting very badly and I did not know how I would ever manage the visit, so Lockwood, my invaluable batman, took the matter in hand and gave me the largest brandy I have ever drunk!
>
> It had a marvellous effect as regards restoring my morale, and with the help of two sticks I felt like facing anything, but when I entered the room swaying on two sticks and breathing brandy I am certain the Pope wrote me off as one of those drunken Orangemen from the North of Ireland ... In any case he was certainly quite charming and never disclosed his feelings.

They discussed 'Russia mainly and its threat to the peace of the world'.[45]

Mgr Humphrey Bright, a former Territorial Army chaplain, who had served with the BEF in France, and then in West Africa, was an SRC CF in Italy. He was at Rome in 1944 when Cardinal Rossi, the Apostolic Chancellor, summoned him to the Vatican to inform him that Archbishop Williams of Birmingham had requested him as Auxiliary Bishop, and the Pope had approved. He was placed under a vow of secrecy.[46] That afternoon he met Archbishop Griffin, whose promotion to Westminster, on the death of

Cardinal Hinsley, had created the vacancy Mgr Bright was about to fill. However, because of the vow of secrecy, the elevation of Bright was not discussed, although Archbishop Griffin would certainly have known about it.

Extreme Unction in a minefield

The German holding campaign in Italy was conducted in masterly fashion, although it wrecked the Italian communications infrastructure. Every crossing of a natural obstacle had to be examined carefully.

> At first light we 'stand to' and investigation shows that the ground from the bridge down to the water, the route for one who wishes to avoid the bridge, is indeed mined. In clearing a path one of the Sappers, a Catholic, is blown up. I go to minister to him taking care to tread in what I assume to be his footsteps to where he is lying. He is alive and one of his companions has already given him the standard injection of morphia, duly indicated on his forehead.[47]

Ministering to a dying fellow-chaplain must be more difficult for a priest than any other wounded soldier, for the thought 'there but for the grace of God go I' must surely pass through his mind. Fr G. Hart, of Glasgow, who had only recently arrived, was on duty at a forward dressing station when a Presbyterian chaplain was brought in mortally wounded. 'He was quite conscious and Fr Hart went to him and told him he was a Catholic priest. He knelt down beside his dying fellow-chaplain and they prayed together until the wounded chaplain had breathed his last.'[48]

Not all commanding officers were as readily co-operative with chaplains as they might be. Sometimes they had their own priorities, depending upon the operational situation, especially if for some reason a visiting chaplain should arrive later than scheduled. Many chaplains had to visit several units spread over a wide area, which meant considerable travel in difficult conditions. Timetables could alter drastically. Fr T. Candlish MC, of Lancaster, is reported to have had 'twelve Masses on Sundays, travelling from camp to camp'. He recalled that on one occasion he arrived at a particular camp to say Mass, only to be told by the CO that it was a very inconvenient time. 'Very good sir, I will just put in my report to the GOC that I arrived at an inconvenient time.' On this occasion there appears to have been no operational necessity for the CO's insensitivity, for 'within three minutes an altar had been set up for Tommy to say Mass'. Just before Fr Candlish left Italy to return home at the end of the war, he placed his Military Cross on a shrine to Our Blessed Lady, as an offering of thanksgiving.[49]

During the winter of 1944–45, amongst the snows of the high Apennines, the Lovat Scouts, all hardy Highlanders, were quite at home. They were, however, without a chaplain, and an urgent message was sent to Corps headquarters. Fr Walter Finn CSSp drove in his jeep to the high ranges. During the night he heard confessions, and noticed that the Highlanders said their Confiteor and act of contrition in Gaelic. In those far-off days it was the happy custom to say prayers at the end of the Mass. 'I launched forth in Irish. Seldom have I heard such a full-blooded response as I did from these men of the mountains whose first language was Gaelic.'[50]

Italy – the final battle

The last phase of the Italian campaign began for British troops near Lake Commachio. It was in this final battle that Fr E. R. Richardson, of Lancaster, was mortally wounded by a mine explosion while bringing in wounded during the battle to smash the German lines. He died within ten minutes. 'The grief in his unit was intense; an officer said simply, "we all feel it as a personal loss".'[51] This is understandable. Nothing so affects a soldier as the loss of one who has consistently worked voluntarily in dangerous circumstances for the welfare of the troops, without thought of discipline, peer-group loyalty, honour or promotion, the usual military motivating forces. The priest was not 'one of the boys'; usually he was his own man, serving God's purpose in a military environment.

> Holding grimly to his supernatural outlook, in circumstances unkind to it, the chaplain sallies forth to bring the Sacraments to his men and his men to the Sacraments.[52]

Missions and retreats

During a comparative lull in the fighting during the winter of 1944–45 three divisional chaplains organized retreats, one at Cesena and one at Forlio. The preacher at the first two was Fr Dennis Gibson CSSR. 'Few men have his gift of embedding solid doctrine in an eloquence strewn with humorous quips. The troops reaped profit and enjoyment from his week of sermons.'[53] Later, after the end of the war and while a chaplain to the Occupation Forces in Austria, Fr Gibson rendered great service to the Archbishop of Vienna, Cardinal Innitzer, by assisting to get him to Rome for the Consistory. The Cardinal conferred on Fr Gibson the rank of Archiepiscopal Consistory Councillor of the archdiocese of Vienna – the first time such a dignity had been conferred on a foreign priest. The Pope awarded him the Lateran Cross for his services.[54]

Fr McNulty CSSR preached at yet another mission, held at Cervia. Day retreats were also organized for chaplains. These were, however, more in the nature of deanery conferences, and an exchange of information. These periods were a very necessary part of the chaplain's life on active service.

However, it was not possible in every theatre of operations, especially in the Far East.

A chaplain who 'took a leap in the dark' and crossed the Irish border when already in chaplain's uniform was Fr Michael Pelly SJ. After service in North Africa, he accompanied 1st Army to Italy and, during a rest period out of the line, had the honour of arranging for 6,000 of his division to meet the Pope. 'All were impressed, both Jew and Gentile. Even those who might have gone "to scoff, remained to pray".' Of his time in Italy, he wrote: 'There was much besides of glorious adventure in the saving of souls, on the way into Florence, in the rest by Loreto, in the set-backs of the Gothic Line before Rimini, and in the thousand and one happenings which any chaplain could tell about. But, rarely, I think has any chaplain been so richly and undeservedly rewarded as I was for a leap in the dark.'[55]

References

1. Martin Dempsey, *The Priest Among the Soldiers* (London, 1946), pp. xi, 30.
2. *Ushaw College Magazine* (December 1941), pp. 283-4.
3. Dempsey, p. 32.
4. The Military History and Information Service AIF, *Active Service: With Australia in the Middle East* (Canberra, 1941), p. 24.
5. Dempsey, pp. 48-9.
6. Fr W. C. Hayes, letter to the Abbot of Downside (16 November 1942), DAA.
7. Dempsey, pp. 48-9.
8. Quoted in Chester Wilmot, *Tobruk 1941* (Penguin Books), p. 200.
9. Ian Pedley and Bill Boyan, *Altars and Artillery* (Brisbane, 1980), p. 52.
10. Fr George Forster, *Priest Behind the Wire* (published privately), p. 15.
11. Ibid., p. 7.
12. Ibid., p. 10.
13. Pedley and Boyan, p. 60.
14. Hayes, letter (16 November 1942), DAA.
15. Newspaper report about Fr Conlon, quoted in his obituary, SCD (1971), pp. 309-11.
16. Pedley and Boyan, p. 63.
17. Hayes, letter (16 November 1942), DAA.
18. *Pax* (1992), p. 27.
19. Ibid., p. 28.
20. Dempsey, p. 34.
21. Rt Rev Dom Rudesind Brookes OSB, OBE, MC, TD, *Father Dolly - The Guardsman Monk* (London, 1983), p. 125.
22. Ibid., p. 126.
23. Ibid., p. 133.
24. VX12841, *Soldiering On - Meet the Padre* (Canberra, 1942), p. 95.
25. Dempsey, p. 30.
26. Denys Rutledge OSB, 'Padre's progress', p. 110.
27. Ibid.

28. Ibid.
29. Ibid., p. 111.
30. Ibid.
31. *Salesian College Magazine* (1943), p. 73.
32. Ibid., p. 79.
33. Hayes, letter (28 August 1943), DAA.
34. Memoriam to Fr Forbes, *Ampleforth Journal*, vol. 96, no. II (1991), Ampleforth Abbey Archives.
35. Recommendation for an award of the Military Cross, Army Form W3121 (26 February 1944); extant copy at Ampleforth Archives.
36. Vincent de Paul Vokes, Javea, Spain, conversation with T. Johnstone.
37. Various Irish newspapers (April 1946). Copies held by the authors.
38. Brookes, p. 150.
39. Hayes, letter (28 August 1943), DAA.
40. Brookes, p. 155.
41. 'Memoriam', Nottingham diocese (16 May 1983).
42. CSSR Necrology.
43. Achonry Diocesan Records.
44. Dempsey, p. ix.
45. Arthur Bryant, *Triumph in the West* (London, 1959), pp. 526–7.
46. Brian Plumb, *Arundel to Zabi: A Biographical Dictionary of the Catholic Bishops of England and Wales 1623–1987* (Warrington, 1988).
47. Rutledge, p. 112.
48. Dempsey, pp. 111–12.
49. *Lancaster Diocesan Directory* (1992).
50. Dempsey, p. 113.
51. Ibid., pp. 113–14.
52. Ibid., p. 105.
53. Ibid., p. 112.
54. CSSR Necrology.
55. Rev Michael Pelly SJ, 'Adventure glorious', *Interfuse*, no. 41 (1986), pp. 46–50.

17

The Royal Air Force

Unlike regiments of the Army with its constituted hierarchical leadership structure, RAF operational units, either flying stations or maintenance units, were an organizational bureaucracy. On an RAF station all operational functions were controlled by individual section chiefs, who outside working hours had no responsibility for the welfare or care of their personnel. Outside of depots and training establishments discipline was largely self-imposed. Station activities for welfare and entertainment were directed from the centre, Station Headquarters. Outside a flying squadron there was little *esprit de corps*.

Fighter pilots were all highly intelligent aggressive young men, sometimes regarded as 'too cocky', even within the RAF. Natural pride in being one of the chosen few was part of this. Their attitude, slang language that was soon RAF-wide, and dress were part of their outward élitism. The floppy hat and un-buttoned tunic were small outward indications of devil-may-care peer-grouping individuality. They were brave men, concealing a consciousness of flying what were little more than weapons platforms, literally sitting just in front of nearly a half-ton of lethal high-octane fuel.

Bomber crews, on the contrary, were serious and reflective. It was the natural effect of being squeezed for extended periods into a bomber, loaded with up to ten tons of high explosives, flying in freezing darkness over enemy territory; a target for anti-aircraft fire, and radar-guided night-fighters. Repeated bombing missions of this nature during an operational tour of duty was exhausting, physically and mentally. They operated in 'crews' of about six or seven; team work was essential to success, and survival, in what was one of the most demanding and dangerous operational roles of the Second World War.

The RAF aircrew regarded themselves, and were regarded by the rest of the Royal Air Force, as a race apart; a fighting élite, as indeed they were. Aircraft ground crews, essential to the squadron flying teams, came to work on aircraft from their various sections on the station. Unlike other station personnel, they were admitted by aircrew to be part of the fighting team. The 'squadron spirit' thus developed was the nearest Royal Air Force equivalent to the Army's regimental spirit. The élitism fostered in this way was reinforced by the concentration on aircrew of the RAF High Command's morale-boosting effort. The mass of RAF ground support staff was a much lower priority. With the huge Air Force expansion under way there was a potential danger of a moral and spiritual vacuum being created by default. That this did not happen was in part due to effective chaplains' ministry on Royal Air Force stations.

Expanding RAF chaplaincy

The Principal Chaplain (RC), Mgr Henry Beauchamp, of Kildare and Leighlin, had been commissioned CF on 29 March 1916. He had served in France and Flanders with the Army, principally with the cavalry, before transferring to the RAF on 25 July 1919. In 1939 he had served as Catholic chaplain at RAF Halton, the main technical training centre, for twenty years, taking a full part in station life. He knew the RAF thoroughly. To him fell the task of expanding and controlling RAF Catholic chaplaincy throughout the Second World War. In the event he did much more than this. By his motivation he created a moral and spiritual force which was to have a dynamic effect, not only on Catholic chaplains of the RAF, but throughout service chaplaincy services of the Allied forces. It spread world-wide and lasted long after World War II.

On the outbreak of war the number of permanent Catholic chaplains serving the Royal Air Force world-wide was ten. When Mgr Beauchamp moved from RAF Halton to the Air Ministry late in 1939 his first priority was to create a good working relationship with his fellow-Principal Chaplains. Two incidents will illustrate the measure of his success. Until the Air Staff increased his establishment, which could only be done with Treasury approval, no additional priests could be recruited. Establishment increases always lagged far behind the actual need. To fill the time-lag, the Anglican Principal Chaplain, the Rev John Jagoe (later Bishop of Bermuda), with commendable Christian co-operation, allowed the Catholics to recruit twenty chaplains against the Church of England establishment.[1]

Beauchamp's second priority could then be undertaken: recruiting. He began a recruiting tour of the British Isles, visiting every diocese and religious community appealing for chaplains. He was more successful with the Superiors of regular Orders than with the diocesan bishops. The records of RAF wartime chaplaincy show that of the 229 RAF wartime chaplains over 73 per cent were from the regular Religious. The Jesuits and Franciscans of the English and Irish provinces and the Columban Fathers provided most. Thirty of these latter were young priests, recently ordained at Maynooth for the China missions; because of the war they were unable to travel to the Far East. Fortuitously, Fr Jeremiah Piggott SSC, Vicar-General of Hanyang diocese, was on holiday in Ireland at the outbreak of war, and was unable to return to China. During World War I, Fr Piggott had served as a Army chaplain, winning a Military Cross and mentioned in despatches. He immediately volunteered again. However, the Army turned him down on age grounds; the RAF accepted him at once. His zealous young missionaries followed his example.[2]

The second example of the good relations between Mgr Beauchamp and his Protestant colleagues occurred over a selection interview with a Catholic priest for a chaplaincy post. The candidate, having travelled from Liverpool to London, discovered that 'Monsignor' was away elsewhere. 'He was advised to see Dr McHardy', Principal Presbyterian Chaplain. He did so, they had a chat, and the candidate, Fr John Marquis of Beauvais, returned to his home in Liverpool. Some days later he received a letter from Mgr Beauchamp instructing him to report to RAF Uxbridge for duty.[3]

> A Presbyterian Minister had passed him as fit material to become a Catholic Chaplain ... Some 20 years later, Fr. Hilary Carpenter, O.P., writing from Rome could pen 'at this Vatican Council there is much talk these days about ecumenism, they are slowly working their way up to where we were in the RAF in 1942'.[4]

Leadership courses

By the end of 1942 there were 148 Catholic chaplains in the RAF. To achieve this number Beauchamp had had to devote much time and effort, in addition to exercising to its full that charming personality for which he was famous. Now, however, he was able to devote more time for something he had been considering for a considerable time – Catholic leadership courses. The Sword of the Spirit movement had been founded in London during the London blitz. Although Catholic in inspiration the movement was acceptable to other denominations and four senior Anglican and Protestant churchmen were on the first council.[5] Mgr Beauchamp was a staunch supporter of the movement. The courses he envisaged were an extension of the Sword. First he had to obtain authority from the Air Ministry to hold them, provide travel facilities, and authorize absence from duty without loss of leave to the individual. All these were granted. To reduce travel, suitable locations were identified in various parts of Britain, usually in religious houses, or convents; and permission to use their guest facilities sought. Much reliance was placed upon the generous hospitality of the Superiors, and this was not found wanting. The RAF authorities at all levels co-operated willingly towards the success of the new venture.

Obviously, a good spiritual pastor would be required for the position of Director of Studies; for this vital role Mgr Beauchamp selected Fr James Brendan McHugh OSB from Prinknash Abbey. He proved ideal for the task. The zeal of Fr McHugh was legendary. Once, going home to Belfast on leave, while on the boat train from Euston to Liverpool, he asked the guard for use of his van, then walked the length of the train, informing occupants of every compartment that if any Catholic wished to go to confession he should go to the guard's van immediately.[6] Mgr Beauchamp was lucky in having at his disposal a considerable number of highly qualified educators, spiritual leaders, and zealous missionaries, from the Orders and dioceses. It was his genius to use their talents fully, and as widely as possible. Moreover, in his search for excellence and experience, he went beyond the religious field to enhance the quality. For part of the course devoted to leadership he invited eminent guest speakers, the Duke of Norfolk and Lord Trenchard, father of the RAF, being amongst the first. The first ten courses were held in January 1943 at the selected centres.[7] The membership of each course was drawn from the high numbers of the idealistic and intelligent young men and women, from all walks of civilian life, serving in the RAF.

> The moral Leadership movement, already of considerable significance within the Royal Air Force, worked to best advantage in the type of cellular structure (also conducive to 'Sword' activities) provided by the RAF, especially in Bomber Command where wing and squadron formations employed multiples of aircrews of optimum size, six or seven men, which were independent entities in many of their activities and, since all were volunteers, contained a fair concentration of intelligent and idealistic young men, the perfect raw material for the 'Sword of the Spirit'.[8]

The courses were an instant success, and despite early lack of interest shown by the Senior Chaplain (RC) RAF in the Middle East,[9] they also spread to that theatre of operations, possibly by pressure from the ranks in his jurisdiction.

> I should say that all this really began about three years ago when four of us decided to start the 'Sword of the Spirit' in the Middle East. The idea was taken up by the Senior Chaplains and now I think that the whole of the Middle East is organised in some form of Catholic Action and though it was all the Sword of the Spirit at first, most organisations are now represented ... The entire activities are directed by Middle East Catholic Councils on which each society is represented and we have had three great Catholic Rallies out here attended by servicemen who gave up their leave for the occasion and came from all over this part of the world.[10]

The leadership courses spread further afield. Fr Edward Wilcock, of Leeds, was selected by Mgr Beauchamp to take charge of the leadership courses at Osterley College, west London. In 1944 a new leadership school was opened at Monte San Pancrazio, near Rome, where Beauchamp had secured accommodation in a Canadian convent. Fr Wilcock was nominated as Principal and remained until the end of the war in Europe. With the ending of British occupation of Italy, Fr Wilcock moved to Palestine and opened a school in a Trappist monastery at Latroun near Lydda. In addition to leadership courses, Fr Wilcock became heavily involved in the 'Sword of the Spirit' in both Italy and Palestine.[11]

British Air Forces in France 1939–40

Throughout the war RAF chaplains were destined to take part in all operations conducted world-wide by their service, though the main war effort of the RAF during World War II was directed from bases in the United Kingdom against Germany and German military targets in occupied Europe. It was in this air war that the grievous losses to its picked personnel, the aircrew, mainly occurred.

On 15 January 1940 a single RAF command was created in France known as British Air Forces in France (BAFF), by unifying two existing RAF elements in France. Three Catholic RAF chaplains served with BAFF; the experience of one, Fr Thomas Hourigan, will serve as a role-model.

Following his ordination in 1932, Fr Hourigan worked in Salford diocese until he volunteered as an RAF chaplain in 1938. Stationed first at RAF Halton he was posted to a technical training school near Barry, South Wales. It was here that much of the training of ground staff for the AASF (Advance Air Striking Force) was carried out in the early months of the war. From a cadre of a few hundred it grew to nearly 10,000: he regarded it as his parish, but with a strong, and personal, difference.

> The change from familiar friends and activities as well as from the atmosphere of presbytery and parish life - to the jejune surroundings of camp life was sudden and, in a sense, violent. Gone was the company of the priests in the presbytery; the friendly Monday gatherings on the golf links; the meetings at the diocesan conference, and funerals; the parish outings, the parish activities.
>
> A Catholic priest finds himself now living in much closer proximity to his flock and feels that he is a member of a family constantly mingling with persons who are quite literally heathen! The fact is that the majority of non-Catholics in Officers' Messes today are scarcely nominal Christians.[12]

During early November 1939, the main element of AASF moved to its base area near Nantes, Brittany. On a lighter note, Fr Hourigan found himself sharing a room with a Presbyterian chaplain from the Hebrides, over whose bed hung an oleograph of Pope Pius X. The minister bore a striking resemblance to His Holiness, which must surely have come in for comment. It was a quiet period and the local curé entertained the Catholic chaplains of the RAF with the essence of *entente cordiale*.[13]

In the spring Fr Hourigan moved with elements of the RAF to the Somme valley. Here he ministered to the small units scattered over a wide area in Amiens, Poix, Péronne, Mons-en-Chaussy and Moncy Lagache, getting around in a small RAF car to say Mass at each place. Near Amiens a dilapidated church 'sheltering many birds' was used by the RAF with the curé's permission. Here ...

> among the flat, fertile fields of the Somme Valley I spent some of the happiest, and also the busiest, weeks of my life. When I took my last look for many years at those fields on the glorious Trinity Sunday of 19th May, 1940, the Germans were then much too close for comfort. There was the August stillness of quiet wings ...[14]

In mid-May 1940, with the Germans advancing down the Somme valley at what seemed lightning speed, the RAF advance elements were ordered to withdraw south of the Seine. In the confusion Fr Hourigan became separated from the main body and found himself with the RAF rear party at Abbeville. Soon he saw wings of a different kind, and with black crosses on them. With a small party of RAF personnel under an officer, Hourigan's car crawled along in refugee columns under daily air attack. Eventually they reached the Seine crossings and regained contact with the RAF at Nantes. A few weeks after he reached Nantes, with the fall of France imminent, the BAFF was ordered home, and Fr Hourigan was back in Southampton by 12 June.

Italy's entry into the war came almost immediately. Consequently, with Italian forces in Libya threatening Egypt and the Suez Canal, the Middle East became a theatre of operations. Following a short interlude in Blackpool Fr Hourigan was posted to Cairo as Assistant Principal Chaplain (RC) RAF.[15]

The Royal Air Force overseas

Life for a chaplain on an RAF station overseas was in most cases very similar to that of a chaplain in the United Kingdom; however, in certain circumstances he was required to travel much to outlying RAF units. To do this one chaplain, serving in north-west Africa, was given a motorbike and sidecar; in Morocco he travelled by lorry, and airplane. In Italy and Palestine he was provided with a driver and car. In Palestine his RAF driver was twice ambushed by terrorists, but because he was a Jew 'and spoke Hebrew, he was able to talk his way out and come back (with the vehicle)'.[16]

Fr Oswald Earle SJ went on his first overseas posting to Blida, thirty miles from Algiers. It was a large station with American, French and Yugoslav units besides the RAF. While there he ministered to a large polyglot Catholic community.

> The Blessed Sacrament was reserved in the church which was open night and day. This had a great advantage because for some months we were operational, dropping supplies to the French Resistance in the South of France. This was dangerous, as it meant flying into mountainous country in the dark and dropping the containers in exactly the right place. So we sometimes had evening Mass with Holy Communion for the Catholic aircrew before they set out. Some liked to visit the Blessed Sacrament after they returned. With these facilities the life of a chaplain was similar to that of a chaplain at home: three Masses every Sunday, and during the week visiting the outlying units.[17]

In addition to the RAF personnel was the ministry to prisoner-of-war working-parties, mainly Italian Catholics of peasant stock. Their uniforms were those they had surrendered in, long before, and in poor condition. Although without a POW policy at this stage, nevertheless the RAF officers decided that they should be treated as humanely as possible. They were cleaned and reclothed; working alongside RAF tradesmen, they soon made friends. As for the prisoners, they were

> used to turning to their priest with their problems, and as they had no Italian padres with them, the R.C. chaplain found himself more and more involved as intermediary between the RAF officers and the POWs ... The RAF officers were not slow to appreciate the position of moral authority that a Catholic priest has, of whatever race or nation his flock may be.[18]

Fr Hourigan, the senior RAF chaplain (RC) for the Middle East, travelled much. His 'diocese' stretched from Cyprus to Kenya and at one time from Tunis to Tehran. Of all the visits he made none perhaps was as rewarding both for himself and for British service personnel as that to Jerusalem. There he met Fr Austin Treamer AA, who had arrived from Rumania via Turkey. Shortly afterwards Fr Hourigan requested the Augustinian friar to become officiating chaplain to the RAF in Jerusalem.

Fr Treamer had been on the staff of a Rumanian seminary before the German takeover, when he was forced to flee, first to Turkey then to Palestine. In Jerusalem he took refuge in the church of Notre-Dame de France, part of which had been taken over by the Royal Air Force. The headquarters of the RAF in Jerusalem was in the German Vincentian hospice. It was through Fr Treamer that the senior Army Chaplain, Fr H. A. Ainsworth, of Liverpool, gained permission to use the old Jerusalem seminary.[19]

In the seminary a Catholic club was created, furnished and run at first by local lady volunteers under the management of a Jewish lady convert,[20] it was taken over and run by the CWL. 'Though it was a Catholic Centre no service man or woman was ever excluded.'[21]

Jerusalem was a place of pilgrimage for all who served in the Middle East since its capture from the Turks in 1917. But this was the first time that Catholic servicemen had a centre, and a hostel, of their own. 'The lounge was used for lectures, meetings, and discussions at which the chaplains or English speaking priests or religious took part ... Fr Ainsworth and his successor Fr McKenna, were ably helped by Fr William Smith, from Carfin, Scotland.'[22]

The Legion of Mary was established by Fr Smith. Its members, although of course restricted by their military duties, did their best to follow the 'then rather rigid rules of the handbook'.[23] The 'Sword of the Spirit' was run as a weekly discussion group, always beginning with written questions to the chaplains, who then had to give off-the-cuff answers 'provoking lively discussions'.[24]

The club organized a choir which led the singing in the Patriarchal cathedral. The organ was played by an Anglican of the British Palestine Police. The club also arranged tours to the holy places which were run by the Religious Orders, chiefly Franciscans and Benedictines.

Midnight Mass in Bethlehem

Christmas 1942 in Jerusalem, just after the Battle of El Alamein, was a memorable one for those Catholics who were able to get leave to visit the Holy City. Following their experience of the previous year, chaplains were more prepared. By request, the Patriarch forbade the local Christians and nuns, 'a very determined lot',[25] from assisting at the midnight Mass. Entrance was by card only; civil, military and RAF police checked all card-holders before allowing entry. 'I know high-ranking officers were turned away.'[26] Fr W. Smith organized midnight Mass for Army personnel in the large church of the Salesian Fathers. Fr Austin arranged for the RAF to hear Mass in the chapels below, near the cave of the Nativity. Lining up in the lovely Crusader cloister, before descending in groups to the chapels, to assist at low Masses and receive Holy Communion, the RAF personnel then went up to St Catherine's to squeeze in at the back of the church and enjoy the beauty of the midnight pontifical Mass in Bethlehem. The service chaplains of all the other Christian denominations in the Holy City conducted divine worship in the Shepherds' Fields. Christmas dinner in the hostel was served to the troops by the chaplains,[27] instead of the officers who traditionally served the Christmas meal.

The RAF in action

To understand the nature of the chaplains' work among the men most at risk in the Royal Air Force, we should take a look at them through the eyes of a front line Army chaplain. Just before El Alamein the Axis armies and their supply lines in North Africa received a severe pounding from the Desert Air Force.

> Enemy planes did come over occasionally to drop a load or two of bombs or machine-gun at random through the night, but it was a mere bagatelle compared with what the Germans were copping from the RAF ... The returning bombers were a great sight and what impressed us most was they always came back from their raids flying in formation as imperturbably as if they had been on a training manoeuvre ... The aerial dogfights were battles of wits in which the honours seemed to break even, though it appeared to the spectators on the ground that the RAF were always prepared to take the greater risks.[28]

Aircrew over Europe. A priest on bombing operations over Germany

Just as Army chaplains considered it their duty to accompany troops into the front line, at least one RAF chaplain felt that if he was to understand fully the nature of what those in his pastoral care were experiencing, he would have to accompany them on a bombing mission. He had had to wrestle long with his conscience, and lose much sleep, before reaching his decision. What finally appears to have decided him was a joke from a lapsed Catholic bomber pilot following an operational de-briefing at the end of a raid over Germany.

> O'Reilly was in exceptionally good form and with his tot of rum in his hand came over to speak to the chaplain:
> 'We had a good trip to-night, Father. Why don't you come with us some night? You will find the air bracing over Germany – why don't you come some night, Father?'[29]
> The question really went home. The fact that he had never accompanied the men on a bombing raid had been worrying the chaplain. True he could hide behind his Roman collar and chaplain's badge and say that he was not allowed to go. Chaplains were not supposed to fly on operations, and if they were captured by the enemy they would lose their Red Cross privileges. ... What must those lads think, coming back night after night, after such ordeals, to find the chaplain sitting comfortably in the operations room? 'Oh, we are all right, fellows! the padre will wave us good-bye and greet us when we come back – yeah, but you don't find him coming.'[30]

In his thoughts there may have been a faint echo of the old World War I joke about the padre's farewell to a company of replacements going to the front: 'Go with God, *I* will accompany you to the station.'

This decided the priest; he would go the following night.

> He would have to go ... It was not courage, for he was scared and he knew that he would shake like a jelly. He would go on the following night. He could not pick and choose the target, else that would ruin the purpose of his trip. The next question was in what plane would he go? Pilots were very superstitious, as shown by their flying jackets. On the lapel you would find a miniature rabbit's foot, a horse-shoe, a black cat or some other mascot. They never flew a thirteenth trip, it was always 12A. But to ask them to take a 'sky pilot' would be tempting fate. He might take you on up to heaven, and the Lord knows there were enough 'Gremlins' in the air without one with you in the aircraft.[31]

In the event, knowing that he was one most likely to acquiesce in flouting standing orders, the Father asked O'Reilly to take him on the next bombing mission. The operations for the following night were, however, cancelled, prolonging Fr Hamilton's nervous agony a further day.

Bomber Command operational briefings for that night were usually held in the afternoon:

> briefing time arrived slowly but surely and the C.O. got up to make the fatal statement: 'Gentlemen, the target for to-night is our old friend Essen.' There was a combined output of breath that sounded like the whistle of a train ... O'Reilly winked across at a very sick chaplain.[32]

After the briefing, he went to the local parish priest and made a heartfelt confession. That evening before take-off time of 2000 hours, having removed all insignia, the chaplain dressed in borrowed flying kit and boarded C for Charlie. Once inside, Fr Hamilton had raised his gloved hand to give the benediction and general Absolution. As the plane roared into the sky, the priest searched the ground for his little chapel, wondering if he would ever see it again in this life. Once in the air, the priest saw a new side to O'Reilly's character. The responsibility of command banished the devil-may-care flippancy. Instead,

> here on the job he was the pilot, captain of the ship, the boss, serious ... In the air each one was so busy at his own particular job that there was almost complete silence, except for the deafening roar of the four engines outside.[33]

Several hours later they were over Germany. Naturally the priest had read Butler's *Lives of the Saints*, and remembered how several had seen visions of hell. As he looked below he contemplated this, and saw below a hell that was not a vision, but stark reality.

> This was no vision, this was a bird's eye view of hell let loose. There were the flares dropped by the path-finders, the flak that was coming up from down below, and right there in front hundreds of search-lights converging together like illuminated sticks on a witch's broom. Those search-lights are trouble. 'Father,' consoled the renegade O'Reilly, 'if you

are picked up in one of those you've had it.' Scarcely had the words died on his Irish lips when there was an explosion that even rocked C for Charlie. One of the aircraft had been hit and exploded in mid-air.[34]

Someone swore a typical farewell to friends in action, 'the poor _____'. There was no time for thought of anything else to say, even if anyone wanted to say it. The target was in front, lit up by the first bombing wave; these last few seconds in the bomber's approach to its target area were crucial. The bombardier took control, directing the flypath of the aircraft. His words 'bombs away' would signal evasive action and a turn for home.

> This is it. 'Bombs away,' and with that C for Charlie shot up into the skies as if the weight of the bombs had been holding it down ... 'Now for home,' said O'Reilly, dodging in and out of searchlight beams, 'and look out for enemy fighters on the way back.' When they touched down at Penrose, O'Reilly coolly said: 'Well, boys, we made it. Are you O.K. Father?'[35]

The priest went directly to his chapel to pray in thanks for his preservation. A short time later, at the debriefing, the chaplain mentally contradicted the assertion of O'Reilly that it had been 'a piece of cake'. Naturally the pilot was reprimanded for his part in the affair. As for the priest ...

> The C.O. came over. 'Father, you were wrong in going to-night. If anything had happened to you we would all be in trouble.' Then with a grin he put out his hand to shake, and in a quiet voice said: 'Off the record, Father, I am glad you went. These boys will appreciate it.' When the de-briefing was over, Fr. Hamilton went to his chapel to celebrate Mass ... It was a Mass of thanksgiving. He put in an intention at the 'Commemoration of the Dead' for the crews of five planes that had not returned and for all the German people of Essen who had died that night.[36]

Relieved the ordeal was over, the chaplain was nevertheless glad he went on the mission. If only because he would be better able to understand and sympathize with any aircrew member who spoke, however jokingly, of being afraid of flying.

> He knew the feeling and could now understand. He had nothing but admiration for the courage and nerve of the young men who night after night risked their lives upon their dread mission.[37]

Aircrew – lack of moral fibre

The dangers of civil operational flying in peace are many and constant. Hardly a day goes by without notification of an accident, however trivial, or a near miss, even in mid-air on well-controlled international flight paths, using the most sophisticated modern technology. The dangers to aircraft and aircrew in wartime are immensely greater, especially as a great part of the enemy war effort is directed towards air defence. During the Second World War casualties to bomber aircrews of all the combatants were horrendous. The odds against surviving an operational tour of duty - 30 missions over enemy territory, before a rest was granted - were high. It would be surprising if any bomber aircrew was emotionally untouched by the experience. Some aircrew worried so much that they sometimes refused to fly.

The authorities had to decide whether a refuser was a coward or suffering from nervous shock. If they came to the conclusion that he was a coward, he would be informed that he was lacking moral fibre (LMF).

> At home it was the custom at one time to send these poor fellows to RAF Uxbridge, where they inhabited a barrack block all to themselves. This was unsatisfactory. The RAF high command employed very distinguished doctors and psychologists to 'vet' pilots after a crash, and treatment was prescribed. As the war went on a great advance was made in handling this difficult problem.[38]

When such problems occurred overseas where the skills and facilities were not to hand, any other way available to help calm nervousness and assist in the restoration of self-confidence was tried.

> The R.C. chaplain might be called in. He was held to be someone in whom people could confide, and pilots sometimes liked to talk informally to the Catholic priest about their crashes. An American doctor said: 'I guess the priest can be a great help to the doctor. When a guy is in hospital, a little encouragement or religion can give him peace of mind which helps him more than all the medicines the doctor gives him.'[39]

References

1. Rt Rev Mgr J. J. Roche SCA, CBE, Principal RC Chaplain RAF, 'Sermon preached at Holy Family Church RAF Halton on Nov 8th 1980. On the occasion of the dedication of the Memorial Window to Deceased RAF Chaplains'.
2. Fr Michael Healy SSC, conversation with Tom Johnstone; SSC Necrology; Cloyne Diocesan Archives.
3. Roche, pp. 4-5.
4. Ibid.
5. Thomas Moloney, *Westminster, Whitehall and the Vatican* (London, 1985), pp. 194-5.
6. 'In Memoriam - Dom Brendan McHugh OSB', *Pax*, vol. XLVIII, no. 286 (summer 1958), pp. 44-5.
7. Roche, pp. 4-5.
8. Moloney, pp. 194-5.
9. Roche, p. 5.

10. Sgt W. Clifford, letter from RAF Provost Headquarters, Middle East (29 December 1944), Archives of St Bede's Grammar School, Bradford.
11. Rev Edward Wilcock, letter to James Hagerty.
12. Fr Thomas Hourigan, 'The Odyssey of a chaplain in the RAF', *St Kieran's College Record* (Kilkenny, 1956), p. 96.
13. Ibid., p. 97.
14. Ibid.
15. Ibid., p. 99.
16. Rev Oswald Earle SJ, *Letters and Notices* (Journal of the Society of Jesus), vol. 68, no. 398 (1990), pp. 27-34.
17. Ibid., p. 27.
18. Ibid., p. 28.
19. Fr Austin Treamer AA, 'Catholic Forces in Jerusalem 1941-1946', unpublished, COA.
20. Hourigan, p. 100.
21. Treamer.
22. Ibid.
23. Ibid.
24. Ibid.
25. Ibid.
26. Ibid.
27. Ibid.
28. Ian Pedley and Bill Boyan, *Altars and Artillery* (Brisbane, 1980), p. 61.
29. P. Hamilton-Pollock, *Wings on the Cross* (Dublin, 1954), p. 76.
30. Ibid.
31. Ibid., p. 77.
32. Ibid., pp. 78-9.
33. Ibid., p. 79.
34. Ibid.
35. Ibid.
36. Ibid., p. 80.
37. Ibid.
38. Earle, p. 31.
39. Ibid., pp. 27-34.

18

The return: Normandy to the Elbe

Just four years after Dunkirk, American, British, Canadian, French, and Polish forces invaded France. The planning for the Second Front began as early as 1942, and when 21st Army Group was formed in 1943 under General Montgomery its headquarters was at St Paul's School, Hammersmith. The Rt Rev Mgr J. P. Stapleton OBE, recently home from the Middle East, was appointed Senior Catholic Chaplain to 21st Army Group and joined in January 1944. An OBE had been awarded to him for chaplaincy services to the Middle East Forces from 1941 to 1944.

Mgr Stapleton organized Catholic chaplaincy for the invasion based as usual on the order of battle, divided into forward and rear areas.

Forward Areas:

HQ 2nd British Army	Fr R. L. Quilly	SCF (RC)
1 Corps	Fr C. P. Crean	SCF (RC)
8 Corps	Fr H. H. Welchman	SCF (RC)
12 Corps	Fr O. V. Murphy	SCF (RC)
30 Corps	Fr C. D. Foley	SCF (RC)

They controlled the chaplains in the forward areas, in divisions and brigades.

Rear Areas:
Lines of communication chaplains in the rear and base areas - mainly hospitals, depots and workshops.
Fr A. Horner SCF (RC)

11 L of C Area	Fr J. Duggan	SCF (RC)
12 L of C Area	Fr F. E. Coughlan	SCF (RC)[1]

Each senior chaplain had a number of priests under his authority, depending upon the number of units in his formation or area of control. First Corps, for example, had twenty chaplains. In all there were 165 priests serving 2nd Army and its lines of communication. In addition, 1st Canadian Army had no fewer than 50 Canadian priests with the Canadian Army. The Canadian chaplains were under the Rt Rev M. C. O'Neill MM, Assistant Principal Chaplain overseas with the Canadian Expeditionary Force.[2] (Mgr O'Neill had won the Military Medal at Ypres during World War One while serving in the ranks.) During the years of waiting for D-Day, soldiers trained and then attended 'refresher courses'; the chaplains were not neglected either. Command senior chaplains arranged for chaplains to attend annual retreats, at suitable locations in their areas. One such was Prinknash Abbey:

> At the wish of the Senior chaplain the Catholic chaplains of the Southern Command are making here their annual retreat. There are about forty in all, they come each week in groups of three. The retreat lasts from Monday evening till Thursday. It is quite informal, no rules are drawn up, the retreatants attend the Divine office, and the guestmaster gives a conference each day.[3]

Operation Overlord

In the early hours of the morning of 6 June 6th Airborne Division landed in Normandy; the first loss to the chaplains occurred when Fr J. C. McVeigh was captured when his glider crash-landed near an enemy position.[4] Fr James Kenny, of Lancaster, dropped into France by parachute; he was slightly injured on landing but carried on. He was in the thick of the furious fighting that followed, administering to the dying and caring for the wounded. On one occasion, carrying a wounded man on his back, he led a party of paratroopers who had been cut off back to safety.[5]

The Royal Navy landed the troops on the beaches, under cover of a tremendous naval bombardment. Fr Thomas Holland (later Bishop of Salford), a naval chaplain, was in a ship loaded with sailors destined to man the small craft used in the landing. He was awarded the Distinguished Service Cross for ministering to them under fire and for his 'gallantry skill determination and undaunted devotion to duty during the landing of the Allied Forces on the coast of Normandy'.[6] Those chaplains who had to climb down rope-ladders over the side of a heaving ship into a tossing landing craft, carrying their Mass kit, in addition to personal equipment, were thankful for the Greek corporal they used instead of an altar stone.

The first priest to die in the assault was Fr P. F. Firth of the diocese of Lancaster. He had just given a cheery wave to a soldier when he was shot and died instantly. He was buried that night by Fr M. Alcock, in an orchard beside the parish church of Hermanville-sur-Mer. Later the French authorities awarded him a *Croix de Guerre*.[7] During the battles for Caen four priests were wounded and evacuated, and a fifth, Fr James Graham, with 51st Division, was wounded but remained in France.

Although not officially with the assault formations, Fr Cyril Crean, a Dublin priest, had been attached to an armoured brigade, and was now SCF (RC) to 1st Corps. He waded waist-deep ashore at Bernières-sur-Mer on D-Day, so as to be close to the infantry soldiers, and because of the responsibility he felt towards their chaplains.[8] Unluckily, one of 1st Corps' chaplains, Fr J. J. Meagher, of Hexham and Newcastle, attached to a brigade of 7th Armoured Division, was wounded shortly after the landing by one of the few enemy aircraft to fly over the beaches. Fr Crean was able to 'borrow one' from a British Casualty Clearing Station (CCS) under command of Canadian 1st Army.[9]

Fr James O'Sullivan had been ordained for Goulburn, in New South Wales, Australia, but had been asked by the Bishop of Goulburn to become an army chaplain instead. He landed with 6th Duke of Wellington's on the Normandy beaches. Before landing he had given general Absolution to Catholics. After wading on to Normandy's beaches, he administered the last sacraments to many. 6th 'Dukes' suffered so heavily in the Normandy battles that it was withdrawn completely. In Fr O'Sullivan's words: 'They took an absolute hammering. The poor boys were like sitting ducks.' Fifty years later he marked the D-Day commemorations with a British Legion service in a Catholic church. Speaking to a newspaper reporter before the service he said: 'I'll talk about the dead first, then I'll talk about the different attitudes to life that we had then and I'll also talk about the lack of hatred we all had for the enemy in the front-line. That was created by the newspapers and politicians back home.'[10]

In the heavy *bocage* country of Normandy, the 51st Highland Division, which had landed in the first wave of 1st Corps, accustomed to fighting in the more spacious desert, suffered heavily. Two of its chaplains were wounded, Frs George Conlon and James Graham, both Glasgow priests. Both were later mentioned in despatches. It was given to the Highland Division to liberate Lisieux, and a Mass of Thanksgiving was said in the shattered Basilica. The congregation, however, was not completely Scottish. Until his death nearly 50 years later Basil Funnell, a Yorkshireman in the Seaforth Highlanders, remembered with pride that he served at that Mass.[11] A chaplain from headquarters 21st Army Group visited the basilica at Lisieux on 16 August; he described it as having all its windows shattered and completely bare except for the benches. 'Never did I see a church looking so deserted.' However, things were quite different in the crypt where hundreds had sheltered during the bombardment: 'Here no signs of warfare – warm atmosphere contrasting with the windy church above. The Blessed Sacrament was here – the bronze fittings and altars and the mosaics added to the contrast.' The chaplain also noticed that although bomb craters were within 60 feet of the basilica and most of the houses around were ruins, the great building itself was spared a direct hit.[12]

The heavy fighting in Normandy continued into July. Five priests were wounded: Frs P. R. Dare, W. C. T. Briscoe, A. A. Coia, M. G. Murphy, H. Donaghey. Fr Coia, of Lancaster, nearly died of his wounds, and suffered from them for the rest of his life. The 50th was the leading division of 1st Corps on D-Day; one of its chaplains, Fr Gerard Nesbitt, of Hexham and Newcastle, was killed near Tilly nearly a month later, on 5 July. He had been attached to 8th Durham Light Infantry, and had been with the unit since February 1941. In his area he had served both British and French troops and because of this the French authorities later awarded Fr Nesbitt a posthumous *Croix de Guerre.*[13]

The living chaplains continued to say requiem for the soldiers they ministered to. Fr Dan Cummings, a Redemptorist Father from Belfast, was attached to 3rd Irish Guards; his story is typical of many battalion chaplains.

> Since we arrived in France, our routine has been arrival in a section of the line, digging of deep slit trenches, the Germans observe our arrival and the air becomes noisy with the whine of shells and the explosion of *nebelwerfers*, a shout for stretcher bearers and my speedy crossing of a field or two to the ruined house or barn where a busy doctor is injecting morphia into a writhing, groaning shape covered with blood that a few minutes earlier was a man. In one place we had this continually for over a week and frankly it was as much as a human being could stand.[14]

Under the Geneva Convention a chaplain's pastoral care must also extend to enemy soldiers of his own religion. Fr Dan spoke German, and he had also come prepared for this aspect of his ministry by obtaining a few small German prayer books. However, the priest had not bargained upon meeting Nazi fanatics of the Waffen SS.

> The cream of the German army faces us here in the west. I have met and talked to quite a number of the S.S. who are the cementing force of the Wehrmacht. They are young - 17, 18, 19 years, long haired, grumpy and amoral. We meet their work in the ruins of a house or a church or along the deep lanes. One S.S. man is brought in wounded. I was standing beside his stretcher helping the doctors to cut away the blood-stained sleeve of his tunic. I felt something knock against my side. I felt a fully primed grenade in his pocket. It was not there by chance for he had no other arms or ammunition nor had he any documents.[15]

Of course not all enemy prisoners were of this suicidal mould. One captured enemy was grateful for a mug of tea and exclaimed 'This is the happiest day of my life'. Fr Cummings asked him: 'Why can't you stop the war?' The German answered, as any British soldier might, 'An order is an order'.[16] In one of his letters the priest posed an ethical question on the nature of warfare, which soldiers are faced with in battle, with little time to think about it.

> Is it lawful or unlawful to shoot any enemy who keeps firing until you are right up on him and then when he sees all is hopeless, puts up his hands? Also, what about the sniper who has lain low behind our lines and snipes our men and then puts his hands up when discovered?[17]

With no end to the war then in sight, Fr Cummings pondered upon the future:

> If we are spared to return, we shall be all the better for the experience. Living close to death is an experience which changes your mind irrevocably. No meditation, no purposeful thinking, no continued reflection brings that vivid stark reality of death so closely to mind as does this kind of life we now live. The years will not be long enough for us to thank God for his mercies.[18]

Fr Edmund Swift SJ had arrived in Normandy with 81 General Hospital. Normally such a hospital is far behind the lines in a base area, but there were no rear areas in the Normandy bridgehead. Nearby was a casualty clearing station (CCS). One afternoon 'a young Redemptorist chaplain' told him of a death he had just witnessed. 'A young Scot had been brought in about mid-day terribly wounded. While he was anointing him, and two nurses were trying to save his life by blood transfusion, he kept repeating the Hail Mary gasping out the words as his strength declined, but changing the last phrase into "Holy Mary Mother of God pray for me a sinner for THIS ... is ... the hour of my death. Amen." As he expired, the nurses were in tears. "Father," one of them said, "we have seen many of your boys die. But we have never seen one die like this Jock." '[19]

After the invasion there were many attempts to use Catholic churches for thanksgiving services. General Eisenhower had issued an order expressly forbidding the commandeering of local churches. The local *curés* objected to this, and they were supported in their stand by Catholic chaplains in view of the orders of the Supreme Commander.[20] However, with the onset of autumn there was an urgent requirement to regularize the use of available churches for Mass. Also, the Catholic Women's League was anxious to establish a 'Hut' in Normandy as soon as possible after the landing. Fr John Jones SM, the Staff Captain on Mgr Stapleton's small office staff, made a courtesy call on the Archbishop of Rouen, Pierre Petit de Julleville, whose cathedral was badly damaged. He was in a small parlour of a convent where he was living when Fr Jones called. 'He was pleased that I had come representing Mgr and the Catholic Chaplains. I spoke to him of the question of using churches, and the desire of the CWL ladies to have a place in Rouen. He promised to earmark a place for them ... to be taken over when they arrived.'[21] In a further interview the following morning the Archbishop told Fr Jones 'how they could not understand how the British people had possibly carried on in 1940, and prepared this invasion. And how much he admired our strategy, having witnessed this whirlwind advance.'[22]

Reinforcements and replacements poured into the beach-head and vast dumps of reserve ammunition and supplies were created. By August movement became difficult. Although the closeness of their congregations reduced the amount of travel the chaplains had to do, when the break-out occurred at the end of July and the Allied armies burst out and began to spread all over Normandy and Brittany, it came as a great relief. Fr Denys Rutledge, chaplain to HQ 2nd Army Troops, arrived on D-Day plus three as a passenger on a vehicle loaded with ammunition. Shortly after he arrived an old French lady reported that she had found a dead British soldier in her garden and had buried him there. Fr Rutledge went to investigate to try and discover the identity of the soldier and register the burial place. He confirmed the existence of a body and was able to identify the soldier.[23]

At the headquarters, he noted: 'The break-out from the bridgehead has come as a great relief. The area has become even more congested. For the chaplain this has certain advantages, his flock is within reasonable reach and he is on occasion able to gather a group together for the sacraments immediately before they go into action.'[24] He recorded also, that there was general criticism at the headquarters of 2nd Army of 'Monty's' strategy and the slow advance.

The break-out from the beach-head

The German Army, caught between the anvil of the British around Caen and the wide swinging hammer of Patton's armoured divisions, and pounded from the air by ground-attack aircraft, was destroyed at Falaise. Although the casualties in chaplains had been high already, another was killed and one wounded during August, as they continued to risk their lives for the sake of the comfort and salvation of the troops. Fr Patrick McMahon SCC was the next victim, on 14 August. 'Paddy went out under fire in an ambulance to rescue a Canadian soldier. On the return journey the ambulance was hit by a shell and all were killed.'[25] Fr McMahon was buried in the churchyard at Issy, Normandy, following Requiem Mass at which 50 chaplains were present, British and Canadian, Army and RAF.[26] The wounded priest was Fr J. F. Devine of Elphin.

Following the break-out, Fr Rutledge's workload increased again. On Sunday 3 September, the fifth anniversary of the war, he said Mass in a village school on the Somme, 'courtesy of the communist headmaster'. That same morning he buried a sergeant killed in an attack on a house where a group of Germans were still holding out. In the afternoon Vespers, followed by Benediction, was held in the village church of St Thibault, followed afterwards by a procession, and prayers at the village war memorial. Benediction was sung at 1800 at Romescamps.[27]

After the 'Dukes' were withdrawn from the line, Fr O'Sullivan was transferred to 1st Leicesters, then on a sector near the Escaut canal, close to

Lille. On his first night with the battalion, he had a narrow escape from death, but at the expense of a fellow-priest.

> 'On my first night,' says a sombre priest, 'I was asked to carry out line of communications duty. I was told I'd need to use my French. Swiftly I told my superiors that I had very little French, so another chaplain, Fr Barry, who I'm certain was from the Liverpool Archdiocese, stood in for me. An hour later he'd been blown to bits.'[28]

Arnhem

In all, fifteen chaplains accompanied the 1st Parachute Division into Arnhem. At the height of the battle two chaplains were killed or died of wounds, three were taken prisoner during the battle, one wounded; seven were taken prisoner when resistance ceased, having decided to remain with the wounded. Three crossed the Rhine with wounded, and at least one, the Rev R. Talbot, an Anglican chaplain, swam back to the north shore to rejoin the remnants of the division.[29] Three priests landed in Arnhem with 1st Parachute Division on 17 September 1944: Frs B. J. Benson, B. M. Egan and D. McGowan; the first died of wounds received tending the wounded in St Elizabeth's Hospital. The second was wounded and captured during the fight to capture the vital bridge. The third was captured just as he had stripped to attempt to swim the Rhine and escape to the British-held bank.

On landing McGowan became entangled in his rigging-lines and in freeing himself dropped his pyx - the container holding the Blessed Sacrament. While others raced to take cover from German small-arms fire, Fr Danny, helped by an RAMC doctor, searched desperately for the precious Host until he recovered it;[30] both then raced to rejoin the field ambulance already busy with wounded and dying. St Elizabeth's Hospital, in the centre of the battle area, was crowded with wounded. Dr Stuart Mawson and Dr Clifford Simmons, two of many doctors and orderlies of the RAMC, all sensitive to the horror of battle at its most gruesome, carried on their duty in the shambles at Arnhem, ignoring danger. The battle immediately outside the hospital increased in ferocity; both doctors sheltered under a table because the air was filled with flying metal:

> While Simmons and I were lying under tables, another case was brought in and a voice, which we recognized as the CO's, 'Clifford, where in blazes are you? Oh there you are! You've got to do something quick. We've got Padre Benson here and he's in a very bad way.' Simmons, who was looking rather sheepish, drew his mouth into a hard line when he saw the padre, whose face and clothes were covered with a mask of blood and plaster, and whose right arm was dangling grotesquely over the side of the stretcher.
> 'What happened, sir?'

'He was brought down like this from one of the rooms upstairs. We've had four hits by eighty-eight millimetre guns on two of the small wards. The top storey's an absolute shambles, half the roof's down. Can't stop. Good luck boys.'

Simmonds took one look at the arm. 'That'll have to come off for a start. Get him under.'[31]

The doctors were without proper amputation saws; these were with the surgical team elsewhere. Fr Benson's arm was amputated with a flexible escape-saw. In the middle of the operation German troops smashed through a back door, using the hospital as cover to break into the rear of the British position. One young enemy soldier burst into the makeshift operating theatre, semi-automatic weapon at the ready. Mawson, sewing the Padre's face together, saw him first. 'Better get your hands up, Clifford. There's a German behind you.' Simmonds, intent on patient-care, reacted more slowly. The German indicated with a silent movement which had only one meaning. Simmonds raised his blood-stained hands. 'Doctor, Doctor', said Mawson pointing first at Simmonds then to himself. Then, indicating the still figure, 'Pastor, Pastor'.

> Just then a Dutch nurse appeared. She entered the room and spoke rapidly in German.
>
> 'He is asking if you have any arms concealed in here.'
>
> 'Tell him, no, of course not', Simmonds said. 'Do we look as if we had? Tell him the Minister of God here needs our help badly and we must get on with our work.' The nurse and the German spoke together for a few minutes again ... The German took another few steps into the room and, reaching up, pulled Simmonds' hands down from above his head and pointed to the body on the stretcher. He did the same to me and then returned to the door, from where he stood watching as we silently began again to mend the padre.[32]

The Dutch nurse, a civilian under German military rule, was aiding the British, and was without protection from the Geneva Convention. She had most to lose. None would disagree with Dr Mawson's verdict. ' "God, that girl's got nerve," I thought, "nerve and a lot more beside." '[33]

By a curious quirk of fate Fr Benson's father, Mr Henry Benson, had seen his only son on a cinema newsreel shortly before news came, first that he was missing, then of his death from wounds.

Fr Egan was ministering the last sacrament to the dying at the height of the battle for the bridge, when he himself was wounded. He was dragged, his battledress alight and suffering terribly, from a burning house near the Arnhem bridge.[34] Captivity followed, and after his release from the prisoner-of-war camp he learned that he had been awarded the Military Cross. On the tenth anniversary of the battle, he preached at the Mass offered by Bishop Koning. Upon the conclusion of the Mass, a service was held at the grave of Fr Benson in the War Cemetery at Oosterbeek.[35]

Fr McGowan, despite his tireless work with the wounded, exposed to enemy fire, somehow survived the battle, and impressed friend and foe alike. General Sir John Hackett, at that time a brigadier commanding 4 Para Brigade, was badly wounded and taken to hospital.

> Quite early on I had seen a chubby, glowing face peering at me and had recognized with pleasure Danny McGowan, Roman Catholic padre to my own brigade, clean-looking, healthy and cheerful as ever. He now came to see me daily, while he carried out some of the strangest and bravest work I have ever known. Every day he used to go out from the hospital and walk over ground where the Division had fought, burying dead, registering such graves as were already marked, picking up the paybooks soldiers always carried (invaluable documents for Records), gathering in whatever was likely to be useful in the hospital from the huge quantity of miscellaneous material spilled around the countryside and doing a hundred-and-one other valuable jobs. He was always impeccably dressed in uniform as an Airborne chaplain, from the red beret on his head down to his polished black boots, clean and shining from head to foot. He went about by day quite openly, accompanied by a Dutch youth, moving freely among the German troops who were now working hard to prepare the defence of the area against the further attack expected from the British. Both wore Red Cross armbands but these were of little significance, after the traumatic events of the last two weeks, to German soldiers who saw them worn under a red beret. He was often stopped, sometimes threatened, but the astonishment, verging on disbelief, with which German troops saw a smart British Airborne captain walking freely amongst them, red beret and all, stood him in good stead. His real armour, however, was the transparent honesty of his purpose and the boldness of his approach. His command of German was poor but I know what a determined person he was. I was almost sorry for any German who tried to obstruct him, when Danny McGowan was set upon doing what he saw as his duty.

The hospital was under fire, 'McGowan was the only English-speaking priest available to us in hospital but he was a Roman Catholic.'[36]

General Hackett then commented upon the strictness of Catholic chaplains he had met previously, who, it seemed to him, upheld canon law inflexibly, to the detriment of non-Catholic troops, possibly not being aware of the historical background, when each Christian denomination jealously guarded its religious prerogative, and viewed with deep suspicion any hint of 'proselytism' by Catholics. Whereas, as early as 1915 at Gallipoli, a Catholic priest could say in a comforting way to a dying soldier 'Tell me anything that is troubling you and I'll treat you as one of my own'.[37]

> It caused me no surprise to learn that in St Elizabeth's Hospital he was bringing men together in the wards and corridors for prayer whether they were members of his own church or not. This was good, but was it, I

wondered, enough? Men were dying. Some were devout Christians but
were Protestants. Would he, I asked Danny, as a Christian priest, deny
them the sacrament of Holy Communion? He had to, he said, but it was
clear that he had already given much thought to what he saw as a terrible
dilemma. I pressed him. He suffered a great deal from his conscience, I
know, but in the end it brought him to a decision which in all the
circumstances he was certain must be right. He began to administer the
sacrament to any who sought it.[38]

This is a terrible dilemma for any priest, especially those engaged in public
life. However, priests, and not only service chaplains, have been known,
where the person was a devout Christian, and reverential, to have given
Holy Communion to non-Catholics.

Amongst the useful items which Fr McGowan was able to take to the
hospital was a big tin of Ovaltine, extremely good for those patients unable
to eat, and a bottle of vintage Burgundy, Nuits St George '34. Hackett, to
his chagrin, was only allowed one glass, but his bedside companion, a
battalion commander destined to die of his wounds, was allowed by the
doctor to drink as much as he cared to.[39] Doctors too can forsake ethical
niceties in certain circumstances.

If soldiers take their weapons to hospital they are removed and placed in
a lock-up store. When the hospital at Arnhem was overrun, the SS delivered
written notice to the senior surgeon, Major Longland RAMC, that they
would arrive next morning to collect the arms. Possibly one of Fr
McGowan's most daring exploits was the mock burial which removed
three Bren-guns, a German machine-gun, grenades and ammunition, from
the lock-up store at the hospital under the nose of the SS, and into the hands
of the Dutch Resistance leader Piet van Arnhem.[40] 'Father McGowan,
chaplain to 16th Parachute Field Ambulance, who had already been in touch
with Dutch Resistance agents, worked out his audacious plan ... "We have
to do the job properly ... If anyone should see us – or if any of our Jerry
friends should be around – then let's give them a right good show".'[41]

> Germans, patients, and prisoners alike, stood in respectful silence as the
> solemn cortège passed among them on the way to the cemetery. Capt
> Lippman Kessel, of the RAMC, helped a corporal to carry the first stretcher
> and its blanket-shrouded figure. Two medical orderlies volunteered to carry
> the other. Bringing up the rear, Father Daniel McGowan, the priest who
> had worked tirelessly among the casualties. As the blanketed figures were
> lowered into graves, Father McGowan appeared to complete the ritual
> which had become all too common to both sides. Everyone stood to
> attention and threw up immaculate salutes.[42]

The 'graves' were shallow, and exhumation easily carried out later by the
Resistance. Shortly afterwards, Fr McGowan marched with the surviving
paratroops into captivity.

*   *   *

The divisions of 30th Corps were heavily engaged in the battle to relieve the carpet of paratroopers on the string of bridges from the Meuse–Escaut canal to the Lower Rhine, a narrow corridor of about 60 miles. Fr Reginald Anwyl of Birmingham had served with 50th Division since the Normandy landings. By this time it was accepted practice that chaplains should supervise burying the dead and registering the graves. Sometimes the work, traumatic anyway, could be ghastly. Prisoners of war were used as grave-diggers.

> Before long I had 18 bodies awaiting burial and was glad when I received a body of prisoners to set to work on the plot that I had chosen as a cemetery. Amongst the dead was a body without a head, which had no marks whereby I could identify it. Next day a message came from the Green Howards … to say that one of their officers was missing and would we look out for his body.[43]

Knowing the terrible uncertainty, which could last for years, that hangs over a family whose relative is 'missing believed killed' the priest redoubled his efforts at this ghastly work. Searching through the clothing on the body, eventually an identification mark on the inside of a gaiter was found, and the battalion was able to correctly inform the next of kin. Later, just before his unit was relieved for a rest, Fr Anwyl witnessed one of those terrible accidents of war which harmed friend more than the enemy.

> After four days we returned to Nijmegen but before we did we saw a huge fleet of Lancasters, and I think Halifaxes, pass over us. One of the leading planes dropped its bombs by some terrible accident behind us at Nijmegen killing many people. As this happened my blood ran cold for I thought that perhaps this plane was a path-finder and might be copied by the hundreds of following bombers. To my utter relief the rest knew their target better and flew steadily over the German lines. The A.A. fire from the Germans was heavy but seemingly powerless to check or influence the planes in any way though I saw three planes hit and some at least of their crew bale out.[44]

The Rhine crossing

During March 1945, 2nd Army prepared massively for the Rhine crossing. During the huge build-up of troops on the west bank of the Rhine, good accommodation in the ruins of Germany was at a premium. The headquarters to which one priest was attached were allocated quarters which undoubtedly added a new experience: 'For the first and last time in my life I lived in a brothel.'[45] In the occupied west bank of the Rhine, life for the German population returned to normal. 'Fraternization is already beginning. So far I have met no one who is, or ever was, a Nazi. Priests invite me to meals. People throng the streets laughing and talking …'[46]

A Jesuit priest attached to 52nd Lowland Division sat by the side of a road as his brigade trundled slowly by. Near him was a roadside sign that had a certain enterprising flavour but which would have appealed to soldiers' humour and drawn them to its author. It read 'Catholic Priest: Maybe the last you'll see'. The priest reported that he did great business. 'Men came out of the vehicles, knelt by my chair for Confession, received Holy Communion from the ciborium that I carried in my breast pocket, and signed their field post-cards. I gave each man a card certifying that he had received the Sacraments.'[47]

The Rhine crossing by 9th US Army and 2nd British Army was a combined land and air assault carried out by 6th British and 17th US Airborne Divisions a commando brigade and four infantry divisions, 51st Highland and 15th Scottish of 2nd British Army and 30th and 79th of 9th US Army. In the Rhine crossing and in the subsequent operations east of the river, three more chaplains became casualties, the last casualties of World War Two. Fr J. W. Kenny, of Lancaster, a parachute chaplain with 6th Airborne, was killed on 24 March shortly after he landed. Fr Maurice McGowan CSSR was wounded. A third chaplain, Fr Terence Quinlan, of Southwark, accompanied the commando brigade which crossed the Rhine under cover of a massive bombardment, concealed themselves until the barrage lifted then stormed German positions in Wesel while the defenders were still dazed.[48] During the commando attack Fr Quinlan was wounded slightly but carried on. Having crossed the Rhine, 2nd Army raced for the Elbe to meet the Russians.

Even at this stage of the war danger lurked everywhere for the unwary; near Bremen, 52nd Division was involved in stiff fighting in a dense forest close to Hopsten. The chaplain of 157 Brigade, Fr Laurence Kearns S J, lost his way while doing the rounds of the forward units; by mistake he crossed in front of an advancing RE mine-clearing section before the road was cleared. Driving back through the British lines he was halted at Bren-gun point by Royal Engineers. 'The sergeant then asked me to look back along the path and tell him if I noticed anything unusual. "Yes," I said, "there are some patches of ground of different colour." To this the sergeant told him with calm professional detachment, "Right sir, there are twenty-three German mines planted under those patches, and you have driven your car over all of them. You have proved to us that they are RM43s, and it will take the weight of a tank to set them off." '[49]

The German surrender

On 1 May, Fr Rutledge was with 3 CCS on Lüneberg Heath. The German Army had retired east of the Elbe. Two days later on 3 May, at Tactical Headquarters of 2nd Army, Fr Rutledge witnessed the arrival of a German military deputation who unconditionally surrendered. General Dempsey made them wait, and they later formally surrendered to Field-Marshal Montgomery.

> What we see is a long German staff car roll slowly up the drive, from which emerge two German generals in their scarlet-lined greatcoats and one admiral less brightly attired. They enter the house. They have come to offer unconditional surrender of all the German forces in the sector. Dempsey makes a point of keeping them waiting. They had wished to come last night but were told to wait until this morning. The formal acceptance will take place later at Montgomery's Tactical HQ ...[50]

Bergen/Belsen concentration camps

On 12 April 1945, when the battle for the north German plain was still at its height, two German officers under a flag of truce were seen approaching the line held by 159 Brigade. At brigade headquarters they stated that they had been sent to represent their High Command, which wished to discuss the question of a truce to hand over a large area twenty by ten kilometres, containing two concentration camps. The camps were said to contain 60,000 political prisoners, anti-Nazis, murderers, thieves and Jews. Guarding them were about 2,000 Hungarian troops and some Wehrmacht and SS troops. Two further German officers arrived stating there were 1,200 cases of typhus, and for humanitarian reasons wished the battle to bypass the area.

> However, on April 13 the Chief of Staff, 1st German Parachute Army asked 8th Corps to take control of the area ... Typhus had broken out among the concentration camp prisoners, and lack of food and supplies made the situation unmanageable for the German authorities. Would the British accept a truce and take over the camp areas immediately. The terms of the truce stated that the Hungarian troops and some hundreds of armed Wehrmacht soldiers would continue to do guard duties for six days and give assistance to the incoming troops. After the six days they would be returned, still armed, to their respective units. As for the SS (Schutz-Staffel) they could be treated as the British troops thought fit.[51]

The camps were inspected on 17 April 1945 by a mixed party of medical and religious experts to assess and organize the medical and spiritual welfare effort for the relief of the prisoners. The party consisted of:

> Lt Col A. M. Michie ADH
> Major R. P. G. Ormrod DADMS
> Capt W. Hughes, from a mobile laundry and bath unit (ML & BU)
> Rev O. D. Wiles, Deputy Assistant Chaplain-General
> Rev H. H. Welchman SCF (RC), 8th Corps
> Rev M. G. Morrison CF (RC), 121 Gen. Hosp.
> Rev L. Hardman CF (Jewish), HQ 8 Corps District[52]

Fr Welchman paid a second visit a few days later, then wrote a short memorandum on his visit for the Principal Chaplain (RC).

> On entering the camp a vast mass of pitiable humanity was seen sitting about or wandering around in a dazed and lifeless condition, seemingly indifferent to the appalling stench and squalor of their surroundings.
>
> They appeared to be mentally degraded almost to a sub-human level. They watched their companions dying all around them without a flicker of interest. Those who had scraps of food ate it squatting unconcernedly beside naked corpses. All sense of personal shame had been lost – men and women, suffering from dysentery, relieved themselves in the open. Seething crowds fought for water from the Army water-carts, refusing to believe the assurances of the troops that there was plenty for all and more to come. The more active rummaged among the piles of filthy rags stripped from the dead, jealously hoarding whatever they could find. It was definitely established that cannibalism had taken place.
>
> A number of huts were visited. The first was a hospital (so-called) containing dozens of bed-ridden patients in wooden bunks. Their apathetic misery gave way to hysterical weeping when they were spoken to kindly and assured that their slavery was really at an end and they would be well cared-for from now on.
>
> Two young Polish girls, sisters, related how they had seen their parents with hundreds of others burned alive in their previous concentration camp in Poland. The dreadful scene haunted them day and night and they were convinced that it would continue to do so for the rest of their lives. Their great concern was lest Kramer [Josef Kramer, Camp Commandant, later hanged], who had been responsible, should escape the punishment his crimes deserved.
>
> Two French women were proud of the part they had played in the underground Resistance movement, in spite of what it had cost them. A large party of French men had been transferred to Belsen a few days previously. They keenly appreciated their good fortune in being liberated before they too sank to the level of those around them, doomed to perish of slow starvation and disease. They asked for a priest (throughout their captivity they had been denied one) and were overjoyed when they heard that a British Military Chaplain was coming to live in the camp and that they would be able to attend Holy Mass and the Sacraments. They proudly produced their tattered prayer books and said that they had used them daily.
>
> On making a second visit to Belsen on 20 April it was found that Fr. M.G. Morrison CF who had meantime arrived with 32 CCS, had discovered among the prisoners about 50 priests of different nationalities still surviving; an unknown number had perished. They eagerly welcomed the opportunity of exercising their sacred ministry again and were most anxious to assist the Chaplain in his work in the camp, though most of them were incapable of exerting themselves much owing to their extremely feeble condition. At first so high was the death rate that the greater part of the day was spent administering the last Rite. It was most

touching to see the gratitude of these poor souls for the consolations of
their religion of which they had been deprived so long.[53]

The first British unit to enter Belsen was a battery of 63 (Anti-Tank) Regt
RA, followed two days later by 32 Casualty Clearing Station; Fr Morrison SJ
was attached. The cleaning and medical process then began.

About 70 SS guards, some 40 men and 30 women, were caught and put
on forced labour to bury the thousands of dead. Their food was reduced to
a minimum, some were beaten. They had to be transferred from the camp
to save their lives, but this failed; some had contracted typhus and died. By
comparison the Wehrmacht soldiers working at clearing the mess were
well treated. On the first day of their

> gruesome task of burying the corpses, a party of Wehrmacht soldiers
> broke down completely. Having deposited about two dozen bodies in the
> grave, a corporal ripped off his Iron Cross and stamped it in the ground.
> The rest of the company followed suit and tore off their badges and
> decorations in sheer disgust.[54]

The first Mass for the Catholic inmates of Belsen was celebrated on
Sunday, 22 April in a torrential downpour, by Fr Morrison. It was
suggested that because of the weather the Mass should be postponed, but
the congregation would have none of it. 'They put a rough covering of
canvas over the altar and clad in rags they knelt in sodden ground
throughout the Mass. They were drenched through but that did not
diminish the fervour and enthusiasm of their singing.'[55]

Death and burial of Heinrich Himmler

On 24 May 'Himmler, the most feared and hated of the Nazi secret service,
committed suicide in the Defence Company office next to my own in 31A
Lünebergstr. at about 1115 last night'.[56] Apparently, Himmler was a
Catholic. He was found to have a picture of the Blessed Virgin in his wallet.
The OC of the defence company apologized to Fr Rutledge for not calling
him. Fr Rutledge gives no indication of any remorse at not being able to
attend Himmler's final hours! The defence company buried the corpse of
Himmler in a secret grave on 26 May. Again Fr Rutledge was not called.[57]

War's end: reflection

In the course of the war far too many priests were perforce thrown into
their duties in war without adequate preparation. One spoke to a brother-
priest of his difficulty:

> He said in a tired voice 'This is my first time in action and I am absolutely
> lost. Tell me what on earth can one do? I am torn between about a dozen

duties each seeming to demand my immediate attention.' Recalling my own bewilderment when I was new to the work I pitied him. The work of a chaplain, of a priest at least, was made more difficult by the feeling wherever one was, that there was a better place to be in and whatever one was doing, that one should really be doing something else.[58]

At the end of the war priests were released in order of the Age and Service Release Group Number; many left in 1945, most in 1946. Very few did not return to their diocese or religious house. One priest asked for *exeat* during the war and promptly accepted a combatant commission. None, judging from obituary notices, regretted their war service, although most were reticent about their experiences. For this reason few books have been written by, or about, chaplains. The question 'Did you have any difficulty settling back to parish (or monastic) life after the war?' always brought an unqualified 'No'. Often, the returned parish priest was immediately confronted with a large outstanding mortgage on church, or presbytery or school (or perhaps all three), all in need of urgent repairs. In addition to this, there was the nettle of parish administration and spiritual ministry to be grasped. Usually the ex-chaplain had little time to ponder the past, or philosophize upon the future. Perhaps the diary of a Benedictine former chaplain contains the quintessential answer:

> The answer is easy. It was just like slipping one's hand into a well worn glove. For one thing, the monastic life was much easier physically than that which we had been living for the past six years. On top of that was a certain wonder at still being alive, an inability to realise why, when so many better men were dead, and the hope that perhaps God had still some work for us to do.[59]

Judging by correspondence received by the authors, there existed a mutually high regard between Catholic and Protestant chaplains. In the days before ecumenism became fashionable this was not always evident outside the armed services. Some tributes from Protestant pastors to their Catholic friends have already been shown; it is therefore fitting that a final tribute should come from a Catholic priest who worked with Anglican and Protestant chaplains among the soldiers in North Africa and Italy:

> I should add, also, that in that period before the great ecumenical advances of Vatican II, it was often a pleasure to work alongside the Protestant chaplains, and to admire their dedication.[60]

Notes and references

1. 21st Army Group HQ, 'Organisation of Chaplains (RC)', RCCA.
2. Canadian Army Chaplains' Report.
3. *Pax. The Prinknash Quarterly* (spring 1941).
4. *Ushaw College Magazine.*

5. *Lancaster Diocesan Directory* (1945), p. 83.
6. Citation, *London Gazette* (14 November 1944), quoted by G. Taylor, *Sea Chaplains* (London, 1978), p. 451.
7. *Lancaster Diocesan Directory* (1970).
8. Letters, Fr Crean to his father; courtesy of Fr Crean's niece, Mrs P. Moorhouse.
9. Rev Laurence Kearns SJ, 'Pretty bad times', *Interfuse* (1986), p. 20.
10. Greg Murphy, 'James O'Sullivan', *Catholic Times* (5 June 1994).
11. Fr Bernard Funnell, conversations with T. Johnstone.
12. Rev John W. Jones SM, CF 1939-47, notes, Chaplains' Department, RCCA.
13. Record of Service, RCCA.
14. Rev Brendan McConvey CSSR, 'A chaplain's wartime letters', *Reality - A Redemptorist Publication* (December 1994), p. 26.
15. Ibid., p. 25.
16. Ibid.
17. Ibid.
18. Ibid., p. 29.
19. *Letters and Notices* (Journal of the Society of Jesus), vol. 90, no. 399 (1990), p. 132.
20. Denys Rutledge OSB, 'Padre's progress', p. 144.
21. Jones.
22. Ibid.
23. Rutledge, p. 144.
24. Ibid., p. 147.
25. SCC Necrology.
26. Jones.
27. Rutledge, p. 148.
28. Murphy.
29. 'Padres at war', *Pegasus, Magazine of the Airborne Forces*, p. 91.
30. Dr Anthony Barling, conversations with T. Johnstone.
31. Stuart Mawson, *Arnhem Doctor* (London), pp. 86-8.
32. Ibid. According to Henry McAnelly, formerly of 1st Para, who fought in the battle and still lives in Oosterbeek, there were also German nuns from Münster staffing the hospital: letter, McAnelly to Fr D. Sexton, Hallam diocese (25 October 1993) refers.
33. Ibid.
34. News item, *Universe*. Undated copy held by authors.
35. News item, *Universe*. Undated copy held by authors.
36. General Sir John Hackett, *I Was a Stranger* (London, 1978), pp. 28-9.
37. Fr J. Hearn SJ, Jesuit Necrology, Melbourne.
38. Hackett, p. 29.
39. *Pegasus*, p. 91.
40. Ibid.
41. Ibid.
42. Ibid.
43. Fr Anwyl RA, War Diaries, RCCA.
44. Ibid.
45. Rutledge, p. 164.

46. Ibid., p. 167.
47. Kearns, p. 23.
48. Chester Wilmot, *The Struggle for Europe* (London, 1952), p. 682.
49. Kearns, p. 23.
50. Rutledge, p. 170.
51. Rev Edmund Swift SJ, *Letters and Notices*, vol. 90, no. 399 (1990), p. 139.
52. Fr H. H. Welchman, SCF (RC) 8th Corps, report to the Principal Chaplain (May 1945), RCCA.
53. Ibid.
54. Swift, p. 148.
55. Fr Michael Morrison SJ, 'At Belsen', *Interfuse*, no. 41 (1986), p. 73.
56. Rutledge, p. 174.
57. Ibid.
58. Anwyl.
59. Fr George Forbes OSB, 'The war diary of Fr George Forbes, OSB' (3 MS vols; unpublished), Ampleforth Abbey Archives.
60. Dom Alban Boultwood OSB, letter to James Hagerty.

19

Burma, the Far East and prisoners of war

Burma was totally unprepared for the Japanese invasion which followed swiftly upon the Japanese attack on the Americans at Pearl Harbor. General Harold Alexander was appointed commander of the Burma 'Army' and Lt Gen 'Bill' Slim became Corps Commander of 1st Burmese and 17th Indian Divisions, and the under-strength 7th Armoured Brigade. However, the best that could be done was to fight a defensive battle and destroy everything of material value to the enemy. In the course of the first half of 1942, Slim conducted the retreat of a defeated army across 900 miles, from Rangoon to Imphal in India, through some of the most inhospitable country on earth.

In this chaotic emergency, religion most assuredly would have been in the minds of the fighting troops and, privately, in their commanders' thoughts, but would not have been high in their priorities for military action. The organization of normal chaplaincy services would have to wait until the battle stabilized. Into the breach stepped two southern Irish missionary priests of the Columban Fathers: Fr James Cloonan and Fr Jeremiah Kelleher. This story is about one.

In March 1942, 1st Royal Inniskilling Fusiliers, at that time the oldest Irish regiment in the British Army, was flown into Burma. Although raised as a Protestant regiment to support King William III, since the Napoleonic wars it had always a large Catholic element. The battalion arrived in Burma without a Catholic chaplain. Happily, a Columban was stationed near the point of the battalion's arrival.

Fr Jeremiah Kelleher SSC was born in Rathmore, Co. Kerry, on 12 July 1912. Educated at St Brendan's College, Killarney, he received his priestly seminary training at Maynooth, and was ordained there. Leaving almost immediately for Burma, he joined a mission station in 1937. By the outbreak of war Fr Kelleher had become the missionary parish priest of

Hkudung near the Chinese border, and officiating chaplain to Kachin troops in the area. When news arrived of the Japanese invasion, Fr Kelleher was in Bhamo, the Columban headquarters of a province which included Myitkyina and Sumprabum. He at once requested permission from his Columban Superior to accompany Kachin troops going to the front. In granting permission, the Superior made it clear that it was granted only to serve Kachin troops - his mission, as the Columbans had no responsibility for British or Indian troops. He left in January 1942 and after a delay, while they sought authority from Delhi, which probably never arrived, the British authorities at Mamyo appointed him to a chaplaincy.[1]

Kelleher joined the Kachin troops in south Burma at the end of January 1942 and remained with them until early March. The Kachins were garrison troops responsible for rear areas' internal security, and were at this time in little danger. The arrival by air of 1st Inniskilling Fusiliers, on their way to the front, gave Fr Kelleher greater spiritual responsibility. On learning they had no chaplain of any denomination, and notwithstanding the orders of his superior, Fr Kelleher felt he had a wider duty. Judging that the Kachins were less in need of his spiritual care than the battalion of Fusiliers, he asked the battalion commander, Lt Col R. C. Cox, a Belfast Catholic, if he might accompany the battalion; his offer was immediately accepted.

> My work with them was very rewarding. Shortly after I joined them they were called upon to hold a Japanese break-through. None of the Catholics had had the sacraments for years so I asked the C.O. to ask the Catholics to remain behind after he had briefed his troops, and to tell them there was a Catholic chaplain who wished to speak to them. He did so. It was a very consoling experience for me. After I had spoken to them they all received general absolution but one of them came up asking for private confession. They went off to the front but all came back safely.[2]
>
> The young man who had asked for auricular confession was from Wexford. After the troops had come back from the front he came to me and said: 'Father, when the CO told us that day that there was a Catholic chaplain here in this benighted country I could not believe it and when he said that you were Irish I felt that God dropped you down from heaven for the Inniskilling Fusiliers'. That was tremendous for me; it was worth joining the army for that alone.[3]

Fr Kelleher was with the Inniskillings in the actions at Prome and Magwe; and during the battle at Yenanchyaung on 17-18 April, in the oil fields south of Mandalay. General Slim had been ordered to defend the oil wells and installations. But in doing this, the Burma Division was surrounded by the enemy, and its possible line of withdrawal across the Pin Chaung, a tributary of the Irrawaddy, was cut. The oil fields were set alight to deny them to the Japanese and the division fought its way out of the trap. On 18 April Fr Kelleher found himself in the middle of a ferocious battle.

> And a brutal battle it was. The temperature that day was 114 degrees; the battle was in the arid, hideous, blackened shale of the oil field, littered with wrecked derricks, flames roaring from the tanks ... burning buildings everywhere ... the British and Indian troops of the division fought doggedly over ridge after low ridge, the Japanese defending each to the last man ... a detachment of Inniskillings struggled through to the Pin Chaung ...[4]

In the course of the battle the Inniskillings lost heavily. Colonel Cox was killed during an air attack. Fr Kelleher had given him Holy Communion just fifteen minutes previously, and shortly afterwards Kelleher himself collapsed from heat exhaustion in the inferno. The troops put him into a tank (possibly of 7th Hussars) that fought its way through the Japanese road-block, with enemy machine-gun fire beating a tattoo on the armoured plating. Evacuated by ambulance to Mandalay, he was placed on an Irrawaddy river steamer converted into a hospital-ship. On board he recovered sufficiently to minister to the wounded during a long journey northwards to Myitkyina, where he arrived on 2 May. With fellow-Columban Fr James Cloonan, he began ministering to the troops in the hospitals of the area. The British were evacuating the sick and wounded by air, and a decision had to be made whether to accompany them to India or remain with the Kachins. Both priests stayed at their post. Fr Kelleher changed into a soutane, but Fr Cloonan remained in uniform and on being captured was beaten up by Japanese troops. Internment in Rangoon jail until the end of the war followed.[5]

The British retreated to the eastern border of India, and with the exception of the first Chindit expedition of 1942–43 stood on the defensive. The 14th Army was formed with General Slim as its commander. However, as early as April 1942 Field-Marshal Wavell and the Joint Planning Staff at Delhi had begun examining the problems of the reconquest of Burma.[6]

In the meantime, the Army had many lessons to learn about the nature of jungle fighting, and became battle-fit. Although chaplains were excused military training one spiritual descendant of Ignatius de Loyola took part.

> One evening the Colonel said, 'Look, we're going to have to start doing route marches again and we are going to begin by doing twenty-five miles tomorrow. Anybody who does not return will be taken back and confined to barracks'. ... I said I would go. So we set off North and I kept in step with the men, talking to them and generally giving a hand. After a while I was near the front of the column, talking to the dentist. Right in front of us a fellow fell flat on his face with the heat. We picked the man up and left him in a wayside cottage. I took his pack and his rifle and reached home after another four or five miles. When I got back to base, I received a great cheer.[7]

In February 1944, the 14th Army went on to the offensive: first in the Arakan, then in March and April at Imphal and Kohima. Fr M. J. O'Carroll, of Kilmore, was SCF (RC) India Command, and Fr J. A. Gardner, of Westminster, became SCF (RC), South East Asia Command.

Fr James O'Callaghan, of Hexham and Newcastle, was attached to 7th Worcesters during the Battle of Kohima, one of the hardest fought battles of the Burma campaign. His formation, 5th Brigade, 2nd Division, had been tasked with opening the road to Kohima, in Nagaland, north-east India, under siege by strong Japanese forces. Setting out from Dinanpur, the British railhead, the battalion staged at Milestone 32 before moving to Zubza next morning, 11 April 1944. The Japanese had Zubza under observation, with a 75 mm gun well sited to defend the road. Earlier, the Worcesters had lost four men, killed at first light by this gun, and when the battalion headquarters came into sight on the approach road the Japanese gun again opened fire. Several stories are told about the death of Fr O'Callaghan, one that he indicated a slit trench to a young soldier saying 'You go there – I won't need it', another tells of him dragging a wounded soldier to cover when killed by shell-fire. What is certain from the regimental records is that he was buried by two sergeants at Zubza. Later his remains were moved to the Kohima War Cemetery.[8]

After the battle, the pioneers of the Worcesters fashioned a teak memorial upon which was carved the names of the battalion's dead. Fr O'Callaghan's name is shown as: 'Captain (Rev) J. O'Callaghan, RAChD'. The Worcesters' memorial was placed initially in the Dak Bungalow (Government rest house) at Maram: then in 1952 it was moved to St George's Chapel, Worcester Cathedral, where it still is.

In ten months from the beginning of the offensive, hard fighting brought the British, Indian, and African troops to the banks of the Irrawaddy. The wide river provided the Japanese with a good defensive line; and the British with a formidable natural obstacle to surmount. But by a brilliant deception plan Slim's Army gained a bridgehead. Fr Horace Relph, a Birmingham priest, was in one of the first units to cross the Irrawaddy, and was able to say Mass in the bridgehead on Christmas Eve 1944.[9]

Although primary jungle gave shade from the sun, secondary jungle undergrowth was mostly impenetrable and a path had to be hacked through to allow forward movement. Humidity approaching 80 per cent meant everyone was perpetually soaked with perspiration. The clearest memory one chaplain had of Burma was the long marches in thick jungle.

> I rode mules. I swam rivers. The most terrible thing was the rattling of the bullets and their ricochetting off the trees. You would often get lost – even if you were very close to your comrades. You would have four or five hundred men clearing a path in front of you with hatchets cutting down

the under-growth so that we could follow with the mules. And on our way through, we came across three or four fellows who had been lost there quite a while. It wouldn't surprise me to hear that there were still some fellows out there even now.[10]

Fr John Hayes – The 'Willie Doyle of Burma'

Fr Hayes joined 36th Division at Poona in 1943 during its training period prior to its deployment in Burma. After the division moved to the Arakan front early in 1944, Fr Hayes adopted the rather unusual, but easily recognizable, dress of 'Ghurka hat, battle-dress blouse and blue rugger shorts';[11] soon he became a well-known figure in the divisional area. In the course of heavy fighting in the Arakan, and in the 36th Division's battle to capture Myitkyina Fr Hayes earned the affectionate sobriquet of 'Battling Hayes'.[12]

Fr Hayes contracted typhus, then pneumonia, and died on 21 January 1945 on the banks of the Irrawaddy just two months before 14th Army decisively defeated the Japanese at Meiktila, on the road to Mandalay, and Rangoon. Rangoon was retaken in early May. A letter of sympathy to Fr Hayes' Provincial was written shortly after his death by an officer serving with 36th Division.

> He joined us in Poona in 1943, and came with the Division to the Arakan early last year, and later flew in with us on our present operation. To one and all he was known as Battling Hayes, utterly devoid of fear. It was only on the express order of General Festing that he took his batman to act as escort when on his rounds. No matter where one went, more especially at the height of battle, there one would find Fr. Hayes ... It was common to see him walking along a road known to be infested with the enemy, without any protection of any kind, happy in the thought that he was doing his job. The highest praise I can pay Fr. Hayes, and in this our present chaplain, Fr. Clancy, agrees with me, is that he reminded me very much of the late Fr. Willie Doyle. Nothing mattered: monsoon rain, heat, disease, the enemy: his one thought was to be among his flock, doing all he could to help them. Nothing was too much trouble, and the further forward a unit was, the greater his delight in going forward to celebrate Mass. By his death all the Catholics of this Division, and many of the Protestants, have lost a great friend and the finest chaplain one could wish to have.[13]

General (later Field-Marshal) Festing wrote to the mother of Fr Hayes. 'I would like on behalf of this Division and myself to express our very deepest sympathy to you in the loss of your son. We all were fond of Fr Hayes who was an exemplification of all that a Catholic Priest and an Army Chaplain should be. He was a tireless worker, and if any man worked himself to death, it was he. Your son was an undoubted saint and he died fortified by the rites of Holy Church. May he rest in peace.'[14]

Soldiers have long accepted that awards for bravery in action are sometimes a lottery in which many deserving cases are passed over, especially in the British Army, to protect the high standing of its military decorations. Often those who deserve a much higher bravery award are only mentioned in despatches, the French equivalent of which is the *Croix de Guerre*. In the Burmese jungle one priest, Fr Peter Brady, was twice mentioned in despatches for bravery in action.

With the possible exception of the Allied armies in Italy, the 14th Army was probably the most polyglot of all armies in the Second World War. Among its wide diversity of personnel was the King's African Rifles (KAR), of 11th African Division, consisting largely of tribesmen from Kenya, Tanganyika and Uganda, led by white settlers. Skilled at fieldcraft, the East Africans quickly adapted to jungle fighting. Among its Catholic chaplains was Fr Tom Maher CSSp who had been a missionary priest in East Africa since 1932. Fr Maher had served with KAR East African Division in Eritrea and Ethiopia, before arriving in Burma with the division. With fine disregard for military regulations he wore no badges of rank and rarely wore a hat. His homily was always delivered robustly in fluent Swahili to a transfixed audience of African Askaris.[15]

Fr A. M. Daley MSFS and Clifton was attached to 1st Northamptonshire Regiment in 20th Indian Division, and was also twice mentioned in despatches. Fr Daley wrote that despite the war, the Japanese, and the jungle, the tradition of annual retreats for chaplains was not neglected. He attended one at Shillong on the north Burma/Assam border. During one of these retreats he made the acquaintance of a Presbyterian minister and his wife, in an uncommon setting which required the greatest courage and human devotion on their part.

> It [the retreat] was at the residence of one Fr. Sontag S.J. A Jesuit preacher, retreat master, editor of a Catholic newspaper, etc. Indeed he was very helpful. Fr Sontag suggested if interested, I should visit his neighbours; a Presbyterian minister and wife who managed a leper colony. I was delighted - what devotion![16]

Malaya 1941-45

For a long time after the outbreak of World War II, such was the nearness of war that in the Whitehall and Westminster nexus of power the Far East was very distant, geographically and mentally. As a result the military requirements of anywhere east of Suez had no priority.

In February 1941 the establishment of Catholic chaplains for the garrisons of Malaya and Singapore was two priests. The pressure of attempting to minister to many distant and scattered units in tropical conditions had caused the collapse of one priest, and the near breakdown of a second. A signal relating the facts to the War Office resulted in the approval of an increased establishment.[17] During August of the same year, two further priests arrived, bringing the total in Malaya/Singapore to four. However, one priest was posted immediately to Hong Kong.[18] In the next five months five more priests arrived, three just before the Japanese invasion.[19] During the second half of 1941, the arrival of 8th Australian Division with its supporting Arms and Services brought an additional ten Catholic chaplains to Singapore and Malaya. After the outbreak of war with the Japanese, one chaplain, Fr J. Lombardi, narrowly escaped capture and was later mentioned in despatches for his services. However, the following British and Australian chaplains were captured and imprisoned:

British Army chaplains	*Australian Army chaplains*
Fr M. L. Cowin, Northampton	Fr F. Burke SJ
Fr A. Jackson OFM	Fr P. X. Corry OP
Fr R. J. Kennedy SJ	Fr M. J. Dolan, Rockhampton
Fr J. O'Mahoney, Middlesbrough	Fr J. Kennedy CSSR
Fr E. Rowles, Nottingham,	Fr L. Marsden SM
SRC chaplain	Fr A. O'Donovan OFM
Fr K. Whelan CSSp	Fr B. Quirk OFM
Fr J. P. Ward, Clifton	Fr B. Rogers OFM
Fr J. Watson, Brentwood	Fr C. Sexton, Sydney
	Fr H. Smith SM
	Fr P. Walsh, Queensland

Hong Kong

Fr E. J. Green, of Menevia, had won the Military Medal serving in the ranks during World War I, entered the Church after his army service, and became a permanent Army chaplain on 29 May 1936. In 1940 and 1941 Fr Green was one of two Catholic chaplains ministering to all the troops in Malaya and Singapore. Naturally they were overworked and one, Fr F. H. Carless, of Birmingham, the SRC chaplain in Singapore, collapsed and was evacuated. His replacement had a serious disagreement with Fr Green chiefly, it would appear, because Fr Green married a girl, the daughter of a sergeant-major, to a sergeant against her parents' wishes, and against a court order they had taken out to prevent the marriage taking place.[20] Possibly, however, Fr Green was in possession of privileged information the parents, and senior chaplain, were unaware of. Fr Green was posted to Hong Kong, on War Office authority dated 3 May 1941, but his replacement did not arrive until August, and he disembarked at Hong Kong on 17 August.

On arrival he found that no office accommodation was allocated to him at Garrison Headquarters, but through the kindness of the Anglican chaplain, Fr Green used a room in the C of E hut beside the headquarters. The Catholic troops were widely scattered on Hong Kong island, in Kowloon, and on small off-shore islands. However, he was unable to discover their exact whereabouts from the Garrison Headquarters staff. In discussing administrative matters with the Rev S. James Squires, the senior Anglican chaplain, Green discovered a fellow-victim of over-secrecy. They decided to confront the Brigadier A.Q., the administrative head at the headquarters. The Brigadier told them plainly that the movements of troops were secret. They replied equally plainly, that if *they* were not to be trusted, he should send them home and replace them with men whom he could trust. Following this confrontation 'the necessary information [was] divulged'.[21] When he collated the information there were sixteen scattered places with troops to be ministered to in Hong Kong, Kowloon and the islands. Even so, such was the secrecy that one place was unknown to him until a few days before the Japanese invasion.[22]

War and imprisonment in the Far East

When war arrived on the doorstep of Hong Kong, Fr Green was inundated with requests for the sacraments. It is a truism frequently remarked upon that the closer the battlefield the more conscious of religion a man becomes. 'Not out of fear or cowardice, but because, possibly for the first time in their lives, they have come in contact with reality, and what they need is a clear conscience and peace of mind ... that only religion can give.'[23]

Fr Green confirmed this: 'Everybody was ready and glad to receive the Sacraments, not in panic fear, but as a chance of being reconciled to God. They all seemed to think it quite normal to receive them at any time and place. In the case of individuals I heard their confessions, but as a rule if there were three or more I gave a general absolution.'[24]

The Japanese invaded the New Territories on 8 December 1941, and thereafter Fr Green carried the Blessed Sacrament with him day and night mostly around his neck. He maintained a brief diary of main events until August 1942. A brief résumé of the next months follows:

> 9 December. Informed by HQ to position himself at Whitfield Bks Kowloon. Reported to the Royal Scots there, visited the forward companies then actually fighting.
> 11 December. Evacuated to H.K. Took position at St Albert's Hospital.
> 12-16 December. Visiting pill-boxes (defensive positions held by 1st Middlesex) for H.C. daily.
> 17 December. Ordered not to visit forward position by day. From then on he substituted the 15 mysteries of the Rosary for the Divine Office.

23 December. Captured. Hands up for two hours.[25]
On Christmas Eve, Fr. Green gave Holy Communion to all the Roman
Catholic bed-patients.

No general massacre took place at St Albert's as happened elsewhere in
Hong Kong, possibly because when the Japanese found the body of one of
their officers, upon whom obvious medical care was evident, the staff were
spared, although one sister had been killed and the matron wounded in
the preliminary bombardment.[26] On 27 December Japanese sentries were
removed from St Albert's, and on the following day Fr Green visited Bowen
Road Hospital. Possibly it was here that on New Year's Eve he read the
Burial Service in general for all unburied RC soldiers.[27] Fr Green was
allowed to remain at St Albert's for over a month after the surrender.

> The Dominican priests at St Albert's were kindness itself and I was able to
> say Mass daily in their chapel. After the capitulation I used to say night
> prayers there publicly also, with Benediction on Sundays and the greater
> feasts. A fair number of the patients and hospital staff attended daily. I
> found that the cessation of active hostilities had practically no effect on the
> religious revival among the men. All were still ready and anxious to take
> advantage of their opportunity of receiving the Sacraments regularly, and
> those who had received general absolutions regularised their positions.[28]

18.1.42. Visit Bowen Rd. Mass kit goes astray, say Rosary and preach.
24.1.42. Sing Requiem for all those killed in siege of Hong Kong.
25.1.42. Say Mass at Bowen Rd with kit borrowed from Jesuits. During
          week arranged for a Jesuit to say Mass each Sunday at Bowen
          Rd.
20.2.42. Take letter from Bp. Valtorta to Japanese consulate asking to
          have me interned in Shamshuipo.
25.2.42. Transferred to Shamshuipo internment camp.
 4.3.42. Solemnly bless 'Hut E3' as a Catholic Church dedicated to St
          Michael the Archangel. Solemnly erect the Stations of the Cross
          in the evening. All ceremonies and processions of the liturgical
          year were fully carried out from this onward.
16.3.42. The Japanese bring in all my vestments etc.
15.6.42. Fr. Grovelle sends in a monstrance and thurible.
16.8.42. I confirm 30 men by virtue of faculties granted me by the Vicar
          Apostolic of Hong Kong.[29]

Fr Green's arrival in Shamshuipo camp was in the nature of 'a triumphal
entry'. The troops were delighted to see him.

> I arrived on Wednesday, 25 February, after lights out, and said Mass
> privately the following morning. In the evening I heard confessions for
> one-and-a-half hours and from that day onwards did not miss hearing
> confessions daily, except when prevented by sickness. By Easter the great
> majority of the RC personnel had made their confessions, including a
> large number who had been away for many years.[30]

In response to his written request, the Japanese brought to him all his private Mass vestments and vessels from the hotel where he had lived, and from 17 March onwards he was able to carry out the full ceremonies of the Church.

Prior to Green's arrival a small hut had been allocated for RC worship, but it now proved inadequate, holding only 100, and after the first night there were more outside than in. He was given the use of one of the largest huts, which he 'solemnly blessed' on 4 March dedicating it to St Michael the Archangel. The General Officer Commanding attended the opening, at which Fr Green preached on the text 'There was no room for him at the Inn'.

Catholics in Shamshuipo numbered approximately 750: Army, RAF, Hong Kong Volunteers and Canadians. In April the Canadians were transferred and Royal Navy personnel took their place. Catholic troops of the Canadian brigade were ministered to by a Canadian chaplain, Fr F. J. Deloughery (Pembroke diocese).

> On Christmas Day the sad news was received of the surrender of Hong Kong, it is not known how many were killed or wounded. Among the two thousand Canadians, there were many Catholics.[31]

The Canadians fought so courageously that the Japanese took special vengeance against them.

The average number of daily communicants was 80, and 120 on Sundays.

> On Easter Day, we had about 500 and after that the average rose to 120 daily and 200 on Sundays. The normal daily attendance until dispersal in September was 250 and a similar number used to attend rosary at night.[32]

Except at meal and parade times the church was rarely empty. The Way of the Cross was frequently made. The ceremonies of Holy Week were carried out in full, and on Maundy Thursday the Japanese allowed the priest to keep the lights on in the church and to watch before the Altar of Repose until midnight.

> After that until reveille a few men remained in church with just the sanctuary light burning. So many men came to me for instruction in the Catholic Faith that after a short time I was unable to deal with them individually, but gave classes three times a week, working through the catechism, and starting again when I got to the end. This went on for about four months, during which time I received over thirty.[33]

Fr Green also sang Vespers every night until the Japanese took the church. He missed saying Mass for the prisoners on two Sundays and one feast-day in three and a half years of captivity. On the feast of the Assumption 1944, he collapsed with malaria on the altar during the vigil. He also missed saying Mass one Sunday on the ship carrying him to England in September

1945, because of tonsillitis. The above account is taken from a remarkable hand-written document headed: 'Report. To be forwarded to the Senior Roman Catholic Chaplain, The War Office, London.' Dated 24 September 1942. On the top right hand side of each sheet of paper in Chinese characters are the words: 'Hong Kong Enemy Prisoner of War Camp'.

In places such as Hong Kong and Singapore there was little restriction on the practice of religion. In the working camps elsewhere much depended upon the camp commandant. A few were humane, the majority were not, and those who harboured resentment against white races were in a position to vent unrestrained barbarism upon their unfortunate victims. Those who opposed their will were killed. Even without deliberate execution on whatever pretext, death was all too frequent among men desperately short of food, malnourished and debilitated by disease without medical supplies. All this was coupled with forced, unrelenting labour in a tropical environment: death came prematurely to thousands. The report of a British priest regarding Japanese policy on religion stressed the similarity in all POW camps in which he had been imprisoned. Mass was forbidden for long periods without reasons being given; when it was eventually allowed, homilies were prohibited. He was not allowed to visit neighbouring camps, and Catholics there were totally without the sacraments. It appeared to him that the Japanese were deliberately seeking to undermine the morale of prisoners.

> Although I made application scores of times to be allowed to visit adjoining camps where there were no Roman Catholic ministers to minister to the men, such permission was always refused, with no explanation and often rudely. With the result that hundreds of Catholics died denied the Sacraments, the supreme consolation of their faith, and burial by the priest. No transport was allowed for the bodies or burial parties, and the former, sewn up in sugar sacks, had to be carried to the cemetery on stretchers ... a mile distant. At a time when morale was low and full freedom of worship would have been of incalculable value, the Japanese went out of their way to obstruct chaplains in their work. They were indifferent to every kind of pleading. Throughout their captivity the prisoners of war were starved – starved of food – starved of clothing – of medical supplies – of news – of letters from home and starved of spiritual consolation.[34]

Australians are noted for blunt forthrightness. In his memoirs one former Australian prisoner wrote about the most dreadful of all those terrible places; the cholera camp.

> Let me tell you about our padre, Fr. Paddy Walsh. He is one of the real thinkers and went north with us [to Thailand]. During the terrifying days of our first cholera epidemic he was our only connection between the

dreadful Cholera Hill isolation area and the main camp. He gave each man a separate burial. I saw him conduct a Jewish service one day. Of the few men who returned from Thailand with an unsmirched reputation he is one. He never ever complained or spoke ill of our friends [the Japanese] and still preaches charity towards them. At Gemas [a battle during the fighting in Malaya] he administered spiritually, and Johnnie Walker, to wounded men. He is a most unassuming man, but was the spiritual father of the Unit, no matter what his Creed may be.[35]

In a letter to the authors Canon Walsh said that his charity had been stretched to the limit. In a matter-of-fact, unhistrionic way, he told of his ordeal in those far-off days, and places the blame not on the Japanese combat troops but those far behind the lines.

It's difficult to imagine the conditions of a POW camp. So much depended on the Camp Commander. There were one or two humane ones but the rest were sadists ... The Jap. engineers were mostly at fault. That railway line had to be finished and they didn't care how many died. Apart from a chaplain's usual work, my chief work was digging graves. On account of cholera, all dead had to be cremated, the ashes collected and put in bamboo containers each of which was 9 inches long. These 'coffins' were then buried, in 'mass graves' 18 inches by 9 inches by about nine inches deep.[36]

But digging even these tiny graves, by a sick debilitated person, in a bamboo jungle was back-breaking work. The same burial service might be given for up to as many as ten human remains.[37]

Another priest who in the absence of other chaplains regarded the men in his unit as being in his spiritual care, no matter what their faith, was Fr J. Kennedy CSSR or 'Pop' to the battalion.

He was of the earth, earthy, and he ate with us, marched where we marched, lived by our side and spoke our own forceful language. But there was a strength and a spirit in this rough man, with his practical faith, and he spoke not so much of the Kingdom to come, or of texts and dogmas, but of the need for kindness, courage, and cleanliness in our present life. Because he was one of us, seeking no privileges and clearly understanding our problems, his words carried conviction and a strange inspiration.

And when an anti-tank bombardier said, 'I'm grateful that you have restored my faith in God, Father, but I can't come to your Sunday Service because I'm an Anglican', Pop wheeled on him fiercely and said: 'Now you listen to me, you young idiot. God is not the property of any one Creed. He made us all, Anglicans and Catholics, so you be there – or else!'[38]

Following the liberation of prisoners of war held in Thailand, most had to be treated in hospital before being repatriated home. While hospitalized they were ministered to by chaplains of 12th Army. As a result of what was heard from the ex-prisoners, a report was sent by the SRC chaplain 12th Army, Fr G. Pritchard, to Fr J. Gardner SRC chaplain HQ Allied Land Forces South East Asia, concerning Fr Malcolm Cowin formerly with 18th Division in Malaya.

> I have heard from very many officers and British other ranks about the magnificent work that he did during these three and a half years. I have been visiting one of the 2000 bed hospitals of Evacuated POWs each day – and I should imagine the men I meet represent a cross-section of the whole. Again and again the names of two have been heard – Fr. Cowin and Fr. Burke (a [New Zealand] Redemptorist). Their work had been carried out in spite of all the obstacles placed in their way by the Japanese. There can be no doubt to my mind (after three weeks continually hearing the testimony of so many people) that these Fathers have achieved something of which we may feel proud and grateful to God.[39]

Like the vast majority of returned former prisoners of war, few of the returned priests were decorated by the military authorities. One, Fr Lionel Marsden SM, was created an OBE, and several were mentioned in despatches. This paucity of recognition seems remarkable, considering the spiritual hope and moral encouragement they gave that helped sustain so many, especially within those terrible camps of Thailand. It would appear that whatever their sufferings and privations, the fact that they had continued to tend their flocks in captivity, under appalling conditions that defy description, was simply doing their duty. They on their part sought out no praise or glory; they had simply attended to God's work on earth in adversity, just as the early Fathers of the Church had. After the war Fr Marsden went to Japan as a missionary. He is said to have wanted to convert one Japanese for every sleeper on the 'Death Railway'. 'I doubt if he ever realised that ambition.'[40]

Another priest who remained in the Far East was Fr Richard Kennedy SJ. He had arrived in Singapore only to become a prisoner almost immediately, and was imprisoned in Malaya, Formosa, and Manchuria. Somehow, probably because they were from neutral Ireland, while in Formosa during 1944 he received two letters, written in 1942. Fr Kennedy's reply was brief, and was eventually delivered in Ireland: 'Cheers! Your letters of 1942 arrived yesterday. I went to bed singing last night.'[41] In Changi prison Fr Kennedy had erected a chapel in the 11th Indian Division area dedicated to St Ignatius Loyola.

Fifty years later, still serving in the Far East, Fr Kennedy gave an all too familiar, and understandable, reply to a request for reminiscences:

> This note is to turn down your kind invitation to write a few pages of war-time reminiscences. Reasons? I am old and for the most part unwell. Besides, three and a half of my years in the army were spent in very unpleasant Japanese gaols, so I would not have much to say.[42]

Several chapels were built in Changi besides Fr Kennedy's. Fr A. Jackson OFM, with 18th British Division, built one dedicated to Our Lady of Lourdes, Fr F. Burke SJ erected one to Our Lady of Perpetual Succour. The church of Fr Dolan SJ in the Australian area was dedicated to St Francis Xavier. Perhaps the most remarkable of the Changi chapels was the one built at Sime Road after the return from Thailand. There was only one chaplain of any denomination in the camp, Fr Lionel Marsden. A Royal Engineer officer, Hamish Cameron-Smith, designed the chapel, and built it with the assistance of Lt Hugh Simon-Thwaites. In front of the chapel a memorial plaque was erected on which was inscribed: 'This chapel is dedicated to Our Lady Help of Christians and in memory of our deceased comrades who died in Malaya, Netherlands East Indies, Thailand and Burma, over whose remains there was no Christian symbol.'[43]

Hugh Simon-Thwaites became a Jesuit priest. In a remarkable tribute to Fr Marsden he wrote:

> One evening when we got back from the cutting [a railway cutting the prisoners were hacking through the jungle], we were told that there was a Catholic priest in the camp and he would be offering Mass. I went round to where he was. He'd set up his little altar – two small crates covered with a white cloth with two candles burning. Around us were the tree trunks going up into the darkness, like the columns of a cathedral, and I remember thinking to myself, 'St Peter's in Rome must be quite grand, but it's places like this that keep the Church going.' There were perhaps a dozen of us at the Mass.
>
> Afterwards, as he was unvesting, he said a few words – words I've never forgotten. He said, 'If you fellows could realise it, you're living through the most precious time of your lives.' Now this was a time when we had cholera in the camp, out of nearly 250 of us left, nearly 150 died. And yet he said that.[44]

Prisoners of war in Italy and Germany

The first Army Catholic chaplains captured were those taken during the Battle of France in the blazing summer of 1940. The greatest suffering endured by prisoners of war in Europe was hunger and thirst in the early weeks of captivity before reaching the relative stability of a POW camp. Once there, conditions were at least tolerable, and although food may have been scarce, camp diet supplemented by bulk and variety contained in Red Cross parcels sustained health. Amongst the early prisoners were Fr C. Scarborough, of Southwark, Fr M. A. Charlton CSSR and Fr K. Grant, Argyll and the Isles. With thousands of British prisoners they marched for weeks across France, Belgium and Germany before reaching a train terminal for an easier journey to camps in Bavaria.

You could never be sure when the longed-for opportunity to procure water would present itself and with food scarce or absent the desire to drink would have been sufficiently strong even without the very hot weather of the 1940 summer. A kindly action of a German once allowed us to get up about 2 a.m. in the morning and move off as soon as it was light, so that we got through much of the day's marching before the sun was high.

Wherever you spent a night you would scour the area for anything of value. Officers would sometimes be in a building: it was always worth while searching thoroughly though it might appear to have been gone through previously. I remember finding a bit of chintz curtain which mended my shirt for about a year. One of my group (a dozen or so of us who moved together and shared our findings) found a quantity of raisins which had obviously been spilt from a sack on the ground which we gathered. On another occasion one of us was somehow contacted by a Belgian boy who said that if we gave him money, he would get what he could in the village. The risk was taken with excellent results. Such events may seem trivialities, but they are the all-important realities in a prisoner's early life.[45]

At first chaplains were refused permission to say Mass or hear confessions. One priest was informed that a German priest would say Mass and hear confessions. One of the first German priests Fr Scarborough met was a Capuchin friar, who arrived wearing the Iron Cross (First Class) on his habit. He had won the decoration in World War I and the wearing of this made it easier for him to minister to prisoners. Until the end of the war priests were forbidden to hear confessions; however, 'private conversations' were allowed![46]

Fr Scarborough was transferred to what was deemed by the Germans to be the most secure of all camps, Colditz Castle. Twice it was his sad duty to say Requiem Mass for fellow-prisoners: once for Lord Arundel of Wardour, who had never recovered from wounds received at Dunkirk and died shortly after repatriation during the war. The other was for Ulsterman Mike Sinclair, who was shot during an attempted escape. 'Scarborough (the RC chaplain) said a requiem mass this morning, a generous thing to do, for Mike was not an RC.'[47]

Fr Kenneth Grant, afterwards Bishop of Argyll and the Isles, force-marched with the Highlanders of the 51st Division from Saint-Valéry-en-Caux through France, the Low Countries, and into Germany before the long train journey to a stay of nearly five years behind barbed wire.

> Of the five years that followed, the Bishop was later to consider them the happiest of his life. By experience he learned what it is to suffer cold, hunger, terror, depression of spirits, and even the temptation to despair. But in compensation he experienced also a knowledge of men at their best and at their worst; he knew the meaning of true comradeship, and the charity which is proved only in adversity; he had the consolation of bringing Christ to men who might never have known Him, and who needed Him most.

In times of great stress he would point to the distant Alps and quote the psalms, 'Lift up your eyes to the hills', and remind his Highlanders and Islandmen of home.[48]

After the early months of captivity, life became less boring with the arrival of books, musical instruments and sports equipment. Various activities were organized and lectures arranged. Because of the presence of so many Scots in one camp, courses in Highland dancing and Gaelic became the most popular.[49] In one Italian camp, Campo 21, Chieti Scala, the Anglicans were very active and well-organized. In addition to Sunday and weekday services, training courses were established for prospective Church students, at which a Catholic chaplain was invited to talk about the Catholic faith.[50] 'Indeed, relations were very friendly between chaplains of all denominations.'[51] After a time it was the loss of freedom that was most keenly felt. However, this was not felt by all. Fr Michael Charlton CSSR, taken prisoner at Dunkirk, was known in his camp as 'the mad monk'. Once, listening to his fellow-prisoners bemoaning their fate, he silenced them by exclaiming 'I don't know about you chaps, but I've never been so free before'. However, he was one of those that 'had the consolation of being able to celebrate Mass each day'.[52]

Fr George Forster, captured at Tobruk, was subsequently a POW in Italy and Germany. Next to being killed or mutilated the most serious thing which can befall a chaplain in action is the loss of his Mass kit. Fr Forster lost all his kit when his car was blown-up by a shell during the bombardment which preceded the overwhelming attack at Tobruk. Because of his loss, in the early days of captivity in a camp at Bari, Fr Forster was unable to say Mass, and an Italian chaplain promised the loan of a Mass kit. The following Sunday morning he duly arrived and set up an altar draped with the Italian flag, much as a British battalion drapes the Union flag over its stacked drums for a drum-head service. Fr Forster flatly refused to use it and his congregation supported him. The Italian priest and the camp commandant were outraged, but were told by Forster the Church is universal not Italian, and for British soldiers Mass in such a way was out of the question.

> There was a heated argument. The Commandant and a visiting General joined in and seemed to be accusing us of insulting the Italian flag by refusing to celebrate Mass on it. But we held our ground and the chaplain removed the flag with bad grace, while General and Commandant scowled at us. I was able to say Mass and give Holy Communion to a large number of officers and men.[53]

Later, more priests arrived in the camp; some had their portable altars and daily Mass became a regular feature of camp life. A mission was held attended by some 150–200 officers, all communicants. The Italian chaplain became more co-operative and supplied wine and altar breads.

Because of the dilapidated state of his desert uniform, Fr Forster was loaned a Franciscan habit, and speaking Italian as he did might easily have escaped to Rome and Vatican City. Such a thought never occurred to him and he remained with his flock, shared their captivity and ministered to their spiritual needs until the end of the war.

It is the duty of prisoners to attempt to escape from captivity and chaplains also have a duty to their flock in captivity; usually the latter duty won. However, because there were several Catholic chaplains in his camp, in the chaos which ensued following the Italian surrender, and before the Germans appeared to guard the prisoners, many British escaped to the hills and were assisted by partisans to regain their freedom, and Fr Edward Gibson CSSR, who had been captured in North Africa, was one who attempted to escape. He found refuge for a time in a Redemptorist monastery, and a guide was found to take him to Switzerland. However, the guide betrayed him to the Germans, who sent him to Germany for the remainder of the war.[54]

In 1944 Fr T. J. E. Lynch, writing from Oflag IX A/Z, reported that he had been there since the previous October, on transfer from Italy, and had not been allowed to minister to camps where there were no chaplains, although he had twice signed documents certifying his willingness to say Mass.

> Unfortunately there are two other priests here, Fr. Michael Charlton and Fr. George Foster [sic]; and as there are only thirty Catholics in this camp you can see how we have been unable to get work for six months. I have managed to say Mass fairly regularly during that time and this has been a great consolation. We keep well, and considering the trying circumstances of enforced idleness, cheerful.[55]

Acting on this and other information, the matter of enforced unemployment of chaplains was almost immediately taken up by the War Office with the 'Protecting Power', Switzerland, through the Foreign Office.

> It has been reliably reported that there are twenty British chaplains at Oflag IX AZ and a further twenty British chaplains transferred from Italy detained at Oflag VA. His Majesty's Government in the United Kingdom consider it important that the British chaplains who remain in Germany should be given full facilities to minister to British prisoners of war and that to this end they should be distributed amongst the camps to the best advantage. His Majesty's Government are for their part according all reasonable facilities to German chaplains who are prisoners of war.[56]

For Allied prisoners of war in Europe, the Geneva Convention, which was generally observed by Germany and Italy, proved a reassuring safeguard. The commitment of the International Red Cross, and Switzerland, towards the safeguarding of prisoners' rights was well tested in the Second World War and, to their lasting honour, was not found wanting, whereas the treatment of prisoners in the hands of the Japanese, who had not signed the Convention, has to be an enduring stain. It ought to be a matter of the gravest human concern for the United Nations if any member-state refuses to sign this Convention.

References

1. Fr Jeremiah Kelleher SSC, transcript of a taped interview (4 September 1989), SSC Archives, courtesy of Royal Inniskilling Fusiliers Museum.
2. Ibid.
3. Ibid.
4. Field-Marshal Viscount Slim, *Defeat Into Victory* (London, 1959), pp. 67–8.
5. Kelleher.
6. Bernard Fergusson, *Beyond the Chindwin* (London, 1945), p. 2.
7. Fr Conor Naughton SJ, *Interfuse*, no. 41, p. 41.
8. Hexham and Newcastle Diocesan Necrology.
9. Necrology, Birmingham archdiocese.
10. Naughton, p. 42.
11. 'Our single casualty. The death in Burma of Fr. John Hayes', *Interfuse*, no. 41, pp. 82–4.
12. Ibid.
13. Letter from an officer of 36th Division, quoted in *Interfuse*, no. 41, p. 24.
14. *AMDG* (Journal of the Irish Province of the Society of Jesus) (1945), p. 461.
15. T. Johnstone, conversations with Fr Maher.
16. Correspondence with Fr Daley.
17. Fr Edward Rowles, SRC chaplain, Singapore 1941–42, letters to Bishop Dey (14 February 1941, 24 April 1941, and 6 June 1941), RCCA.
18. Rowles, letter (19 August 1941), RCCA.
19. Rowles, letter SCF/RC/298-L (1 January 1942) to Mgr Coghlan, the War Office, RCCA.
20. Rowles, letter to Bishop Dey (19 August 1941), RCCA.
21. Fr Eric Green, report to the Principal Chaplain (RC), RCCA.
22. Ibid.
23. Dom R. Brookes OSB, quoted by Sir John Smyth, *In This Sign Conquer* (London, 1968), p. 286.
24. Green.
25. Ibid.
26. Smyth, p. 286.
27. Green.
28. Ibid.
29. Ibid.
30. Ibid.
31. Second Annual Report of the Canadian Chaplaincy Service (RC) (1 January 1941–31 December 1941), p. 13.
32. Green.
33. Ibid.
34. Fr M. Cowin, quoted by Smyth, p. 290.

35. Stan Arneil, *One Man's War* (Chippendale, NSW, 1981), p. 181.

36. Canon Patrick Walsh, Queensland, correspondence with T. Johnstone.

37. Ibid.

38. Kenneth Harrison, *The Brave Japanese*, quoted in Smyth, pp. 293-4.

39. Fr G. Pritchard, letter 60093/CH (RC) (3 October 1945) to Fr J. Gardner, SRC chaplain HQ Allied Land Forces South East Asia, RCCA.

40. Walsh.

41. Fr Richard Kennedy SJ, 'So sorry', *Interfuse*, no. 41, p. 15.

42. Ibid.

43. Lionel Marsden, 'Under the heel of a brutal enemy our boys kept the faith', *The Catholic Weekly* (15 November 1945).

44. Fr H. Simon-Thwaites SJ, letter (11 October 1995) to T. Johnstone.

45. Fr C. Scarborough, 'Chaplain in captivity', *Southwark Journal* (1959), pp. 68-9.

46. Ibid.

47. Margaret Duggan, *Padre in Colditz: The Diary of Ellison Platt* (London, 1978), p. 263.

48. SCD (1960), Obituaries, p. 326.

49. Scarborough, p. 69.

50. Fr George Forster, *Priest Behind Barbed Wire* (printed privately), p. 36.

51. Ibid.

52. *Ushaw College Magazine* (July 1941), p. 199.

53. Forster, p. 23.

54. CSSR Necrology.

55. Fr T. J. E. Lynch, letter to Mgr Coghlan (15 May 1944), RCCA.

56. Foreign Office memorandum, 0103/3098 (P.W.2) (15 July 1944), RCCA.

20

Royal Navy chaplains (RC): World War II and after

According to the *Catholic Directory for England and Wales* (1940), the ecclesiastical superior for 'His Majesty's Forces' was Rt Rev James Dey DSO, Bishop of Sebastopolis. However, since 1935, the Admiralty recognized only Rt Rev Arthur Hinsley, Cardinal Archbishop of Westminster, the successor to Cardinal Bourne, as the ecclesiastical superior and delegate of the Holy See to Royal Navy Catholic chaplains.

On the outbreak of war, including those recalled from the reserve, there was a total of eleven commissioned chaplains to serve all Catholics in the Royal Navy, ashore and afloat. At that time the Royal Navy was the strongest naval force in the world, spread from Bermuda to Hong Kong. Expansion to match the size of the Navy was painfully slow. Six were commissioned in 1939; seven in 1940; twelve in 1941; six in 1942; nine in 1943; eleven in 1944; and four in 1945. Perhaps the reluctance of some bishops to allow young priests to volunteer had something to do with this slow recruitment. Whatever the cause, the burden thus thrown on serving chaplains could only have been severe. Not to mention the neglect felt by serving Catholic sailors: as the Principal Chaplain told a volunteer priest in 1944: 'I'd almost come to believe our bishops had put an embargo on us.' He had had no reinforcements for months.[1]

In 1940 Mgr Edward John Dewey, a Westcountryman from Dorset, was appointed Principal Chaplain (RC) at the Admiralty. Mgr Dewey had been commissioned a Chaplain RN (Temporary) on 3 February 1921, and was still a 'Temporary' commissioned officer because only Church of England chaplains could become full permanent chaplains RN. Dewey, of Plymouth diocese, was a graduate of St Alban's, Valladolid. In 1913 his long attachment to the Navy began, six years after his ordination. Becoming parish priest at Devonport automatically meant he was officiating chaplain there until his commissioning into the Navy in 1921. By 1939, he was a very experienced sea-going chaplain, having served in *Hood, Tiger* and *Royal Sovereign.* He had been Senior Naval Chaplain (RC) Mediterranean Fleet since 1931, and upon the outbreak of war was posted home and became chaplain to HMS *Caledonia* – the boys' training establishment. Although there were two chaplains senior to him in the Navy List in 1940, Mgr Dewey was appointed Principal Naval Chaplain (RC). It was said that 'the whole Navy knew him as a keen footballer, and a selector of teams for the Fleets'.[2]

It seems incredible that a service at the leading edge of naval warfare technology since the launching of HMS *Dreadnought* 40 years before, and socially cosmopolitan, could be, at the highest level, bigoted in religious attitudes. The Admiralty proved more resistant to religious equality than any other public department of Great Britain.

In a paper written in 1907 detailing how poor facilities were for Catholics in the Royal Navy to attend the sacraments, even in the Channel fleet, the writer, then recently ashore from service with the Navy, remarked:

> A lot may happen in two years and conditions may have changed since I came on shore. Personally, I sincerely hope they have changed but I am afraid that they have not. The Navy is a very conservative institution and, following the traditions of the senior service, every naval officer, from the Admiral of the Fleet down to the last joined naval cadet, looks with a chilly suspicion on proposals for any innovation, be it what it may.[3]

In the 32 years up to the outbreak of World War II, nothing had changed in this respect. Facilities were just as poor. Moreover, chaplains of 'fancy religions'[4] were still not regarded as worthy of permanent commissions in the Royal Navy. Not until over a year after the declaration of the Atlantic Charter, on board a battleship, guaranteeing freedom of conscience, did their lordships of the Admiralty decree that chaplains of all denominations could become full Chaplains RN.[5] This was after the appointment of Admiral Andrew Cunningham as First Sea Lord, the greatest British fighting admiral of the Second World War. Significantly, Cunningham's religious background was Presbyterian.

Whatever the reasons for the Admiralty's religious attitudes they were not shared by Anglican chaplains, as evinced by the comments and writings of Catholic chaplains. Indeed, the co-operation between chaplains of all denominations was, according to Catholic chaplains, very good. 'I never met unpleasant chaplains of other denominations ... they were excellent men.' Another, writing of one Anglican chaplain, Rev M. A. P. Wood (later Bishop of Norwich), quoted Shakespeare: 'he was also "the glass of fashion and the mould of form".'[6]

This high regard is also true in respect to naval officers, as testified by chaplains who served in World War I and shown in an earlier chapter. A report in a Catholic newspaper of 1943 confirms the continued good relations.

> In port he will usually muster all his flock in a convenient church, and
> Catholics in the Royal navy are envied their not infrequent chance to
> 'shake a leg,' especially after being cooped up in battleships serving in
> tropical seas. Confessions are easily managed, for the 'Bishop' (a naval
> Chaplain is rarely a 'padre' and nearly always the 'Bishop') has a
> privileged cabin definitely arranged for private interviews. On visiting
> other ships I have never failed to borrow the cabin of another officer, or to
> have space 'rigged' for Mass ... No one has the run of the ship like the
> chaplain. With official blessing he may go anywhere, converse with
> anyone.

Although obviously part of the morale-boosting effort of the time, this does
not detract from its obvious sincerity.[7]

As in previous wars, the enemy were less discriminating than the
Admiralty, killing seamen irrespective of creed. Within weeks of the
declaration of war a German U-boat penetrated the harbour defences of
Scapa Flow and sank HMS *Royal Oak* with heavy loss of life. In reply the
Navy exhibited its accustomed valour whatever the odds. The converted
merchant cruiser *Rawalpindi* took on two German battle cruisers and was
sunk with colours flying. In December *Ajax*, *Achilles* and *Exeter* suffered
casualties in the running battle against *Graf Spee*. The destroyer *Glowworm*,
its upper works a shambles of wreckage, rammed the heavy cruiser *Hipper*
causing serious damage before going down herself. Another armed
merchant cruiser, *Jervis Bay*, took on the pocket battleship *Scheer* and
sacrificed herself to save a convoy. In the succeeding two years the Royal
Navy suffered its greatest casualties of the war by the sinking of the battle
cruisers *Hood* and *Repulse*, and the battleship *Prince of Wales*. Catholic
chaplains would gladly have joined their Anglican colleagues, Canon
C. J. S. Bezzant and Rev W. G. Parker, who went down with those great
ships. Their feelings at not having one of their number aboard to minister
to the Catholics of the ship's company before action may be judged by
those of Australian chaplain Fr Thomas Campbell CSSR who 'to his
chagrin missed the last sailing of *Centaur* before she was sunk by a
Japanese submarine'.[8]

Training, or even briefing, for naval chaplains before joining an
operational unit was as neglected as in the Army during the early part of
the war. One former wartime chaplain, Fr George Pitt, recalled its
casualness.

> My entry into the Royal Navy was most unlikely and unexpected. I had
> been ordained only three years previously and of a rather delicate
> constitution. I had been convalescing all the previous year from an attack
> of tubercular pleurisy. My Bishop, Lee of Clifton, during the war said, 'no
> curate need apply [for a chaplaincy]. Parish Priests may do so only if they
> renounce all claims to the parish if they survive'. However, on the subject
> of my convalescence a problem arose between my medical consultant and

the Bishop. To settle the matter he challenged me to become a chaplain; he expected me to say if I could not stand up to the life of an ordinary priest how could I stand the rigours of a military life. To his surprise I said I would give it a try, and told him I knew I was unfit for service in the Army, but as both my brothers were already serving in the Royal Navy I would offer my services to the Principal Catholic Chaplain at the Admiralty.

It still seemed most unlikely that I would pass the required naval medical examination but by a mixture of confidence, skill and sheer cheek, I managed to do so and on 20 July I received notice of my appointment as a Chaplain R.N. (Temporary), and ordered to join the *Oxfordshire*, a naval hospital ship somewhere in the Mediterranean. I was told to purchase a naval uniform, and prepare to join the steamship *Cameronia*, a troopship preparing to sail for Gibraltar in two weeks time.

There was no opportunity to make contact with any naval chaplain, and I presented myself at the dockside at Greenock with absolutely no training on how to be a chaplain in the Royal Navy. I simply replaced my civilian suit with its black buttons, for a naval jacket with brass buttons, and hey presto I was a fully fledged chaplain facing a world at war.

Perhaps I was over-confident, but on finishing my training to be a priest at the Venerable English College (Rome), I was told, 'you are now fully equipped to cope with any situation as a priest, go out, set to and do it.' Here I could put this into practice. 'You are a Catholic priest, always live and behave as a Catholic priest, and all will be well with you, whatever situation you find yourself.'[9]

The Battle of the Atlantic

Ministering to the fleet anchored in Scapa Flow during foul weather in winter was not for the faint-hearted. Although there were several Catholic chaplains on station there, the demand for their service was great. Mgr Dewey forbade them to say more than three Masses on Sunday.[10] These were the days of long fasting before Communion! In addition to saying Mass in his own ship, HMS *Dunluce Castle*, an auxiliary cruiser, Fr Rory O'Sullivan celebrated Mass on shore in a 'Mass hut' built by Italian prisoners of war, and in the admiral's cabin of HMS *Iron Duke*, once used by Admiral Jellicoe.

'To board it was a murderous trip. It was no joke climbing up rope ladders in foul weather. My altar kit went first.' However, once he got there the results could only have been heartening. 'I had the men sing Gregorian chant at Mass – *Kyrie Fons Bonitatis*.'[11] In addition to his other duties, such as visiting two hospital ships, Fr O'Sullivan undertook religious ministration to naval families ashore. 'In [my] spare time, I gave catechism instruction to the children of wives ashore on request.'

One of the bases in the front line of the Battle of the Atlantic was Lough Foyle, Northern Ireland. The officiating chaplain there from the outbreak of war was one of the most remarkable persons ever to serve as a chaplain RN, Fr William Devine. An Ulsterman, Fr Devine was ordained at St Patrick's College, Maynooth on 23 June 1912 for the diocese of Derry. However, immediately after ordination Fr Devine went to Australia 'on loan'. On the outbreak of war in 1914 he volunteered and was commissioned chaplain. Wounded at Gallipoli, he later served in France and was awarded the Military Cross, and the *Croix de Guerre avec Palme*. After the war he returned to Melbourne to serve as a parish priest before going to China to lecture at the new Catholic University. Possibly it was here that he wrote his 72-page history of the world! Recalled to Ireland in 1932, on the outbreak of war he was first an officiating chaplain then commissioned temporary chaplain on 1 January 1941. Fr Devine served with the Atlantic Fleet until the tide of success turned against the U-boats in 1943, when he went to serve with the Mediterranean Fleet.

It was said that while an officiating chaplain at Lough Foyle he so impressed the captains of the flotillas based there and 'made such good contact with the ships calling into the station that the captains would willingly take him to sea for weeks at a time. On becoming an active chaplain he was unwearying in his care of the ships at sea.'[12] At the Derry base Devine insisted that the men of his flotillas attended confession and Communion before going to sea. When he himself went to sea he confessed to Fr Joe McCauley: 'I will have to do what I oblige my men to do.'[13]

As their numbers increased more Catholic chaplains went to sea, such as in the operations to sink the *Bismarck*, following the destruction of HMS *Hood*. Indeed, service life revealed, or developed, strengths in chaplains hitherto not obvious to their priestly confrères. Fr Gerard Costello CSSR, 'A very gentle sort of man', was commissioned in May 1940 and then transferred to the Royal Marine Commandos. With them he took part in several operations including the Walcheren operation. 'Some of these quiet types can surprise one!'[14]

With the Mediterranean Fleet

The entry of Italy into the war almost upon the fall of France instigated the naval war in the Mediterranean. But it was against the French Navy that action first took place. Faced with the possibility of the powerful Navy of its former ally falling into enemy hands, and despite many French ships having continued the fight with Britain, the decision was taken in London to prevent this. Admiral Cunningham, C in C Mediterranean Fleet, was ordered to deny to the enemy the French warships sheltering in North African ports. The French refused to accept any of the British alternatives, and were bombarded. At Oran, French ships were blown up or disabled with considerable loss of life. Even amongst the Free French Navy feelings ran high over the British action. Writing from Portsmouth to the Archbishop of Westminster (still in the eyes of the writer his ecclesiastical superior), Fr William Purcell told him:

> We have a lot of Frenchmen still here. They are those who have made up their minds to soldier on with us. They seem very happy. I see a great deal of them; which is natural. But I had a most unhappy time with the officers at the time we took their ships. They were terribly *hurt*. Some of them had spent hours in my Chapel and had questioned me frequently on the moral aspect of blowing themselves up with their ships, of making a resistance which would inevitably have meant their own deaths, and so on. Thank God none of those things happened; though I had to intervene in one case.[15]

During the battle for Crete many cruisers and destroyers were lost. In the course of the action Fr J. D. Dobbins OFMCap greatly distinguished himself and was amongst the last off the Cretan beaches. He had already become famous in both the Home and Mediterranean Fleets for wearing his Franciscan habit instead of naval uniform. An article about him, together with a photograph in *Renown* wearing his habit, even appeared in a Spanish newspaper. 'On arrival at Scapa he had insisted on keeping his clerical garb, and we had great difficulty in persuading him not to. He never frequented the officers' bar, but preferred to move around the lower deck.'[16] On leaving HMS *Duke* early in 1943, his commanding officer wrote: 'He has done splendid work here; unsparing of himself wherever help is needed irrespective of Denomination; he will be sadly missed by officers and men alike.'

The captain of his next ship, *Renown*, was equally praising: 'He quickly endeared himself to everyone, regardless of rank and religion, and we will all miss him greatly.' His last ship in the war was HMS *Proserpine*; again the praise was unstinting: 'His enthusiasm for the Service, and the men, is colossal.'[17]

In 1943, North Africa had been cleared of Axis forces. The invasion of Sicily and Italy was about to follow, and this necessitated a considerable naval fleet train build-up. Fr Devine, 'famous throughout the Navy for his drive and efficiency',[18] was one of several naval chaplains posted to the area. Based first at Algiers, then Taranto, Italy, he was responsible for the east coast of Italy and regarded the entire Adriatic as his parish. In the history of Royal Navy chaplains he is described as 'an elderly very charming Irishman'.[19]

The charm of Fr Devine could be felt in the most unlikely places. In 1957 he visited Australia, and on the same ship was Sir Basil Brooke. At that time, Sir Basil was a member of the Northern Ireland Government, and later he became Prime Minister. The two Ulstermen became friends, to such an extent that Fr Devine asked the future Lord Brookeborough,

'What would your Orange friends think if they knew that I was your chaplain on the voyage?'[20] Alas for history, the reply is not recorded.

As in Malta, Royal Navy chaplains at Gibraltar were usually local officiating chaplains, and although they were good priests, knew little about the Navy, its regulations, and strong, sometimes unwritten, traditions, and foibles.

> On arrival at Gibraltar I looked forward to finding a long standing Catholic naval chaplain who would give me all the information I needed about R.N. chaplains and life in the Royal Navy. I was flabbergasted to learn a civilian priest was looking after all naval personnel, he seemed to know even less about the work than I did. At the Naval Personnel Office, they told me they had no idea where the *Oxfordshire* was operating. So I must remain in Gibraltar until she calls here, she must in the near future. I found this very annoying, because my elder brother working at the Admiralty had already told me that he knew she was operating from Bizerta [Tunisia]. After a fortnight I persuaded them to send me to Algiers in a tiny corvette. In this I felt seasick for the first time, and spent all the time I could in my bunk. I apologised to the young lieutenant who was the captain of the vessel. He said 'no apology is necessary, I'm most of the time sick myself, only I have to be captain of this ship, facing continuous danger of attack by German or Italian submarines and their crews'.[21]

At Algiers, Fr Pitt's search for a priest to advise him on ministering to seamen at last met with success when he met Fr Devine, recently of HMS *Sea Eagle*, Lough Foyle.

> With complete confidence and lucidity, he said there are four important rules you must know and live up to.
>
> First. Always be a priest, a friend to all and sundry, prove your sincerity and love of your work.
>
> Second. Remember you are recognised as a senior officer, and therefore act like one. Make contact with the commanding officer of any ship, and ask his co-operation without fear or favour.
>
> Three. On visiting any ship your first job is to make contact with the Catholics on board. Ask the Captain to summon all the Catholics in some place to meet you. Stand by the doorway and greet as many as possible coming in with a handshake. Congratulate them on their good work, then say you have come on board to hear their confessions and give them absolution. Tell them you know they will have forgotten how to do this, so you will do it for them and with them. Go through a good preparation of confession examination of conscience, good act of contrition, assure them of forgiveness. Then stand by the doorway so nobody can leave without passing you. Most of them will go to confession through its being easier to do so than refuse.
>
> Four. Keep clear of all Army chaplains. They are junior officers and they act like them. They are ineffective in getting things done.[22]

Fr Pitt joined *Oxfordshire* at Philippeville (Algeria) and spent his first eight months in the Mediterranean ministering to ships involved in the landing at Anzio, and to the sick and wounded soldiers being ferried from various ports in Italy to base hospitals in Algeria, Libya or Tunisia. Although really staffed and equipped to act as a floating hospital in its own right, in this campaign *Oxfordshire* was little more than 'a large floating ambulance'.[23]

Working from various ports all over the Mediterranean, it soon became clear to Fr Pitt what an excellent base a hospital ship is for a Catholic chaplain. It was something Army chaplains, whom Fr Devine scorned, had learned in World War I, for almost the same reasons.

> There were so few of us, we were appointed to work for any ship that may need us. Going to and from these ships could be done only by boat and these were always over-worked in any ship. The boats came and went from the hospital ship almost incessantly, so one could visit ships comparatively easily.[24]

The Normandy landings

Most accounts of the D-Day landings concentrate on soldiers battling their way ashore. This is perhaps right, but the part played by the Royal Navy and the Merchant Marine in getting them ashore safely should not be overlooked, nor should the overpowering support effort of the Allied navies, to amass such strength in the bridgehead that the break-out, when it came, unleashed into Europe a gigantic flood of concentrated military power never seen before in the history of war. At the foremost tip of the naval effort were the seamen and marines manning the landing craft. They were essential for ferrying the assault troops and supporting guns, tanks and engineer equipment on to defended beaches. To achieve this in the face of resistance by a brave enemy in well-prepared positions demanded resolute courage and high professional skill. Epitomizing these last qualities was the redoubtable Commander Maude RN, the Beach Master of Juno (in the film *The Longest Day*, Maude's part in the day's events was played by Kenneth More).

Accompanying the combined operations force responsible for the landings was a team of chaplains of all denominations. This fragment from a mighty story is about one, Fr Thomas Holland, who before his commissioning had been a professor at the English College, Lisbon, and was later Bishop of Salford.

Three ships were to accommodate the marines and seamen who were to crew the landing craft: *Ascanius*, *Thysville*, and *Cap Touraine*.

> Our job as chaplains was primarily with Royal Marines manning L.C.P.s [landing craft personnel]. In addition to R.M.s there were Royal Navy and Merchant navy crews on the three accommodation ships. Any other vessel in our area without a chaplain would also look to us.[25]

Fr Holland was positioned in *Ascanius*, a Holt liner based before the war in Liverpool, and the merchant seamen of her crew were 'mostly Catholics from St Malachy's parish'.[26] Its personnel were to be deployed opposite Juno beach, flanked by Gold and Sword in the British area. Unlike the other chaplains, Fr Holland's responsibility ranged over all crews of the off-shore ships of the expedition, and there proved to be many of various nationalities in addition to British: French, Belgians, Poles, and French colonial Africans. Like many priests before him just before action he had miscalculated the quantity of altar breads required. It was impossible to go ashore to collect more; however, he had not taken account of the facilities offered by a pre-war passenger liner.

> The *Cap Touraine* must have been a pleasant ship for peace time voyaging. I had my own reasons for gratitude to her. I had seriously miscalculated the number of communion hosts I was going to need. Already the imminence of battle was having its effect on the men.[27]

Having explained how he was prevented going ashore, by civil and military police, he continued:

> But the chief steward of the *Cap Touraine* at least temporarily solved my problem. He unlocked one of the elegant glass cupboards in the main lounge and produced a large tin hermetically sealed. He gave me his honest expert opinion after sampling. The hosts were in perfect condition.[28]

Having landed on Juno, Fr Holland decided that since Sword beach on the left was under heaviest fire from north of the Orne, that was the place he ought to be; he was ferried over to *Jean Bart*, a French battleship grounded to form a breakwater for Mulberry Harbour.

> Once aboard her I had plenty to hear about those H.F. shells and a lot to do. On a return visit days later, I had a full house for Mass preceded by confessions. The only entry to the chapel area was through a lobby in which I sat with my stole on and bagged the lot, all individually shriven. All is fair in love and war. I could claim both.[29]
>
> I told them at the Mass of a young girl who died a few miles inland from us in the Carmel at Lisieux. She promised she would shower favours ('roses' she called them) on people in need. In view of the prevailing havoc on Sword I decided to enlist for a 'rose'. I can't think what got hold of me but at the end of the homily I found myself saying: 'There will be no more casualties aboard this crate. St Thérèse has it all in hand. In the name of the Father ...' There *were* no more casualties. Within half-an-hour the order came to evacuate *Jean Bart*.[30]

Amongst the many ships Fr Holland visited were the Polish units *Slazak*, a destroyer, and a Danae class cruiser *Dragon*. This latter ship was struck by a human torpedo, suffered severe damage and heavy casualties, and was brought into Mulberry Harbour cradled between two destroyers. 'Thank God I got aboard her before that.'[31] The main magazine was flooded with oil. The ship was a literal shambles. 'I there saw sights that killed forever the "glamour of war", if that ever existed.'[32]

It is sad to have to relate that at the end of the operation a flotilla of the ungainly landing craft, en route for Portsmouth, sank in mid-channel, with heavy loss of life to the Royal Marine crews.[33]

Fr Holland became shore based, first at Rouen, from where he visited Lisieux and was able to help the convent of Carmel in material ways. Antwerp, which was under bombardment by German V weapons, became his next appointment, to cover all naval units in Holland and Belgium. Here he remained until after the end of the war in Europe.

The Indian Ocean: Kilindini, Kenya

Two naval Catholic chaplains were killed by enemy action in World War II: Fr Thomas Bradley CSSR, and Fr Thomas Aidan Brennan OMI (lost while taking passage in SS *Nellore* during 1944). Fr Bradley had been both a military and naval chaplain in World War I. One of Fr Bradley's ancestors, Admiral Sir Thomas Hardy, was Nelson's Flag Captain at Trafalgar. Because of his connections he transferred from the Army to the Navy when the opportunity arose, and was slightly wounded while serving in *Lion* at Jutland.

Returning to the Navy in 1940 after service at home, Fr Bradley was sent to the East African base at Kilindini, near Mombasa, Kenya. He sailed on many ships, which because of security restrictions in force at the time were not mentioned in his letters to his Father Provincial. Much of his letters was about his personal expenditure accounts, and the best way of transferring his surplus money back to his Order at such a distance in wartime.[34] In 1943 Fr Bradley asked for and was given two months' leave to visit the sailors on Madagascar. On the way he called at Mauritius and spent a week with Archbishop Leen before embarking in SS *Hoihow*, a small steamer of 2,198 tons. About 100 miles from Mauritius, on her way to Tamotavi, Madagascar, *Hoihow* was struck by a Japanese torpedo at 1115 on 2 July 1943. Of the master and crew of 91, five gunners, and 100 passengers, only four survived.[35]

The Pacific Fleet 1945

Following the defeat of Germany, the Royal Navy deployed a large fleet and fleet train to the Pacific for operations against Japan. Fr George Pitt, still in the hospital ship *Oxfordshire*, accompanied her to the Pacific.

> Suddenly we were ordered to join the Pacific Fleet in Sydney, Australia.

This was wonderful news to us, now we could be a proper naval hospital ship; part of the great company of supply and repair ships which formed the Fleet Train.

The Pacific Fleet comprised two battleships, four large aircraft carriers – *Eagle, Victorious, Invincible* and *Indefatigable*; also a host of smaller ones known as Woolworths aircraft carriers. A couple of squadrons of cruisers, and all the accompanying destroyers, corvettes, submarines and the small boats. While we were at Sydney we had the most wonderful welcome from the noble clergy and laity. Archbishop Gilroy had served in the Australian Navy as a sick bay attendant and could not do enough for us.[36]

A huge Royal Naval establishment was created. There, personnel of its depot, *Golden Hind*, were ministered to by Fr Thomas Moriarty. The Senior Chaplain (RC) Pacific Fleet, Mgr Hon Valentine Elwes, a Westminster priest, had with him in addition to Fr Pitt, Fr Michael Barry of St Andrews and Edinburgh, Fr Matthias Bodkin SJ, Fr Henry Leonard of Glasgow, and Fr Bernard Wilkins OSB.

We actually confronted the Japanese navy in the wide Pacific Ocean. The Japanese Navy knew they were losing the war, but that made them all the more determined to fight to the death.[37]

In the actions that followed, particularly when attacked by *kamikaze* suicide planes, British aircraft carriers had a decided advantage not possessed at that time by their American counterparts: armoured decks. The suicide planes did little damage and the wreckage of the planes could be pushed over the side with minimal interference to operations. However, this, and other demonstrations of enemy fanaticism, created an atmosphere of foreboding, in which the dropping of the atomic bombs on Japan was welcomed.

We all knew that we would have to suffer the most tremendous losses when we made the invasion landing in Japan itself; and the Royal Navy had built the largest ever hospital in Sydney. We expected thousands of wounded to be taken in there and *Oxfordshire* knew it must carry most of them to Australia. We had to wait until service with the British Pacific Fleet to act as a hospital, fully independent and equipped to deal with all wounded and sick without reference to any shore hospital.

The dropping of the atomic bomb came as a complete surprise to us all and seemed a great relief. So many thousand American and British lives would be saved by it.[38]

Visits to Japan

Two chaplains have given accounts of visits to Japan after the surrender: Mgr George Pitt, of Clifton, who went to Hiroshima and Nagasaki, and Fr Matthias Bodkin SJ, to Tokyo.

Hiroshima was totally destroyed with not one building still standing. Nagasaki was different, it resembled many a European city destroyed by aerial bombing. The reason was the atomic bomb fell, not on Nagasaki itself, but on the great Mitsubishi armament factories 18 miles away. I learnt that a Catholic convent was still standing in the city though very badly damaged. The superior in charge was a Canadian Sister so I called on her to gain her reaction to the terrible blast. She gave me all the expected answers, then I enquired how the young Japanese nuns had taken it, 'I cannot tell you,' she replied, 'because I know the polite Japanese answer to such a question is not to say what actually happened, but what would please one to hear.' I think this applies also to the claim that the bombs should not have been dropped, because the Japanese were about to surrender. For the Japanese, surrender is worse than death, putting the horror towards it on the prisoners of war.[39]

When HMS *Anson* arrived in Tokyo Bay on 3 December 1945, Fr Bodkin decided to visit a Jesuit house in Tokyo. With the Principal Medical Officer, Cdr Malone RN, a Belfast Anglican, Fr Bodkin paid a courtesy call on the senior US Army chaplain in Tokyo, Fr Lambert, then accommodated in the Finance building. By coincidence, it was the feast of St Francis Xavier, and the American chaplain had prepared a bundle of presents for the mission. Fr Bodkin and the PMO were invited to accompany him on the visit. In the talk which followed Fr Lambert mentioned that Dr Ross, the Jesuit Bishop of Hiroshima, had been removed on the orders of the Japanese authorities and a vicar appointed, and that the bishop was alive in Tokyo.[40]

In the drive to the mission Fr Bodkin observed that apart from the commercial centre and the fortress-like Diet buildings, the city was in ruins from Allied bombing.

Nine tenths of the great commercial buildings, insurance companies, shipping and banking offices, etc., stand intact. European in style, of stone, block brick, and most frequently marble, on wide avenues and squares, the finest group of commercial buildings I've seen anywhere.[41]

Driving through the ruined city they eventually found the area where the mission was located. With the exception of four, all the churches and the cathedral had been destroyed with the rest of the city. Eventually they saw a ruined church and convent. Walking through the debris they found the mission buildings almost intact.

In the open hall was one of the Fathers. After one glance I recognised Fr. Geppert. Almost at once Fr. Michael appeared and a Fr. Helvig who knew our Hong Kong men well. They all looked worn out but in better shape than our Hong Kong Fathers when we landed. They and the whole community have survived and are of course quite free and working hard. The Minister was summoned for his sack. They gave me a great welcome. We had only a few minutes, but I heard with immense joy and relief that all the Fathers of the Mission are alive, well and active. They included

such old friends as Fr. Heidrich and Fritz Guhrmann. Fr. Muller went
back to U.S.A. shortly after the war. Most wonderful of all, four of our
Fathers in Hiroshima, the first atomic bomb city, were living in a house in
the centre of the utter devastation; everything round them came down
and everyone was killed, but all four, including the Superior of the
Mission, Fr. Arrupe, survived without injury. The P.M.O.'s remark was to
say before everyone, and again at the jetty: 'I think you'd have to call it a
miracle' ... I will only add that I got very comforting accounts of the
loyalty and fervour of Japanese Catholics. When any connection with the
foreigner and his religion was anathema, they remained faithful.[42]

Back at Yokohama, Fr Bodkin and the PMO had lunch with the US Army
chaplain there, Fr Nern, and his Presbyterian colleague. It is delightful to
record that the Protestant chaplain, also from Belfast, established an instant
rapport with his fellow-Irishmen, the PMO and Fr Bodkin.[43]

Korea

During the Korean war, HMS *Belfast* and HMS *Glory* played a significant
role in support of the UN land forces. In addition, 41 Royal Marine
Commando, serving with the US 1st Marine Division, excited the
admiration of watching US Marines as they carried out an attack on
Communist positions. 'I heard one say in surprise, "They are as good as we
are", which was praise indeed from US Marines, who regard themselves as
better than any other fighting troops.'[44] Serving with 41 Commando was
Fr Henry Leonard. Since serving in *Glory* during the Pacific war, he went to
the British mandated territory of Palestine, and during the evacuation in
1948 had been in the perimeter around the port of Haifa. He was the last
British chaplain out of Palestine.[45]

HMS *Belfast* had won a high reputation for inshore bombardment in the
dangerous waters of the North Korean coast. Possibly during a rest period
between engagements she was in company with HMAS *Melbourne*, an
aircraft carrier, in the South China seas; *Melbourne* was asked to send its
Catholic chaplain over to *Belfast*, and Fr Francis Lyons was duly
despatched by helicopter. In recalling the event long afterwards, the then
Mgr Francis Lyons told of most helpful and praiseworthy ecumenism
shown by the ship's Anglican chaplain.

> As we flew over *Belfast* I could see that a canvas swimming pool had been
> rigged on the upper deck; the pilot playfully hovered directly over the
> pool and lowered me to just a few inches above the water. Then, after
> several minutes, I was lowered onto the foredeck. Reporting to the
> Captain he asked 'Is he a friend of yours?' 'He was' I replied. I found the
> Anglican chaplain, known to all as 'Eric the Cleric', very helpful, he had
> assembled all the Catholics ready for me; and afterwards Eric also served
> at Mass.[46]

With the Royal Navy in the Falklands

It was Holy Week, 1982. Fr Phelim Rowland, chaplain RN, was 'doing his sea time' on HMS *Yarmouth*, when the ship was ordered to ammunition and resupply at Gibraltar, then join the Task Force steaming to the South Atlantic.

> The ship's company worked hard over the next few days and everyone was in good spirits - hoping that the whole Falkland affair would fizzle out. I attended the Mass of Chrism on Wednesday evening praying earnestly for peace. But the next day we were ordered to sail at 1600. I celebrated the Easter Ceremonies on board as best I could, but it was certainly a very strange experience ... I went around the Mess decks visiting, the sailors appeared philosophical: 'That's life in a blue suit.' Most felt that Mr. Haig [US Secretary of State] would sort it all out. We reached Ascension Island - which was in a flurry of activity ... We left at ominously short notice and continued south with mounting trepidation. The pace of preparation for war speeded up and every aspect of the ship was put through its paces.[47]

There were five Catholic chaplains with the South Atlantic Task Force, three with the Amphibious Assault Group: Fr Chris Bester, in the hospital ship *Uganda*, Fr Noel Mullin with 3 Royal Marine Commando Brigade; and Fr A. J. Hayes, with 5 Infantry Brigade. Fr John Ryan was with the Support Group. Fr Rowland was therefore the only Catholic chaplain with the Naval Battle Group. When he realized this Rowland began circulating through the ships of the group before they entered the new 'total exclusion zone'. He celebrated Mass and gave general absolution in every ship he visited.

> And so it was that I found myself at war. 2nd May was quiet until the evening when we heard on the World Service of the sinking of the Argentinian cruiser, *The General Belgrano*. It came as a great shock - especially with the news of the great loss of life. We still hoped that it would bring the Argentinians to their senses and end hostilities. We awaited some reaction: it came at 1430 on Tuesday, 4th May. The action stations buzzer sounded and we were warned of an air raid closing. Then we were told that HMS *Sheffield* had been hit. HMS *Yarmouth* was ordered to close, and again launched our 'chaff' rockets. The Officer of the Watch saw an exocet missile pass us on the starboard quarter at about 600 yards. We very quickly found out it was such a missile which hit *Sheffield*.[48]

The crew of *Yarmouth* could see the huge pall of smoke from *Sheffield* on the horizon and on closing saw a 15-foot hole in her side; the entire ship was engulfed in flames. 'It was like a nightmare seeing one of our finest warships ablaze.' *Yarmouth* was almost alongside when its torpedo alarm sounded and for the next hour circled, firing mortar bombs at suspected submarines, then returned to help *Sheffield*. When her captain considered that a magazine might explode he gave the order to abandon ship. *Yarmouth* picked up survivors and headed for the Battle Group.

> It was a shocked group of officers that ate their 'pot mess' again that evening. We were sad beyond words - and angry. I remember saying a prayer over the ship's main broadcast system for the twenty men killed - and those injured.[49]

The next day the survivors of *Sheffield* were transferred to two Royal Fleet Auxiliaries; the chaplain accompanied them to give whatever assistance he could. That evening the moment came for Fr Rowland to attempt to relieve the trauma of the survivors in the Church's immemorial way. At home, friends, neighbours, and the extended family would help the families of the bereaved. A memorial service held immediately after a battle at which all present have lost friends, comrades or shipmates is an occasion where the chaplain is most valued, and exposed.

> That evening we held an impromptu Memorial Service at which every member of the Ship's company was present. It was the most emotionally charged Service I have ever taken. The men were still stunned and deeply saddened at the loss of life - and the loss of their ship.[50]

In addition to ministering to his friends, as a Christian minister the chaplain also has a duty to 'the enemy'. Directly Fr Rowland transferred by helicopter to *Invincible*, he was asked to look after 24 Argentinian prisoners who had been picked up from a fishing boat inside the 'total exclusion zone'.

> I was able to relieve their anxieties - as some of them believed they would be shot as spies. We celebrated Mass together and I gave them general Absolution. The prisoners were well looked after, well supplied with cigarettes and chocolates from the ship's company, and kept - ironically - in the Ship's Chapel. Eventually they were sent to the hospital ship and then home to Argentina.
>
> I remained in *Invincible* for a week and moved onto HMS *Hermes* the flagship. The Ship was a hive of activity as the amphibious group had arrived and the invasion was imminent. I met Admiral Woodward, the Task Force Commander, who looked tired and drawn but nevertheless confident that success would be achieved.[51]

A landing 'off the target' at San Carlos Bay on 21 May achieved tactical surprise, and the landing of ground troops was unopposed. Supported by warships, a bridgehead was secured; however, later that day the Argentinian Air Force reacted vigorously, and pressed home their attacks heroically. In the course of the day HMS *Ardent* was sunk. *Antrim* received a direct hit but fortunately the bomb did not explode. Two other ships, *Broadsword* and *Brilliant*, were strafed with cannon fire. On the following day *Antelope* was also sunk, nor did it end there: two RFA landing craft took hits from bombs which mercifully did not explode. In the immediately succeeding days, while the build-up ashore was taking place, these terrible events continued. HMS *Coventry* was sunk, and a bomb passed completely through *Broadsword* without exploding. In the failure of these bombs Fr Rowland's prayers may indeed have been answered.

Fr Rowland returned to *Yarmouth*, which with *Glamorgan* was tasked with an in-shore bombardment role. From its position off-shore and out of range of air attack, the bombardment group steamed in at dusk and, directed by a shore observer, 'pounded Argentinian positions all night. Latterly, this was in support of our troops' advance on Mount Kent and Tumbledown ... It was after such a night that HMS *Glamorgan* was hit by a shore based exocet missile with nineteen killed.'[52]

After two weeks of close support, the news came of the surrender of Stanley; and six weeks' fighting had ended. However, there was one final operation for *Yarmouth*: the removal of Argentinians from Southern Thule in the South Sandwich Islands, taken over by them in 1977.

> The weather was awful, as Southern Thule is just north of the Antarctic circle and only 30 miles from the ice pack. Thankfully, the Argentinians were only too delighted to surrender, and it was officially returned to British hands on Sunday, 20th June. We took the prisoners back to Port Stanley and once again returned to the group.
>
> I was now able to continue my 'parish visiting' of the ships and returned briefly to the carriers. It was from *Invincible* that I flew into Port Stanley to say 'hello' to Monsignor Spraggon, the Parish Priest. He is a delightful man with a great sense of humour, despite the ordeal. He made a point of showing me the bullet holes in his study wall and even one through his Breviary.[53]

On 7 July *Yarmouth*, *Exeter*, and *Cardiff* steamed in line ahead past *Invincible* and headed north-east and home. In summing up his adventurous 'sea time' Fr Rowland justifiably felt he had got his 'sea legs'. He had other feelings too, which he had never felt or experienced before.

> I was needed and used as a priest. I saw professional men doing what they consider a professional job. I discovered few who enjoyed the realities of war. We all know war is futile and negative. Theologians will argue over the principles of the just war. The abiding reaction was that the Force were there to defend our defenceless people – wherever they happen to be. I found no deep antagonism towards the Argentinians – in fact, often quite the reverse.
>
> As a Priest, I discovered people everywhere who wanted to attend Mass and receive Absolution. They wanted the understanding and sympathy that must be part of the Priestly Ministry. I have never before been in a situation where I felt so close to the people I was serving. We shared so much in common from food to fear.[54]

Notes and references

1. Rt Rev Thomas Holland, *For Better and for Worse* (Salford, 1989), p. 95.
2. *Plymouth Diocesan Year Book* (1965).
3. Rev Alured Ozanne, 'Catholics in the Royal Navy', *The Edmundian*, vol. VII (1907), p. 172.
4. Ibid.
5. Admiralty Fleet Order 13/1944; quoted by G. Taylor, *Sea Chaplains* (London, 1978), p. 545.
6. Holland, p. 98; Fr Rory O'Sullivan, letter to Bishop Walmsley (25 February 1992), COA.
7. 'Chaplains in the Royal Navy have a hard but fruitful job among God-fearing sailors', *Catholic Herald* (26 February 1943).
8. Australian CSSR Necrology.
9. Mgr George Pitt, taped interview, courtesy of Bishop Walmsley.
10. Fr Rory O'Sullivan, letter to Bishop Walmsley (25 February 1992), COA.
11. Ibid.
12. Pitt.
13. Derry Diocesan Records.
14. Fr Henry Parker CSSR, Provincial Archives, St Mary's, Clapham. Fr Costello landed with 48 Royal Marine Commando on D-Day. He later gained renown by saying Mass in a deserted church in no-man's-land twice a week until the break-out. Later, Fr Costello was slightly hurt when a mine exploded under his tank, killing the driver.

    In 1945 Fr Costello and Rev J. Armstrong RN, an Anglican chaplain, clashed when the latter attempted to assert unwarranted authority over RC naval chaplains. In consequence of this unpleasant incident all RC naval chaplains were replaced by RC Army chaplains responsible to the Senior RC Army Chaplain in the field. Memoir, COA.
15. Fr William Purcell, letter to Cardinal Hinsley (9 July 1940), COA.
16. O'Sullivan.
17. Captain's reports, CSSR Archives.
18. Pitt.
19. Taylor, p. 444.
20. Derry Diocesan Records.
21. Pitt.
22. Ibid.
23. Ibid.
24. Ibid.
25. Holland, p. 100.
26. Ibid.
27. Ibid., p. 102.
28. Ibid.
29. Ibid., p. 104.
30. Ibid.
31. Ibid., p. 105.
32. Ibid.
33. Ibid.

34. Fr Thomas Bradley CSSR, letters to Father Provincial, CSSR Archives.
35. Correspondence, CSSR Archives.
36. Pitt.
37. Ibid.
38. Ibid.
39. Ibid.
40. Matthias Bodkin SJ, *Interfuse*, no. 41, pp. 76-8.
41. Ibid.
42. Ibid.
43. Ibid.
44. Rev Kevin J. Keaney, USN, attached USMC, conversation with T. Johnstone.
45. Canon J. Canning, Paisley diocese.
46. Mgr Francis Lyons, former chaplain RAN, conversation with T. Johnstone.
47. Fr Phelim Rowland RN, *A Catholic Chaplain in the South Atlantic* (1982). Courtesy of Fr Rowland.
48. Ibid.
49. Ibid.
50. Ibid., p. 5.
51. Ibid.
52. Ibid.
53. Ibid.
54. Ibid.

21

The post-war period

In 1946 the Rt Rev James Dey, Bishop to the Forces, died and was not replaced for some years. The Principal Chaplains (RC) of the Army and RAF became Apostolic Administrators for the chaplains of their own service. However, at the insistence of the Admiralty, the naval Catholic chaplains continued to be administered by the Archbishop of Westminster.

Korea, 1950–53

On 25 June 1950, North Korean forces launched a surprise attack across the 38th Parallel on the Republic of Korea (South Korea). Two days later the Security Council of the United Nations called upon all members of the United Nations to give military assistance to South Korea. By 4 August all of South Korea was in the hands of the Communist forces with the exception of an area around the main southern port of Pusan. The skeletal British 27 Brigade arrived from Hong Kong on 29 August, consisting of little more than two battalions, 1st Middlesex and 1st Argyll and Sutherland Highlanders. With them came Fr Terence Quinlan, of Southwark diocese, attached to the Middlesex. Two days later an all-out Communist offensive began to break into the Pusan bridgehead. A landing by a US Marine division at Inchon, coinciding with an offensive by the United Nations forces in the Pusan Box, forced the North Koreans on to the defensive. By the end of the month the Communist forces were in full retreat.

The Security Council, on 7 October, authorized the UN commander, General Douglas MacArthur, to use his forces to pursue the Communists into North Korea, and twelve days later Pyongyang, the capital, was captured. By this time the 3rd Royal Australian Regiment (3rd RAR) had reinforced the under-strength 27 Brigade, bringing with it Fr Lynch. Advance parties of the British 29 Brigade arrived in October and the main body landed in November. With the arrival of 29 Brigade and the Princess Patricia's Canadian Light Infantry in December, there were four Commonwealth Catholic chaplains, from the Australian, British, and

Canadian Armies. In February the 'Princess Pats' joined 27 Common-wealth Brigade.

The British 29 Independent Brigade Group had only one Catholic chaplain, Fr John Ryan, of Brentwood. A chaplain since 1942, Fr Ryan had served in Normandy and north-west Europe; after the war he had continued to serve with the British Army of the Rhine. Shortly after his arrival in early November with 1st Royal Ulster Rifles, Ryan contacted the senior United States Army chaplain, Fr Sherry, and learned that the Apostolic Administrator in Japan had appointed Fr Sherry the spiritual head of the chaplains to the UN force. All the dispensations and privileges granted to the American Army now applied to the British. A more immediate problem, the regular supply of wine and altar breads, was happily resolved.[1]

The brigade concentration area near the walled city of Suwon was close to a Columban Fathers' mission. The Columbans had been imprisoned by the Communists, and one, Fr P. O'Brien, who had served with 3rd Division in Normandy, had been killed. It was run by two Korean priests, and although partially ruined by the Communists, was habitable; Fr Ryan used this as a Mass centre. Because the brigade units were sweeping the area for Communist 'stay-behind parties' and stragglers, the chaplain positioned himself at 26 Field Ambulance.[2]

By the end of November the brigade had advanced to Kaesong and suffered many dead and wounded from 'bandit' activity. A brigade cemetery was established at Kaesong and there Fr Ryan had the sad duty of burying one of the 'Glosters' and an Ulsterman.[3] The 29 Brigade Group was twice the size of a normal brigade. It contained many elements normally found in divisional and corps areas, established at Pusan, Taegu and Taejon, on the lines of communications. It was impossible for one priest to cover all units. Those behind the battalion echelon areas had to depend on local American chaplains, usually with medical units, for their spiritual needs; it was unlikely that the personnel of these units were in danger of becoming battle casualties.

Of the five major 'teeth' units in 29 Brigade, the Rifles contained the largest concentration of Catholics, the other four (Irish Hussars, North-umberland Fusiliers, Gloucesters, and 45th Field Regiment RA) had substantial minorities. The host of minor units also contained many Catholics. Fr Ryan's 'parish' became widely scattered when the brigade moved into North Korea in December. Units and sub-units ranged at one time from Pusan to forty miles north of Pyongyang. As a yardstick, there were five Anglican chaplains on the brigade establishment, and the senior C of E chaplain brought an additional chaplain over from Japan, leaving the 'Other Denominations' chaplain there to care for Anglicans.[4]

In early November 1950, as the UN forces drew near the Yalu river, the international border with Manchuria, several Chinese field armies crossed the frontier and drove them back; Pyongyang was retaken by the Communists in just a month.

The UN withdrawal on the west central front was almost headlong. The retreating UN forces did not stop until the majority were south of the 38th Parallel, where on the 15 December a defensive line was formed. At this time the two Commonwealth brigades were in the front line but widely separated. The 27 Commonwealth Brigade on the central front, and 29 Brigade on the west central front.

Once again 29 Brigade concentrated in a comparatively small area at Kaesong, making it easier for Fr Ryan to get around all units. The intense cold, and difficulty in finding a building, meant Mass was held on open frozen paddy fields in bitter weather. Despite this Fr Ryan was delighted with the response of the troops.

> In spite of all the difficulties, the lads are responding magnificently to their religious duties. As I am saying Mass so often in the open, the non-Catholic lads are getting their first sight of the Mass. At the same time the slack ones amongst the Catholics who are not attending have their consciences pricked.[5]

During the course of the next four months Seoul was lost and retaken. Fighting in a brigade action north of Seoul, and the subsequent retreat through the burning city, the Ulster Rifles, rearguard for the brigade, distinguished themselves in 'Happy Valley'. In the course of a fierce battle on 3 January 1951, the Ulsters lost heavily in killed, wounded, or taken prisoner. The Chinese attack had been expected and Fr Ryan had done the rounds of the brigade units, giving general Absolution and Holy Communion to the Catholics. He was the last priest hundreds of soldiers from 29 Brigade were to see for two-and-a-half years.

In the middle of January the Chinese offensive was brought to a halt, and a counter-offensive caught the enemy off-balance. By early April the British were again back in their positions of the previous December.

The Battle of the Imjin

On 23 April 1951, St George's Day, the Northumberland Fusiliers wore roses in their berets. The Ulster Rifles, in reserve and out of the line, held a remembrance service for the dead of the January battle. Then the Chinese began their spring offensive. On the west central front they struck at the widely dispersed 29 Brigade, who were holding positions easily infiltrated. In the course of heavy fighting two British battalions were surrounded, the Belgian battalion withdrew from its position just north of the Imjin river, and the Ulster Rifles, rushing forward, covered the Belgian withdrawal on the right flank.

The Gloucesters were concentrated on Hill 235 (Gloucester Hill) near

Choksong, and held out for three days. Neither British nor American tanks were able to break through the ring of Chinese. When the Gloucesters broke out of the hill position, they were forced to leave about 200 wounded behind. The commanding officer, the RSM, the medical officer, and the Anglican chaplain of the Gloucesters, Rev S. J. Davies, stayed with the wounded. Only 39 succeeded in fighting through the Chinese lines. Hundreds of Glosters were taken into captivity. Fr Ryan had been able to visit the Glosters just before the battle.

On 28 April the Chinese Communist forces struck on the central front. A massive Chinese attack made a large hole in the UN line. The newly-arrived British 28 Brigade, with Fr Louis Madden of Achonry diocese attached, was rushed to plug the hole. The 1st Middlesex of 27 Brigade, half-way to Inchon and the ship for Hong Kong, were recalled to help. In a desperate battle the British battalions, together with 3rd RAR (later awarded a US Presidential Citation), supported by the guns of the New Zealanders, held fast. After the battle, the Middlesex, and Fr Quinlan, returned to Hong Kong. On 21 May the UN forces began the counter-offensive which drove the last Communists north of the 38th Parallel. On 10 July, truce talks began at Kaesong. After just over two weeks an agenda was agreed, and talks proper began at Panmunjom.

The Commonwealth Division

The Commonwealth Division, under command of Maj Gen A. J. H. Cassels, formed in July 1951, was declared operational at the end of that month. One additional British Army Catholic chaplain, Fr R. Woods, of Glasgow, arrived to minister to the units in the divisional area. Fr Ryan remained with 29 Brigade. Because the Canadians had the majority of chaplains and Catholics in the division, a Canadian chaplain became the SCF (RC).

The percentages of Catholics in each national contingent in Korea/ Japan were:

Australian	25 per cent of 1,859
British	10 per cent of 15,925
Canadian	40 per cent of 8,031
New Zealanders	20 per cent of 1,805[6]

There were no Catholic chaplains behind the rear divisional boundary. British troops elsewhere in Korea continued to be ministered to by American chaplains.

The Commonwealth base, Japan

The area of Kure in Japan had been held by the Australians as the Commonwealth occupation force after the British withdrawal in 1948. On the outbreak of the Korean War it was expanded to include many British units, including the 29th General Hospital, Reinforcement Holding Unit, and the Battle Training Centre in the hills at Haramura. There were two Catholic churches, the Sacred Heart at Kure and St Patrick's at Hiro. In addition to a chaplain at RAAF Station, Iwakuni, the Australians had two chaplains; the British and Canadians had one each attached to the General Hospital.

Fr Ryan had suggested in 1950 that it would have been better to have deployed the British chaplain to Taegu, where he would attend to the Base areas, and be better positioned to support the brigade/divisional chaplains in the event of a casualty occurring. But this was not acted upon. When Fr Ryan left Korea at the end of 1951 he took over at Kure and again suggested this arrangement. Again the suggestion was turned down. Nevertheless, such was his concern for the troops in these areas that he visited these areas himself from Japan.[7]

Prisoners of war

Like prisoners taken in previous wars, to British prisoners in Korea the period immediately after capture was the worst. Because they were captured in the depth of the Korean winter, on 3 January 1951, the Ulster prisoners perhaps suffered the greatest hardship. All prisoners were made to do a forced march of about 300 miles to camps near the Manchurian border.

On arrival at the POW camps the officers were separated from the men. One UN Catholic chaplain, Fr Emil J. Kapaun, died in Camp Five because of lack of attention to his wounds.[8] The intention of the Communists was to deprive the troops of their appointed leaders, as the first step in the 'brainwashing' to which the prisoners were subjected.

Although without a priest and unable to attend Mass or the sacraments, the Ulster prisoners of Camp Five had an outstanding young NCO, 22202796 Lance-Corporal W. Massey, who gave them spiritual leadership. He held prayer meetings every Sunday, and on St Patrick's Day 1953 the Royal Ulster Rifles held a church parade taken by Corporal Massey.

After their release the British prisoners returned home on the troopship *Asturias*. A Catholic chaplain who accompanied the prisoners home submitted a report to the Principal RC Chaplain, the War Office:

> One man, more than any other, won the deepest respect and affection of all his fellow prisoners. He was LCpl Bill Massey, a Dubliner, who organised services in Camp 5 after the death of the American Chaplain. LCpl Massey was a prisoner for two and a half years and for most of that time it was he who kept the Catholics together, both British and Americans, constantly encouraging them by word and example. An Altar was built and a crucifix made by melting down and moulding old tooth-

paste tubes. The Chinese supplied the candles. Cpl. Massey earned the gratitude of hundreds – Catholics and non-Catholics alike. They called him 'Doctor' no less than 'Father' because he volunteered for the job of medical orderly and displayed a remarkable devotion to the sick and dying. On the day of his release he went to Confession and Holy Communion – using the little Prayer book, which he had used in the prison camp.[9]

Massey's spiritual role in adversity was an important manifestation of the role of the laity in the absence of the priesthood. It gave much comfort to his fellow-soldiers, and contributed greatly to the failure of the Communists to break the spirit of British prisoners. A high-level study took place into the treatment and conduct of prisoners taken in the Korean War. It was found that those with a strong religious faith were better able than any others to withstand the Communist attempts at indoctrination, and subversion. As a result moral leadership courses began in many of the armies of the world, on the same lines as those begun by Mgr Beauchamp in the RAF more than ten years before.

Bishop, later Cardinal, Heenan, while on his way to the Eucharistic Congress in Sydney, Australia, visited Korea in April 1953. Unlike other senior churchmen he did not wear combat clothing, but appeared everywhere wearing his purple-piped cassock and purple biretta. His visit, coming as he did at the express wish of Pope Pius XII, created a profound impression. 'When I left England the Holy Father summoned me to Rome and although he was ill at the time, he specially commanded me to give his blessing to all the Catholic soldiers fighting at the front.'[10]

He was able to visit units of any nationality in the Commonwealth Division and be accepted by them as a Catholic bishop. He told the British troops he addressed, 'When I get back home to England I will write personally to the family of every man I have met'. He spoke to the French Canadians of the Royal 22ème Regiment in French. At an Italian field hospital in Seoul, working for the Koreans, he spoke Italian. He told the Australians of his forthcoming visit to Australia and his impression of them: 'Before I came to Korea I was looking forward eagerly to my visit to Australian troops. But now I have seen the Australian troops, and talked to the Catholic soldiers among them, I realize just how high their reputation stands among their fellow soldiers.'[11]

He spoke about all the Commonwealth troops when he said: 'They are a fine body of men, worthily upholding the principles of their faith, and the honour and reputation of their country. May God bless them all'.[12]

Bishop Heenan was critical of some of the conditions he saw in Korea and at Kure. Some of these criticisms were not too well received in Britain. The general opinion among the officers and troops in Korea, however, was that 'it was time someone in authority spoke up'.[13]

Northern Ireland

During the 1970s there were four Army Catholic chaplains serving in Northern Ireland: the SRC chaplain at HQ Lisburn, brigade chaplains at Derry and Armagh, and a fourth at the Royal Victoria Hospital, Belfast. Numbers have since been reduced to three: one in Lisburn, one in Derry and one in Armagh. Much could be written about a chaplain's work there, but two anecdotes must suffice.

While based at Derry, and making the rounds of the scattered army posts of his 'parish', Fr Alf Hayes' car broke down on the Glenshane Pass, and he rolled downhill into Dungiven, an out-of-bounds area to all British troops at the time. As he searched his documents for the telephone number of an army recovery unit, some men approached and on seeing his 'dog collar', offered to take the car and fix it. He felt he should not refuse a generous offer of help, saying 'No, it's all right. I'm waiting for the Army to rescue me.' The strangers pushed the car down to a nearby garage. It was raining; an old lady living nearby seeing a stranger standing in the rain invited him into her house. There he sat for an anxious couple of hours wondering about his car. In the meantime he drank strong tea, eating 'rashers of bacon and eggs with doorstep-size slices of fresh bread and butter in company of her husband'. As is inevitable in Northern Ireland they spoke of 'the troubles', and the lady told him of her daughter, Siobhan, who at that very moment was leading the strip-search protests in Armagh jail. Not once did they question him, in spite of his English accent, of his religion, nationality, or reason for being in Northern Ireland, 'though they knew fine well who I was'.[14]

Eventually his car reappeared, and having given his thanks to everyone concerned, he got in (without checking underneath for bombs as was usual in the Province), drove to the garage and paid his bill before returning to Derry.

> So many ordinary Northern Irish people are like that, kind, helpful and hospitable. So sad their story rarely gets told.[15]

The chaplain based at Armagh covered the posts along the border from the Irish Sea to Enniskillen. During a tour of duty lasting a year one chaplain, Fr Bernard Funnell, motored 23,000 miles visiting soldiers, schools and families in 27 different locations.

> My 'Sunday' journey began after Saturday lunch, heading east for an evening Mass at Downpatrick. After a night in an RAF bed, Masses followed at Ballykinler, Portadown, Armagh and finally Omagh. A total of 150 miles. Every mile was one of tourist beauty. Fermanagh was what I imagined Finland to be, beautiful lakes and few people. In Co. Armagh, whilst the milk churns at a farm gate were a worry, boxes of apples for sale, with a trusting plate to receive the money, bettered any Supermarket presentation.

The only mar were the two groups of Nationalists. One waved a Union Jack, the other the Plough hidden behind a Tricolour. Nationalism is not a love of one's own country, but exists only when there is another group to hate. There wasn't a British National Party to wave the Union Jack before the West Indians and Asians came. Oswald Mosley's Black Shirts only marched in Jewish streets. But Satan's henchmen didn't have it all their own way. Thank God for love. Many of my best Army parishioner families had an Ulster wife and Mother. One came from an area only patrolled at night![16]

A soldier of the Parachute Regiment wanted to marry a Catholic local girl. He was nominally a Catholic but had no record of baptism, and no knowledge of the faith. Weekly instruction began, and for four months Fr Funnell arranged his itinerary to suit the soldier's off-duty periods.

But the end of the course lacked a suitable Chapel of Reception. A religious order provided their hospitality and the local father of a teacher in my civvy parish school stood as Godfather, willingly. Penitents came into the Chapel during the reception Mass and being good Irish Catholics, stayed. As I entered the facts in the register, one of these strangers slipped a £5 note into the soldier's hand. Unknown, never to be seen again, but spontaneous kindness never to be forgotten. Then the good Fathers gave us a high tea.[17]

The Falklands, 1982

In the folk-history of the British Army there was never a send-off for troops going to war that could compare with that given to the South Atlantic Task Force. The *Queen Elizabeth II* slipped from her Southampton moorings on Wednesday 12 May 1982.

Some on board realized for the first time that 'this was for real'. There were three brigade chaplains on this beautiful ship: Rev Peter Brookes, an Anglican attached to the Welsh Guards; Rev Angus Smith, Church of Scotland, with the Scots Guards; and Fr Alfred Hayes, attached to the Headquarters and Signal Squadron, the Brigade Catholic chaplain – better known as 'Father Alf'.

In the next two weeks, from Southampton to South Georgia, Fr Hayes helped organize shipboard activities which gave him the opportunity to arrange a 'prayer for the day' on the ship's radio, and a 'thought for the day' in the brigade daily newspaper. Briefings and intensive military training occupied most of the troops' waking time. Nevertheless, daily Mass was said for anyone who could find the time to attend; in the restaurant for the Scots Guards, in the theatre for all other units, in the ship's laundry for the crew. Hymn sheets were printed, and a guitarist and flautist provided musical accompaniment. Attendance at Mass was low considering the number on board, 3,500 all ranks, but Fr Hayes put this down to the intensity of the training. Nevertheless he noted that some very good confessions were made. The Forces' Catholic Ordinary, Bishop Francis Walmsley, had provided him with written authorization to give general Absolution, which he did on a number of occasions.

On board *Canberra*, Fr Hayes, a Spanish-speaking priest, had his first meeting with Argentine prisoners. Three were in the ship's hospital, all with gunshot wounds in the leg. In the same hospital was a Royal Marine sergeant who had been shot down while flying in a helicopter. In the water the survivors were fired on by the Argentinians and the pilot killed, later to be buried at sea by the Commando Catholic chaplain, Fr Noel Mullin. Coincidentally both Fr Mullin and Fr Hayes were from the diocese of Lancaster, one of the smaller English dioceses, which provides an inordinate number of chaplains to the forces. On the following day they concelebrated Mass.

Exactly three weeks after leaving Southampton, 2 June, 5 Brigade landed without trouble in San Carlos Water under cover of mist and darkness. Knowing the hard time 3 Commando Brigade had the previous week they could hardly believe their good fortune. Nevertheless, Fr Alf, directly on landing, followed the example of everyone else, in digging a shell-scrape for himself. Shortly after preparing his scrape the priest reported to the Field Ambulance for duty and had a rude shock.

> There I encountered difficulties with the CO who told me he didn't want a Chaplain since, in his experience, the sight of a priest at a dying man's side made the man give up. I said that, in my four years as a hospital chaplain in a large general hospital before joining the Army, I had never had that experience, and usually found that patients got genuine comfort from the priest. Said I'd have another word with the Brigadier about where to position myself, and at this he changed his mind.[18]

Next day the Brigade Headquarters advanced to Darwin/Goose Green, leaving the Ambulance at San Carlos; Fr Hayes, realizing there might be more urgent work at the 'sharp end', went also. At Goose Green he inspected the battlefield and finding enemy dead decided to bury them.

> Then went to look at the battlefield since somebody had found six bodies. Decided we should bury them and took a couple of lads with shovels to do so. However, from the top of the hill we saw a tractor and trailer bumping along the track from Goose Green laden with seventeen more corpses. Decided to wait until we'd found all the bodies then bury them in a mass grave. 2 Para. Battalion who had fought the battle told us there were about 250 corpses, but we only ever found 37, even after scouring the battlefield and flying over it in a Gazelle. Later, speaking to the senior Argentine prisoner, I was told he had a list of 200 missing, but didn't know how many of those were dead, wounded, missing, presumed dead or prisoners elsewhere. Another 50 could possibly have been amongst the remains of a Harrier strike on a schoolhouse (which was flattened) half-

way between Darwin and Goose Green. There were certainly enough scraps of human flesh around there to make up that number.[19]

Lying among the litter was a letter from a schoolboy in Buenos Aires to a soldier which 'assured him that every day they prayed for their compatriots, but also for "the English, who are not our enemies but our brothers and for the peace of the world"'.[20]

On the evening of Thursday, 3 June, the brigade commander, Brigadier Wilson, briefed his staff on the situation and his intentions. Reinforcements were due to arrive at Bluff Cove by sea; 2 Para were to move forward to secure the landing place, although the Para battalion was in a bad state with trench foot and frostbite, and was without their Bergen haversacks.

On the following morning Fr Hayes and an Argentinian chaplain concelebrated Requiem Mass for the Argentinian dead. That afternoon the priest and the Staff Captain (Administration) from the brigade headquarters, Captain C. Gundry, visited the prisoners to ensure they had sufficient food and water.

The funeral service for the 37 dead Argentinians took place on Saturday 5 June. It was to be a very long day. There were no body bags available. So Fr Hayes insisted that the bodies be wrapped individually in ponchos, in order that they might later be exhumed for burial elsewhere. The chaplain regretted that some of the dead were without identity discs, to record their names, 'and it was too unkind to ask the prisoners to search the blood-stained clothes'.[21] No explanation is given as to why the Argentinian chaplain had not already completed this duty to his compatriots.

All were buried in a mass grave dug by a local farmer with a tractor. The rest of that day Fr Hayes spent visiting British troops. Two of the soldiers he spoke to were Army Air Corps NCOs destined to die in tragic circumstances, Corporal Simon Cockton and Staff-Sergeant Chris Griffin, a helicopter pilot. In the evening Fr Hayes had dinner with the NCOs and some of the officers. The meal was cooked by Major Mike Forge, the OC 5 Brigade HQ and Signal Squadron.

> Simon was a bit homesick, missing his wife. He had just got married the day we left and had had to leave during the reception. Later this evening, on a task with the OC of the Signals Squadron, his helicopter would be shot down and he would be killed, leaving his young bride a widow before she knew what it was to be a wife. The Welsh Guards Recce patrol, led by Lt. Willie Sym, came in exhausted and drenched after two nights yomping ... Mike Forge who was to be killed in the same helicopter with Simon later this night, cooked us a lovely meal which was preceded by sherry that the RSM had somehow got from Goose Green. For Mike, Simon and the two others in the helicopter it really was the last supper and their deaths were our Brigade's first taste of war.[22]

That night, going forward by helicopter to reconnoitre a new position, their aircraft was picked up on the radar screen of a Royal Navy frigate and shot down with a surface-to-air missile, in the mistaken belief that it was Argentinian. All the occupants of the aircraft were killed.

> Sunday 6th June: We are all stunned at the deaths of the four lads we'd all been talking to and eating with last night. The reality of war has finally come home to us. More so as I buried the Argentine dead on what has turned out to be the worst day here so far.[23]

In war there is no time to grieve over-long; Fr Hayes had the living to consider. It may be taken for granted, however, that the Mass he said that day for 2 Para was offered up for his recently-dead friends. Mike Forge, a Belfast-born Protestant, had served with the Para Brigade when it first went to Northern Ireland in 1969. At that time the Catholic people of Belfast and Derry welcomed them as deliverers. Mike, and some other non-Catholic officers, had gone to Mass there to express sympathy for the Catholics.[24]

After saying Mass for 2 Para and giving general Absolution to about 30 soldiers, Fr Hayes learned from the acting commanding officer, Major Chris Keeble, who had assumed command upon the death of Colonel H. H. Jones ('Colonel H' to his battalion), the story of the Argentinian surrender at Goose Green.

> He hadn't a clue what he was going to do at first and spent a lot of the night praying for inspiration. As dawn was approaching, he suddenly thought that the Argentinians might like to surrender if he made it worthwhile and honourable. He sent a couple of prisoners over with a note saying something like … 'We are sitting here waiting to kill each other. I am a Catholic like most of you. We have you completely surrounded. At 1200 I will lay a fire-power demonstration on to the football pitch at Goose Green. When you have seen what is coming at you I'd like you to surrender. If you surrender we will treat you according to the Geneva Convention. We will feed you, keep you warm and get you back home as soon as possible. If you don't surrender we will kill every one of you!'[25]

Purely by chance the only three artillery pieces on the island at that time arrived to support the Paras and were seen by the released prisoners. In response to Keeble's inspired message the Argentinians surrendered. The amazed paratroopers learned there were 1,400 Argentinians at Goose Green, double what they had expected. The battalion's remaining ammunition was barely that number of rounds. 'It was a bit of luck, a bit of bluff, and the power of prayer.'[26]

On Tuesday, 8 June, the land element of the Task Force suffered its first serious losses when enemy aircraft scored direct hits on the landing ships *Sir Tristram* and *Sir Galahad* carrying the Welsh Guards and the Field Ambulance, and tons of ammunition. Much heroism was displayed in rescuing the wounded and badly burned.

> Forty-nine Welsh Guards and Field Ambulance personnel are un-
> accounted for. I ran straight up to the Field Ambulance Dressing Station
> where 79 casualties (including Chinese seamen) were being treated. All
> had burns. One had his leg blown off. They were all casevaced to Ajax Bay
> very quickly. The helicopter pilots flew brilliantly and were very brave.[27]

The next day, in a nice mixture of the spiritual and the practical, the priest
spent the forenoon visiting the troops and the afternoon building a bomb
shelter.

During the battle for Stanley, Fr Hayes positioned himself with the
Forward Surgical Team and at first light on 12 June the first casualties
began to arrive, both British and Argentinian.

> Some of the casualties were very serious, lots of shrapnel wounds, a
> couple of leg amputations, an arm, a lad shot in the throat. I had to hold
> his throat together for half an hour before they could get him on the table
> for a tracheotomy, during which time I thought he was going to choke to
> death several times and prayed that he wouldn't.[28]

After the operation which saved the young man's life, he tried to speak.
Thinking he was asking if he was a priest, Hayes replied 'Yes'.

> He was still very agitated and I eventually realised he was saying 'feet' and
> not 'priest'. His feet were freezing, after I covered them he smiled with
> relief and relaxed into sleep.[29]

Surgeons and nursing staff of the Royal Army Medical Corps and the
medical service of the Royal Navy could feel justly proud of their superb
record in the Falklands War. The wounded who were brought to the
advance dressing stations, no matter how critical their condition on arrival,
all recovered. The chaplains who assisted them, although they don't make
the claim, surely are part of that astonishing record.

Just after midnight on Monday, 14 June, the Scots Guards began the
battle for Tumbledown. The chaplain's language skills were useful at this
stage of the battle; then he reported for duty with the Forward Surgical
Team just after four, but as yet no casualties had arrived. At dawn came the
news that the Scots had taken Tumbledown, but with heavy losses in a
very hard fight.

> A lot of seriously wounded casualties through the FST. Spent all day, until
> 0200 the next day, helping with both the British and Argentinian
> casualties. Fr. John Ryan RN came in for an hour or two. It's amazing the
> values that a man holds on to. I remember cutting the clothes off a badly
> wounded soldier who had gunshot wounds and shrapnel wounds and
> needed major surgery. In spite of his state, his main concern was to
> apologise, out of embarrassment, for having soiled his underpants. We
> were just glad to see him alive.[30]

During the next two days Fr Hayes spoke with Argentine prisoners from opposite ends of the rank spectrum, commander-in-chief and rifleman. Their various attitudes and needs were pathetically different. Unable to visit the hospital ship *Uganda*, because she put out to sea overnight, the chaplain went instead to the assault ship, HMS *Fearless*, where he was asked if he wished to speak privately with General Mario Menéndez, the Argentine commander, and a few senior officers with him.

In answer to a question why they had fought for the Falklands, consisting only of sheep and bogs, the general replied: 'For the Argentine, this was a crusade of the spirit. When he was a little boy all the comics he read had been overprinted with the words *Las Islas Malvinas son argentinas*, so every child grew up believing this to be true. "Never before", he said, "had the country been so united." I asked him about the alleged disappearance of thousands of his fellow-citizens each year. They all laughed at the question and assured me it was no longer true, although it had happened in Perón's time. In a discussion with the Swiss Red Cross representative about ten days later in Stanley, I found out from him that it was just as true today, averaging about 5,000 *desaparecidos* per year.'[31]

The following morning Fr Hayes was taken by helicopter to a naval medical centre at Ajax Bay, where he again met the Commando chaplain Fr Noel Mullin. Together they visited the remaining casualties there, six young Argentinian conscripts all with bullet wounds to the feet. All had been on the point of death from starvation on arrival, and had to be fed in small quantities to gradually build up their strength.

> We were not sure if they shot themselves in the feet in order to get taken into hospital or whether they were shot by their officers to prevent them running away. They were too weak to discuss it. Very hard to have to give them such a small portion of food and make them build their strength up day by day. They kept asking for more food, that would only have made them vomit, so we had to refuse them. They were ravenous.[32]

Eventually Fr Hayes could visit *Uganda*, where he was met by Fr Chris Bester RN, the ship's chaplain. He found that the wounded that had passed through the FST were doing well, even the most desperately wounded were on the road to recovery. Fr Hayes' Spanish came in useful. The Argentinian wounded on board were also recovering well and were at particular pains to thank their captors.

> Several Argentinian wounded pressed me over and over to stress to our people how grateful they were for the treatment they'd received. One prisoner in particular said that they had been told that we would torture them, kill the wounded, and leave them to starve if they were captured. We presumed they were told this to make them stay and fight out of desperation.[33]

Our Lady of Lujan is venerated by the Argentinians. When their Army invaded the Falklands they carried with them a statue of Our Lady and installed it in St Mary's, Stanley. After the recapture of Stanley, Fr Hayes stayed with Mgr Spraggon, the parish priest. He saw the statue of Our Lady and asked Mgr Spraggon if he could take it back to England, which was agreed. The monsignor explained that he had another, smaller but identical one, which Argentinian tourists had donated some years previously. On the point of his departure, Fr Hayes was approached by the Red Cross representative who asked him, on behalf of the Argentinian officers, to return the statue.

> I went with him to see the officers in the house where they were being detained and suggested they might like to have the spare one from St Mary's, as I had already packed theirs very carefully in my kitbag. They seemed happy with that arrangement, and the statue I brought home now stands in St Michael's Church, Aldershot as a memorial to all who died in the Falklands War.[34]

The Gulf 1990-91

For all Catholic troops who took part in the land-battle of the Gulf War, religious preparation was very similar to that seen by millions of television viewers: a priest in battledress wearing a stole giving general Absolution and saying Mass beside a main battle tank of the Irish Hussars in the Saudi desert. He was one of half-a-dozen British Army Catholic chaplains serving with the Allied force preparing for a ground offensive to liberate Kuwait. As one chaplain wrote afterwards: 'As this was Lent I began to appreciate Our Lord's time in the desert ...'[35] It was surely a point all chaplains there, whatever their denomination, would have reflected upon.

The hundred-hour land-battle which followed the air onslaught was a classic military operation.

After the short war, services were held in the desert under a blanket of smoke from burning oil wells. The troops formed the old-fashioned hollow square, with the chaplain standing in the centre, sometimes standing behind a collapsible table for the Blessed Eucharist.[36] The disciplined silence, a memorable homily, prayers, hymns. All present with private thoughts. In this war there were not many dead to remember in bitter sadness. Regrettably though, most of the British dead were not caused by enemy action. Easter was approaching and as Christians the thoughts of many would surely have turned to the suffering, death, and resurrection of Our Lord.

When hostilities ended the British 7th Armoured Division concentrated in battlegroups in the desert outside Kuwait City. The city itself was declared out of bounds. The padre of the 14th/20th King's Hussars Battlegroup, however, Fr Michael Wymes, of Hexham and Newcastle, was granted permission to enter the city and make contact with the bishop, Rt Rev Mgr Francis Micalleh, in order to receive new Holy Oils at Easter. On his return Fr Michael told of the suffering of the civil population within the city. Deeply moved, the Hussars resolved to help.

> The Commanding Officer gave the scheme his total support and a personal donation. The Brigade Commander gave permission for a small group of soldiers and a few vehicles to go to the City with aid ... and a request for all unwanted food was broadcasted. A tremendous response followed and within 3 days we had enough to fill an 8-tonne truck. More volunteered to go to Kuwait City than could possibly be taken. Eleven were selected; with Fr. Michael and Warrant Officer J. Mawes of the King's Hussars.[37]

The selected party set out early on the morning of 12 March 1991, in an 8-tonne vehicle and Fr Wymes' Landcruiser. Arriving on the outskirts of Kuwait City, the first person who saw the little group responded in an unexpected way. 'An old lady, upon seeing our vehicles, touched her heart and lips with her hands and then raised both her arms and head to the skies. This act of gratitude made any apprehension about our reception disappear.'[38] Soon they were at the entrance to the Cathedral compound.

> After brief introductions to the clergy we set to work unloading the truck into a storage area. It was at this time that children appeared from the Community Centre. They didn't make a sound. They got so far then turned on their heels and ran back towards the Centre. I instructed the soldiers to grab handfuls of sweets and follow me. When we entered the room we saw about 40 working at their desks, aged between 4 and 17. They looked frightened, confused and sad. I extended my arms, opening my hands to reveal nothing more dangerous than jellied sweets. For what seemed an eternity the room remained motionless. At last a little boy came forward shyly, bowed in front of me, took a sweet and ran back to his place. Then another came forward, then another and very soon the whole room was a cacophony of sound and frenzied motion. The ice was broken. The majority of children spoke English very well. They asked us to sign their books and give them our names and addresses. After 20 minutes we returned to the truck to finish unloading.[39]

Formal introduction to the Bishop of Kuwait followed. The bishop explained that he was a Carmelite, and the priests with him were from Malta, India and the Philippines. His congregation were exclusively non-Kuwaitis from places as far as the Philippines, India, Pakistan, Lebanon and the USSR, either top professionals, or manual workers. The Catholics of the diplomatic community were also part of his spiritual flock. At the end of the brief chat the bishop asked the soldiers to tea.

All were invited to wash their hands; the housekeeper poured water for each man, the bishop dried every hand. It was a nice paschal touch.

> We sat down and were served with tea and homemade biscuits. The Bishop reiterated how welcome the gifts were and thanked the Regiment for the compassion that it had shown. Inevitably the conversation turned to the conditions that Kuwait had endured since 2 August. We were spellbound by this charismatic man as he recounted stories of human deprivation, degradation and suffering. How the Iraqi occupying force murdered, tortured, looted, raped both men and women and how they vandalised everything they didn't see an immediate use for. The Cathedral and residence were also subjected to such acts of theft and destruction: smashing holy artefacts, shredding Persian carpets and smearing excreta on walls. The Bishop himself showed great fortitude against adversity. He was ordered to go to Basra by Saddam to attend an ecumenical conference. He had refused to go. He had stopped an Iraqi soldier urinating in the compound and had promptly had an AK 47 held to his throat. He didn't know why he hadn't been shot.[40]

After tea the party returned to the compound. Schoolchildren and young people were laughing and joking. The soldiers noted the marked difference in the spirit of the youngsters compared with a few hours before.

> What a pleasure it was to see. Their overwhelming desire was to know how Manchester United and Liverpool were standing in the League. LCpl Clowes took great delight in bringing them up to date ... The priest from Malta asked if I could get a message to his brother who lived near Salisbury, which I agreed to do. The message read, 'I am alive, thanks be to God'.[41]

Soon, after a photo opportunity, it was time to depart.

> The children sang a song for us as we climbed aboard our vehicles and moved out of the compound to the accompaniment of applause, cheers and expressions of gratitude ... We headed back into the desert ... Passing through the Mutla Ridge area we saw what looked like the whole of the US 7th Army Corps 'proffing' car engines, tyres and anything else that was not bolted down. So ended for me a quite remarkable day that will remain etched in my memory forever.[42]

Fr Wymes returned to Kuwait City for Easter Mass with the Indian community, and to collect Holy Oils for the forthcoming year.

> Easter Sunday Mass with the joy-filled Indians will be a vivid memory of how suffering can be overcome. Their gratitude to us was humbling, the generosity of the British soldier to them was encouraging. For me the Gulf peace had as many lessons as the Gulf war, and those lessons will stay in my heart and mind.[43]

Bosnia 1995

The civilized world has been saddened, and at times horrified, by the savage communal strife in the former Yugoslavia. The United Nations

Protection Force (UNPROFOR) defined its mission as:

> developing the peace in central Bosnia between the BiH (Moslems) and
> the HVO (Croats)
> monitoring the conflict between Bosnia (BiH and HVO) and the Bosnian
> Serbs (BSA)
> supporting humanitarian agencies
> supporting the European administration in Mostar.[44]

Since the beginning of the British involvement with UNPROFOR in Bosnia-
Hercegovina there have been five British chaplains, two Anglican, two
Presbyterian and one Catholic. The Catholic chaplain is responsible for the
entire area, the others are localized to the regiment to which they are
attached. The Catholic chaplain must rely on the good will of his
colleagues to pass on information regarding Catholic soldiers and any
matters arising. 'It follows then, that the Chaplaincy cover has to be fully
ecumenical, with services taken by all Chaplains, for all who turn up, as it
is impossible for me to travel the whole area of operations on a given day.'[45]
Curiously, in view of his widespread responsibility, it has been reported
that the Catholic chaplain is the only one not to have a vehicle and driver,
although another chaplain reported that: 'The Signals here have been a
great help, and try to get me a vehicle and driver if I can let them know in
time when I want one.'[46]

The arrival of 24 Air Mobile Brigade with the multi-national back-up
force, brought a second British Army Catholic chaplain. While this helps
the UN chaplain spiritually it does not reduce his area of responsibility or
lessen his work. One chaplain wears a light blue beret, the other a dark
blue.[47]

During the week 8–15 September 1995 Fr Ian Evans, chaplain to the
British contingent of UNPROFOR, carried out his usual round of visits.
The life led by Fr Evans, and the other priests who have served in this
bewildering and saddening situation, is one of prayer, sacraments, talking
with 'the lads', and movement between outposts. Although ostensibly
based at Split on the Adriatic, the chaplain and his driver sleep in five
different places every week for the duration of an operational tour of six
months.[48] A weekly circuit of his 'parish' involves a drive of almost 900
kilometres of dangerous routes, in most places little more than mountain
mule-tracks improved by Royal Engineers, snow-bound in winter, always
requiring driving skill and constant vigilance.

The men in his spiritual care are cavalry, engineers, signallers, infantry,
medics, as well as the service troops hauling supplies along dangerous
roads, higher than Ben Nevis.

> Church attendance does not feature as a high priority out here with the
> 'boys', or with the higher echelon. Numbers at Mass can in a given place
> range from two to thirty, depending on what is happening at the time. A

couple of Commanding officers try to make Church attendance compulsory for a group of lads on a given Sunday, so that a company will parade for Church. This is a move that I fight most strongly.[49]

This last has always been the view of Catholic chaplains, although chaplains of other faiths do not always agree. The historic Catholic view is that the sacraments are received voluntarily, compulsion is anathema. Ultimately, a more lasting faith is achieved in this way. Although on occasion it is done informally:

My responsibilities are not solely to say Holy Mass, of course, or to celebrate the Sacrament of Reconciliation. Though, with Reconciliation, it is pleasing to note how many of the boys do come and ask for it. They often have to pluck up courage in the bar in the evening to ask about it, and then we celebrate the Sacrament the next morning, or at the earliest opportunity. Normally as I travel it is to see if there are any problems or difficulties. I then try to take them up with the respective bodies, whether that is their commanding officer, or via a phone call home. Visits do tend to be much appreciated, especially in the outlying detachments, where sometimes I am the only one ever to go and see them.[50]

The weekly round of his 'parish' by one chaplain is a good example, although it can vary, depending on the deployment of the British within UNPROFOR. Having stayed the weekend at Split, Fr Evans' week begins early.

On a Monday morning I travel to the border crossing at Komensko and on to Tomislavgrad where elements of an engineer regiment are based adjacent to the British and French contingents of the Multi National Brigade. From there I travel to the Engineer forts on route triangle. These lads live in fairly basic accommodation and yet their contribution to keeping the route serviced, open and passable is invaluable.[51]

In an international force not all the Catholics who attend the sacraments are British.

From the forts I pass into the town of Prozor, scene of fierce fighting over a year ago. My first main stop is Gornji Vakuf, there I say Mass in Spanish for the Spanish contingent, make contact with my Church of England colleague. Then on up the road to Bugojno where I say Mass and stay the night with the Light Dragoons and the 1st Fusiliers.[52]

Not far away is Donji Vakuf, newly captured from the Serbs. No UN official has been able to get into the place since. Having toured the Fusiliers, and some outlying observation posts, Fr Evans attempts entry into the captured town:

I drive up to the Bih checkpoint on the chance I might [get through] but am politely refused entry into the town. I then make my way up the hill above Donji Vakuf to Mike Bravo 8, the observation post (OP) overlooking the town. This tends to be a bit exciting as drunken locals use the OP for target practice in the evenings.[53]

Not all the troops are on checkpoint or OP duty. Some, such as the Devon and Dorsets, are in reserve and have to be in a constant state of readiness to move, which adds to the strain of life. At one place, with good reason, a Mobile Surgical Team is attached to the 9th/12th Lancers. They are responsible for peacekeeping in the 'fairly dodgy' area on the confrontation line near Zepce and Maglaj. Getting to the latter place can be dangerous.

> I head up the road to Maglaj school where thirty or so personnel maintain a presence in the town. Frequently shot at and once mortared, it is approached by entering sniper's alley, a 100 yard long stretch of road only passed when wearing helmet and body armour.[54]

Because they travel greater distances than most other officers, chaplains are more personally aware of the dangers faced by drivers. It comes not only from sniper fire, but more usually the dangers are from stone-throwing vandalism perpetrated by undisciplined children living 'in the culture of hatred, distrust and violence ... brought up to perpetuate the futility'.[55] There are other dangers for the unwary:

> Travelling around a war torn country has been an eye-opener – the level of the destruction to Mosques and Catholic churches is particularly saddening. I have been hustled out of desecrated places by AK 47-wielding local Muslims. The first Church was situated to the east of Gorni Vakuf. I was taking pictures of the mess when I was yelled at by a Muslim militiaman. I turned my camera on him and he disappeared, or so I thought. On my way out of the building I felt the muzzle of a rifle on my shoulder pushing me out the door. I shouted to my driver to show his weapon while starting the landrover. I tried calmly to walk away but I must admit to waiting to hear the sound of his AK 47 as they usually shoot above our heads ... we drove away and then he 'opened-up' over the roof of the Rover.[56]

The peacekeepers of Bosnia pray that the ceasefire of 11 October 1995 may hold sufficiently to allow a permanent peace to be negotiated. However, given their personal observations and experience, who would blame them for evincing pessimism about the future?

> The real tragedy here is for the children. They are the ones that always lose out. It is they who are brought up to perpetuate the futility. Around all the UN checkpoints or observation posts, the children gather as bees round a honey pot. Most reasonably friendly, many doing jobs, like cutting wood. As I arrive, they are usually interested to see who I am and look in wonder at the pips on my shoulders. Then the eagle-eyed ones spot the dark crosses in the lapels of my combat jacket. If I am in a Moslem area there is an immediate reaction. There are cries of 'chetnik', often some spitting, and nearly always there will be an attempt to rip out

the crosses, with graphic demonstrations of how they would snap them. Trying to talk to them is impossible. From being a potential new friend who might give them things, I suddenly become one of the 'enemy'. For the first time in my life, I experience real antipathy to the thing I hold so dear. Their distrust of the sign of the Cross, has been bred in so deep. The cycle is set.[57]

The Military Ordinariate of Great Britain

The creation of the Ministry of Defence in the 1950s produced, amongst other benefits, enhanced service administration. Additionally, the Holy See brought about changes to the governance of Forces chaplains. Since the death of Bishop Dey in 1946, ecclesiastical oversight of chaplains devolved upon the Archbishop of Westminster, who delegated pastoral care of Forces personnel to a Principal Chaplain who acted as Apostolic Administrator. In 1951 the Vatican issued the Instruction *Solemne Semper* setting out laws governing Military Vicariates. These reflected very much the interim structure devised for the governance of churches in missionary territories. Their bishops, as the name Vicariate implies, were not Ordinaries; they did not govern in their own right, but were Vicars or delegates of the Holy See. The first *Vicarius Castrensis* for the British Forces was Archbishop David Mathew, a former Apostolic Delegate for East Africa who had served as a midshipman at Jutland. Archbishop Mathew, who was expected to succeed Cardinal Hinsley, was appointed in 1953 and under him, for the first time, Royal Naval chaplains came into line with their Army and Royal Air Force colleagues. This British Vicariate, supported by Cardinal Griffin and later Cardinal Godfrey, was erected by the decree *Inexhausta Caritate* and conferred jurisdiction over service personnel and their dependants at home and overseas. Archbishop Mathew retired in 1962 and was succeeded by Bishop Gerard Tickle, formerly Rector of the Venerable English College, Rome, and a Second World War chaplain. Bishop Tickle became titular Bishop of Bela.

A further development in the ecclesiastical governance of Forces chaplains came in 1986 during the episcopate of the present Bishop of the Forces, Francis Joseph Walmsley, a former Principal Naval Chaplain, who succeeded Bishop Tickle in 1979. The Apostolic Constitution *Spirituali Militum Curae* swept away the interim Vicariate arrangement and made provision for a permanent quasi diocese of the Forces. This was effected in Great Britain on 24 October 1987 by the decree *Pro Solicitudine Omnium Ecclesiarum* when Bishop Walmsley was solemnly enthroned as the first Military Ordinary. He was now a member of the Episcopal Conference of England and Wales and acquired a special relationship with the Scottish Bishops' Conference. By right he could now represent chaplains and their people; he could appoint Principal Chaplains as his Vicars General, and chaplains as parish priests to garrisons, bases and ships. Chaplains now had a canonically elected Council of Priests and Forces laity their own Bishopric Pastoral Council. Thus in 123 years

> The deep concern felt by Bishop Grant of Southwark for the spiritual welfare of soldiers and sailors, and their families, in the great bases of the south of England, which had at that time formed the diocese of Southwark, containing the greatest concentration of British Naval and Military strength in the world, had finally come to full fruition.[58]

References

1. Fr John Ryan, report to Principal Chaplain (RC) (3 November 1950).
2. Ibid.
3. Ryan to PC (RC) (29 November 1950).
4. Ibid.
5. Ryan to PC (RC) (15 December 1950).
6. Senior RC Chaplain's Return to PC (RC) (11 May 1953).
7. Ryan to PC (RC) (30 April 1953).
8. A. Farrar-Hockley, *The British Part in the Korean War* (London, 1995), vol. II, p. 281.
9. Fr R. J. Petry to PC (RC) (October 1953).
10. Australian newspaper report (April 1953). Extant copy at RCCA.
11. Ibid.
12. Ibid.
13. Ryan to PC (RC) (30 April 1953).
14. Fr Alfred Hayes, letter to Tom Johnstone (24 August 1994).
15. Ibid.
16. Fr Bernard Funnell, letter to Tom Johnstone (26 September 1995).
17. Ibid.
18. Fr Alfred Hayes, 'The diary of a priest in the Falklands' (unpublished MS), p. 2.
19. Ibid., p. 4.
20. Ibid.
21. Ibid.
22. Ibid.
23. Ibid., p. 7.
24. Ibid., p. 8.
25. Ibid.
26. Ibid., p. 9.
27. Ibid., p. 10.
28. Ibid.
29. Ibid.
30. Ibid., p. 11.
31. Ibid., p. 12.
32. Ibid.
33. Hayes, letter to T. Johnstone (24 August 1995).

34. Ibid.
35. Fr Michael Wymes, 'A long march.'
36. Photo, *Journal of the 14th/20th King's Hussars*.
37. Warrant Officer II Class J. Mawes, 'The children of Kuwait', *Journal of the 14th/20th King's Hussars*, p. 168.
38. Ibid., p. 169.
39. Ibid.
40. Ibid.
41. Ibid., p. 170.
42. Ibid., p. 171.
43. Wymes.
44. Fr F. P. A. Barber, 'Report from Bosnia-Herzegovina', p. 1.
45. Ibid., p. 1.
46. Ibid., p. 3.
47. Fr Ian Evans, letter to T. Johnstone (22 September 1995).
48. Ibid.
49. Barber, p. 2.
50. Ibid.
51. Evans.
52. Ibid.
53. Ibid.
54. Ibid.
55. Fr F. P. A. Barber, 'Impressions of Bosnia'.
56. Evans.
57. Barber, 'Impressions of Bosnia'.
58. COA. The authors are grateful to Rt Rev Francis Walmsley, Bishop of the Forces, for his kind assistance on this section.

Epilogue

Since St Augustine, Catholic theologians have expounded the thesis that military service is not against the teaching of Christ, or mankind's humanity and desire for peace. St Augustine himself did not codify a theory on the just war, or Christian participation in it. His beliefs are segmented, fragments being in sermons, pamphlets, and letters, such as:

> Peace should be your aim; war should be a matter of necessity so that God might free you from necessity and preserve you in peace. One does not pursue peace in order to wage war; he wages war to achieve peace. And so, even in the act of waging war be careful to maintain a peaceful disposition so that by defeating your foes you can bring them the benefits of Peace ... 'Blessed are the peacemakers' says the Lord 'for they will be called the sons of God' (Mt 5:9). If peace is such a delightful dimension of man's temporal happiness, how much sweeter is the divine peace that belongs to eternal happiness of angels. And so, let it be because of necessity rather than your own desire that you kill the enemy fighting against you.[1]

The stalemated Cold War between the ideologically-based East and West power blocs has ended. At worst NATO forces gave Europe the longest period without active warfare the continent has ever known. Considerable euphoria surrounded the collapse of the starkest symbol of Communist Europe, the Berlin Wall. Upon its fall, the world was filled with hope for a new era of peace. Alas, the haste to turn swords into ploughshares, or their modern equivalents, was premature. The end of the Soviet epoch has proved dangerously unstable. Thankfully, peace, at last, may come to two of the most intractable problem areas of the twentieth century, Palestine/Israel and Ireland. Sadly, events elsewhere have been disastrous to mankind's hopes and desires for peace. Bloody events in parts of Africa, Asia and Europe have taken a terrible toll of the innocent. Horrifying scenes, brought through the medium of television into our homes, have shocked and outraged the civilized world, while world leaders were apparently helpless or uncaring. Whatever room of God's mansion his people might occupy, surely all deserve to reside peacefully therein?

The world's hope for a peaceful future towards the twenty-first century can only lie in strengthening the power of the United Nations through its General Assembly. The imposition of peace on warring factions in any conflict has to be an early priority, either through peace-making or peace-keeping. These means have been defined by Secretary-General Dr Boutros Boutros-Ghali in his 1992 report *Agenda for Peace*, as:

> peace-making: 'Action to bring hostile parties to agreement, essentially through peaceful means'
> peace-keeping: 'The deployment of a United Nations presence in the field, hitherto with the consent of all parties concerned, normally involving United Nations military and/or police personnel and frequently civilians as well. Peace-keeping is a technique that expands the possibilities for both the prevention of conflict and the making of peace.'[2]

Events in Bosnia have shown these precepts are imperfect. Peace-making in the last resort may have to be imposed by the use of force. As a corollary to this, immediate close collaboration between sovereign states to bring war criminals to justice should follow the restoration of peace, as an example and a deterrent to others who would foment or support war against mankind. The increasing availability of nuclear, biological and chemical weapons to irrational warlords, or terrorists, poses serious threats to world peace and stability. Threats that cannot be ignored by even the most God-fearing and peaceful.

In recent years the British Army has refined and defined principles for operating in a peace-keeping role which could act as a model for all such operations undertaken by the United Nations. Based upon firm guidelines evolved through its long, and sometimes unhappy, experience of internal security duties throughout the world.

> Acting with the consent of the parties involved; through conciliation not force.
> Showing impartiality in the conflict.
> Attitudes of restraint, guidance and supervision, not belligerence.
> Mediation, negotiation and conciliation, based on sensitivity to cultural background and traditions.
> Mutual respect between the peoples involved and the peace-keepers.
> Notwithstanding the above, maintaining the credibility of the peace-keepers by a capability to respond effectively, with minimum necessary force, to any attack.[3]

These are principles, surely, that St Augustine himself, or any modern chaplain, could, or can, feel comfortable in preaching to an army *en route* to hold the line of civilized beliefs against barbarity.

References

1. St Augustine, letter to Legate Boniface, *Letters* 189.6; quoted by Louis J. Swift, *The Early Fathers on War and Military Service* (Wilmington, DE, 1983).
2. Rev Michael K. Masterson SCF, 'Peace making and peace keeping'.
3. Ibid.

Appendix: Roll of Honour

Priests Killed in Action, Died of Wounds and Died on Service

If they experienced punishment as men know it, their hope was rich with immortality. (Wisdom 3:4)

Crimea, 1854–56

Canty, Rev M.	Westminster
Doyle, Rev J.	Westminster
Meany, Rev P.	Salford
Sheehan, Rev D.	Southwark
Shiel, Rev J.	English College, Valladolid
Strickland, Rev J.	SJ
Wheble, Rev J. J.	Westminster

India, 1857–58

Fairhurst, Rev P.	Liverpool
Morgan, Rev C.	Unknown

World War I, 1914–19

Royal Navy

Gwydir, Rev Canon R. B.	OSB, Douai
Phelan, Rev S. J.	OMI

Army

Baines, Rev T. L.	Liverpool
Bedale, Rev C. L.	Westminster
Bertina, Rev U.	OSB, Malta
Burdess, Rev M. F.	Middlesbrough
Carey, Rev T.	SJ, Irish Province
Clarke, Rev S.	Kilmore
Collins, Rev H. H. J.	Westminster
Cowd, Rev A. M.	Scots College, Rome

Doyle, Rev D.	SJ
Doyle, Rev W. J.	SJ, Irish Province
Finn, Rev W. J.	Middlesbrough
Fitzgibbon, Rev J. J.	SJ, Irish Province
Gordon, Rev M.	Glasgow
Grobel, Rev P.	Salford
Guthrie, Rev D. M.	OSB, Quarr
Gwynn, Rev J.	SJ, Irish Province
Hartigan, Rev J. A.	SJ, Irish Province
Kavanagh, Rev B.	CSSR
Knapp, Rev S. S.	OCD
Leeson, Rev J. T.	Liverpool
Looby, Rev P.	Liverpool
McAuliffe, Rev C. R.	OFM, Irish Province
McDonnell, Rev J. J.	CM, Irish Province
McGinty, Rev H. C.	SJ
Montagu, Rev W. P.	SJ
Monteith, Rev R. J.	SJ
O'Dea, Rev L.	OSF
O'Meehan, Rev I. J.	OFM, Irish Province
O'Sullivan, Rev D.	Kerry
Prendergast, Rev M. V.	Waterford, on loan to Middlesbrough
Ryan, Rev M.	OCD
Shine, Rev J.	Waterford, on loan to Dunkeld
Strickland, Rev J.	SJ
Watson, Rev C.	CSSR
Watters, Rev J. A.	Plymouth
Whitefoord, Rev C.	Shrewsbury

Australia

| Bergin, Rev M. | SJ, Irish Province |
| Sydes, Rev E. | SJ |

New Zealand

| Dore, Rev P. | Auckland |
| McMenamin, Rev J. J. | Holy Cross College, Mosgiel |

World War II, 1939-45
Royal Navy

| Bradley, Rev T. | CSSR |
| Brennan, Rev T. A. | OMI |

Army

| Barry, Rev G. | Liverpool |

Benson, Rev B. J.	Leeds
Boyle, Rev A.	SC
Costello, Rev B.	Middlesbrough
Curran, Rev J. G.	CSSp
Firth, Rev P. F.	Lancaster
Gilgunn, Rev W. G.	CM, Irish Province
Hayes, Rev J.	SJ, Irish Province
Hirst, Rev J.	Lancaster
Hobson-Matthews, Rev G.	OSB, Downside
Hourigan, Rev D. F.	SC
Kenny, Rev J. W.	Lancaster
McMahon, Rev P. J.	SSC
Nesbitt, Rev G.	Hexham and Newcastle
O'Callaghan, Rev J.	Hexham and Newcastle
Richardson, Rev E. R.	Lancaster

Selected bibliography

Published sources

Acta of the Bishops' Conference (18-19 April 1939), item IV.

'Some aspects of the war', *All Hallows Journal* (Dublin, 1914).

'Ampleforth at war', *Ampleforth Journal*, vols 20 and 21.

Army List (London: HMSO, various editions, 1861-1994).

S. F. Arneil, *One Man's War* (Chippendale, NSW, 1982).

Margot Asquith, *The Autobiography* (London: Thornton Butterworth Ltd, 1922).

Australian Dictionary of Biography.

Mark Bence-Jones, *The Twilight of the Ascendancy* (London: Constable, 1987).

Robert Blake, *The Private Papers of Douglas Haig* (London: Eyre and Spottiswoode, 1953).

Sr Evelyn Bolster, *The Irish Sisters of Mercy in the Crimean War* (Cork: Mercier Press, 1964).

Bill Boyan and Ian Pedley, *Altars and Artillery: The Life of Mgr Owen B. Steele* (Brisbane: Boolarong Publications, 1980).

James Boyle, *Railroad to Burma* (London: Allen & Unwin, 1990).

Russell Braddon, *Naked Island* (Hawthorn, Victoria: Lloyd O'Neil, 1975).

James Bradley, 'Mass on active service', *St Bede's Magazine*, no. 6 (March 1918).

Rt Rev Dom Rudesind Brookes OSB, OBE, MC, TD, *Father Dolly* (London, 1983).

Gnr Eddie Brown, RFA, 'Fr. Francis Woodlock', *St Bede's Magazine* (December 1915).

Arthur Bryant, *Triumph in the West: Completing the War Diaries of Field-Marshal Viscount Alanbrooke* (London: Collins, 1959).

John Buchan, *History of The Great War* (24 vols; London: Nelson, 1915-19).

Gerald Achilles Burgoyne, *The Burgoyne Diaries* (London: Harmsworth, 1985).

Patrick K. Callan, 'Ambivalence towards the Saxon shilling: the attitudes of the Catholic Church in Ireland towards enlistment during the First World War', *Archivium Hibernicum*.

Rev Bede Camm OSB, *Pilgrim Paths in Latin Lands* (London: Macdonald & Evans, 1923).

Second Annual Report of the Canadian Chaplaincy Service (RC) (1 January 1941-31 December 1941).

Canadian Dictionary of Biography.

Rev Canon B. J. Canning, *Irish Born Secular Priests in Scotland 1829–1979* (Dundee:

Bookmag, 1980).

Canon Bernard J. Canning, 'Scotland's wartime spiritual contribution', *Scottish Catholic Observer* (5 August 1994).

'Catholic Army chaplains: a diary', *The Catholic Bulletin and Book Review*, vol. VII, no. 4 (April 1917).

Catholic Directories of England and Wales; Ireland; Scotland (various editions).

The New Catholic Encyclopedia (New York: McGraw-Hill, 1967).

N. Cave, *Battleground Europe: A Guide to Battlefields in France and Flanders* (Barnsley, 1990).

Charles Chenevix Trench, *The Great Dan* (London: Jonathan Cape, 1984).

Randolph S. Churchill, *Winston S. Churchill*, vol. I (London, 1966).

Winston S. Churchill, *My Early Life* (London: Odhams, 1965).

Winston S. Churchill, *The World Crisis* (London: Butterworth, 1927).

Winston S. Churchill, *The Second World War* (London: Cassell, 1950-54).

Hugh Clark, Russell Braddon and Colin Burgess, *Prisoners of War* (Sydney: Time-Life Books Australia, 1988).

H. Clifford, *Letters and Sketches from the Crimea* (London, 1956).

Rev Michael Clifton, *Amigo - Friend of the Poor* (Leominster: Fowler Wright Books Ltd, 1987).

Rev Michael Clifton, *The Quiet Negotiator* (Liverpool).

Senator Helena Concannon, 'The Irish Sisters of Mercy in the Crimea', *The Irish Messenger*.

Rev J. W. Cosser, 'Campaigning in East Africa', *St Francis Magazine*, War Memorial number (Northampton diocese) (1919).

Rev O. Creighton, *With the Twenty-Ninth Division in Gallipoli* (London: Longmans, Green & Co., 1916).

The Very Rev Canon Croft, *Historical Account of Lisbon College* (Barnet: St Andrew's Press, 1902).

Fr Edmund Cullen CM, 'The Battle of Loos', Castleknock, *St Vincent's College Chronicle* (1916).

Henry C. Day SJ, MC, *A Cavalry Chaplain* (London: Heath Cranton Ltd, 1922).

Henry C. Day SJ, MC, *Macedonian Memories* (London: Heath Cranton Ltd, 1930).

Len Deighton, *Fighter: The True Story of the Battle of Britain* (London: Jonathan Cape, 1977).

Martin Dempsey, *The Priest Among the Soldiers* (London, 1946).

Fr Philip Dominic Devas OFM, *From Cloister to Camp* (London, 1919).

The Douai Magazine.

Rev Raymund M. Dowdall OP, DCL, *Memories of More Recent Irish Dominicans* (Dublin: Dominican Publications, 1951).

Raymund M. Dowdall, OP, DCL, *Memories of Still More Recent Irish Dominicans 1950-1960* (Dublin: Dominican Publications, 1961).

The Downside Review.

Fr William Doyle SJ, *A Year's Thoughts* (London: Longmans, Green & Co., 1922-23).

Tpr Charles Drake, Sherwood Rangers Yeo., *St Bede's Magazine* (July 1916).

Margaret Duggan, *Padre in Colditz: The Diary of Ellison Platt* (London: Hodder and Stoughton, 1978).

Dundee and District Catholic Year Book (1918).

J. C. Dunn, *The War the Infantry Knew* (London, 1989).

G. Dwyer, *Diocese of Portsmouth, Past and Present* (Portsmouth, 1981).

Brig Gen Sir John Edmonds, *Military Operations France and Belgium 1914–18* (16 vols; London: HMSO).

Rev Bartholomew Egan OFM, 'A West Limerick chaplain of World War I', *Limerick Association Year Book* (1982).

Capt C. Falls, *Military Operations: Macedonia* (2 vols; London: HMSO, 1930).

'Our Burma Story', *Far East* (Magazine of the Columban Fathers and Sisters) (November 1987).

Anthony Farrar-Hockley, *The British Part in the Korean War* (London: HMSO, 1995).

Bernard Fergusson, *Beyond the Chindwin* (London: Collins, 1945).

Charles FitzGerald-Lombard, Abbot of Downside, *English and Welsh Priests 1801–1914* (Downside, 1993).

W. J. Fitz-Patrick, *The Life, Times, and Correspondence of the Rt. Rev Dr. Doyle* (Dublin, 1880).

Rev M. J. Flanagan, 'Our military chaplains', *St Francis Magazine* (1919).

Fr George Forster, *Priest Behind Barbed Wire* (Sunderland).

Hon J. W. Fortescue, *A History of the British Army, 1906–1920* (14 vols; London: Macmillan, 1930), vols VI–XIII.

A. C. Fox-Davies, *The Complete Guide to Heraldry* (London: Thomas Nelson & Son, 1956).

Margaret Goodman, *Experiences of an English Sister of Mercy* (London: Smith, Elder & Co., 1862).

Robert Graves, *Goodbye to All That* (London: Jonathan Cape, 1929).

F. Le M. Gretton, *Campaigns and History of the Royal Irish Regiment, 1684–1902* (London: Blackwood, 1911).

Rev J. A. Gribben, 'The evacuation of Anzac', *Ushaw College Magazine*, vol. XXVI (July 1916).

Rev T. G. Griffen, *Ushaw College Magazine*, vol. XXXII (December 1922).

General Sir John Hackett, *I Was a Stranger* (London: Chatto & Windus, 1978).

J. Bryant Haigh, *Men of Faith and Courage: The Official History of New Zealand's Army Chaplains* (Auckland, 1983).

Patrick J. Hamell, *Maynooth Students and Ordinations 1895–1984* (Maynooth, 1984).

P. Hamilton-Pollock, *Wings on the Cross: A Padre with the R.A.F.* (Dublin: Clonard & Reynolds, 1954).

H. M. Hanham, 'Religion and nationality in the mid-Victorian Army' in *War and Society*, ed. M. R. D. Foot (London, 1973).

Henry Hanna, *The Pals at Suvla* (Dublin: Ponsonby, 1916).

Hansard, 4th series (1901) 89, 1189 90.

Gen Sir Charles Harington, *Plumer of Messines* (London: John Murray, 1935).

Fr T. A. Harker, 'Notes from Ushaw at the front', *Ushaw College Magazine*, vol. XXVII (March 1917).

Rev T. A. Harker, 'College notes', *Ushaw College Magazine*, vol. XXV (July 1915).

Jock Haswell, *The First Respectable Spy* (London: Hamish Hamilton, 1969).

Maurice Hennessy, *The Wild Geese* (London: Sidgwick and Jackson, 1973).

Rev Gerard Hetterington, 'Bishop Brindle, DSO., 1837-1916', *The Lisbonian Magazine*, vol. XXVIII, nos. 1 and 2.

Capt F. C. Hitchcock, *Stand-To: A Diary of the Trenches* (London: Hurst and Blackett, 1937).

Bishop Thomas Holland, *For Better and for Worse* (Salford, 1989).

Fr Thomas Hourigan, 'The Odyssey of a chaplain in the RAF', *St Kieran's College Record* (Kilkenny, 1956).

Lionel Hudson, *The Rats of Rangoon* (London: Leo Cooper, 1987).

Interfuse (Journal of the Irish Province of the Society of Jesus), no. 41 (1986).

Irwin and Chichester, *Stonyhurst War Record* (London: Constable).

Dr Christine Johnson, *Scottish Catholic Secular Clergy 1879-1989* (Edinburgh: John Donald, 1991).

Air Vice-Marshal J. E. Johnson, *The Story of Air Fighting* (London: Hutchinson, 1964).

Tom Johnstone, *Orange, Green and Khaki* (Dublin: Gill and Macmillan, 1992).

Lt Col H. F. H. Jourdain, *History of the Connaught Rangers* (3 vols; Whitehall: RUSI, 1925-28), vol. III.

John Keegan, *The Mask of Command* (London, 1987).

Capt Cyril Lancaster, 'Ampleforth and the war', *The Ampleforth Journal*, vol. 21.

Lancaster Diocesan Directory (1945, 1970 and 1992).

Letters and Notices (Journal of the English Province of the Society of Jesus), vol. 6, no. 330 (1963); vol. 90, nos 398, 399 (1990).

'Letters from the Front', *Stonyhurst Magazine* (1914-20).

The London Gazette, various editions.

Laddie Lucas (ed.), *Wings of War* (London: Hutchinson, 1983).

Rev Brendan McConvey CSSR, 'A chaplain's wartime letters', *Reality (A Redemptorist Publication)* (December 1994).

Charles McCormac, *You'll Die in Singapore* (Morley Books, 1973).

Lyn MacDonald, *Voices and Images of the Great War* (London, 1988).

Capt Desmond McWeeney, 'Fifteen days of the march retreat', *The Ranger*, no. 76 (1968).

Rev Lionel Marsden, 'Under the heel of a brutal enemy our boys kept the faith', *The Catholic Weekly* (Australia) (15 November 1945).

Rev James B. Marshall MC, 21st Division, *St Francis Magazine*, War Memorial number (Northampton) (1919).

Sr Mary Aloysius, *Memories of the Crimea* (London: Burns & Oates Ltd, 1897).

Warrant-Officer J. Mawes, 'The children of Kuwait', *Journal of the 14th/20th King's Hussars* (1991).

Stuart Mawson, *Arnhem Doctor* (London: Orbis Publishing).

Hon Mrs Maxwell-Scott of Abbotsford, *Henry Schomberg Kerr, Sailor and Jesuit* (London: Longmans, Green & Co., 1901).

Rev W. I. Meagher, 'College notes', *Ushaw College Magazine*, vol. XXV (December 1915).

Rev W. I. Meagher, 'Notes from the log of a naval chaplain', *Ushaw College Magazine*, vol. XXVI (July 1916).

Rev W. I. Meagher, 'Things seen', *Ushaw College Magazine*, vol. XXVII (December 1917).

The Military History and Information Service AIF (Middle East), *Active Service: With Australia in the Middle East* (Canberra, 1941).

Thomas Moloney, *Westminster, Whitehall and the Vatican* (London: Burns & Oates, 1985).

Allan Moorehead, *Gallipoli* (London: Hamish Hamilton, 1956).

Michael Moynihan, *God on Our Side* (London, 1983).

Greg Murphy, 'James O'Sullivan', *Catholic Times* (5 June 1994).

C. Naughton, *Interfuse*, vol. 41 (1986).

Northern Catholic Calendar (1917).

D. J. O'Doherty, 'Students of the Irish College Salamanca 1776–1837', *Archivium Hibernicum*, vol. VI (1917).

Ernest Oldmeadow, *Francis Cardinal Bourne*, vol. I (London, 1940).

Prof. Alfred O'Rahilly, *Father William Doyle, S.J.* (London: Longmans, Green & Co., 1939).

Mgr M. O'Riordan, *Appunti riguardanti la sistemazione delle Cappellanie dell'armata britannica. Pro Memoria* (Rome: Tipogravia Pontificia nell' Istituto Pio IX, 1916).

Rev Alured Ozanne, 'Catholics in the Royal Navy', *The Edmundian*, vol. VII (1907).

Pax, The Prinknash Quarterly (spring 1941).

'In Memoriam – Dom Brendan McHugh OSB', *Pax, The Prinknash Quarterly*, vol. XLVIII, no. 286 (summer 1958).

Fr Frederick Peal SJ, *War Jottings* (Calcutta: Catholic Orphans Press, 1916).

Ian Pedley and Bill Boyan, *Altars and Artillery* (Brisbane, 1980).

'Padres at war', *Pegasus*, magazine of the Airborne Forces, copy held by the authors.

Jacques Pelletier and Rev Francis G. Morrisey OMI, *Le Vicariat Militaire du Canada* (Faculté de Droit Canonique, Université Saint-Paul, 1976).

Brian Plumb, *Arundel to Zabi: A Biographical Dictionary of the Catholic Bishops of England and Wales 1623–1987* (Warrington, 1988).

Plymouth Diocesan Year Book (1965).

Grace Ramsay, *Thomas Grant, First Bishop of Southwark* (London: Smith, Eden & Co., 1874).

Capt S. W. Roskill RN, *The Navy at War 1939–1945* (London: Collins, 1960).

Salesian College Magazine (1943).

Fr Cyril Scarborough, 'Chaplain in captivity', *Southwark Journal* (1959).

R. J. Schiefen, *Cardinal Wiseman and the Transformation of English Catholicism* (Shepardstown, 1984).

Alice Shiel, *Henry Stuart, Cardinal Duke of York and His Times* (London: Longmans, Green & Co., 1908).

Cecil Woodham Smith, *Florence Nightingale* (Constable: London, 1950).

Sir John Smyth, *In This Sign Conquer: The Story of the Army Chaplains* (London, 1968).

Frederic C. Spurr, *Some Chaplains in Khaki: An Account of the Work of Chaplains of the United Navy and Army Board* (London, 1916).

Statistics of the War Effort of the British Empire (London: HMSO, 1922).

R. H. J. Steuart, *March Kind Comrade* (London, 1931).

George Stevens, *With Kitchener to Khartoum* (London: Blackwood, 1898).

Lt R. I. G. L. Stirling, 2nd Leinster Regiment, 'Rosary in the trenches', *The Castleknock College Chronicle* (1916).

Louis J. Swift, *The Early Fathers on War and Military Service* (Wilmington, DE: Michael Glazier Inc., 1983).

G. Taylor, *Sea Chaplains* (London, 1978).

Rt Rev Maurice Taylor, *The Scots College in Spain* (Valladolid, 1917).

Ushaw College Magazine (July 1941).

VX12841, *Soldiering On - Meet the Padre* (Canberra: Australian War Memorial, 1942).

The War Office, *Manual of Military Law* (London: HMSO, 1914).

B. Ward, *History of St Edmund's Old Hall* (1893).

A. P. Wavell, *Allenby* (London: George G. Harrap & Co., 1940).

The Western Catholic Calendar.

'The Cardinal Archbishop's visit to the Fleet, August, 1916', *Westminster Chronicle*, vol. X, no. 9 (1916).

Lt Col F. E. Whitton, *The History of the Prince of Wales's Leinster Regiment* (2 vols; Aldershot: Gale & Polden, 1926), vol. 2.

Who's Who (London: A. & C. Black Ltd, 1936).

Alan Wilkinson, *The Church of England and the First World War* (London: SPCK, 1978).

Rev Dr Michael Williams, *Saint Alban's College, Valladolid* (London: C. Hurst & Co., 1986).

Benedict Williamson, *'Happy Days' in France and Flanders with the 47th and 49th Divisions* (London: Harding & Moore Ltd, 1921).

Chester Wilmot, *The Struggle for Europe* (London: Collins, 1952).

Chester Wilmot, *Tobruk 1941* (London: Penguin Books, 1993).

J. Anselm Wilson, *The Life of Bishop Hedley* (London, 1930).

Sir Evelyn Wood, *From Midshipman to Field Marshal* (London: Methuen, 1906).

Newspapers

Catholic Bulletin.

Catholic Herald (4 September 1914; 17 October 1914; 21 October 1914; 21 November 1914; 5 December 1914; 26 December 1914; 22 January 1915; 30 January 1915; 27 February 1915; 24 April 1915; 14 August 1915).

'Chaplains in the Royal Navy have a hard but fruitful job among God-fearing sailors', *Catholic Herald* (26 February 1943).

Catholic Weekly (Australia) (15 November 1945).

Cork Examiner (1915).

Daily Telegraph (9 May 1931).

Daily Chronicle (13 December 1900).

Hampshire Chronicle (12 January 1798).

The Irish Catholic (26 September 1914; 2 October 1914; 6 October 1914; 10 October 1914; 2 March 1917).

Irish News (30 September 1981).

New York Freeman's Journal (24 November 1914; 26 August 1916).

Scottish Catholic Observer (4 May 1918).

Scottish Catholic Observer (August 1945), quoted in *Scottish Obituaries* (1971).

The Tablet (26 September 1914; 10 October 1914; 7 November 1914; 21 November 1914; 26 December 1914; 16 January 1917).

The Universe.
Various Irish newspapers (Apr 1945), copies of cuttings held by the authors.
Weekly Register.

Unpublished sources

Achonry Diocesan Records.
Ampleforth Abbey Archives.
Archdiocese of Southwark Archives, Chaplains papers.
Archdiocese of Westminster Archives, Chaplains papers.
Sr M. St Austin, letter published in *Weekly Register* (4 May 1900).
Fr F. P. A. Barber CF, 'Report from Bosnia-Herzegovina', and 'Impressions of Bosnia'.
Maj Anthony Barling RAMC, 1st Airborne Division, conversations with T. Johnstone.
Abbot Alban Boultwood OSB, letter to James Hagerty.
Curé of Bouzincourt, letter to Mrs O'Sullivan, mother of Fr Donal O'Sullivan. In possession of the O'Sullivan family, Ballydowney House, Killarney, Co. Kerry.
Rev J. E. Brady, 'Soldiers in Christ', Catholic History Bureau, Linden, Johannesburg.
Chaplains' File Box, Archdiocese of Melbourne Archives.
Lt Col Christie, 51st Bn AIF, letter re Fr Bergin, JAD.
Fr R. F. Collins, letter, *Catholic Herald* (5 December 1915).
Fr C. P. Crean, collected letters, courtesy of Fr Crean's niece, Mrs P. Moorhouse.
CSSR Provincial Archives, St Mary's, Clapham, London.
Archbishop Cullen Papers, 1852-57 – Sec. 449/8 No. 45, 11 May 1856. ADA.
Derry Diocesan Records.
Fr P. D. Devas OFM, post-war letters, IWM.
Downside Abbey Archives.
English Jesuit Necrology, Provincial Archives, Farm Street, London.
Fr Ian Evans, letter to T. Johnstone (22 September 1995).
Fr S. Farragher CSSp, Blackrock College, Dublin, correspondence with T. Johnstone.
Lord Desmond Fitzgerald, letter to Fr Delaney SJ (16 October 1915), JAD.
Maj M. L. Forge, Royal Signals, conversations with T. Johnstone.
Fr Bernard Funnell, letter to T. Johnstone (26 September 1995), and conversations with T. Johnstone.
Edward Gallagher, thesis, 'The Irish College, Salamanca under the rectorship of Dr Patrick Curtis', Russell Library, St Patrick's College, Maynooth.
Dr Gartlan, Rector, Irish College, Salamanca (1829-70), letters, Archives, St Patrick's College, Maynooth.
Rev Henry Gill SJ, letters, JAD.
Rev Francis Gleeson, diary, Meagher Papers, ADA.
Bishop Thomas Grant Papers, ASA.
Fr Alfred Hayes, letter to T. Johnstone (24 August 1994).
Fr Alfred Hayes, 'The diary of a priest in the Falklands. May-July 1982'.
Fr Michael Healy SSC, conversations with T. Johnstone.
Fr J. Hearn, 'Australian Jesuit necrology', Melbourne, Australia (1942).

Rev John W. Jones SM, CF (1939–47), notes, RCCA.

Fr Kevin J. Keaney, USN Retd, conversation with T. Johnstone.

Fr Jeremiah Kelleher SSC, transcript of a taped interview (4 September 1989), courtesy of Royal Inniskilling Fusiliers Museum.

Leeds Diocesan Archives.

Cardinal Logue Papers, AAA.

Mgr Francis Lyons, former Principal Chaplain RAN, conversation with T. Johnstone.

Henry McAnelly, paratrooper, 1st Bn Parachute Regiment, Arnhem Bridge (1944), letter to Fr Desmond Sexton (23 October 1993).

Rev James McRory, Diary, Public Record Office of Northern Ireland, Belfast.

Rev Michael K. Masterson SCF (RC), 'The just war v pacifism'.

Rev Michael K. Masterson SCF (RC), 'Peace making and peace keeping'.

Meath Diocesan Necrology.

'Memorial to the Irish Hierarchy re shortage of Catholic Army chaplains', copy held by the authors.

Rev L. E. Montgomery CRL, Diary, IWM.

Nottingham Diocesan Necrology.

Fr Rory O'Sullivan, letter to Bishop Walmsley (25 February 1992), COA.

Mgr George Pitt, taped interview, COA.

Portsmouth Diocesan Records.

Fr G. Pritchard, letter 60092/CH (RC) (3 October 1945) to Fr J. Gardner, SRC chaplain HQ Allied Land Forces South East Asia, RCCA.

Fr William Purcell, letter to Cardinal Hinsley, 9 July 1940, COA.

Dom B. S. Rawlinson OSB, Rawlinson MSS, DAA.

Recommendation for an award of the Military Cross. Army Form W3121 (26 February 1944). Extant copy in Ampleforth Archives.

Lt Col J. P. Riley, 'Coalitions - World Wars: a study of 1813'.

Colin Johnston Robb, 'The story of the Royal South Down Militia', Linen Hall Library, Belfast (typescript copy).

Rt Rev Mgr J. J. Roche SCA, CBE, Principal RC Chaplain RAF, 'Sermon preached at the Holy Family Church RAF Halton on Nov 8th 1980. On the occasion of the dedication of the Memorial Window to Deceased RAF Chaplains'.

Royal Air Force List of Catholic Chaplains, COA.

Dom Denys Rutledge OSB, 'Padre's progress. Diary of an unknown British Army chaplain in the Second World War'.

Fr John Ryan SCF, Reports to Principal Chaplain (RC) (1950–53), RCCA.

St Bede's Grammar School, Bradford, Archives.

Salamanca Papers, Legajo C/35/3. Russell Library, St Patrick's College, Maynooth.

Rev Vincent Scully CRL, letters, CRL Archives, Eltham.

SMA Necrology, Servite Archives, Begbrooke.

Rev Lionel G. Smith, 'War journal. France and Belgium 1915–1917', Archives of the Archdiocese of Westminster, Archives of St Edmund's College, series 12, 167A.

Rt Rev Mgr James Sullivan, last Rector, The English College, Lisbon, conversations with T. Johnstone.

Fr Austin Treamer AA, 'Catholic Forces in Jerusalem 1941–1946', COA.

Ushaw College Archives.

Vincent de Paul Vokes, Javea, Spain, conversation with T. Johnstone.
Archbishop Walsh Papers, ADA.
Mgr Patrick Walsh, correspondence with T. Johnstone.
Rev C. E. Warren, 'Extracts from my War Diary', IWM.
Fr H. H. Welchman SCF (RC), 8th Corps, report to the Principal Chaplain (May
    1945), RCCA.
Westmeath Diocesan Records.
Fr A. Whitehead CRL, conversation with T. Johnstone.
Mgr Edward Wilcock, letter to James Hagerty.
Fr Michael Wymes, 'A long march'.

Index